CW01498204

SUNSETS AND OLIVES. THE PAIN

After a hugely successful period of early retirement in the wilds of Inland Andalucia, Chrissie and John have suddenly encountered problems, of a financial nature, having their Spanish bank account frozen, amid allegations of money laundering. Added to this, returning home after a wonderful tour of the Westcountry, they stumble upon a mugging, a break-in and a robbery, none of them especially serious, but it is no wonder John in particular questions whether he still wishes to remain in Spain.

It is not all doom and gloom, however. After a *Fifty Shades of Grey* moment, we discover the pitfalls of lying to a Spanish insurance company, and driving without benefit of tax and MOT. On a show-business note, *Jonathan Ross* makes an appearance next door, and we are introduced to the Spanish version of *The Waltons*. There is even a love-affair, from the most unexpected of quarters.

Meanwhile, we learn that buying a dolly is not as simple as it seems, how a photo of a tiger provokes a massive row in the library about General Franco, and that ordering vegetarian food in a restaurant does not necessarily guarantee the absence of meat. Local wildlife, of an airborne nature, puts in an appearance, and the Great Western Railway announce plans for a branch line to Santa Marta.

Conflict is never that far away, however, as an unruly family move into the street, John almost starts a brawl in a filling station, and Chrissie tackles three burly Spaniards in a bar. John is also forced to explain his 'accidental' appearance in a local brothel.

Finally, as the world descends inexorably into a global pandemic, the deaths of two close friends causes our couple to reassess their priorities, and Chrissie herself writes the epilogue in a stunning denouement, explaining, perhaps, the reason for the long delay in the publication of this work.

PROLOGUE. WASHING THE MONEY.

The ferry port, Cherbourg, northern France, after two tortuous days in the saddle, aboard my trusty if rapidly ailing motorbike, about to board the sailing to Poole. And a text message from my wife Chrissie 'Give me a ring, as soon as you get this.' *Oh blimey. Sounds serious, whatever it is that has happened.*

Quick as a flash I dial her number, and she answers almost immediately, in a small, frightened voice, almost as if she has been crying. 'It's our Spanish bank account' she sniffs. 'They have frozen it, completely.'

This sounds ridiculous. 'What? Why in the hell would they do that? Are you sure?'

'If you would let me finish' she shouts, clearly in some distress, 'I went down there today, tried to pay in a hundred euros, to cover any water or electric bills while we are away, and they wouldn't let me. No paying in, no withdrawals. Account suspended. I had to go to see the manager, it was so embarrassing, frogmarched almost, I was so scared, he was babbling away but I was so flustered I couldn't take anything in.'

'Did you manage to catch anything else he said?' I enquire, somewhat aggrieved to hear about this officious jobsworth banker, when I am over a thousand miles away, with a ferry to catch.

'Oh, I don't know' she wails, '*limpiar dinero,* cleaning money, was what he said, God knows what that is supposed to mean, but that is it. We have been sussed, they have caught up with us. Rumbled. Without a bank account, we are finished, here.'

Suddenly I am gripped by panic, sick to the very depths of my stomach. Somehow, however, I manage to retain a sense of normality, in my voice. 'Oh, don't worry. You know what the Spanish are like. It will be something and nothing, just some ridiculous bureaucracy, a few forms to fill in. Forget it, and when we get back from the UK we will nip down there and get it all sorted. How much was in the account, anyway?'

She brightens, considerably. 'Well, there was about a hundred in there, but there might have been an electricity bill come out recently, I was going to get the passbook written up, but of course he wouldn't do that, either. But eighty euros, definitely.'

'So there you are then' I reply, reassuringly, 'that is plenty to cover any bills while we are away. We can go down there next month, and tell him to stuff his useless bank where the sun don't shine! Forget all about it. So, are you all ready for the bus ride to the airport tomorrow? Got your boarding pass all sorted out? Have you given Lydia the key, so she can pop in and water your plants? Looking forward to that lumpy old spare bed in your mother's?'

She laughs, and we discuss the various details of our journeys, and when we will finally meet up, but I cannot help wondering; *was I wrong to have lied to her?*

Stomach clenched with an icy grip of fear, I stumble, unseeingly, around the terminal, my mind a jumble of thoughts, all of them negative. *Why did this have to happen now, when everything was going so well?* The result of the biopsy on the polyps came through just a few days ago, the burden of the past month suddenly lifted from our shoulders, such overwhelming relief. Suddenly, I become aware of a voice, calling out, and I turn to see the girl behind the ticket desk, gesturing frantically in the direction of the ferry. Time to board, presumably. I wave vaguely, forcing a smile, but really all I want to do is head straight back home, and get this hideous mess sorted. How can I possibly enjoy a holiday, with the sword of Damocles hanging over us? I stagger outside, and see that the car park is in darkness. My fellow passengers have departed, and the guy on the customs post is waving irritably for me to get a move on. Instant decision time. Chrissie will not be there, by the time I get back, if I go back, and I have no idea where the bank book, or account details, are kept anyway. I have no choice but to continue with this pretence, this ridiculous charade of normality, for the next three weeks in the UK. Slinging my leg over the saddle, I straighten the bike, haul up the bungee to retract the stand, fire up the engine, and after a cursory glance at my passport, I am allowed to board.

Following the directions of the yellow-jacketed stewards, I park the bike in the depths of the ferry, stuff the key in my pocket then head straight out onto the deck, where I slump against the railing, staring blindly at the murky water of the harbour. *Cleaning money?* Money Laundering, of course. A serious criminal offence. Taking the proceeds of crime, and by a series of financial transactions, eventually obtaining 'clean' money. So how in the name of all things holy have we been accused, or suspected, of this grave matter? On an account containing less than a hundred quid? *Hang on a minute.* The icy grip returns, with a vengeance. We transferred twenty-five thousand sterling, via a currency exchange, into this Spanish account, to buy the house, less than two years ago, and that must be what this is all about. My stomach is in knots.

Wracked with dread, I glance mournfully at the outline of the French coast, disappearing into the dusk, lights of the little town twinkling. Is this really it? Is this the beginning of the end of our lives in the land of sunsets, and olives?

CHAPTER 1. THE PAIN IN SPAIN.

And now, a month later, here I am, in this pathetic excuse for a bank, awaiting my turn. This so-called manager, or chief clerk, this Bruce Forsyth lookalike, in his dapper pinstripe suit, is seated across the room, behind his desk, self-importantly dealing with an old fellow, who seems keen to impart his entire life story, and that of six generations of his ancestors. But I am next. *El ultimo.* And Brucie knows I am here. Refuses to make eye contact, but he knows. He didn't shout 'Nice to see you, to see you, nice!' when I entered. There were no cries of 'Good Game, good game!' And he certainly won't be hollering 'Didn't he do well!' when I leave. My eyes, like laser beams, are boring holes in the side of his head, and this is not gonna end well, for him. This bastard, who completely ruined my holiday.

But you had a great trip to the UK, you said. You got your bike repaired, didn't you? Shot the breeze with your old mate Anton and the other guys in the shop, ripped the Michael mercilessly, didn't they, what with you traversing an entire continent on illegal tyres? Then didn't you head up to Dartmoor for a spot of wild camping, in that secret spot, that location you refuse to divulge, under pain of death, up the track to the side of one of your favourite pubs, The Fox, just off the Okehampton to Tavistock road? Shortacombe, wasn't it, the name of the village? And didn't you partake of several pints of Dartmoor Ale, and one of their humungous Fox-Whopper burgers? And return in the morning, after performing your ablutions in the stream, for a monster gut-busting breakfast?

Then didn't you meander through mid-Devon, across Exmoor and down to Porlock, and that thatched pub where Samuel Taylor Coleridge was interrupted by some bothersome peasant whilst writing his masterpiece, 'Kubla Khan'? Wrote the first verse, and promptly forgot the rest, didn't he? Then on to Minehead, another of your all-time favourite pubs, The Old Ship, down by the harbour? A steam-train ride on the West Somerset Railway? The mandatory stop in the Harley dealer in Bridgwater, for a sneaky peek at all those gleaming bikes you can no longer afford, now you're a pensioner? Cheddar Gorge for a huge slice of that cave-matured cheese, the strongest they make, then across the Mendips? Then didn't you leave your bike in auntie Ann's garage, meet up with Chrissie, and your younger daughter Charlie and her partner Andrew? A trip to Truro on the train to reconnect with old friends and former colleagues? Then back on the bike, the return journey, through France and Spain?

Yes, I did all those things, but will you ever stop going on about my favourite pubs? God, I wish I was there now, instead of here, suffering this indignity, this complete lack of customer care, for something we didn't do. I am sick of it. And don't forget, this moron made my wife cry.

But don't you have some mechanism for shutting out bad thoughts, you said? Put them away in a box, or something?

Not a box, no. I imagine I am a cricketer, a batsman, out there in the middle, alone. England versus Australia, the Ashes series. *Lord's.* And every time a bad thought about money-laundering, or Brucie, or anything, comes my way, I pretend it's a ball, fast or slow, seam or spin, matters not, whack! Off it goes to the boundary. Four runs, six runs, they cannot get me out, those legendary bowlers. Crash bang wallop. And now, here it is, final match, final ball. 'Forsyth to Richards, he comes in, bowls... and oh my word! Richards is half-way down the pitch, dispatches that delivery with the meat of his bat, and it's still travelling, over the stand.' The Ashes series secured in a whitewash. Sent the lot of them back Down-Under, with their tails between their legs, we did. And Forsyth is down on his knees, a broken man.'

Which is as it should be.

Yes but it might not actually be his fault, might it? You know, a new law? Maybe he had no choice in the matter.

I am getting fed-up with this. Just stop trying to defend the indefensible, will you? This idiot is supposed to be the manager. All it needed was a letter. *Dear Client, Following recent changes to legislation, we are required to ascertain the source of deposits made by non-Spanish nationals. Perhaps you could furnish us, at your earliest convenience, with this information. Yours etc.* Did they do that? No. They froze our account, without telling us. You simply don't do that to a customer where I come from, and I'm gonna make sure he knows that. We could have been in all sorts of trouble, with standing orders and direct debits. Still could, for all we know. Despite the little white lies I told Chrissie on the phone at the ferry port, back in August, there could have been water and electricity bills due, and not paid. We could be in the process of being cut off. And a tax bill is due to come out very shortly too. So no, Brucie is not getting a bonus this day. He is not going to keeep dancing. And there are no cuddly toys on his conveyor belt. Just a massive shock, which I have lined up. Been planning this for a month, so he is getting it, with interest, right between the eyes, right about now I reckon, as the old fellow is gathering his papers. Will need to be on my toes too, with these nippy locals, under five feet tall most of them, they know I'm next, the *ultimo*, but what's the betting they will try to duck under my guard and wheedle their way in? *Oh I just have a little question. I'm in a bit of a hurry. Look at this letter I've received.* Not happening, today. Usually I would be trying to engage, laughing at the jokes, enjoying the morning, what's the rush, after all? Nope. I'm all fired up, and besides, I've memorised all these new phrases... and here goes! The old man is scraping back his chair, and I am across the room, slaloming around the startled pensioner, and locking my eyes on Forsyth, with the pent-up fury of the past weeks, I slap my papers aggressively on his desk. 'You suspended our account, without telling us. Why?'

A little question. Bit of a hurry. Letter received.

I turn my head slightly and hold up my arm. *Don't worry people. This will be totally worth it. You can tell your Grand-kids you were here, this day.* Forsyth is like a startled rabbit, caught in the headlights. Time to administer the coup-de-grace. 'Do you have a complaint form, in this pathetic bank? A complaint form. Get one, now. You're gonna need it.' And I turn my head again, grinning, clench my fist, pump my arm, and sling my passbook onto the pile, with all the contempt I can muster. About as much as I show Australian bowling, actually.

A sharp intake of breath is audible from half-a-dozen pairs of wheezy lungs behind me, and I swear that was several sets of false teeth I could hear clicking back into place. Or maybe it was hip joints. Oh yes, the Spanish complaint form. All retail businesses are required by law to provide one, upon request. We first came upon this phenomenon in a filling station, not long after we'd arrived in this country, a printed sign, maybe 2 feet square, affixed to the forecourt office wall, in Spanish, and English. *This establishment provides complaint forms for use by customers.* Made us chuckle, actually. I mean, what manner of complaint could there possibly be in a garage? HOW MUCH FOR A GALLON OF FOUR-STAR? And assuming the unsuspecting punter managed to complete one, wouldn't the attendant simply tear it to shreds, the very second the motorist departed the premises? Not so, according to the good folks at the library conversation group. 'Thees much important, complaining form!' explained Juan, the financial guru. 'Ees organise by Gobby-Enry, not sure local or national of he, but forms complaining have numbers consec… consecu…'

'Consecutive?'

' YEES! Numbers of consecutive, so person of shop cannot to

throw away thees. Gobby-Enry he inspect forms, not sure how much times during year, but if numbers consecutivo not agree, ees big trouble for they! Yees!'

Information duly noted, and filed away. And three years later, ees big trouble for Brucie. Yees! Like a bulldog who has just swallowed a lemon whilst being stung on the testicles by a giant bumblebee, having already stumbled painfully into a patch of thistles, our friendly local banker clearly regrets leaving the comfort of his basket this morning. Clenching his teeth with as much dignity as he can summon, in the face of outright, naked hostility, and a sea of grinning locals, he gathers my documents, rises unsteadily to his feet, and indicates an office behind the cash desk. 'Thees way, plees?'

Not a chance sonny Jim. Unless you are prepared to lift me bodily and carry me across the room, and best of luck with that, you weed, I ain't moving, and to prove it I shake my head. 'I would like the other customers to hear your reply' I smile, sweetly, and judging by the clacking of dentures from behind, I have the audience in my hand. Yees!

Wincing, in the manner of a canine with a tender rear end, he sits back down, extracts my passbook from its clear plastic wallet, opens it to the inside cover, and smirks, wagging his finger, in the manner of Spaniards who feel they have right on their side. An annoying trait, to be honest, and I always caution my students to avoid finger-wagging when visiting the UK, if they wish to retain all their digits intact, that is. He looks me in the eye for the first time this morning. 'Say-oss' he proclaims, proudly. 'You don't have say-oss.'

Now I know this one. A postage stamp, no less. We get ours from the tobacconist, where, and I promise I am not making this up, he cuts the stamps from a long strip, with a pair of scissors. Two are required, for letters and cards to the UK. Damn good service too, they often arrive within several days.... HANG ON A MINUTE. What in the name of all things holy has a postage stamp to do with a bank-book? Is this a form of Spanish sledging? Is he about to belittle my batting style, my waistline or my family, by, I dunno, assaulting me with a Penny Black? I narrow my eyes in a *don't give me any of this crap, matey* kind of way. 'Say-oss?'

He taps the inside page. 'Say-oss. Here.' And he bangs his fist on the page in the manner of a Post Office counter-clerk updating an Ordinary Account passbook in about 1969. You remember, the blue one? The Investment Account passbooks were grey I believe, not that I had sufficient funds for the posh account, when I was a callow youth. And didn't you have to give about a month's notice to get the money out? Or post it to Glasgow? The Ordinary Account funds were available on demand, I used to carry mine on cycling tours, back when ten-bob would last a week, whilst Youth Hosteling. So who knew? A say-oss is an ink-stamp, as well as the postage variety. Blow me down. So one of us, and trust me on this, it won't be me, needs to stroll across the bank, fish said say-oss out of a drawer, extract an ink pad, dab the stamp on the ink, and, here's an idea, despite the fact that there is no mark on the page where said imprint might go, STAMP THE BLOODY THING.

I turn to face my audience, blow out my cheeks ironically, despite the fact that Spaniards do not really get British irony, but clearly several of them are catching on as they're grinning widely, then fixing Brucie with a glare that could strip cheap varnish from a bank counter-top, I return the finger wagging gesture, with interest, and point in the general direction of the cashier. 'Go on then.'

I fully expect him to slink sheepishly in the general direction of the say-osses, but no, he stands, or rather sits, his ground. And out comes out the finger again. All right, call me childish, and you'd be right, but I cannot help it. If he is wagging, so am I. With my middle finger. In a playground sword-fighting way. This wastes a further few seconds of our lives, until he comes out with the immortal words. 'You need to go to Almorate.'

We do, actually. Very pleasant little town, Almorate. Independent shops, excellent tapas-bars, narrow, winding streets leading to a hill-top castle, we tend to go there every other month, on a Saturday morning, park outside.... WHAT? WHY? *'POR-QUE?'*

He is on the front-foot, he feels. He wags the passbook under my nose. 'This is a new *libreta*. Your branch, where you opened the account, is Almorate. You need to go to the bank in Almorate to get a *say-oss.'*

I throw him a look which could cause cheap varnish to burst into flames, all the while collecting my Spanish thoughts. Our conversation thus far has been rehearsed, now I am going to have to wing it. *Right. Got it. Here goes.* 'YOUR machine was not working.' I hiss, indicating the printer next to the cashier's desk. 'HE told me to use the machine in the *entrada*,' jabbing my finger in the general direction of the foyer, 'and YOUR machine broke the book.' I am using the verb 'to break', as I don't know the Spanish for 'chewed-up', but that is what happened, on that fateful morning towards the end of last year. The cashier's machine wasn't working, so to update the book he told me to use the hole-in-the-wall machine in the entrance. All went well, suitable printing-noises from an earlier century were audible, until several seconds later the cursed book emerged looking like it had been fought-over by a ravenous pack of hyenas. Didn't apologise, the cashier, for wasting even more of my morning while a new passbook was printed up. Not even the flicker of a grin, as I recall. Acutely embarrassed, I imagine, but he didn't want to lose face. That must have been it...

I turn to face the crowd, which has been swelled by several more oldies queuing by the cash-desk, again gathering my thoughts. *What the hell is a round-trip of sixty miles, in this lingo? Never like this in the Post Office Savings Bank, was it?* 'Almorate is one-hundred kilometres, *ida y vuelta*' I remind him. 'I am *autonomous*, self-employed. You are not open Saturday mornings. Are you going to pay me the petrol, and my time? Sixty euros?' *Well, gotta add a few bucks for myself, don't I?*

You don't believe me, do you? You think I'm making this up, for cheap laughs. Whatever your view of Brucie, and his complete lack of the duty of care regarding our finances, he is the manager, right? Worked his way up through the hierarchy, during his career? Started out making the tea, ended up at the top of the tree? He cannot possibly be arguing about an ink-stamp, can he? That just doesn't happen. Well, I agree with you. Typing this out now, I scarcely believe it, myself, and I was actually there.

If looks could kill. He stands, and stalks across towards the cash desk. *Should have asked him to make it a hundred.* He snatches something from a drawer, A4-sized, so clearly not money, returns and slaps it on his newly-stripped desk. *OK, just credit my account, Mr Forsyth.* And what is this, pray? Ooh, looky here. A Spanish complaint form. In three parts by the seem of it, carbonated, one for the customer, one for the business, and one for Gobby-Enry? With a machine number in the top corner. Spaces for name, address, knee-number, all the usual, plus a larger box which I take to mean 'nature of complaint.' Yees! Swiping a pen from the desk, which bears the legend *Banco Santander*, which he himself must have nicked as we most definitely are not in the Banco Santander, I start to complete the large box, get some ink on it before he changes his mind. Cathartic. This feels so good. Never in the history of literature have the words *you suspended our account without telling us, why?* had such a calming, soporific effect. Samuel Taylor Coleridge didn't achieve this level of well-being, even before the Person from Porlock turned up, that's for certain.....

Fifteen minutes later I emerge, squinting, into the bright autumn sunlight, plonk myself on a bench in the square and switch on my phone, which I'd kept turned off during my encounter, *because I am polite like that.* To be aurally assaulted by a cacophony of ringing and buzzing, which eventually reveal themselves as two texts, a missed-call and a voice-mail, all from the same person, Marie of library-group fame. Probably wanting to arrange a get-together. I plump for the voicemail, purely for entertainment reasons, after the morning I've just had. 'Jonneee! You have good holly-days? I think you return to Espain thees day? HODER! My Eengliss ver bad! I am een library, weeth womans Eengliss. Ees much problems. Plees help!'

Hell's teeth. I was hoping for a lie-down, under the fig tree, open the pool, doze off on the sunbed. Still, shouldn't take long, and Marie is so good to us, in so many ways. For a second or two my mind is a blank, what with all that cricket I've been playing recently, and I cannot think where the library actually is. Slowly, the fog clears from my brain-box. Yep, got it. End of the street, two minutes tops. Probably take me that long to type out a reply, the speed my fingers, and Spanish mobile signals, move.

Up the half-dozen steps to the entrance foyer, I am spotted by the white-coated cleaner, who seems mightily relieved to see me, she dashes inside and summons Anna the chief-librarian, who almost stumbles in her haste to usher me inside. 'Jonneee, thank you much for coming! Marie thees way, plees!' I am shown into a small room, where indeed our dear Spanish friend is seated across from a smartly-dressed woman, our age, British certainly, perfectly coiffured hair in a light-brown bob, immaculate, understated make-up, flowery Laura Ashley-style print dress just above the knee, and strappy wedges. Not an earthly clue.

Marie scrambles gratefully to her feet and we exchange the usual formal double-kiss, with a big hug thrown in for good measure and a deafening cry of 'JONNEEE!', as if I'd just returned from the North Pole, not Exmoor. I then turn to the womans Eengliss, and smile, but honestly, I don't have the foggiest.

She rises to her feet, squeezes my arm, and plants a peck on my cheek. 'Ello John, me ole China!'

BLOODY HELL! Jackie! Ex-wife, or partner, of Phil, he of chicken fame. The Spanish 'ens, what were they called, Bessie, Jessie, Flossie and Bossy, wasn't it? Turned out they were cockerels, so were re-christened John, Paul, George and Ringo, until the latter ended up plucked and stuffed, in their kitchen, and Phil cried. Jackie then had a romantic liaison with the son of the Spanish 'en guy, Phil discovered said indiscretion and promptly booted her out, since when not a thing has been heard from her, went back to London, according to the Santa Marta gossip mill. OK, Del-Boy. But look at her now! Last seen grubbing round her flea-bitten acres in a scruffy London Transport 'Mind the Gap' man's tee-shirt, and Primark jeans, she could have stepped off the pages of a fashion magazine. Certainly done better than her ex, who has gone right to the dogs, according to, well, Del. Last seen contracting a group of Moroccans to saw up an illegal Ford Transit van.

I smile warmly. 'Jackie! You look sensational!' *Gotta be careful here. Don't want to imply she didn't look sensational before, and you know what I'm like. Straight in with my size-elevens. Both of them. Where the Devil is my wife, never around when I need her? Oh to hell with it. She does look incredible, and I'm a bloke, can probably get away with the odd fox-paw, as Nan used to say.* 'Are you here for a fashion shoot? *Cosmopolitan? Marie Claire?*'

There endeth my knowledge of fashion magazines, unless you count *Railway Modeller*, but I needn't have worried. She squeezes my hand. 'Oh John, yer silly bugger! I do love you! I'm 'ere for a few days, not sure really, come up on the bus from Malaga yesterday, stayed last night in the *Rodrigo*, I checked out this morning, left me bag there for now, but they got a room fer tonight if I need it.'

Suddenly there is a polite cough from across the room. Marie. 'Sorree, I must to collect my cheelds from school. Good lucky

Jackie, I hoping to see you soon! And Jonneee, please Cristina call me, meet for coffee!'

We all hug again, express our grateful thanks, and promise to meet again soon. And Jackie and I are alone. I am rubbish at this emotional stuff, but she continues her story. 'I been living with me sister, she runs this boozer in Greenwich, good pub it is actually, lovely crowd gets in there, and yeah, I been doin' alright, got meself together, yer know, saved up a few bob, couldn't stay moping about fer-ever, like, could I?'

I am rubbish at this. 'I think you are absolutely right, Jackie. You look wonderful, I have to say, and I'm so pleased for you!'

She squeezes my hand again. 'Bless you, John. Anyway, I 'ad a few days owing, so I gets a flight over, thought I might look up the old feller, just to see 'ow 'ee's doing, not to get back with 'im or nothing, but this morning I wakes up, and loses me bottle, like, so I thought I'd call in 'ere and see if you or Chrissie was about, and Marie says she thought you was in England, but you was coming back yesterday or today. Anyway, yer 'ere now! Thank gawd!'

Why am I so rubbish at this? 'Well Chrissie is out with someone for coffee, I thought it was Marie, actually, but clearly not! But look, it's ridiculous you staying in the *Rodrigo*, we have a spare bedroom, we are sleeping in the lower ground-floor apartment at the moment, so you have the whole of the upstairs to your-self. Come and stay at our place, you can come and go as you like, eat with us or we can go out, there's a spare sunbed in the garden, and if you packed your costume you can have a dip! Chrissie would love to see you and you can both have a good old girlie chat. We've only been home a day and she's fed up with me already!'

She grins, but shakes her head. 'That is so kind of you, but I couldn't possibly intrude like that. You don't want me hanging about, like, and you ain't even asked Chrissie yet! I'll be fine down the 'otel.'

Now it is my turn to do some hand squeezing. 'Jackie, honestly, it is no problem. Of course, if you want to be alone, take some time for yourself, we will understand. Anyway, there's no need to decide right now, Chrissie will be home any time now, so come up and have a cuppa. I can always collect your case later.'

'Well a cuppa sounds great' she chuckles, 'go on then, you convinced me!' She turns serious. 'Actually, this morning I did feel lonely, 'ere all on me own, like. Just talking it through with someone will help I'm sure.'

'Grab your bag then, and let's go!' I laugh. 'Just a word of warning though, it's still pretty warm at nights, on the top floor of the house, I hope you'll be able to sleep up there!'

'I been living in bladdy Greenwich for six months!' she splutters, 'warm is great, I can do warm, hot will be better, bring it on!'

We exit the little room, and almost collide with librarian-Anna, who appears to have had her ear to the keyhole. Concerned about the womans Eengliss, no doubt. We head up the hill towards our place, and to fill the silence, I start to babble, as you know how rubbish I am at this. 'I went to Greenwich once, on the London Marathon, in 2001. It starts in the park there as far as I can remember. We ran along this big wide road, there were quite a few pubs along there, and outside one pub there were loads of people, with dogs, about a dozen dogs, so I started singing at the top of my voice that song which was popular at that time, 'OOO LET THE DOGS OUT?', and all the runners nearby sang 'OOO, OOO OOO OOO!' Fantastic it was, singing with the marathon, you had to be there I suppose..... then we ran past the 'Cutty Sark', the old tea-clipper ship, and it reminded me of when I was a little boy, in Westward Ho!, north Devon, there was a cafe called the Cutty Sark, mum and dad, nan and grandpa used to take me in there, and I always thought what a romantic name it sounded, and I used to dream about all the places the ship had visited, imagining I might go there one day... it was a car-park last time I was there... and I thought they had a cheek calling it the London marathon actually, as you don't get to see that much of London, I mean you cross Tower Bridge about half-way then the route goes out through Docklands, you could be anywhere really, and you only get to see the sights of London in the final few miles... and I overtook Frank Bruno, you remember, the boxer, at the Tower of London, they put rubber mats down on the cobblestones, and he was really suffering, as he is absolutely huge, his arms were bigger than my thighs, and to gee him up as I overtook I punched his arm, only gently of course, 'come on Frank you can do it!', so I can actually say that I punched Frank Bruno, and lived!'

Told you didn't I? We are approaching the steep, cobbled section of the climb, rendering speech virtually impossible, which is probably just as well.... Jackie turns her head towards me, and for a split-second I imagine she is going to tell me to shut the hell up. 'We only done it the once, you know.'

Oh. My. God. Did she actually just say that? Who did what, to whom? 'Er, sorry?'

'Ramon, Man-well's son, you know, that day out in the barn. Me an' Ramon, we only done it the once.'

My toes are curling with embarrassment, and I don't know if you've ever tried walking up a cobbled street about as steep as the north face of the Eiger with curled toes, but it ain't easy. And I cannot think of anything to usefully add to her statement. I mean, were we in the rugby club I imagine that half-a-dozen ribald replies would trip off the tongue, but here, stone-cold sober, my feet are killing me and I'm confronted by a woman in a Laura Ashley dress, describing a sexual, extra-marital encounter in a farm building. I think. *See what I mean?* She squeezes my arm. 'Sorry, John, I'm embarrassing yer. But we was drunk, see, me an' Ramon. Man-well keeps a barrel of this rot-gut red wine in the barn, we 'ad a coupla glasses like, well more than a couple, and one thing leads to another, an' we ends up in the hay!'

My digits are now twisted around my ankles and I am hobbling like a three-legged duck in a field of turnips, when suddenly, joy of joys, deep salvation in the form of an unruly Spaniard invades the peace. 'NEIGHBOUR! THAT IS NOT YOUR WOMAN! WHO IS SHE? I WILL TELL CRISTINA OF YOU! PUT HER DOWN!' Pirate Pete, you beauty, I want your babies. My hero. Never before have I been so utterly relieved by an intervention by this old reprobate. Jackie throws her hands across her face and bursts into tears, shaking uncontrollably, whereas I want to plant a slobbery kiss on his whiskery, sunken cheeks. I cannot of course, and it is none of his business what Jackie is doing here, or why, and I have no intention of entering into any conversation whatsoever, so I merely smile politely as we pass by, and pray that none of the other neighbours hear the commotion and decide to stick their heads out.

Jackie meanwhile is rummaging in her bag for a tissue, locates one, dabs her eyes daintily... turns to face me again... she is actually laughing, not crying! 'Oh my gawd, I've missed this so much, these nosey old Spaniards, doncha just love 'em? That ole bloke is just like Man-well, they just says what they thinks!'

They do indeed, and by a miracle, which must indicate it is almost Spanish lunch time, we make it to our front door without further inquisition, and I usher our friend inside. *Hopefully the storm has passed.* 'Right, make yourself at home, while I pop the kettle on. Chocolate Hob-nob?' *Just don't mention bloody Ramon again, please...*

Suddenly the front door is flung open and Chrissie bursts in. 'What's all this I've been hearing about you smuggling a strange wom.... oh blimey, hello, Jackie, I didn't see you there!' she adds, sheepishly. 'When did you get back? I love your hair like that, and that dress really suits your complexion. Come on, shift up the sofa, and tell me all what's been going on!'

'Milk and sugar?' I enquire, to nobody in particular. The girls are deep in conversation, and I am surplus to requirements, as usual. 'I'll just pop down the *Rodrigo* and collect Jackie's case than, shall I?' *Might as well talk to the cat. He loves me.*

I step into the street again, and when I am out of earshot, not that it makes a scrap of difference, I dial up Del-Boy. He loves me too, or he will do, when I impart my news. ''Ello mate! Did yer 'ave a good 'oliday?'

There you go, told you, didn't I? And he hasn't even heard the news yet. 'I did, thanks Del, and yes, I made it to Poundland!'

I can feel the love, even at Spanish mobile speeds. 'Ahh, you beauty! Did you get it? Did you? Come on, tell me! Did you get it?'

Ahh bless. 'I did mate! Two, actually. Might be a bit shaken up, travelling across France, but there were two bottles of Daddies sauce in my saddlebags, last time I checked. And a few boxes of fag papers. Just what the doctor ordered!'

You'd imagine he'd won the lottery. 'Mate, mate, you made me day! Me year, actually. The weekend just gone stratospheric! Ohhhh, Daddies sauce! Get in, yer beauty!'

I cannot help feeling good about life. This is what I do, you see? Punch Frank Bruno, and transport tomato sauce across Europe. Stuff Ramon and his hay. 'So your Sunday morning fry-up is all sorted!' I giggle. 'What will it be, sausages, bacon, fried eggs, mushrooms, baked beans, what, fried bread or toast? Cuppa PG? Can I come?'

He falls silent for a second or two. 'No mate, not me breakfast, the Daddies is for me lunch.'

I am still chuckling. 'Sorry, I forgot, you don't get up till midday on a Sunday, do you? So will it be the full monty and Daddies for brunch?'

'No mate, I jus told yer, the Daddies is for me lunch, you know, roast beef, Yorkshire, roast and boiled, carrots, all the trimmings.'

I feel like I've been hit between the eyes by a bouncer from some heathen Australian. 'Are you telling me you put tomato sauce on a roast lunch? You bloody Cockney savage! I've just aided and abetted a crime! D'you think I'd have gone to that trouble if I'd known you were putting it on roast beef? Is that what they do up there by the Great Bells of Bow? Doing the Lambeth Walk, OI! Have you never heard of horseradish?'

He's roaring with laughter. ' 'Ackney, mate. London East Five. Clapton Road. God used to live there, when he was a boy! We all puts Daddies on our roast beef, out there, it's the law!'

'Heathens, the lot of you!' I snigger. 'I was planning to drop it up in the next couple of days, but I'm not so sure now. I might get struck by a bolt of lightning! Anyway, listen, the reason I phoned is because I want to get hold of Phil the Chicken. Someone was asking me about his paintings, before our holiday, so I thought you might know where I could find him?'

'Bladdy 'ell, mate!' he splutters, "ee ain't done no painting fer months, far as I know. Too pissed to see straight! 'Ee can't even draw the curtains, these days!' We both chuckle about Phil being too inebriated to pull the drapes, then Del sucks his teeth. 'But if yer def-nately wants to see 'im, maybe try the Flower Bar, or a park bench if 'ees sleeping it off! But never mind 'im, when yer coming with me Daddies?'

Now it's my turn to inhale deeply. 'Depends on my conscience, and my soul, Del. If I can persuade them both to overlook your satanic habits, maybe tomorrow. If not, then gawd knows, as they say in 'Ackney!'

So down the hill again to the Flower Bar, where a quick glance through the window reveals a couple of older locals, plus a scruffy old man perched precariously on a bar stool, sunken eyes, unshaven, faded Deep Purple tee-shirt from 1972 which looks like it hasn't seen the laundry since, and a pair of jeans which.... well you don't want to know, seriously. I am still traumatised, ten months later. Taking a deep breath, to psyche my-self up, and because the air surrounding my friend might not be the freshest, I swing through the door. 'Hello Phil!' I exclaim brightly. 'Long time no see. How you doing?'

Daft question actually, but what can I say. 'Oh, you look as if you died, some while ago? Hardly. He glances up, slowly, disinterest-edly.'Oh, it's you. What d'you want?'

Not very nice is it? I might just have this man's future in the palm of my hand. Not that he knows it yet of course. 'Oh, just wonder-ing how you're doing, you know. Not seen you for a while, what with one thing and another. Did you sell those paintings I gave you last year?' *Five thousand quid's worth, according to Nigel. Just saying.*

'What do you care?' he snaps. 'It's all your bloody fault I'm in this state.'

I'm gonna bail out any minute now, tell his wife to forget this waster and go back to Greenwich. 'So how d'you reckon that, Phil? Last I heard you were trying to blame Del for all your problems. Sounds to me like it's everyone's fault but yours.'

'That day in this very cafe,' he growls, attracting the attention of the customers and barman, who is wondering if I've actu-ally come in for a drink, or to wind up his clientele. 'With the Spanish 'ens, me chickens, and you was laughing about Jackie asking for cock, an' she was saying she wouldn't mind a bit of that bastard Ramon's cock. That's what put the idea in her head. You. All your fault. You and your big mouth.'

Actually, put it like that, he might well have a point… 'Crap. That is total crap, Phil. Look at the state of you. Have you lost all your self-respect, man?'

His eyes are burning with malice, and slowly, inexorably, he rises from the stool, bristling, and advances a step towards me, then falls, collapses, into my arms, so that I have to grab him in a massive bear hug to avoid an ungainly heap on the barman's freshly swept tiles. 'Oh John, oh John' he sobs, 'I'm so sorry, look at me, what am I doing? You were a true friend, and I behave like this. What have I become? I miss her, John, I miss her so much. I'd do anything, anything, to get her back.' And he convulses into tears.

I nod at the bewildered barman to reassure him that this melodrama is entirely normal in the lives of British expats, then gently ease my burden back onto the stool. 'It's fine, Phil, everything's fine. Just sit there a second. Listen, I have some news for you. And somehow, through the fog of tears, he seems to sense what I might be about to say. He runs his hand across his weeping eyes, and runny nose, then grips my arm. 'Hey, careful!' I giggle. 'This shirt is brand new, from Edinburgh Woolen Mill last month, a James Pringle super-soft cotton, £7.99 in the sale! I don't want your bodily fluids all over it!' He grins, coughs, and grabs a serviette from the bar, dabbing his eyes. The moment of tension has been diffused. 'Phil, Jackie is back, for a brief holiday, and she wants to see you.'

He grips my arm again, tighter this time. *Oh what the hell, the shirt needed a wash, after the day I've had.* 'You're not.... joking? This isn't some wind....'

'Phil, I am serious. She is with Chrissie right now, in our place. She is staying with us a couple of nights, while she decides what she is doing.' I place my hand on his shoulder, as he appears to be about to leap to his feet. 'But listen, she is here to talk only, she is not moving back. You understand? She is just here for a short break. OK? Come up to the house now, and sit down with her.'

He looks panic-stricken. 'But the state of me, I cannot see her like this, I need a shave, a haircut, a bath, a change of clothes. Christ, I'm a wreck.'

I smile reassuringly. 'You don't have six weeks! She knows you've gone to the dogs, Phil. I think she will see past that!'

'But what do I say? What do I do?'

'You're a grown man, Phil, you will need to work it out yourself. But if I were you I'd listen to her, tell you know how it hurts when you lose the one you love, you took her for granted, and everything got destroyed between you. Become the man she fell in love with, all those years ago. Swear to be a better man, but above all listen to her.'

He grabs my arm again, luckily the bare bit. 'Come on then, what are we waiting for?' He digs a grubby, crumpled tenner from the murky depths of his jeans pocket, slaps it on the bar, grins at the barman, and with a sheepish *gracias*, we stumble out into the blinding sunshine.

Up the cursed hill again for what seems like the umpteenth time today, both of us are silent, each with his own thoughts, Phil no doubt on the cusp of a new life, possibly, me dreaming of a shower and a change of shirt. I am the proud owner of three *Edinburgh Woolen Mill James Pringle super-soft cotton, £7.99 in the sale* shirts, which as I told the lady in the shop, should last me until I die. She thought I was joking…..

It is siesta time, for some lucky people at least, and we manage to reach the house unhindered by inquisitive locals. I unlock the door, and usher my friend inside. Jackie, sat on the sofa with Chrissie, throws her hand to her mouth, realising, possibly, she might have bitten off more than she can chew. 'Oh Phil' she whispers, starting to rise.

'Stay there, Jackie' I command, holding up my hand. 'Phil, you sit over there, in that armchair. Right, listen up, you pair,' as Phil gets himself settled, nervously. 'The past is gone, nothing we can do to change it. We cannot return. All any of us can do is look back, from where we are right now, and learn from our mistakes. And the future? Well, we have plans, and dreams, but we have no control, no real say in how it turns out, in reality. No, all we have, all any of us has, is the present, right here, right now, this moment, this second. This one chance, which is what you both have. I've spoken to you both today, and I believe you want to be together, that you need each other. So take this opportunity, it might never come again.' I glance up at the clock. 'Chrissie and I have to leave you now for an hour or so, we both have students, in town, so we'll be back just after six, OK? There's tea and coffee in the kitchen, beer and wine in the fridge, make yourselves at home, anything you want, help yourselves.' I look them firmly in the eyes, Jackie first, then her husband. 'Just don't waste the time, promise me?'

I head for the door, not waiting for the replies. 'Oh Jackie, just one thing' Chrissie giggles, perhaps compensating for the severity of my speech. 'If you want to throw the crockery at Phil, use the cheap stuff in the kitchen, not the posh stuff in the dining room, OK?' Which gets a couple of laughs from our audience, then we are out into the street, yet again. My wife takes my arm. 'Ooohhh, I do love a strong man!'

I blow out my cheeks. 'You can jest! I took a lot of that from Joni Mitchell, *The Circle Game.* 'We can't return, we can only look, behind from where we came, and go round and round and round in the circle game.' Great song, but it always makes me feel profoundly sad, for some reason. It's about the circle of life, like a carousel. 'The painted ponies go up and down.' And you should have heard me spouting at Phil, earlier. A Beyonce song, *If I Were A Boy.* 'I'd listen to her cos I know how it hurts, he's taken you for granted, and everything you had got destroyed.'

She smiles. 'Well, you were great, I thought. But tell me, who are these students, we are allegedly visiting? On a Friday? When we don't actually have any? Is there something I should know?'

We head down to the *Rodrigo*, where I exchange the cloakroom ticket Jackie gave me earlier for her suitcase, then as we still have the biggest part of an hour to kill, we drag the bag, wheels clip-clopping on the tiles, through to a pleasant, shady bar, where the sullen-looking barman, polishing glasses in a desultory fashion, does his best to ignore us. 'God I need a sit-down'

I exhale, closing my eyes and leaning back luxuriously in the chair, 'this is not how I imagined my first day back panning out!'

Chrissie turns serious, 'well before you drift off over there, tell me how it went at the bank today? I've barely seen you to ask!'

I roll my eyes, exaggeratedly, and sigh. 'Well I wiped the floor with that Forsyth bloke, I can tell you that!'

My wife looks puzzled. 'What Forsyth bloke?'

I am half asleep already. 'Bruce Forsyth, of course. How many Forsyths are in that bank? You know, that manager fellow, or chief clerk, whatever he is, sits opposite.....'

She gazes at the ceiling in exasperation. 'That's not Bruce Forsyth, the manager, he looks like Larry Grayson! You know, SHUT THAT DOOR! What's the scores on the doors? Seems like a nice boy!' Used to wear his glasses on a chain round his neck. Isla St Clair was his assistant. Can't you get anything right?'

I sit up straight in my chair. 'Right, I wiped the floor with that Grayson bloke, I can tell you that! There were no scores on his doors, apart from a big fat zero. Anyway..... you sure he's not Brucie?

'LARRY GRAYSON. For pity sake!'

'Well, anyway, you seem like a nice boy, so I believe you! Two years free banking, and I filled out one of those complaint forms. The place was rocking, all the old folks were laughing.'

'So why the long face? That's great, two years free, will save us, what, fifty euros?'

I rub my hands across my aching eyes. 'Because, all I actually wanted was an apology, just a recognition they acted badly, to-wards us. I don't really care about the money, yes of course it is good, but I simply needed him to say sorry. No. Didn't want to lose face, I suppose. All he was interested in was that we didn't have a poxy ink stamp in the passbook, from that time the old one got chewed up. You should have heard the fuss about that. Shows you where their priorities are, never mind causing us all this grief, the worry, and yes, me seriously reconsidering whether I wanted to live in a country with customer service from the Dark Ages. We don't have an ink stamp. And where is that bloody barman?'

I glance across at the shadowy figure, busily doing nothing whatsoever, and raise my hand, politely, as I was brought up to do. 'The bar is closed' he murmurs.

'So why didn't you say that five minutes ago?' I glare. I then tap the handle of the suitcase, signifying we are tourists who might be about to check-in, or maybe deciding against it on account of the crap staff. 'Two glasses of tap water, with ice.' Now the thing is, you are supposed to be able to walk into any bar in Spain, and demand a glass of water, on account of the fierce temperatures outside, I imagine. We are about to find out, I guess. What a day of discovery this is turning out to be, firstly complaint forms, now tap water. And don't blame me for not adding 'please' to my somewhat surly request. It is simply not done here. Takes some getting used to, I can tell you, but the locals never say please, and actually take the Mickey out of us for so doing. *Los por-favores* they call us Brits. My mother would spin in her grave if she heard me walk into a bar and say *one beer, one lemonade*, and no please. What have I become?

'Can you believe that?' Chrissie moans, shaking her head. 'Anyway, the account. Is it all working again? Can we pay in, and withdraw now? Did he look at the papers?'

'As far as I know' I grimace, 'he updated the passbook, without chewing it up, despite it not having an official stamp, and he did glance at our P60's, although his level of education meant he didn't have a clue what 'Legal & General Annuities' or 'Civil Service Pensions' were!' Just at that moment the barman sullenly places two glasses of water on the table. I grin, sarcastically, like the Cheshire Cat. 'Gracias!' My wife has her hand across her mouth, giggling helplessly. I take a sip of my water, which does indeed feature ice cubes. *Well who knew?*

'Oh, I forgot to tell you' I continue, 'yesterday, or it might have been the day before, riding back, between Burgos and Madrid I think, I had another extremely unpleasant experience. The road goes up through these mountains, up and up, and I was getting really low of petrol, mile after mile, climbing, climbing, with no sign of a garage. I really was starting to panic when at long last I crested the summit, and started the descent, and finally a garage came into view. Only a small one, just a couple of pumps and a small shop, but I was mighty relieved. Anyway, the attendant wasn't there, the fuel was switched off, so me and this other bloke in a car were just standing there like dummies, waiting. Now you know me, usually I would have driven off to the next garage, but I didn't have that option with only fumes in the tank, anyway eventually the attendant came back, tall fellow, miserable as hell, my age, really enjoying his work you could tell. So I filled up, fifteen euros or something, and went into the kiosk to pay, and you know sometimes with a UK card, the card machine gives you the option to pay in British pounds, or euros, and it gives you a conversion figure? And you have the choice, euros or GBP. Now the retailer gets his fifteen euros whatever you choose, it is simply giving me the option of how I want to be charged by my bank. Anyway the conversion rate was quite good, thirteen quid, so I pressed GBP, and this bloke went absolutely ballistic. Seriously, I thought he was coming over the counter at me, bawling and shouting, 'THIS IS SPAIN, NOT ENGLAND.' So I replied, quite calmly, something like it was my choice, not his. THIS IS EUROPE, WE PAY IN EUROS HERE, NOT ENGLISH MONEY. I couldn't believe it was happening, I mean it was the main motorway to the south, from the French border, not some backwoods village garage, he was hollering like some crazy, demented maniac. Clearly I'd had enough of this lunatic so I reared right up across the counter at him, and hollered 'EFFFFFFF OFFFFFF! WHY

DON'T YOU JUST EFFFFFF OFFFFFF?' And I snatched up my card, and the receipt, calmly put them away, then called him something else profoundly unpleasant, and strode out to the bike. I really thought he was going to follow me out, he was that aggressive, all over a simple bank transaction. Absolutely unbelievable. I was determined not to turn round, until I got to the bike, then I put my helmet on, and my Aviators, leg over the bike and I rode slowly away.'

I take a refreshing draught of cool, free, water. 'Of course, the adrenaline was still pumping and it took a couple of miles to calm down, but then I realised I hadn't signed the chitty, which you have to do to confirm you have agreed the conversion rate, so there is no argument at a later date. The retailer then keeps the slip. In all the aggro I'd forgotten that, and it was still in my pocket. Now in usual circumstances I'd have gone back with it, but to hell with that, for that moron, so I continued along the road, then after a few more miles I spotted a castle and a pretty-looking village, Be-Trago, or something, which re-minded me of the discount stores in Devon and Cornwall, and decided to stop for a look, maybe get some bread and cheese for lunch. Then, just as I'd turned off the slip-road, a police car came hurtling along the motorway, lights and sirens blazing, luckily I was just out of sight and he went screaming past.'

Chrissie's eyes are wide open. 'What, do you think the cops were chasing you? Am I harbouring a fugitive?!'

I instinctively duck down. 'Well, possibly, because I'd gone off with the till receipt of course. The state that bloke was in, maybe he thought I'd gone off with the receipt deliberately, to avoid paying, who knows. After lunch, when I got back on the motorway, I was a bag of nerves until I'd got well past Madrid, let me tell you! But I checked my online bank last night and the money had gone through of course, but maybe we should steer clear of Madrid for a while, until the heat dies down! But ser-iously, I am getting heartily sick of some of the customer ser-vice in this country, the water board threatening to cut us off if we didn't install a water meter over the Christmas holidays last year, this bank suspending us, that garage bloke, even this bar person, all indicative of a sloppy attitude to the customer. There have been other incidents as you know, and I'm not sure how much longer I can put up with it.'

My wife grimaces. 'Absolutely, I know what you mean, but we only arrived back yesterday! I think you should give it a couple more days!'

A picture of a Fox-Whopper and a pint of Dartmoor comes into my mind, and I shake my head to dispel the image. 'Anyway, our time is up, better get back, see what the love-birds are up to! What do you reckon, we'll find them having it off on the sofa, or all our mugs smashed to smithereens?!'

Dragging the case, studiously avoiding the barman, we head back up the cursed cobbles for hopefully the final time today. Entering the house, like anxious parents, we find our friends sitting primly on the settee, like a couple of schoolkids on a first date, although Jackie does have a gentle flush on her cheeks. *Probably the make-up, right?* I mop my brow theatrically, 'right, got your case, Jackie, shall I pop it upstairs for you?'

The pair of them stand, and take our hands, like we are about to play *Ring a Ring o' Roses.* Jackie smiles. 'Thank you both so much, for everything you've done, today, truly. But we think we would like to go home, now. We have so much to catch up on, a lot of making-up to do, but bless you, the pair of you.' And suddenly we are all hugging. Ah, to hell with my *Edinburgh Woolen Mill James Pringle super-soft cotton, £7.99 in the sale* shirt. They wash-out lovely. Apparently.

And finally, we are alone. Only one thing to do, in the circumstances. A glass of wine, out on the terrace, and watch the sun setting across the olives, which isn't a bad way to end the day, when all is said and done. If I can get past the rest of the conflict, I could probably do this for the remainder of my days.

Chrissie is also feeling mellow. 'I wonder what the pair of them are up to, now?' she giggles.

'Making the most of this moment, this second, this one chance, like Joni Mitchell told them,' I grin. 'But honestly, it was just one occasion, one moment of drunken madness, her and that Ramon, wasn't it? Is it worth throwing everything they have away, for that?'

My wife frowns. 'What do you mean, one occasion?'

I take a deep breath. 'Well, my toes were curling, let me tell you, but she said they only did it the once, in the barn, Ramon's dad keeps this rot-gut wine in there, she said, and one thing led to another....'

'It was going on for a couple of months' she hisses. 'You've heard of Fifty Shades of Grey? Well it was like fifty shades of hay, in that barn. He used to tie her to the workbench, then come up behind her, and....'

'SHUT UP!' I leap to my feet, crash across the terrace, and grip the balcony railings like a miscreant in the county lock-up. Which is where I feel I am. In prison. Trapped, in this nightmare. With all my strength I try to rip the bars away. 'AAHHHH! THE BLOODY LYING COW. Why would she lie to me? Tell you one thing, me another? It's obvious we would compare notes, at some stage.' A thought crosses my mind. 'Or maybe she was exaggerating, for your benefit? Maybe she read the book, and though to impress you...'

'Ah well who cares?' she soothes, 'she was obviously lying to one of us, just forget it, come and sit down, pour yourself another glass, next to me, like this.' And she takes my hand.

I slump into my chair. 'What a bloody waste of a day, pandering to these idiots. Christ, I wish I was up Shortacombe right now.'

'Yeah, but all you'd have up there for company is sheep!' she chuckles, 'here you have me!'

'Ooh, I don't know' I object, all serious-face. 'Some of those ewes are quite attractive!'

Which rightly earns me a dig in the ribs, to add to my other woes.

Later, drifting off to sleep is proving impossible, with the events of the day churning round in my mind. Especially one particular aspect. 'Did he really tie her to the workbench.....?'

CHAPTER 2. THE SPANISH MUGGING

The following morning, after an uncomfortable night, images of rope, workbenches, rot-gut wine and straw going around in my brain, the dark clouds are still low, over my head. The sun is out of course, and the sky a vivid blue, but I cannot see past the fog in my mind, and wishing I was elsewhere. My Corn Flakes taste like mush, my toast dry and dusty, and my coffee is uninspiring. I am indeed down in the dumps.

'Right, if you wouldn't mind joining the rest of the world, I am thinking of popping down Multibuys, then the supermarket, for a few things, this morning,' Chrissie smiles, brightly.

I glance up, morosely. 'Oh woopy-do, Multibuys. Hold me back. Will they have their Nativity and Christmas stuff out already, like Truro cathedral last month, which was *August*, let me remind you, do you think?'

'You need to get out of this mood, right now' she growls. 'We had a great holiday, now we're back. And this is hardly Purgatory, is it? Look at the view. The sunshine. I bet you didn't get any of that on bloody Dartmoor, did you? If Tom Pearce's grey mare had appeared ghostly white, I bet you couldn't have seen it, in all that fog. You sorted the bank, stuff Jackie and Phil, this is all about us now. Come on, shake a leg!'

I eye her unenthusiastically. 'What do you need in the supermarket? Surely I will go, late afternoon, when it's quiet, like I always do, before the Spanish get in there, for the weekly shop?

Why do we need to go twice?'

She rolls her eyes, standing there, that familiar pose, hands on hips. 'Come here a minute' she commands, beckoning me into the kitchen, and holding the fridge door, wide open, 'and tell me what you see?'

My turn for sarcasm. 'I don't need to see what is in the fridge, because there is precisely nothing, apart from a carton of UHT milk, and UHT orange juice, which I why I am going later this afternoon. Duh.'

She smiles sweetly. 'Right. So about one o' clock today, under the fig tree, flopped out on your sunbed, when you start looking at me expectantly, stomach rumbling, and I tell you there is nothing for lunch, apart from milk and orange juice, that will be OK, will it? Cornflakes and dry toast? Delicious. I just thought I might get myself a pack of cheese, and maybe some ham for you, and of course we missed *Jose the Pan* as you were snoring away in your pit, so a nice fresh crusty loaf might not go amiss, but if you are happy with UHT juice, that is fine by me. DUH!'

I rub my hands across my eyes. 'All right, all right, it was a hell of a day, yesterday, and technically I am still a fugitive from the law, so cut me some slack, please. Yes I'd be delighted to come to Multibuys with you.' I stand up. 'Actually I'm ready, what about you, come on, hurry up, get a move on, dawdling as usual, trying to find the right handbag, always waiting, I am.' And I even manage to dodge the in-swinger....

Inside the emporium of all things naff, apart from the three weeks before Christmas when a glorious display of all things Nativity appears, when it becomes my favourite shop in all the world, I am approached by a little boy, aged around seven maybe, dressed in a *Ramones* tee-shirt several sizes too big, and a pair of board shorts. 'You English?' he queries. 'Can you tell me the significance of the English word *fuck-off?*' Which takes me aback, somewhat. Did I swear when I was that age?

At strangers? Well actually he is asking what it means, of course. In Spanish they use the term *significance*, whereas we say *meaning*. What is the meaning of this English word. Well two words to be precise. And now his mother is approaching, in a *Ramones* tee-shirt several sizes too small. Maybe they got dressed in a hurry, this morning, having been told to eff-off, and determined to go out immediately and discover what it meant?

'Well, it is a bad word, a *palabra mala*' is all I can think to say. 'Who said this to you?'

'An English man in our street' Mrs Ramone confirms. 'Juanito here was playing football, and this English man came out of his house and said this. Only this. *Fuck-off.*'

'Well in this context it means *Betty*, go away' I confirm, struggling to keep a straight face, as this is a first for me, I can tell you, explaining the meaning of *eff-off* to a woman in a bulging top, in a discount store, halfway up a mountain in the wilds of Spain. And there was me didn't want to get up, this morning. You just never know, do you? And there you go. Want to tell a Spaniard to clear off? Try *Betty*. Actually I think the spelling is something like *ve-te*, but you're not gonna put it in writing, are you? 'Which street is this?' I continue, out of interest, in case I know this alleged Englishman, who could equally be from any part of the British Isles, or Ireland, USA, Canada, Australia, New Zealand, in the interests of fairness. But yeah, he sounds English.

'Calle Cazzy -something' she slurs, and I smile, as only I know I haven't a clue.

'Well this man is a *tonto*, forget it' I grimace, looking her straight in the eye, as gazing anywhere else is not an option. 'Sorry.' Don't know why I'm apologising, quite honestly, especially if the bloke is an Aussie. Still, just whipped them at cricket, didn't I? It's the least I can do.

'What was all that about?' enquires my wife, when we get outside. I explain the gist of the conversation. 'I don't know, you're not safe to take anywhere!' she giggles. 'I turn my back, for two minutes, and there you are, engaging with a woman with artificially large breasts.'

'Can't say I noticed, quite honestly' I splutter, 'but her kid was sweet, didn't you think? What kind of a moron would tell a little boy to eff-off like that?

She eyes me suspiciously. 'Anyway, grab this, will you?', handing me a folding umbrella. I glance sarcastically at the sky, like Pooh Bear, looking for black clouds, and hunny. 'Yeah, all right, all right' she giggles. 'But they had them on offer, two euros, and they're handy, aren't they, that size, to slip in your bag, just in case.'

Oh yes! I can feel a little victory on the horizon. 'So why don't you, er, slip it in your bag? You know, just in case?'

Silently, she unzips her leather bowling-ball bag with the scotty-dog motif dangling from the handle, which I know all about having purchased it myself, last Christmas, a rare success, of which I am justifiably proud, to reveal a giant pack of paper serviettes. 'And' she sighs, 'I need to save some space, for the cheese, and the ham, so just take the bloody umbrella and shut up!'

'Well thanks very much' I wail, 'I will look a right plonker carrying an umbrella, in thirty-five degrees. Can't I carry the serviettes?'

We approach the main shopping streets in companionable silence. Well that was my take on it anyway. 'Right' she smiles, 'I am off to the supermarket, if you could pop in the *panaderia* for a crusty loaf, that would be a help, and I will meet you out here in ten minutes or so. And please don't tell me they sell bread in the supermarket, it is much fresher from the baker, as we all know. Can I trust you to do that, without accosting any women with an impossibly massive chest, and allegedly explaining the eff-word?'

I am still scanning the horizon for black clouds, just in case. 'Oh sorry, were you talking to me? I will be fine. What can possibly go wrong, here? A simple transaction, buying bread, you can toddle off to get your cheese and ham, safe in the knowledge that I will be waiting for you, when you return. Besides, as you know, I am more of a leg-man!' *Been waiting to get that one in all morning....*

So I pop into the bakery, purchase said *pan,* which I drop onto a shady bench, next to the umbrella, then slump down next to them, and whip out my phone to run through my holiday snaps, while I am waiting. Not sure this is a particularly good idea, in my current state of mind, as most of the pictures seem to be of my bike standing outside various pubs, or heritage railways, or the Cheddar cider and cheese emporium. Still, it passes the time, so much so that I am hardly aware of a couple of teenage boys, sidling up the street. Their presence barely registers as I giggle to myself about Coleridge and the Person From Porlock, Tom Pearce and his grey mare at Widecombe, and the Devil, who, as we all know, accidentally dropped a load of stones into the river Barle on Exmoor, forming in the process the ancient clapper-bridge, Tarr Steps.

I come to the end of the photo display, then close the phone and drop it in my pocket, only at that moment becoming vaguely aware of the kids, mooching along, and still I fail to register any danger, or threat, whatsoever. They are a strange pair, I have to say, thirteen maybe, one tall and blond, quite un-Spanish looking actually, his mate stocky and dark, undoubtedly a local. Suddenly, blondy approaches, smiling. 'Race you to the top of the street' he suggests, politely.

I grin in response. 'Sorry, I have a bad *Rhodesia*' I tell him. This is true, more or less, even though I cannot recall the Spanish for *foot,* I don't know the word for *ankle,* and *leg* escapes me for now. Still, *knee* is close enough for these purposes. Must have gone down on it hard, stepping off the bike, outside a pub or a cheese shop somewhere. But what a strange request? Nobody has challenged me to a race since I was about eleven.

'Oh go on' he protests, 'only to the top of the street!' And in the background, I spot his stocky mate, lurking, but still my alert levels are switched completely off.

I cross my leg and start rubbing it. *Pierna,* that's the word. 'Sorry, I have *dolor* in my *pierna.* I cannot run.' *Now Betty, before I tell you to eff-off. You are starting to get on my nerves, now. And what's the big deal about racing blokes who are fifty years older than you? Pick on someone your own age.*

Suddenly, he reaches down, snatches up the crusty loaf, and goes tearing down the road with it in his hand. And I, ignoring the *dolor* in my *Rhodesia,* and the *pierna,* go charging after him. Luckily, this stretch is slightly downhill, and I feel the adrenaline kicking in, as for a brief period we are re-enacting a scene from *Chariots of Fire,* in slow-motion, with Jon and Vangelis playing in the background. In a few seconds however, we reach a busy cross-street, the main road through town, across which he dashes, dodging the traffic, floppy hair flying, still clutching my bread, and disappears into the shopping area. I haven't finished with him yet, however, as taking a deep breath, I bellow at the top of my voice 'YOU BLOODY LITTLE BASTARD!' Well, not an Australian, am I? Then, glancing up the street, who should be approaching, like Noddy and Big Ears in a clockwork Panda-car, but Santa Marta's finest, the extremely ancient Old Bill. Complete and utter waste of time involving these geriatrics in the crime of course, as by the time they have eased their aching *Rhodesias* and *piernas* out of the car, sharpened their pencils and took down the details, Blondy will have nicked some ham and tomatoes, prepared elevenses for his mates, and consumed the evidence.

I turn and hobble back up the street, then spot Chrissie standing, open mouthed, on the pavement. 'What was all that English swearing? Was that you? It sounded like you. And why are you limping like that?'

'Been robbed, mugged, haven't I?' I croak. 'Some little peasant ran off with the loaf.'

She stares in disbelief. 'Five minutes. Five minutes I've been gone, and you manage to get into trouble in that...AND WHERE'S MY UMBRELLA?'

We are approaching my bench, where sure enough the cursed brolly remains, untouched, precisely where I left it. 'There it is, look' I giggle. 'Even a pair of thieves wouldn't touch it. A fifteen-bob loaf and a two-quid umbrella, and which one got nicked!?'

She is dumbfounded. 'You left it there? I cannot believe you left it there?'

I employ a healthy dose of sarcasm. 'Well the thing was, a crime was being committed, you see, so I didn't have time to gather up all my belongings, before attempting to apprehend the miscreant. But don't you worry about me, I am fine thanks, no cause for you to be concerned.'

She runs her hand across her face. 'Sorry. You are right of course. It's just, I don't know, you always seem to be in trouble, lately. It follows you around.'

'Well it wasn't me, it was my phone what attracted them, in the first place' I chuckle. And I go on to relate the sequence of events, from the relative comfort of my bench.

She is thoughtful, for a moment. 'So what would you have done, in the unlikely event of you catching him?'

I consider this implausible prospect for a few seconds. 'Well, I reckon I'd have held out my hand, he'd have given the loaf back, sheepishly, with an *aw-shucks* look on his face, then we'd have fist-bumped maybe, and I'd have taken him for a pint. Well possibly he's a bit young. A lemonade, maybe.'

She is still frowning. 'So what if it was my bag, he snatched?'

'Well, in that case' I fume, all thoughts of going for a pint dispelled from my mind, 'I would have followed him through the shopping area, providing he didn't vanish down some alleyway, and took the bag back, by fair means or foul.'

'OK. So what if it was a little old lady, he mugged?'

Outrage courses through my veins. Chrissie is nodding, meanwhile. And suddenly, I remember the whole sordid, hateful incident. 'Oh. My. God. That little old lady, last Spring. That was here, this street, wasn't it? A teenage boy, wasn't it? Didn't she fall over, in the attack? Badly shaken-up, wasn't she? Didn't catch anyone, the Police, did they?' I can feel my fists bunching. 'I wonder if it was the same kid? Paco the Policeman at the conversation group didn't say any more about it, did he? Well of course, if I'd witnessed that, I would have thrown the kid to the ground and sat on him, until the cops arrived.'

She still has that strange look on her face. 'So are you sure there are citizens' powers of arrest, in this country?'

'Well there must be, surely? What is anyone supposed to do, let him go? I don't care what country it is, a member of the public has the right to apprehend a criminal, attacking an old lady , by using reasonable force?'

She raises her eyebrows. 'And what if half a dozen of his 'uncles' turned up? Look, I agree with you, any right-thinking person would intervene, if they were able, but sometimes I think you need to remember you are nearer seventy than seventeen...'

'Only just!' I giggle. Or are you saying I'm seventeen stone?'

She grins. 'I'm just saying, you're not as young as you were. Remember just before we retired, when you were opening the office that morning, you disturbed that burglar who came at you with a chisel, and you ended up with that great slice across your chest. That could so easily have been a stab-wound, and for what? A bottle of whisky, was all the boss gave you!'

I am smiling at the memory, even though it wasn't funny, at

the time. 'Yeah, and do you know what the boss said? He said 'Aren't you supposed to be playing cricket tonight? Didn't you have your kit with you? So why didn't you hit the burglar with your bat?!' And I replied something like 'Yes I was batting at number-three, but do you think I want the imprint of some scrote's face across my trusty Grey-Nicolls?' Mind you, it was a Single-Malt, he gave me, so I forgave him!'

Chrissie gathers up her umbrella, then pauses. And waits. And looks me in the eye. I blink first. 'What? Can we go home please? I'm sick of this day, already.'

'Well of course, I'd love to get home. Hopefully you can get the pool uncovered and we can spend the rest of the day doing absolutely nothing. But you, er, need to get some bread, seeing as how you allegedly lost the last lot! I mean, you say you were robbed, but there is absolutely no evidence of that, is there? Some kid made off with it, like in some Dickensian tale. A likely story, I have to say.'

Grumbling mightily, I root around in my pocket, and come out with twenty-five cents. 'Here you go, you gave me a euro coin, didn't you, and here's the change. And I am certainly not going back in that baker's, they will think there is something fishy going on. They will think I am up to something. They won't know quite what, of course, other than it involves bread!'

We head steadily home, each immersed in our own thoughts. So was I mugged, or robbed? Obviously the monetary value is irrelevant, it is the actual deed which matters, and I cannot help feeling profoundly sad this has happened here, in what is supposed to be our retirement in this little town on a mountain. Not the crime of the century of course, but there have been several break-ins recently, which is a crime I detest, plus the old lady last Spring, which I abhor. Can happen anywhere of course, but I am struggling to recall anything like this happening to me, during my lifetime, in some of the livelier parts of the UK. Maybe I've been lucky, my size helps of course, as the villain generally preys on the weak, doesn't he? Oh yes, I remember, 1970 or thereabouts it would have been, going home from Sea Scouts one Friday evening, I was set upon by half-a-dozen skinheads, one of whom was swinging a bicycle chain, which he'd sharpened into various points, and proceeded to whack me across the face with it, missing my eye by a whisker. Jack Reacher would have seen them off, naturally, wouldn't he? All six laid out in the road, in under five seconds. I am no Reacher, of course, and took the only available course open to me, in the circumstances. I ran like hell. Mind you, Reacher would not have been encumbered, as I was, with a sailor's cap under one arm, and a 1966 Genuine Leather World Cup Willie Official Football under the other. Rather restricts the options, no? Actually, I bet you don't even know who World Cup Willie is, or was, Jack, do you?

Reaching home, Chrissie heads to the kitchen to prepare lunch, which for what we just spent on bread, we could probably have flown to some chic bistro in the south of France, and I head downstairs to prepare the pool. Will need topping up, almost certainly, a handful of chemical pellets too, and I will probably need to run the pump.... 'NEIGHBOUR! GOOD HOLIDAY? ENJOY YOUR DAY WITH THOSE BASTARDOS IN THE BANK YESTERDAY? YOU TOPPING UP THE POOL? MOKKA! HOUSE OF YOUR FRIENDS, MOKKA, NEIGHBOUR!'

Startled, heart pounding from the aural assault, I glance up and spot Juan, the dustman, gurning out from behind his patio curtains. I say curtains, but only in the most optimistic sense of the word, because in a former life, these faded, flapping, frayed, heavy-duty canvas drapes undoubtedly saw service hanging from the side of a lorry, as protection from the elements, bearing as they do the legend PANA TRANSP, which presumably is the Spanish version of *Eddie Stobart*. Still, waste not, and all that, bearing in mind the remainder of the back of his house looks like it was thrown together by the *PG Tips* chimpanzees, or lunatics. He seems to have lost even more of his front teeth since I last saw him, which is hardly surprising really if he keeps jumping out at people and hollering, as he drags his rubber bucket around the town. And blimey, how many questions were in the same sentence? *Yeah great holiday, although probably best keeping quiet about the Person From Porlock, all bankers are bastards, everyone knows that, but how the hell did news of my escapade there spread round the town so fast, er yes, topping up the pool, after I put the parasol up for a bit of privacy, and mokka? Isn't that some sort of coffee and chocolate concoction, and what does it have to do with our friends?* Questions, questions, and now I have one for him. 'Not working this morning, Juan?'

He grins, gummily. 'Jubilado, neighbour!' Ah yes, I know this one, as we too are *jubilado* here. Retired. But there is more to come, it seems. 'Not working, September, back to work, October and November, then finish *totalmente* in December.' A staggered retirement, sounds like a great idea, actually, get him and his family used to the concept.

'So does Susanna like the thought of having you home, *permenente?*' I giggle.

There comes a shout, and the 'curtain' bulges, exactly like in the *Morcambe and Wise* show, and I have to stuff my knuckles in my mouth as a head finally emerges. 'No she doesn't!' giggles his wife, her crimson hair and orange suntan glinting in the bright sunshine. But at least there is no little white dog trapped under her bosom, this morning.

This does of course raise a serious point, not the little white dog I don't mean, as whilst preparing for retirement seems an eminently sensible idea, how is he proposing to fill his days? Like many of the locals here, he cannot or does not like to read, his DIY skills are at best rudimentary, and his garden consists of an olive tree in severe need of pruning, surrounded by jungle. Usually arriving home just as the church clock is striking two, he will stand on his terrace like a diminutive town-crier and bellow 'DOSS', for the benefit of those unable to count, followed by 'WAHEYYYY!' to attract the attention of 'Seve', his neighbour on the other side, who bears an uncanny resemblance to the late, great Spanish golfer, Severiano Ballesteros. There then follows a shouting match between the pair, across their balconies, and Chrissie and I, giggling, from the safety of our garden, like to imagine they are discussing their respective lunches, using British ingredients.

'SAUSAGE, EGG, CHIPS AND BEANS!'

'EH?'

'SAUSAGE, EGG, CHIPS AND BEANS!'

'NO, FISH ON A FRIDAY!'

'EH?'

'FISH ON A FRIDAY!'

'STEAK AND KIDNEY PIE!'

'I PREFER BEEF AND ONION!'

'EH?'

'CHICKEN AND CHIPS IS NICE!'

'EH?

I snuck out from beneath our fig tree once, and was astonished to see the pair of them standing at the opposite ends of their respective patios, rather than within a few feet of each other, as they could easily have done, thereby avoiding wear and tear on their individual throats, and ear-drums.

'CORNISH PASTY!'

'EH?'

I set the hosepipe running, then carry the sunbed mattresses and pillows down to the bottom of the garden, and am just laying it out when Chrissie appears with our expensive lunch. 'What was Juan bellowing about?' she chuckles.

I frown. 'Are Jane and Nigel here at the moment, do you know? He was saying something about a coffee morning, at their house, mokka, that is coffee, right? Problem is he has lost even more teeth and I couldn't really follow the gist of it. He knew all about Bruce Forsyth, or Larry Whatsit, and it's just gone two o' clock in case you're interested!'

Her turn to frown. 'Well strangely enough, I only arrived back the day before yesterday, same as you, so I really have no idea. But I doubt it, as Janie usually messages me when they are coming, but as we were away, maybe she didn't bother. Anyway, let's eat up our gold-plated sandwiches, HAM AND CHEESE! EH? And afterwards I will message her.'

Too late of course, as immediately my lunch has disappeared down the hatch, it's back with my sunbed, head on the pillow, and I'm away to the land of nod before you can say sausage, egg, chips or beans.

Some time later, I wake to find my wife sat up on her sunbed, rolling her eyes. 'Oh, welcome back to the land of the living! I turned the hosepipe off, in case you were interested, to avoid us getting swept away. Three o' clock has been and gone, you know! Janie and Nigel are coming next weekend, but he is going to call you, shortly, as he has something to ask about Miguel's, no idea what it's about. Oh, and changing the subject, have you noticed anything different, around here, these past couple of days?' I frown, yet again. Since I've been back in this country, all I've seemed to do is argue with people, and frown. 'The silence?' she hints. The lack of shouting, from this side of the garden wall anyway?' She nods towards Loli's side.

'Well, now you come to mention it, I did think it was eerily quiet, earlier. Mind you, I've been asleep for most of it!'

'Loli, Isabel, and Fernando' she continues. 'They're not there, are they? Not moving around the house, no banging and crashing, no hollering, no sweeping the path. Do you think they've gone on holiday?'

'Oh my God, can you imagine that?' I smile. 'Arriving at your beach-front hotel, to find them bellowing in the next room, or sat around the pool? Fernando in his spandex mankini? On the next table in the dining room? All that hawking and gobbing round the omelette queue? Sat there at the bingo! Can you imagine Loli playing bingo? HOUSE, NEIGHBOUR! QUICK, SWEEP THE STREETS! MOP THE PATIO! Bloody hell, you'd want a refund, or a change of venue, at the very least!'

Our deliberations are disturbed by my phone ringing. Nigel. 'Hello John, hope you had a good holiday, back in the UK! Look, I'll keep it brief, cos I know you have that fig tree to lie under! We are coming out next weekend, for ten days or so, and I really want to crack on with Miguel's, get the electrics finished on the top floor, get the water piped in, lay the bathroom out if there's time. I've got it pretty well sorted in my mind, but what I was hoping is if you could cast your eye over it, see what you think the priorities are, and we can compare notes when I see you. I've been up on our roof and looked down on Miguel's, it all seems fairly good actually. One thing we need to do is get some plasterboard organised, cover those horrible beams on the top floor, where they got the smoke damage during the fire. Janie and I tried to wash them off last time, but it was hopeless, so all I can think to do is board them over.'

It's not often I find inspiration. It comes to me rarely, especially these days. So when it does approach, I tend to grab it with both hands, invite it in, sit it down, make it a cup of tea. 'Well' I smile, for this is going to be good. 'Have you thought about sanding the beams down? Plastering in between them with that white mortar? Making a feature of them, rather than covering them over? I think they would come up lovely, an antique-wood finish obviously, but maybe with a very light stain to bring out the grain, the patina, it would look sensational up there.'

Silence on the line, as he considers the genius that is his friend John Austin Richards. Or perhaps he is mulling-over how best to sack me. 'Wow! You're right! Do you really think they would come up, sanded? But won't it be a lot of work? I mean, surely it would be easier to just cover them over?'

'Easier?' I wail. 'Easier? Easier, possibly, better, no! This is a one-off. A one-time only job. I bet if you went home to Janie tonight and told her you were thinking of sanding down the beams, nick my idea, I don't care, but she would make all your Christmasses come at once!' Next to me, Chrissie is rolling her eyes, but cue male laughter down the phone line. 'Tell you what' I continue, 'why don't I sand down a couple of beams, in that area above the stairs as you come up, then plaster in between them, and you can see what you think next weekend. And so confident am I, that if she doesn't like it, I won't even charge you. And if she does, that is a pizza you owe me, down that Italian restaurant. But nothing with pineapple on, OK?'

I can feel the relief, surging across the continent. 'You got yourself a deal, matey! D'you know, I've been hammering up plasterboard, in my dreams, for weeks! I'm so glad I phoned, and I cannot wait to tell Janie all about it!'

No, I bet you can't!

Lying back down on my bed, I reflect on what has been a crazy few days, after what was undoubtedly the biggest crisis in our time here. Have we turned a corner at last? Can we move on now? I certainly hope so. The bank business will take some getting over, in my mind, as once I've been wronged, I find it difficult to forgive, or forget. Changing banks would be the logical step, but there is none of this 'one click' business here, seemingly, and I'm not sure I need the hassle in my life. Besides, I have two years to think about it, don't I? Yeah, that's what I'll do, just close my eyes....

CHAPTER 3. MEET THE WALTONS, AND THE SPANISH COW-FLOP

Dungarees. Where are you, on this subject? Are you thinking Depression-era Virginia, the backwoods, moonshine, huntin', shootin', fishin'' good ol' boys, twanging guitars, fiddles, home-fries, catfish on the table, dirt roads, lumber mills, the county sheriff? The Blue Ridge Mountains, maybe Shenandoah? Or late 2019 Instagram-ready style icons, pastel shades, fitted de-signer-style, catwalks, fashion houses, the versatile, go-to, go-anywhere outfit for the West End or down the pub? Or perhaps you're wondering what the hell this has to do with Spain?

Well, let me ask you another question. Have you ever been to Bilbao? City in north-eastern Spain, ferry-port, home to the Guggenheim museum, and, curiously, our sometime-neigh-bours here in sunny Andalucia. Yes, next door to us, on the left, not the right where Loli, Isabel and Fernando reside, is a holiday cottage, the owners of which we have christened the Waltons, on account of their default-setting choice of clothing, with bib-fronts. Not the pastel variety, in cool shades of cotton, but the heavy, denim versions, like a team of wood-cutters, which I have to say is a curious choice, given that they usually holiday here in August, when temperatures regularly nudge forty degrees. And I was just wondering, if you had paid a visit to that Basque town, whether you'd noticed other members of the local populace dressed in that manner? Curious. Nice people however, friendly, affable, a father, Antonio, who must be well into his seventies, and unsteady on his pins, so much so that we always resolve to steer well clear of the Bilbao road in August, and his two adult children, Tonio, which I assume is a diminutive of his father's name, and Sonia. Not forgetting their dog, Luna. Well, actually, the Waltons did actually forget Luna, one year. They also come for ten days at Easter, and on their previous visit Luna managed to escape. After a cursory search of the surrounding area, they toddled off back to Bilbao without her, possibly concluding she would make her own arrangements for getting home. All six-hundred miles. I swear I am not making this up. About a week after their departure, came a knocking on our door and an old woman, perspiring freely, slumped against our wall. The conversation went something like this. 'Got your dog in my garden, neighbour.'

'We don't have a dog, sorry.'

Yes, it's your dog, neighbour.'

'No, we have cats. We don't have a dog, we have never had a dog in Spain.'

'Yes, your dog, neighbour. Lola saw it coming out of your front door one morning, when you were playing your David Bisball records.'

'I don't have any David Bisball records. I hate David Bisball. We don't watch Spanish X-Factor!'

Yes you do, neighbour, you play his records every morning.'

'What colour is this dog?'

'White, neighbour.'

'Does it answer to the name of Luna?'

I advised her to hang on to the creature until August, which, given that it was only April, didn't go down too well. Failing that she could post it back, address the parcel to 'The People in the Dungarees, Bilbao, Spain.' Surely that would find them?

All right, I did make that last bit up.

Their day usually begins on their kitchen patio with five minutes of brisk throat-clearing from Papa, which means that Chrissie and I tend to breakfast early during August, in the cool of the morning. Then Tonio will begin shouting across at us, as perhaps he is concerned we might have overslept. 'NEIGH-BOUR! ALLA MADREEEE!'

To which I, not being a particular fan of Real Madrid, usually reply 'FORZA BARCA!', which basically amounts to heresy in these parts.

Sonia will then chime in with 'NO, ATLETTI!', which I assume might be something to do with Athletic Bilbao, although bearing in mind they generally reside at the lower levels of the Spanish league, could be derogatory. Or obscene.

Then, to wind up the conversation satisfactorily, to perhaps celebrate the venting of his lungs, Papa will holler 'LUNA GUAPA CHICA!', *pretty little Luna*, to which I, were I a certain diminutive white canine, would respond by sinking my teeth into somewhere fleshy. *What, leave me behind with that mad old woman for four months? Have some of this!*

Their breakfast can then begin.

It is bedtime which gives us the most satisfaction, however, with the promise of eight relatively tranquil hours, and the complete absence of David-bloody-Bisball. Usually got an earworm going round in my head though, don't I? You can see now why we usually go away in August. We always know when Tonio is off up the wooden hill, as a small earthquake, followed by the *Mastermind* theme, accompanied by a herd of elephants, starts up, and we imagine a blizzard of plaster dropping off their walls. There then follows around five minutes of stifled

49

grunting, which please God is Sonia brushing mortar off her brother's back, then, praise be, silence. We like to imagine the family, in their respective bedrooms, bidding each other sweet dreams, exactly as in the original, heart-warming Sunday-evening TV series, from the 1970's.

'G-night, Papa.'

'G-night, Tonio.'

'G-night, Papa.'

'G-night, Sonia.'

'G-night, Tonio.'

'G-night, Sonia.'

'Luna guapa chica!'

'AHHHHHOOWWWW!'

Come Monday morning, we are exhausted. The Waltons departed in the early hours, which meant not only did the herd of elephants put in an appearance at bed-time, they paid us a return visit in the middle of the night. Followed by more stifled grunting, the odd strangled oath, the banging of the front door and the clip-clop of their cases as they wheeled away unsteadily down the cobbled street. Mercifully however, no David Bisball. And I dashed to the window to see a little white rump trotting happily behind them, so all is good. Unless she escaped before they got to their car. And I have other things to worry about, quite honestly, like sanding down a few beams at Miguel's, for which I am fully prepared, with sander, the one shaped like a steam-iron, the triangular front end being perfect for getting between the lumps and knots on the tree-trunks, and if not, too bad as it's all I have, spare pads, extension lead, protective glasses and a face mask, all stowed safely in a bag-for-life.

First of all however I have to negotiate the delights of Chrissie's new student Victor, not 'Vic the Fish' mark you, he of Man's Sall-mon and latterly undertaker fame, because I would have nabbed him, and let her do the sanding, but 'Little Victor', candidate in the world's most boring man competition. Diminutive, blond, blue-eyes, around thirty, with absolutely zero outside interests, which makes trying to have an English conversation with the fellow nigh on impossible. 'What do you like to do in the evenings, at the weekend, Victor?' I enquired on one occasion. 'Go for a beer, maybe?'

'No no' he replied, 'when I go to the bar I always have a glass of warm milk.' Which killed that conversation stone dead. Just imagine him out on the razzle on a Friday night with his mates, can't you? 'Six pints of San Miguel and a saucer of semi-skimmed for Tiddles!'

He arrives for his classes clutching a man-bag, which he resolutely refuses to put on the floor, or another chair, causing us to speculate whether he is bearing, I dunno, the Spanish nuclear codes, or the Coca-Cola recipe. Plus an English-Spanish text book, curiously entitled *Ship or Sheep*, two seemingly unrelated words, but which appear to cause the locals some difficulty. Possibly explains the abject failure of the *Spanish Armada*. I can imagine Sir Francis Drake playing bowls on Plymouth Hoe. 'Sire, the Spaniards are coming!'

BAAAAAAAAAAAA!

Like most of our local connections, we first met Victor at the library group, where he asked me to check over his CV, as he was intending to apply to become a teacher in the UK. An impressive resume it has to be said, but bearing several glaring omissions. Firstly, he possessed no English language skills whatsoever, and secondly, no teaching qualifications. I advised him to take an intensive English course, and then apply for an engineering career where he could apply his degree on a practical level. And to be fair, he did enrol with an academy and gained an impressive level of conversation, which really only needs polishing up. Just. A. Shame. He. Is. So. Deadly. Dull.

And here he is this morning, in the armchair, knees together, *Ship or Sheep* opened to a page depicting British kids dancing round a maypole. And Chrissie already yawning. He spots my bag of tools. 'What are you doing, Jonneee?'

'I am sanding some wooden beams at our friends' house this morning' I smile. 'To sand is the verb, sanding is the action, and this machine is a sander.'

He closes *Ship or Sheep* but keeps his thumb in the page, and frowns. 'But you are not a carpenter. How do you know about sanders? Where did you learn thees, plees?'

I take a deep breath. 'Well, we have a saying in English. *It's not rocket science.* I am not fitting the beams, they are already there. All I am doing is removing the accumulated dirt. This is very easy!' *Oh, famous last words...*

I bid him farewell, then escape twenty questions gratefully, step out into the street, and almost stumble into the arms of Juan-the-soon-to-be-retired-dustman, who I have to say looks utterly bored, and it's only the first week of September. It seems as if Susannah has ordered him outside to get on with something useful, but neither of them can work out quite what. Maybe I should introduce him to Victor, they could form a support group possibly, over a couple of glasses of Gold Top. 'Mokka neighbour, your friends' house.' he bellows, despite the fact that we are actually shaking hands.

'Ya boy' I tell him, managing to dodge most of the projectile spittle, but only most. Now then, had I been heading generally in the direction of Miguel's, via the cafe, possibly, at some stage today, I might have said 'me boy.' I am going, soon-ish. 'Ya boy' however conveys the fact that I am off there right that second, if not sooner, and that I will not be passing *Go* or collecting two-hundred pounds. Quite keen to get down there actually, avoiding eye infections, and the possible mention of sausage, egg, chips and beans, which I could absolutely murder right now, or I could before my chin got wet... Luckily, Juan spots a microscopic speck of dust on his windowsill, which needs flicking away, and gratefully I continue my journey unhindered, pulling my tee-shirt up over my face as soon as I get around the bend, possibly not the most hygienic way of cleansing my facial pores, but the best I can manage in the circumstances. Besides, the dust will soak up any unpleasant residues, in about ten minutes, hopefully.

As I approach Miguel's, I notice a large swarm of flies buzzing around aggressively, big ones too, bluebottles I suppose you would call them, but growing-up they were always referred to as 'meat-flies' in our house. Don't ask me. I have no idea whether these insects displayed a preference for butchery products, all I know is that the Sunday roast was always stored under a net 'to keep the meat-flies off', in those pre-refrigeration days. And mother had a favourite expression for someone who was, in her opinion, smiling or laughing unnecessarily. 'Look at her, grinning like a meat-fly.' As a small boy I found this puzzling, as to me the creatures were travelling too fast to be able to discern whether their features were relaxed in any way, but they sure as hell weren't grinning, when father managed to swat one, with a rolled-up newspaper.

I place my tools carefully on the pavement, then unlock the front door, and step back smartly and flap my arms ineffectually as yet more angry bugs, who most certainly are far from amused, make a bid for freedom. For a second or two it is like the Battle of Britain over the White Cliffs of Dover, and all it needs is for Vera Lynn to start crooning, but eventually the multitude disperses, leaving only the odd individual searching vainly for a nice bit of sirloin, and peace reigns again.

I lean against the railings and mop my brow with my hands, thus ensuring an even distribution of bacteria. Been a hell of a day do far, what with the Waltons during the night, Juan's dribble and now this Biblical plague, and I haven't even got inside the house yet. Suddenly, out the corner of my eye, I spot something round and brown on the floor, in the middle of the doorway. An extremely old pancake? It is almost flat, about six inches across, so what is this, someone's sick idea of a joke, sliding rancid crepes under peoples' front doors? No, hang on a minute, it is not confectionery, it is a cow-flop. And believe me, I am familiar with form of entertainment, in the fields near our house, as a small boy, being one of the chief organisers of the world cow-pat discus championships. And let me tell you, there was far more skill involved than the Olympics, as in our championships, you not only had to skim the disc of bovine faeces the maximum distance, but you had to select your weapon of choice from whatever was available, lying on the grass. Texture and consistency were of paramount importance, as I am sure you can imagine.

I am chuckling to myself at my childhood memories when suddenly it dawns on me. Who has been letting cattle loose in Miguel's front room? This is impossible. I haven't seen a single cow, since arriving in this country, on account of there being barely a single blade of grass, between here and Malaga. I step forward for a second glance, and recoil in sheer utter disgust, as I spot the two beady eyes, the twitchy little nose, which twitched its last some considerable while ago, and protruding teeth. *It is not a cow-flop. It is a rat, eaten from the inside, and collapsed in on itself, leaving only the fur.* Feeling rising bile in my throat, I just about have time to slump on the railings before vomiting spectacularly onto the cobbles below. My stomach is heaving and churning, my whole body convulsing, and I am unable to dispel the grotesque image from my mind. I am making more noise than an entire rugby team after a dodgy vindaloo, sure to attract attention from passing Spaniards, and for certain this section of the street will need steam cleaning, at the very least, especially after the sun gets around and everything starts to solidify, but I cannot worry about that yet as my boots are still coming up, from the very depths of my soles.

'WHAT IS HAPPENING NEIGHBOUR?!' I am vaguely aware of shouting, but with my eyes full of tears and drool dangling from my chin, I am unable to focus. With a supreme effort I manage to raise my head and can just about discern Juan edging his way along the railings, glancing down in disgust at the vile mess I have made of his sparkling cobbles. Having momentarily lost the power of speech, I gesture behind me with my thumb in a *you're the dustman, you must have seen worse than this over the years, but I wouldn't have your job for all the tea in China, and by the way can you get your brush out and sweep the thing up before I die* kind of way. Nope. With a cry of HUUUURRRRR!, he joins me on the railings, the pungent aroma of his vomit attacks my senses and I lose the battle yet again.

'BILLY-OOOO NEIGHBOUR!' I cannot stand much more of this, quite honestly. Could this get any worse? A whole audience will turn up, any minute now. Who is it now? Pirate Pete, deep joy. Summoning just the presence of mind to grab my bag of tools, but leaving Miguel's door wide open as facing the thing again is unthinkable, I stagger off up the street, unlock my front door and collapse inside. Chrissie looks surprised. 'Blimey, that was quick! Finished already? You have done ..... CHRIST WHAT IS THAT STENCH? Oh my God what is that down your front?' Victor meanwhile is clenching his knees, gripping his man-bag ever tighter and seems in severe need of a restorative glass of milk. As am I actually. Settles the stomach, doesn't it, milk? Unlike beer. Without speaking, I dive into the bathroom, strip off my tee-shirt and hurl it out the window, as it will need incinerating later, then rejoice as the cold water from the shower courses over my shattered body. I clean my teeth, slip on my dressing gown, then head back to face my wife and her student.

I slump in the chair, ashen-faced. 'There was a rat. Urrrr. A dead rat. Urrrr. A flat, dead, rat, in the doorway. Urrrr. Urrrr. Been dead for years, by the look of it. Urrrr. The most disgusting thing I have ever seen. It is like the world spewing competition down there. Even Juan was sick. Urrrr.'

Chrissie manages to look incredulous. 'Is that all? God, you are a right drama queen. So what, it is dead. You have been sick? What a bloody fuss about nothing!'

Victor meanwhile is thoroughly enjoying his morning. 'A deadth rath! A flath, deadth rath! Oh my Gaad! A flath, deadth rath!' And he reaches into his man-bag, digs out a travel-pack of tissues and dabs his eyes theatrically.

My wife remains unsympathetic. 'So what have you done with this creature?'

I bury my head in my hands. 'Well I'm glad you two are finding this funny. Traumatised, I am. I just left it, door wide open. I cannot face it again. I will need counselling after this. Urrrr.'

She stalks angrily to the kitchen cupboard, returning several seconds later with a long-handled broom, a corresponding dustpan, and a black plastic sack. 'Right, you great big girlie. Get dressed immediately. Get down there now, just sweep the corpse into the dustpan, then tip it into the sack. Easy. Five seconds maximum. Then maybe you can actually get on with some work?'

I shake my head. 'I cannot. I just cannot face the thing again. You haven't seen it, have you? It is vile. The street is awash. I will need a haz-mat suit, and wellingtons.'

My wife points to the door, wordlessly. I know that look. I surrender meekly, but seriously, I don't think I can do this. I stagger back upstairs to change, then taking the dustpan, brush and sack, I slink back down the street, to find a small congregation of Spaniards outside Miguel's. Juan seems to have recovered somewhat, Leopard-skin Woman and Auntie Vera are taking it in turns to slosh buckets of soapy water across the cobbles, and in charge of proceedings, but patently doing absolutely nothing, is Pirate Pete. 'Welcome back, neighbour!'

he grins, 'changed your shirt I see! The last one was covered in billy-oooo!'

I edge my way to the door, and from the corner of my eye I can see that none of the locals have removed the corpse, and spared me this ordeal. It is still there. The miserable bastards. Always sweeping, Spanish women. You'd have thought, surely, one of them would have taken pity? I still don't think I can do this. Really and truly. I cannot even bring myself to look down, let alone go anywhere near it, even at the end of a three-foot brush handle. URRRR! Ignoring the cat-calls and ridicule from the assembly, I stride back up the street, and through our front door again. Victor spots the plastic sack, and thinking I have brought the body back with me, leaps spectacularly to his feet, all the while juggling his man-bag and *Ship or Sheep.* Chrissie of course realises I have wimped-out. 'You great baby. You damned, great big baby. Give me that, I will go down there and do the job myself. Are you coming, Victor?'

His face is a picture of horror. 'Sorree, I have my best trousers today. I would love to see thees flath deadth rath, but I will stay here, weeth Jonneee!'

A couple of hours later, Chrissie and I are on our sunbeds, under the fig tree. My tools meanwhile lie undisturbed, still in the bag-for-life. I will start in the morning. My wife no doubt is basking in female superiority, and fair play to her. I could no more have swept up that flath deadth rath than fly to the moon. 'So what do you think Juan will be considering for his lunch, today?' she giggles. 'Sausage, egg, chips and beans, maybe?'

I open one eye, gingerly. 'Nah, too greasy, after the morning we've had, the pair of us. Something plain, I think. Farley's Rusks, possibly?'

'That'd be right' she laughs. 'Baby food!'

CHAPTER 4. THE SPANISH BREAK-IN

A couple of Fridays later we are sat outside the Italian restaurant with Janie and Nigel, perusing the menu, having won my bet about the beams in Miguel's. Janie expressed her delight at how the sample area came up, and Nigel is looking particularly chipper, for some reason.... We have finished the wiring, too, me on angle-grinder duties, channeling out the walls, for Nigel to come along behind with the flexible plastic trunking, the back plates for the sockets and switches, and a mix of the wonder-material, the ultra-quick-drying *Yesso*. 'Where did you learn about electrics?' I enquired, at one stage. 'I mean, I can wire a plug, change a socket, that kind of stuff, but I don't actually understand the *principle* of it.'

'In the navy' he giggled, conjuring up a brief, fleeting image of 'The Village People' cavorting on Top of the Pops, which I quickly dispelled.

'But I thought you were in a submarine?' I enquired.

'I was in several boats actually' he confirmed.

'So is this how you re-wire a sub, with a disc-cutter, and electric chisel? I giggled.

'You could do' he laughed, 'but the boat would tend to stay at the bottom of the sea, if you did! Nah mate, we don't tend to worry if the cables are visible, on a sub. But seriously, I learned a trade with them, proper qualified too, which came in really handy in my second career, in the fire service.'

'What, as a forensic investigator or something?' I frowned. 'Or is this a new service offered by the fire brigade, a house burns down and you offer to re-wire it for them?'

He smiled conspiratorially. 'Moonlighting, of course! Most of the blokes at the fire station have a second trade, the women too. You know, plumbing, decorating, carpentry, electrics, car mechanics, all that kind of stuff. One of the girls was a wedding planner, another a florist. We had one woman who was a brickie, damn good too, she won an award for it. Didn't you know? If you want something doing, just call in your local fire station and ask.'

Well you learn something new every day. 'But what about the bosses, the officers?' I whispered, in case a Watch Commander was lurking around the corner. 'Didn't these extra-curricular activities get you into bother?'

'Ha! The bloody officers were the worst!' he guffawed. 'Our boss bred dogs, Alsatian puppies, all legit, Kennel Club and all that. You'd often see him walking a pup around the yard. He trained them as sniffer dogs too, he had one who used to wiggle into the canteen, and snatch your breakfast off your plate. The little bugger, he could sniff out a fried breakfast at five-hundred paces, turn your head it'd be gone! We had to eat with our arms around the plate, hunched forward, like prisoners, or soldiers!' *Good to see the old inter-service rivalries alive and kicking…*

So we select our pizzas, and I swear this is true, Janie chooses the Hawaiian, without the pineapple. Which is a Margarita, surely? I am seriously considering ordering mine without any cheese whatsoever when suddenly the spawn of the Devil, a mobile phone, rings. My mobile phone actually. Which comes as something of a shock, as I thought I'd left it home as I usually do on a night out, believing, as surely all right-thinking people do, that idiots who turn up in polite company and proceed to whip out their mobiles and start swiping away, should be exterminated. I fish around in my pocket, to turn the cursed device off, all the while apologising to our friends, when quite by accident I spot the caller-name on the screen. Babs and Andy, from Oxfordshire, the people with the holiday cottage here. My heart sinks. Has something bad happened? 'I'd better take this quickly, sorry.'

The male voice at the other end of the line sounds panicky. 'Really sorry to bother you John but we are in a bit of trouble. A lot of trouble actually. We've just had a garbled message from Paco, you know the fellow who owns the bar near us? We gave him our number for emergencies, and now one has occurred. Actually he doesn't speak a word of English, he had to get his daughter to speak to us, but basically some low-life has broken into our house, and is living there. Been there three or four days they think, you can see the lights on at night. Anyway Paco called the law, and they are coming next Tuesday, can you believe? So we have been scrabbling round trying to get flights, but the earliest we can get there is the end of next week, so we were wondering if maybe you could have a look, see what is happening? Really we don't want you to get involved, put yourselves in any danger or anything like that, but if you could tell us what is happening, if you are able, that would be such a help. Babs is doing her nut, as you can imagine.'

I glance enquiringly at Chrissie and our friends, as the phone is on speaker so I imagine they were following the conversation, and all three nod in agreement. We are all homeowners of course, and hate this type of crime. 'Well first of all don't worry, Andy, of course we will have a look, and there is a young policeman who has just started at the conversation group, so we can have a word with him if we need to. Actually you're in luck, as we're out with our friends Janie and Nigel, I don't think you have met them yet, but Nigel is a burly ex-fireman so he'll know what to do! We've just ordered pizzas, actually they are just coming now, and we have this bottle of wine to polish off, so give us say an hour and we'll head up there, and of course I'll call you back later whatever happens.'

Babs comes on the line. 'Thank you all so very much, I cannot tell you what a relief this is, but like Andy says, please don't put yourselves at risk. Just check-out what is happening, and maybe if you could see what the police say, that would be such a huge help.' I do my best to reassure her, then end the call, as I have this volcanic concoction going by the name of 'Vesuvius' to deal with, which thankfully contains no traces of pineapple whatsoever.

Babs and Andy. Nice couple, she blonde, bubbly and cuddly, he tall, slim and austere. We met them this time last year when they knocked on our door, requesting a translator in Auntie Vera's house, which they were interested in buying, until the pair of them were scared witless by a life-size statue of the Virgin Mary, lurking in the corner of the room, following which we heard nothing more, concluding they had possibly given up on the plan to move to this corner of Spain. Or died of shock. Then, out of the blue, they turned up in July, bearing gifts in the form of Santa Marta souvenirs from the 'sixties, having bought a four-storey shop tucked under the city walls, following which we were invited there for tapas, enjoying ham, cheese and wine while enjoying the breathtaking panoramic views from their roof terrace. And now it has come to this.

'Are you feeling OK?' Chrissie enquires. 'You are very quiet. I've never seen you defeated by a pizza before. Is Vesuvius about to erupt?'

I return to earth from my thoughts. 'Sorry, yes I'm fine' I smile, 'but I just cannot help thinking that this break-in is partly my fault.' Nigel raises his eyebrows. 'We went up there in July, before we went away, and I cannot help noticing this stuff' I continue. 'Now Chrissie could no doubt tell you all about their decor, cushions, what Babs was wearing, which I couldn't if you gave me a million. But I noticed their door lock. It was bizarre.' Janie chokes, momentarily. Maybe she found a sliver of pineapple somewhere.

My wife rolls her eyes. 'Oh not this cursed door lock again, please. He didn't stop going on about it, for two days.'

Our friend dabs her lips, daintily. 'So what about this bizarre lock? Do tell!'

I am not finding this at all funny, however. More like a mounting sense of shame. 'Well, it had clearly been changed, recently, either by Babs or Andy, or maybe the estate agent, I have no idea, but whoever did it used the wrong type of lock, as the cylinder, or barrel, was protruding from the door by about two inches. Now, clearly, the lock should only stick out a millimetre or so, should be flush to the door, but this one was just begging some burglar to whack it with a hammer, and gain entry. And I said nothing. I mean, they were leaving the following day, so there wasn't time, and I didn't want to worry them, and it was none of my business anyway, I could hardly say 'what idiot fitted that?' but I could have said 'have you had the locks changed?' something like that, and maybe raised it that way. I could have volunteered to have gone to the ironmongers, but I didn't want to push myself forward, have them thinking I was touting for work, so I said nothing, and now I wish I had. Of course, I have no idea if that was how the intruders got in, we will see in a few minutes, but it was so blindingly obvious that I bet it was.'

Nigel takes a deep breath. 'Well, I can understand how you feel, but I really don't think it was your fault, at the end of the day, you can hardly be responsible for other people's mistakes, can you? Anyway, if we've all finished, let me get the bill, and we can head up there, see what's what.'

So we trudge up the hill to our friends' house, via our place to pick up their keys, although what good they will do against squatters heaven knows, which should maybe have been easier, fueled by volcanic pizza, but far from it, in reality. All that dough I suppose. I am puffing as we reach the front door, but am mightily relieved to see the lock barrel, still in place, where it was previously, and can start to breathe easier, when I get my breath back. Nigel springs forward, grabs the lock between his fingers, and it comes away, easy as anything. 'The crafty bastards' he cries. 'You were right, John, someone has given it a whack, broken in that way, but put the cylinder back to make it look normal.' He hammers on the door with his fist. 'HOLA! HOLA!' Blimey, maybe we should have discussed tactics on the way up, were any of us capable of speech, that is, but I wasn't expecting to go in all guns blazing. 'Anyway, there's nobody in.'

'Nobody in?' his wife wails. 'Nobody in? Christ, they are probably cowering behind the sofa, the noise you are making. How the hell can you say there's nobody in?'

He regards his wife without affection. 'Because I am a trained professional, that is why. I am half man, half bloodhound. There is no-one home.' Then he presses his eye against the spot where the lock barrel was. 'So what we need here is a quarter-inch flat screwdriver. Does anybody have one?'

Chrissie delves theatrically in her bag. 'Damn, I only have a three-sixteenths. And you can stop wagging your tail in that fashion! And get your wet nose away from me!' And the ladies fall into each others arms, giggling helplessly, like two school-girls sharing a can of *Colt 45* on their way to a David Cassidy concert in about 1972.

I am decidedly unamused, however. This is all still partly my fault. All partly my fault? Is that a thing? I am partly responsible, is what I mean. 'Well, I am glad you all find it so amusing, but what the hell are we....'

'Don't worry!' cries the part-bloodhound, sticking his key into the hole where the cylinder was. 'I...am...IN!' and hey presto, the door opens and he steps across the threshold, followed by the girls, with me bringing up the rear, keeping a wary eye for bandits, at six o' clock. He surveys the scene, professionally. 'Right, wedge that pair of steps behind the front door, John, to stop anyone else getting in, and I will go upstairs to check the rest of the house. Maybe you ladies can check out the back door, see if there is one?'

Chrissie stands to mock attention, and salutes. 'Blue Watch, Blue Watch 'shun! For your duties, fall out!

I tell you what though, he certainly is a trained professional. I could never have got in, and secured the house, the way he did. Wouldn't have had a clue. *So is this one of the moonlighting services provided at fire stations? Breaking and entering?* I grab the steps from what appears to be a laundry room of some sort, and wedge them behind the door, against the first step up, and there we are, we really have secured the place. I call that a result, quite honestly.

Nigel bounds down the stairs, just as the girls emerge from the basement. 'There is a concrete patio out there' Janie puffs, waving her hand, exaggeratedly. 'We left the door open, get rid of this stale cigarette stench. Are they smokers, your friends?'

Chrissie and I ponder, a few moments. 'Never seen them smoking' she confirms, 'so no, I don't think they are.'

'It's the squatters' Nigel confirms. 'There are ash trays, full of dog-ends, either side of the bed. Dirty glasses, too. And look at the mess in this laundry room, clothes left in the washing machine, cutlery, crockery all piled up, towels, bedding. Would Babs and Andy have left the place in this state?'

Again I glance at my wife. 'Trouble is, we don't really know them that well' she smiles. 'John knows them better than me quite honestly, he went down Auntie Vera's that first morning, and he was at home that day they came round with the souvenirs, but no, I don't think they would have left it like this. Andy in particular seems quite precise. And do you think all this stuff here they bought, and just dumped, intending to put it away later? Or is it stuff from the house which the squatters were intending to nick, steal away with it in the dead of night? And by the way, aren't we treading all over a crime scene here? You know, won't forensics want to comb it for fingerprints, and DNA?'

I am really grinning now, as the image of a Spanish Sherlock Holmes creeps into my mind, complete with deerstalker and magnifying glass. 'Elementary my dear Watson. What we need is one of those sniffer-puppies from the fire station, you know, let slip the dogs of... AAAAAAHHHHHHHHH!' An old woman, no more than four-foot-six tall, wizened, dressed entirely in black, with head-scarf and bent nose like some ancient witch from a Grimms fairy tale, has appeared at the top of the basement stairs. If she cackles, produces a black cat from under her skirt, and starts handing out rosy-red apples, I will surely die on the spot. The others all turn, speechless in shock, gazing in disbelief at this sinister apparition, who smiles sweetly, eyes scanning us rapidly as if she is choosing the plumpest, juiciest specimen to spirit away to her cauldron. *Don't look at me, Missus, I am all fat, and gristle. Janie is quite tender, I imagine....*

'Sorry to scare you, people' she croaks, although it might have been *hubble bubble toil and trouble* for all I know, as my heart is banging like a big bass drum. 'I am Consuela, *vecina* from next door. I know your friends Bar-bera and Andrieu. I see you have secured the house against those *gitanos*. Come with me, I will show you my secret exit!' And she turns and beckons us down the steps.

Yeah right. 'After you, Nigel' I whisper, 'you're the professional, after all! You are half-bloodhound, if she tries to stick us in a pot, bite her on the arse and run like hell!'

At the bottom of the steps we exit into a small patio, which I recall from our brief tour back in July. What I didn't spot on that visit however is a thick, ancient wooden door built into the ten-foot-high garden wall, complete with huge iron studs, like the back door to a castle, a tradesman's entrance if you like. The door is ajar, she pulls it back, hinges creaking, and ushers us through. 'Lock the door please to your friends' house, then it will be secure, and you can exit through my patio, and my house.' And she leads us through her museum with a small house attached, featuring antiques which might fetch a small fortune in the UK, such as an ewer and basin on a polished wooden night-stand, various urns and jugs and a wrought iron chandelier which could easily have featured in an Adam Ant video.

'Why didn't the burglars break in here?' whispers Janie, 'this stuff must be worth a mint. Far better than that supermarket crap next door!'

'Oh yeah, and get turned into a frog?' Chrissie breathes.

Under the street lights, Consuela doesn't look half so scary, although all four of us are keeping our distance, just in case. 'Thank you very much for your help' I tell her. 'The house is secure now, I don't know when our friends are coming, so I will let you know. Their first job is to change that lock!'

'Yes, it was ridiculous' she confirms. 'I don't know why some-one didn't tell them.' *Yeah thanks for that. I was just beginning to feel better about the situation.*

The other three are buoyant however, having achieved an out-come none of us could have dreamed of. I whip out my phone, and dial Andy, who picks up first ring. I convey the news, which is received ecstatically, to say the least. 'Oh my God, thank you, thank you! Hear that Babs? Jeez, we've been going out of our minds here. I cannot tell you, thanks a million!'

'Well its not me you need to thank' I tell him, honestly. 'It was Nigel, without his experience we would be still standing in the street. Janie and Chrissie too were a massive help. I wouldn't have had a clue what to do.'

He is still on cloud nine, understandably. 'All of you, all of you! We've never met Janie and Nigel obviously. And I will not rest until we do, and can take you all out for a slap-up meal, and a massive party on our roof terrace! When are they coming over next?'

The phone is on speaker, and I can see Nigel debating with his social secretary. 'November the fifteenth, for a week' Janie giggles.

'Right, we will move heaven and earth to get over for that week, but if we can't, I will send you some money, John, so you can have one on us! Oh my God. Phew!' He calms down, slightly. 'This was all my fault, you realise. That bloody stupid lock I fitted. I asked for the wrong one, fitted it, but it wasn't until I was locking the door from the outside on our last morning that I realised it was sticking out. I don't suppose you noticed, but it was just asking to get whacked, so all this is down to me. It was too late to do anything of course as we had to get to the airport, but I thought it would probably be all right. I was a fool.'

I start to breathe easier, but still my conscience won't let the matter rest. 'Well, actually Andy, I did notice it that evening we came round, and I've been feeling guilty ever since that I didn't say anything. All this could have been avoided if only I'd spoken up, so maybe you should take the other three out for a meal, and leave me at home!'

All of us are laughing, both ends of the phone. 'In the doghouse Mister Richards!' Janie chuckles.

'Ahh, no, no, no!' Andy insists. 'It was nothing to do with you. It was my fault, my balls-up, all down to me. Just one thing though, are you likely to be seeing Paco, in the bar, any time soon?'

I smile, for the first time in what seems like ages. 'Well, by a co-incidence, we are standing outside Paco's right at this minute! And I am sure, after the evening we've just had, we could all benefit from a quick one, to calm the nerves?' And I glance at the others, who are all nodding furiously. 'In fact, you can speak to Paco yourself. Tell him *toda esta bien, Paco!*' And I hand over the phone to the grinning barman.

'Toda esta bien Paco' I can hear from the other end of the line,

and we all fall about laughing.

'We've secured the house against those *Lad-Ronnies*, Paco!' I tell him, then suddenly I am struck by a thought. What if those intruders are close by, watching us? What if that is actually them, that suspicious-looking couple, muttering away in the corner? What if they don't actually know yet, and will totter up the hill in a few minutes to find the door barricaded against them, then face a night on the cobblestones? Or what if they do know already, and are planning on following us home, to find out where we live? I decide to keep these thoughts to myself, but resolve to quietly check our security, in the morning.

So we all head home, say our final goodbyes as our friends are off early in the morning, and promise to empty their fridge of perishable goods, as usual. Chrissie and I are getting ready for bed when she turns to me. 'Did you notice that pair, skulking in the corner of the bar?' I confirm that I might have, vaguely. 'So do you think that might have been them? They looked highly suspect, I thought. I know you say I see monsters lurking everywhere, which you don't, but maybe you should check our door lock, in the morning? I know it is flush, but maybe we need longer screws, in the wood? I know you'll say I'm daft, but after that kid with the bread, and now this, I am starting to feel unsafe here.'

I take her hand. 'I don't think you're daft at all. It makes sense to be vigilant. I think we've just been unlucky, with two unpleasant incidents on top of each other, and if you think about it, all that has been taken is a loaf. So yes, I'll have a look at the lock in the morning, and you don't have to worry, with me here to protect you!'

'Oh yeah, like you did with the flath deadth rath!' she mutters under her breath, and we both have a good old giggle.

Makes you think though, doesn't it?

CHAPTER 5.
MEET JADE

'Excuse me, but are you English, please? Ha ha ha nnnnn.' Chrissie and I are in the supermarket, which in itself is strange as my wife takes the view that as I do the lion's share of the cooking, it is only fair that I also do the buying, and the hauling of it up the steep cobbled street to our house. Not half as strange as our inquisitor however, and I have to tell you my initial split-second reaction is to pretend I am French, as from the corner of my eye I spot a woman, our age possibly, short, spiky white-blonde hair, elfin features, wide, staring eyes which appear to be focused on the ceiling, wearing a multicoloured cotton kaftan and crushed-velvet loon pants, in a delicate shade of purple. Were she wearing a cow-bell round her neck, we could be back in the Summer of Love. And that laugh, like a stoned, drunken parrot imitating a donkey? *Move along Jonno, you know it makes sense.*

Chrissie however jumps in with both feet, a decision which was to have a profound effect on other lives, not just our own. 'Yes we are! Chrissie and John, pleased to meet you!'

The woman brightens visibly. 'Oh thank God, my name is Jade, ha ha ha nnnnn! I am in such trouble.' *Told you, didn't I?* 'I have bought a house here, Cally Castle-o, I moved in three days ago, all the furniture was there, so I had a choice of bedrooms, and picked the back one as it has the lovely view.' *The news gets better. She lives in our street.* 'Then the first night, I was asleep and there was a massive crash, I looked in the front bedroom and the ceiling had fallen down, and in the darkness there were all these thin, white, ghostly things floating about under the roof. I was so scared I ran downstairs, and slept on the sofa, and I've been too frightened to go upstairs again. I need to get someone to go up there and see what it is? Ha ha ha nnnnn.'

'Oh you poor love' Chrissie exclaims, taking her by both hands. 'But don't worry, we live in Castle Street too, number fifty-five, and John here repairs old houses for friends, don't you darling? I am sure he can have a look at it for you.'

Jade fixes me with an intense, hypnotic stare. 'Oh thank you, thank you! Ha ha ha nnnnn. So can you fix my broken ceiling?'

No point beating about the bush, is there? 'I'm sorry Jade, I haven't seen the damage but I know what these old ceilings are, and yours is probably like Humpty Dumpty, not even the King's horses and the King's men could put it back together.'

She focuses on the ceiling again. 'Humpty Dumpty? Oh, you mean the egg-guy, kissed the girls, made they cry? Ha ha ha nnnnn. So what about the ghostly white things?'

I take a deep breath. 'Well, I don't want to sound like I am mansplaining things to you....'

'Oh no!' she interrupts, giggling to Chrissie, who rolls her eyes theatrically, 'I love it when men splain things to me! Ha ha ha nnnnn.'

I shoot my wife a *wait till I get you home* glance. 'Well, these old houses were built cheaply, with whatever materials were to hand, and basically there are no lofts, or attics, like we have in the UK. The spaces above the ceilings are voids, cannot take any weight, as the ceilings are suspended from the beams above using bits of twine, old rope, and I swear I am not making this up, horses tails. They twist it all together to form a length, dip it in quick-drying plaster, and when it goes solid they stick one end to the ceiling, and nail the other end to the beam, and suspend the ceiling that way, using dozens of the white twisted lengths. So that is what you saw, in the dark, and I'm not surprised you were shocked, as it is the strangest concept, gave me the willies the first time I saw it, even in the daylight it looks scary.'

'Ha ha ha nnnnn.'

'The thing is' I continue, 'even though this is house-building at its most primitive, these old builders were extremely skilled. I work sometimes with a friend, Derek, and try as we might we cannot get these ceilings back up. We know *what* they did in the old days, but not *how* they did it. We imagine they put the ceilings up from above, before they laid the roof tiles, but really we are just guessing. Now I imagine there are old-style Spanish builders still around who know how to do it, so probably the best thing is if I ask some of our friends at the library if they know of anyone who can do this, and I let you know. OK? Victoria's dad is a builder, he will probably be able to advise you.' I smile pleasantly, and shape up to move off.

Chrissie, irritatingly, refuses to follow. 'But you can also take the whole ceiling down, darling, can't you, like you did for our other friend, and have exposed beams? And you should see what John is doing at our friends' cottage, on the hairpin bend, sanding down the beams, and plastering between them. Anyway, look, we are having tapas tonight, why don't you join us? What number are you? John can pop up at say seven, have a look, and you can come back to ours. You'd be very welcome!'

'Ha ha ha nnnnn! That would be fantastic, if you're sure it's no trouble. I'm at forty-one, with the green door. Horrible colour, isn't it? I feel like that Shaky Stephen guy.' She grips our hands, then moves unsteadily off down the cat-food aisle.

'Thank you very much' I hiss, from the corner of my mouth. 'Thank you very, absolutely, bloody much. Are you hoping I die, very soon? Is that it? Collect my life insurance, and sail away somewhere exotic? And what was all that bloody *darling* business? You never call me *darling*. What do you think, we were in an episode of *Terry and June*? Christ, I despair of you sometimes, oh John repairs houses, don't you *darling*. Don't you think I have enough to do? I've only just recovered the use of my head after that massive lump of concrete at Jake's place fell on it. And that woman is bonkers, look at her in the cat food aisle, she is actually picking up the tins. Do you think she smuggled a herd of moggies over here in her hand luggage?'

'Awww, I think she's really sweet' my wife giggles. 'Just remember how alone we felt, when we first moved here, and we had each other. She is on her own, and it can't be easy, especially with a disaster like a ceiling falling down. Besides, you know how desperate I am for female company, it would be great to have another Brit in the street, for a good old girly chat now and again.'

I rub my hand across my brow. 'I know, I know, you're making me feel bad, now, but I'm really up to my eyeballs at Miguel's at the moment. I can manage that on my own, I am starting to get the balance right, but I just don't need any more jobs with Del, him wanting to work all day, that is not why we came here and just the thought of it is stressing me out. And Humpty Dumpty kissing the girls and making them cry? Green door? Shaky Stephen? Some girly chat that is gonna be!'

Chrissie looks puzzled. 'But why do you need to involve Del? I thought, Jade is just up the street, you can pop up there and sort it, whenever. No?'

I close my eyes, and count to five. 'Do you have any idea how much work is involved, taking down one of those ceilings? Jade's is two storey at the front, same as ours, she is next to Mercedes, right? So just think how high our bedroom ceilings are, and imagine the void above. Miguel's is three storey, so the ceilings are nothing like as high, because the builders shoved another floor in, which means I can reach the beams in Miguel's from a stepladder. In Jade's I will need a scaffold tower, and do I have one of those? No. Who does? Del. And who is begging for work? Eh? *Oh any work you got, mate.* So getting the tower down to Jade's will be a morning, we will have to slip his Moroccan mate with the van something, and of course the same again after we finish. Taking down the rest of the ceiling, humping it downstairs, getting a skip, sorting the electric cables, sanding the beams and plastering between, then the side walls, Jeez, that is two weeks for two of us, going flat out. I don't need it, I don't want it, I told her I would ask Victoria's dad, but no, you wouldn't listen, and if we carry on like this we're going to have a blazing row, I'll end up a gibbering wreck, and we'll get kicked out! Happy now? Ha ha ha nnnnn!' And I burst out laughing.

'What you doing, mate?' Two weeks later I am up a scaffolding tower in Jade's front bedroom. She has conveniently popped back to the UK 'to sort out a few problems', leaving her workforce to get on with it.

I glance truculently down at the annoying little Cockney. 'What does it look like I'm doing? I'm pulling these rusty nails out of the beams.'

He frowns. 'I don't want you to pull the nails out, mate.'

We're only into day three, and already I'm sick of this job, and my colleague. There's something not right about the whole thing, something he's not telling me, and I am determined to get to the bottom of it. 'Well tough titty to you, short-arse. I've already skinned my head on these bloody nails once today, so they're coming out. Besides, I cannot get a trowel across the bricks, to knock the snots off, so I can plaster over them, and I need the nails out to sand the beams off. So wind your neck in, and get on with your own bit.'

He is still frowning. 'I don't want you to sand off the beams, or knock off the snots. Just give the whole lot a brush over, and that will do.'

I fire off a full-on Clint Eastwood stare. 'What the hell are you talking about? We discussed all this. I said what a beautiful job I could do with all this up here, and we promised Jade. So what aren't you telling me? Come on, out with it, before I jump down there and use these pliers on you.'

He turns away. 'Because I didn't price in the work on the beams.'

WHAT? 'Why the hell not, Del? You are usually so meticulous about pricing. I told you I would need a couple of packs of sanding pads, so to add a tenner for that. So how much did you quote?'

He has the decency to look sheepish. 'Three hundred, mate.'

I brighten considerably at this news. 'Three hundred each? Well that's pretty good, well done. I reckon I can do a superb job up here for three hundred....'

'Nah, three hundred in total, mate.'

I puff out my cheeks. 'Blimey Del, that's cutting it a bit fine, isn't it?' I gaze across the grotty beams and the manky bricks with dried mortar hanging between them, which us craftsmen call *snots*. 'A hundred and fifty each... hang on, that IS three hundred, plus materials, ISN'T IT?'

He buries his head in his hands. 'Nah, three hundred, all in, including materials.'

I drop my pliers onto the platform, and they clank noisily to the floor. 'HAVE YOU TAKEN LEAVE OF YOUR SENSES? We will need almost a hundred quid's worth of white mortar, we talked about that. You must be completely and utterly out of your tiny mind. I quit. I'm out of here right now. If you think I'm working here like this, putting up with an imbecile like you, for a hundred nicker, you have another think coming, and you can explain that to Jade, too. You absolute....'

'She was after me, mate, that day I came round to price up. All over me like a rash, she was. Like one of those cougars you read about, in the papers. So I got all flustered, right? Had to get out of there, sharpish, so I said the first thing that came into my head, and had it away on me toes.'

I feel stunned, like I have passed into another dimension, another universe. Good job I am holding on to the platform, otherwise I would surely have plunged to the ground, like my pliers. 'YOU? She fancies YOU? Why in the name of all things holy, with all the men on God's green earth, would she......'

'TEA UP!' A familiar voice climbing the stairs announces a refreshment break, and my wife appears bearing a tray with two mugs, and a small pile of biscuits. 'Tea time, workers! Come and ....whatever is wrong?'

I cock my leg over the platform rail and begin my descent. 'I tell you what is wrong. HE is wrong. In the head. I have just resigned, so take that tea away right now, he is not having any, and I will be right behind you. This moron quoted three hundred INCLUDING materials for this job, so that is it, I'm damned if I'm doing all this for less than a hundred, I am out of here, and never coming back, just let me gather my tools and we are off.' And I begin furiously winding the cable on my sander. 'Of all the stupid....'

'STOP!' Chrissie places the tray on the ground. 'John, stop. Listen to me, the pair of you. SHUT UP!' Silence descends momentarily. 'On Jade's last night here, she came out for a drink with me, and she told me, she knew, that Del's quote was all wrong. It was obvious, she said. She'd had building work before, in Britain, so it was clear that three hundred was wildly understated. And it was all because Del fancied her, he was getting all hot and bothered, all flustered, tongue-tied....'

'WHAT?' yells my former colleague, 'it was her fancied me, I was fighting her off, almost, and....

'SHUT UP I SAID.' My wife clearly has the bit between her teeth. 'So she gave me another three hundred, in cash, which I have at home, hidden in a secret location, which I was to give you 'at the end', but she meant when the job was completed, not the end when you pair of prats fell out. SO. You have nothing to worry about, so I suggest you drink your tea like good little boys, eat your biscuits, AND GET ON WITH SOME BLOODY WORK!'

About three weeks later I take a call, from Del. 'Ello mate, just a quickie, er, we was wondering if you and your good lady wanted to come out wiv us tomorrow night, end of the week like, have a few swift halves?'

We? Us? Who are these people? 'Who is 'we', Del? You mean that Moroccan mate of yours, who carted the scaffold tower back and forth?'

He giggles, 'Nah, don't be daft, Ahmed don't drink, ya plonker!'

I have another little think. 'Oh Valentine, you mean? The bloke we bought the car from? What is this, a farting contest, in your front room? I don't think Chrissie will be that keen, actually. Or do you mean your dog? Tie him to a bit of string, get a carrier bag full of strong cider, and go and sit in the park? There is nobody else, that I can think of?' *Or is there? No, surely not? Impossible. Isn't it?*

He is really laughing now. 'Dog on a string, you prat! Jade, ya numpty. Me an Jade wants to know if you and Chrissie wants to come out wiv us, termorra night.'

I am confused, which does happen, on rare occasions. 'But I thought Jade was still in England?'

'She got back last night, mate' he confirms. 'I come down to see her, she loves what we done, in her bedroom, especially the ceiling, she reckons it's better than the one Michelangelo done, so she wants to thank you, thank us, and yer Missus as well for putting up with it all. So you coming, or what?'

I have the phone on speaker, and can see Chrissie nodding. 'Not sure that I approve of you sniffing around in our street at night, Del, like some randy old tomcat. In fact, if I see you out there again, I will throw a bucket of water over you. But my wife is grinning, so I reckon that means we'll be there!'

So we fix up a time, and he rings off. My wife, meanwhile, is looking pleased about something. 'Did you know about this? Some feminine secret, between you two ladies?'

'Of course' she confirms, 'Jade and I have been messaging, on Facebook, ever since she went back to England. I was keeping her up to date on the progress, both the bedroom, and the love-sick puppy.'

'Lovesick puppy? What lovesick....? So you knew about that?'

'Oh please, try to keep up, will you? He said she fancied him. She said he fancied her. It was obvious. Well to me, anyway. You were still bitching about getting nails embedded in your head, and the price of sanding pads.'

The trapdoor opens, and I fall straight through. 'So you engineered the whole thing?' I growl. 'You roped me in for two weeks hard labour, just so Del could get his end away?'

'That is quite enough of your coarse vulgarity' she hisses. 'But yes, I was alert to the possibility the two of them might fall in love. I saw it before she'd even spoken to us in the supermarket that day, that her and Del would be perfect together.'

I slump back in my chair. 'So once again all this has been going on completely off my radar. Fall in love, indeed, this is halfway up a Spanish mountain, not some soppy Mills and Boon novel. Jeez, and have you seen the price of sanding pads these days?' I chuckle to myself at the absurdity of it all. 'Well, it's all very well you sat there looking smug, but I have just one thing to say to you.'

She still looks smug. 'And what is that pray, this pearl of wisdom? I am all ears!'

'HA HA HA NNNNN!'

CHAPTER 6. THE EE-TEE-OOBIE

'Plees, you must to visit my city, Baena, in the province of Cordoba. Ees new castle, open-ed recently!' I am with Jesus, pronounced in these parts Cassoo, or HHassoo, depending on how phlegmy you want to be, and it does appear to be optional, a slim, dark-haired young man, who is keen to improve his English. We have heard of Baena of course, having passed it many times on the way to Cordoba city, but never stopped there.

'Your city?' I smile.

'Yees, I was bor, bored, boring HODER!'

'Born?'

'Yees, I was born there, my family live there, my parents, my brother, not my sister, she marry-ed, live in Granada.'

His English is very good actually, just needs polishing up, and to lose the 'ed' suffix, which many non-native speakers struggle with. Open-ed, close-ed, finish-ed. Strangely however they don't have a problem with started... 'So you are from Baena, that is what we say. So this new castle, can you explain about this please?'

'Yees! Ees not new, was ver old, more than meel years, how you say?'

A thousand years old?'

'Yees, a thousand years old, but was going down, many years, how you say?'

'Falling down? A ruin? It was ruined many years ago?'

'Yees, a ruin! Same as Espanees, ruina. So the Gobby-Enry they restor-ed the castle, restoring, HODER!'

'They are restoring at the moment, or they have restored and finished it?'

'Yees, they finish-ed. Ees now open for touristas, only I think one or two euros, possibly less for pensionistas!' I narrow my eyes, but grin. 'But, the restore-ass-on, ees different.' he continues. Not traditional. So I want for you to visit, and say me what you thinking of thees!'

'Tell you. You want us to visit and tell you what we think of the restoration, which has not been done, performed, carried out, in the traditional manner? What, have they used plastic bricks?'

He giggles. 'No, I not say nothing, you must to visit, then we speak.'

Sounds like a plan, doesn't it? 'So is the castle easy to find? Is there parking?'

He frowns. 'Baena have many small streets. I think maybe you can leave you car weeth Lee Dell.'

Never heard of the bloke. 'Lee Dell?'

'Yees, supermarket, Lee Dell, you no have Lee Dell in Eengland?'

I am really laughing now. Crazy foreigners. 'Lidl, we pronounce it Lidl. It rhymes with middle. In fact the 'middle of Lidl' is part of the advertising, 'see the bargains in the middle of Lidl this week. Big on quality, always Lidl on price! So am I allowed to park in Lidl then visit another part of the city? Is there no time limit, with cameras, and fines?'

'Oh my Gaad! Of course no! You have thees in Eengland? Yees you can leave you car in Lee HODER! Lidl. Ees no problem!' *Maybe they're not so crazy after all...* 'So from Lidl go up heel, at top of heel turn iz, iz, HODER!, left, go up famous heel where come down blue.'

'Blue?'

'Yees, blue.'

I cannot help it. Learning English should be fun. I'm not a boring school. He's had the middle of Lidl, so now he will get a short song.

'Blue is the colour, football is the game,

We're all together, and winning is our aim,

So cheer us on through through the sun and rain,

'Cos Chelsea, Chelsea is our name!'

He clearly appreciates talent when he hears it, clapping and cheering. 'Chelsea, yees, I know thees club of football. Fernando Torres, yees!' Then he turns serious. 'But what have Chelsea connection weeth blue?'

Crazy foreigners. 'Because Chelsea play in blue shirts. Blue is the colour!'

'No no no no! I not say blue colour. I say blue, from your hare.' And he taps his chest.

'Heart?' I titter, 'are you saying heart? A hare is a big rabbit.' And I make bunny ears with my hands, and buck teeth. And are you saying blood? Blue is the colour, as I keep telling you. Blood is pumped round you body, by your hare, sorry HEART!' And we are both rolling around laughing.

He buries his face in his hands. 'Oh my GAAD, thees Eenglees! Hare-t, and blue-d!'

'No, heart. Harrrt, blood. Bluuud.' Anyway, enough of this frivolity. 'So you were telling me about this blood, and the hill? What happened?'

He turns serious again. 'Yees, during the war, were kill-ed many people, more than seven hundred, and the blood of they come down heel.'

What an absolutely horrific story. I knew that Spain had a violent, turbulent history, but to think we might actually be walking in this area next weekend is almost unimaginable. 'So the blood of over seven hundred people was running down the hill?' I whisper. 'Which war was this, the re-conquest of Spain, over six hundred years ago?'

'No no. The Civil War. My abuelos, sorry grandparents, remember this story. Epoch nineteen thirties.' *And there was me pretending to be a giant rabbit, and singing about Chelsea, while he was trying to explain about seven hundred of his countrymen, slaughtered and left to rot. Within living memory. I cannot help it, you see. Being a complete arse.* I do my best to look ashamed, and fail miserably. Jesus however seems unconcerned. 'Yees, thees was part of our history, but we do not think of it much. We are different country now, a new democracy. We looky ahead, not back. Ees better, no?' Indeed it is, my friend. Indeed it is.

So here we are, the following Saturday morning, en-route to Baena, and this intriguing castle, restor-ed by Gobby-Enry, and I reckon I caught Jesus out by saying they used plastic bricks, or fibreglass certainly, like something out of Walt Disney World. Didn't deny it, did he? Either that or they used chipboard crenelations, painted grey. Complete bodgers, the Spanish. There was a case in the paper just a few months ago, where a priceless painting of a medieval saint was handed to a so-called 're-storer', who returned it, a year and about a million euros later, with a child-like face such as you might find in an infants' school. So we're not expecting much, quite honestly. And I'm still writhing with embarrassment about this river of blue. Every time I think of it, which is only about ten times a day admittedly, I want to curl up.

We reach the Baena turn-off, take the slip-road, then in a sudden fit of panic I take two turns of the roundabout and come to a juddering halt, in an industrial estate. 'Oh, this is nice' giggles my wife. 'Haven't they done it well, the restoration. I must admit, I was expecting something a little more castle-y, rather than a prefab, I'd hoped there might be slightly more stonework rather than corrugated iron, maybe a drawbridge, possibly a moat, that bit where they pour the boiling oil over the invaders, a window where a damsel in distress might lean out.....'

'Never mind all that' I bark, 'can you get me the car documents out of the glove compartments please?'

She has every right to look offended. 'I beg your pardon? Are you speaking to me? What did your last slave die....'

'Didn't you see the sign, on the roundabout?'

She employs a touch of sarcasm. 'I did indeed. 'Baena' it said. Which funnily enough, is where I thought we were going. I know my female sense of direction is inferior to yours but I could have sworn we were traveling in the right direction.'

'Not that damned sign' I groan, with a mounting sense of anxiety. 'The sign which said 'ITV'. You know, ee-tee-oobie. The Spanish MOT. Which we don't have, as ours has expired. Quick, can you find the bit of paper. You remember when we bought the car last autumn, it had nine or ten months ITV on it? So it must have expired, and we've been driving around....'

'End of June, it expired' she confirms.

'How the hell do you know that? I explode. 'You haven't found the sodding bit of paper yet.'

She calmly taps the top corner of the windscreen in front of her. 'Duh, because it says so, here, on this bit of plastic, with the little hole punched in it, from the ITV company. The hole is next to the word 'Jun', so I assume that is when it expired. 'Jun'. Or June, for stupid people, like you.'

'Well why the hell didn't you say something, if the sticker is right in front of your face? Christ, we've been driving about, up and down the motorway to the coast, what if they have number-plate recognition cameras here? There could be half a dozen fines winging their way to us, as we speak. And don't forget the car is in your name, so it will be you who ends up in clink, not me.'

'Number-plate cameras?' she laughs. 'They didn't even turn up for Babs and Andy's burglary, did they? And besides, you're the bloke in this relationship, this is a bloke job, sorting out the car. Why the hell else do you think I put up with you?'

'Oh yeah, I'm sure you can enter a plea-bargain, on those grounds. 'Oh sorry we've been driving around illegally, officer, but your colleagues owe us two hours, waiting around like lemons, boiling away in the hot sunshine, while they failed to investigate squatters breaking in.' I am sure the judge will be entirely sympathetic. Now give me the damned folder and let me go in the office and try to keep your sorry arse out of jail.'

She places the folder behind her back. 'Just calm down, will you? If you go blundering in there like that, you will end up in handcuffs. Take a deep breath, then try to keep my very small arse out of jail!'

'JUST GIVE ME THE BLOODY FOLDER' I seethe, then immediately see the funny side, if one exists, and smile. 'OK OK, I am calm now. I will bring you a cake with a file inside! Please give me the folder, and I will stroll nonchalantly across and make friendly enquiries, on your behalf.' *Easier said than done though, isn't it, given that I usually need some time to collect my Spanish thoughts, and vocabulary.*

Clutching the file, I enter the office, where a few people seem to be milling around aimlessly, which is entirely normal, in this part of the world. Behind the counter is a burly, severe-looking Eastern-European woman with piercing eyes, who is probably, but I'm only guessing, as I cannot see her bottom half, wearing a military-style skirt, hairy knees covered by thick, opaque tights, and jackboots. I place my papers carefully in front of her, before I totally lose my nerve, and decide to throw myself entirely at her mercy, appealing to her sense of justice and fair-play. 'I am sorry' I whimper. 'I didn't remember the ee-tee-oobie.' I meant to say 'I forgot' of course, but amid rising panic I have forgotten the Spanish word for 'forget'. Then at that precise split second a song by the late, great Benny Hill flashes through my mind. His song *My Garden of Love*, where he is discussing the plants he would grow there, and the immortal line *'A forget-me-not to remind me to remember not to forget.'* There are those who say the world changed the day John Lennon wrote *Lucy in the Sky With Diamonds,* and who am I to disagree, but I tell you what, the Benny Hill line *'A beetroot for the day you said that you'd bee-troot to me'* takes some beating.

My Soviet friend rifles through my papers, stuffs half of them in a plastic folder, hands me the rest, and with a penetrating glare, which had I been a prisoner of war would have caused me to give up the location of the escape tunnels without a murmur, demands 'thirty euros'. I fumble for my wallet, dropping it on the floor as my hands are shaking so much, although by a stroke of good fortune the counter is not glass-fronted, so I am unable to confirm yes or no about the jackboots. Or the hairy knees. I hand her the money, and she points at some uncomfortable-looking plastic chairs, which thankfully appear to be free of manacles, and commands me to wait.

People are still coming in and out of the office, and after a few minutes I spot Chrissie outside the glass door. Checking for the guards, I beckon her inside, with my finger to my lips. 'I have paid thirty euros for something' I whisper, 'and told to wait here. I have no idea if the police are coming, or if I'm going to get a dish of gruel, a bone-hard bread roll and a cup of tepid water, or what. There is no point you hanging about, I'm sure I saw a cafe on the far side of the industrial estate, why don't you wait over there, grab a coffee or something, and I'll catch up with you later, if they let me go!' She places her hand on mine in a 'sorry to drop you into all this when the sticker was in front of me on the windscreen all the time' kind of way, although possibly her gesture means 'I know your PIN codes, so don't worry about me', who knows, then she toddles off.

I lean back in my chair in a vain attempt to avoid the complete destruction of my nether regions, and think about Benny Hill songs. *Ernie* was the all-time classic of course, but the B-side of *Garden of Love* was a ditty entitled *The Andalucian Gypsies,* which even as a six-year-old spoke to me of a far-off land of dark-eyed senoritas, strumming guitars, and donkeys.

'*The Andalucian gypsies,*

Have a saying that's ever so true,

That for every man there's a woman,

And I had to get lumbered with you!'

Smiling inwardly, all the while maintaining a serious demeanour, to avoid punishment beatings, I am woken from my reverie by the sound of urgent Iron-Curtain-style throat clearing, to find Svetlana pointing menacingly outside, and to the left, so I gesture to myself, then outside and to the left, which elicits a grunt. 'Seeeee!' Snatching up my plastic wallet, and the remainder of my documents, I flash her a Cheshire-Cat kind of a grin, even though I doubt whether she read Lewis Carroll in the gulag, and hurry outside, to find the car park empty, apart from our little white SEAT, with the keys in the ignition where I left them. So, what? Am I being dismissed as they are closing for the weekend, having been royally stiffed for thirty euros, or have I been squeezed into the final appointment, out of the kindness of her heart, if she has one?

Turning to the left, then, daringly, left again at the corner of the building, I am amazed to spot a pair of huge garage doors, wide open, revealing a workshop space with three pit lanes, completely devoid of any activity whatsoever. Suddenly, a po-faced, pale, roly-poly, oily, dungaree-clad Venusian, who looks as if he may have spent a large portion of his life in a darkened room playing *Space Invaders* with himself under the sheets, or maybe just playing, without the *Space Invaders*, in Bilbao possibly, appears from nowhere, clutching a clipboard. 'SEAT?' he enquires. Now under normal circumstances I might have replied *two legs, not two doors. Nope, I'm a bloke,* and giggled, but if I'm not very much mistaken it seems as if I'm getting my ITV today, which really would be a result as this situation is totally Chrissie's fault, as it's her car, right? Then again, I am the bloke, which makes it all my responsibility.

I smile sweetly. 'Yes, around the corner, the keys are in it, see you in half an hour?' And I mime sipping an espresso.

'No, bring the car here' he commands, sternly, pointing to a precise spot on the ground. *What, lazy are you? Cannot be arsed to walk five yards? Exercise your legs, not your thumbs for a change? Maybe you need to get out more, get some sunlight on your face, good old vitamin D? A healthy all-over glow, like a British expat?* With gritted teeth, I return to the car, and am almost tempted to push it around the corner, as it's certainly not worth starting the engine, but I don't want to upset the fellow, get beamed-up somewhere, so I waste half a gallon of fuel and drive round. I swing open the door, as I could really do with that espresso, but he is actually leaning on it, preventing me from exiting. 'Stay there, open the windows.' *What? I haven't broken wind all morning, honest. Maybe they have hypersensitive noses on his planet?* He bends over so his face is level with mine. 'Dead point, wanky.' he orders. *Did he really say that? Punto muerte, dead point. I know this, but wanky? Or does he have a slight speech impediment, and is he really saying ranky? As in, it stinks in this car, like something died? I mean, Chrissie recently bought a new air-freshener for the car, but it smells of pine trees, not corpses.*

'Perdon?'

'Dead point, wanky' he repeats, but I shake my head, defeated. He reaches through the window and grabs the gear knob, giving it a good shake, as if he is back under his sheets. 'Punto muerte, punto muerte!'

Neutral! He means neutral. Whatever next. Dead point. Who knew? I flip the gear lever from side to side, in a totally non-sexual way. 'Si.'

'Wanky' he grunts, or it could be ranky, I honestly cannot say, as his voice seems to be coming through a vent in his chest, rather than his lips. Then he mimics turning a key. *Start the engine! Stick it in neutral and start the engine! Blimey, this is going to be the longest MOT in history, at this rate. And why am I involved? Please let me go for that espresso. Why is there never a branch of Halfords, when you need one?*

He disappears, then returns several seconds later with a coil of rubber tubing, with an attachment one end, like you might find in a milking parlour, but which he proceeds to clip under the car, the exhaust pipe I assume. He leaps to his feet, raises his arm, and flaps his hand up and down, a gesture many of us might recognise, but not in connection with exhaust pipes, or udders. 'Progresso.' Got it. He wants me to press the accelerator, in a progressive fashion. But why am I involved in all this? In the UK, you drop the car off for the MOT, and they tell you to come back in an hour, or later that morning, and it is all done, pass or fail. And that in a country where they find it difficult to recruit staff in many areas. Here, there is over forty percent youth unemployment, so surely they could have found someone to train up? I mean, a job for life, an MOT inspector, like a hairdresser, a never-ending supply of customers I would have thought. Yet this place is deserted, apart from us, seemingly. Maybe that was it, everyone has cleared off early for the weekend, and they've roped me in to help out, just to get the car through? But I'm wearing one of my *Edinburgh Woolen Mill James Pringle super-soft cotton, £7.99 in the sale* shirts, so I hope they are not expecting me to go scrabbling around on the floor.

So I press the throttle as progressively as I can, which predictably is all wrong, as he mimics giving it a bit more welly. *Well why didn't you train up your own assistant in that case?* Seemingly satisfied at last, he consults a monitor, then tears off the print-out and clips it precisely to his board. 'Loose Lucy.' he continues. *I used to know her, years ago, drank in the Kings Head, didn't she? That is between us, you understand, please don't say anything to Chrissie, if you see her round town. Anyway, I only knew the woman in passing.* Not a clue, obviously. 'Loose Lucy' he repeats, bunching his thumb and forefinger together, like a gourmet Frenchman, in a turning motion, gesturing towards the steering column. Light? Lights? Now that is strange, because where we live light is *looth*, not loose, and lights loothy, with the Spanish lisp. Something to do with the king, hundreds of years ago, someone told us. Maybe they don't have kings, on Venus. I switch on the lights, side, dipped and full beam, then decide to go rogue and press the hazard button, and toot the horn, which doesn't go down well as it all has to be done in the order on his list, at his say-so.

'*Brisas.*' Now I know this one, as we recently bought new wiper blades, because the old ones were welded to the windscreen, after months without rain, and I needed to remove about a million flies. Similarly the *klaxon*, which is obviously the horn, and suddenly we are racing through his list, at his pace mind you, and eventually the cockpit controls have all been tested.

'Wanky, and advance over the inspection area.' Oh no, no, no, please not. Seriously, I get so nervous with anything like this. It's the same on a ferry, but at least on a boat there are a dozen burly French seamen, with massive chains, should anything go wrong. I really don't think I can do this, the car is only about six inches wider than the hole, and I have visions of crashing over the edge, and damp patches are starting to appear on my *Edinburgh Woolen Mill James Pringle super-soft cotton, £7.99 in the sale* shirt. Suddenly, two heads appear in the pit, like creatures from the black lagoon. Christ, have they been here all this time? Must have, unless they've been dragged in off the street. So why couldn't they have assisted with all the other crap? And one of them is actually directing me from below, like those blokes you see with the table tennis bats at the airport, walking around in front of the plane, a bit to the left, straight on, a touch right. Mate, I seriously wouldn't stand there, have you ever seen me parking? What I wouldn't give for a burly French sailor, right now. With that, the car lurches violently to the right. I AM GOING OFF THE EDGE, AND I HAVEN'T EVEN CHOSEN THE HYMNS FOR MY FUNERAL YET. *Abide With Me*, Chrissie knows I like that one, and *Jerusalem* probably. Just as my innards are about to give up the ghost, we are heading left, praise be. I must be on some sort of movable plate, checking who knows what, my underpants would be a good place to start. The next second we are jerking back and forwards, like Mr Venus under his sheets, hell, this is worse than a fairground, and at least there you know more or less what is about to happen, having bought a ticket from some surly youth. This is like the House of Horrors, the ghost train and a bucking bronco rolled into one. In a little white SEAT.

Nerves shredded, we come to a juddering halt. What now? Please let this nightmare be over. I can see daylight at the other end of the workshop so it cannot be much longer, surely?

'Frenos.' Ah yes, I forgot about the brakes, and there is the rolling road ahead of me, two parallel cylinders buried in the concrete. At least I know what is about to happen, having encountered this equipment in Anton's garage on my motorbike, all the while having the Michael extracted mercilessly, for turning up with bald tyres. At least that will not happen here. 'Wanky, advance.' Or maybe not. I am still over the pit mind you, although the cave dwellers appear to have vanished into some labyrinth down there, so I decide to go for it, surely I can drive in a straight line for a few more feet, which I manage to achieve unscathed, apart from a slight bump, which may or may not have been some Troglodyte's head scraping on the back axle.

Finally, my ordeal is all over. 'Park here, exit the car, and stand there' commands the Drill Sergeant, squinting in the bright sunshine, before disappearing back to his lair. I turn, and almost jump out of my skin again to see Chrissie standing behind me. 'Jeez, don't do that' I hiss, 'my nerves are shot, after all that. What are you doing here, anyway?'

'I've been watching you' she chuckles. 'From my table outside the cafe I could see straight through the garage. It was so funny, all the cars before you drove around, then you came shuffling along like that, on foot with no car, I almost died laughing!'

I rub my hands across my eyes. 'Well I'm so pleased you had an entertaining morning. What was that, over half-an-hour's unpaid labour, just because they are short of staff? And he kept calling me a wanky, every time he wanted me to start the engine. I am shattered, I tell you. Mentally drained.'

She is really laughing now. 'Doesn't take much, does it? That is how they do the MOT here, Jose from the library was telling me, last year when we bought the car. The driver has to help out with the test. You obviously weren't listening. And the Spanish for starting the engine is *aranque*. It is written on a printed sticker, attached to the door pillar my side, how to *aranque* the car in cold weather. God, you are so unobservant at times!'

I take a deep breath, and hold my head up to the heavens. 'So that is two stickers you neglected to tell me about. Anything else you think I should know?'

She sneers, dismissively. 'Huh, boys' jobs, I told you. Theresa May said so. Anyway, do you think the car will pass?'

'Not telling you' I huff. 'This is boy stuff.' I relent, and smile. 'Well, I honestly don't think there will be a problem, mechanically, there are no ominous clanks, or judders. The known unknown will be the emissions, the regulations are getting tighter, especially in Europe, and they want these older cars off the roads as they are less efficient than newer ones. Whether they make allowances.... ah, I think we are about to find out. Here comes Mister Venus. Fingers crossed!'

My new friend, and I can describe him as such after the event, approaches, smiling, and hands me the log book, some other bits of paper, and a small windscreen sticker bearing the legend '2020' with a hole punched in October. WE PASSED! 'Congratulations!' he grins, then turns serious, and starts speaking in broken English. 'I woo like, to speaking Eengliss. You speaky Eengliss to me, plees?'

Awww bless. All this time. And there was me... 'I am sorry but we live in Santa Marta' I tell him, with genuine regret. 'Are there academies here in Baena?' I am sure there are, as English language schools abound in this part of Spain. 'That would be best for you, at this stage. Learn basic vocabulary, how to construct a sentence, and develop your conversation as you become more confident.' Our stock answer really, bearing in mind hardly a week goes by without a request of this nature. It's flattering to be asked of course, but there aren't enough hours in the day, and we are supposed to be retired after all, even if, as with this fellow, we would genuinely like to help.

Driving out of the car park, I ignore the signs for Baena, and head homewards. 'Not visiting the castle today?' Chrissie jokes, 'you do know how to show a girl a good time. Some crappy industrial estate, and a cafe full of stinky old men. What a morning that was!'

'Just shut up will you' I growl, 'and start picking that old sticker off the windscreen, then see if you can put the new one up, straight.'

She shoves the whole lot into the glove compartment, and folds her arms. 'Nope. Boy job. Do it yourself.'

CHAPTER 7. THE SPANISH ROAD TAX

The following Monday, we return from a short excursion into town to discover another of those indecipherable yellow slips in our post box, bearing the town crest, and ancient Greek handwriting. 'Oh hell, what do they want now?' I wail. 'Is this the council tax again? I thought that was all sorted? And after all, this is a girl job don't forget!' We are still bickering light-heartedly about the division of labour between the sexes. Well I am certainly joking, although I get the impression my wife actually means it.

She narrows her eyes, menacingly. 'You know very well the first half-year has already been paid. There is the second half due by the end of this month, but it might have escaped your notice we weren't actually here in August, and everything was closed anyway. That cannot be what this slip is all about, there must be some other boy-job you've cocked-up.' See what I mean?

Fortunately, the following morning is the first library conversation group of the new season, so we have a bevy of Spaniards to ask. And here they all are, Teri and Marie for the ladies, with Jose and Juan representing the guys. Of Amador there is no sign, which is par for the course. Sadly for us, but such a huge triumph for her, Rafi has managed to secure a teaching position at a school in her home town of Linares, way up in the top corner of Andalucia, near the border with Castilla La Mancha, after about seven years on the waiting list, so she and *hoosband*

Pablo have sold their house in Santa Marta and moved up there. Chrissie will keep in touch on Facebook of course, and one day we hope to pop up and visit them. But they never made it to *Glass-ton-boor, Stonn-henhh and Sallis-booor*, after all that. Pity. I was so looking forward to hearing whether he enjoyed his pasty with no bloody carrots.

The first half-hour of the class is taken up by much hugging, kissing and back slapping, and that is just the fellows. So tactile, the Spanish, of which I am the complete opposite, especially with fellows, but hey, when in Rome, or Santa Marta... Next they want to know all about my *voyage to Eengland on you mo-torr-bike,* and by some miracle I have managed to download a selection of photos from my phone to my Kindle Fire, of my bike standing outside various picturesque Westcountry public houses, and the Cheddar Cheese shop, which leads them to believe I might be a bit of a boozer, until I am able to convince them the bike was in those locations for display purposes only, and that not a drop of ale passed my lips. 'And there you are, look' I smile. 'Cheddar Cheese. That is the actual village of Cheddar, where the cheese originated. A shop, not a pub!'

'So what is that standing by the front wheel of your bike?' Teri wants to know.

I study the picture carefully. 'A pint of cider.'

Eventually, Chrissie is able to extract the yellow slip from her bag, and it does the rounds. 'Thees writing is disgusting!' Juan moans. 'I cannot read nothing.'

Jose is similarly unimpressed. 'It look like *booey* wrote this', although whether he means ox-booey or crab-booey, he doesn't say. Could be either quite honestly.

Marie is scathing. 'My dow-terr Peppa can write better than thees!'

'Oh, how old is Peppa now?' Chrissie smiles.

'Seex.'

'I hate thees' Teri fumes. 'Thees people have no education. There is many intelligent person in Espain weeth much qualification, but they give jobs to thees olive-pickers.' *Well that was fairly unanimous, wasn't it?*

Just then the door bursts open and in bounds Amador, like some exuberant puppy. 'Oh my GAAD! Sorry I LATE! Did you all have good OWW-GOOSE?'

'August, not Oww-Goose!' Chrissie chuckles. 'If you go to Britain and talk about Oww-Goose, people will think you are referring to a big white duck, who has just pecked you, painfully!'

Laughing, he slips into the chair next to me, then his eyes come to rest on the yellow slip, in the middle of the table where it is lying. 'Oh my GAAD! Who no pay they SAY-OSS?' Four pairs of Spanish eyes come to rest on yours-truly. Here we go again, this cursed say-oss. As we all know, a postage stamp, and as I discovered recently, an ink stamp in a bank book. So what has this to do with the town hall? I stand and strain across the table, which is actually four big desks pushed together, to retrieve the manky slip, and Amador scrambles to his feet and pretends to whip my elevated behind. 'YOU. NAUGHTY. BOY. NO. PAY. YOU. SAY. OSS!'

Cue uproar. I am facing away from him of course and cannot actually see what he is up to, so have to crane my neck around, which provides a perfect position to spot chief-librarian Anna crash angrily into the room. 'Will you please stop disturbing....' then she spots a large Englishman bent across a table, with a small Spaniard seemingly inflicting corporal punishment, or worse, on his posterior, like a scene from Tom Brown's Schooldays. *Well this is a library after all. I wonder if they have the Harry Flashman stories, translated into Spanish. Must ask her later.*

She covers her eyes with her hands, and turns away, as I snatch up the paper and wave it guiltily. 'I no pay my say-oss' I smile, by way of explanation, hoping she will leave it there, and I can avoid a detention, a hundred lines, or six of the best. I crash back into my chair, to find Amador already sitting there, like some perverted game of musical chairs, and my humiliation is complete. Got my own back though didn't I? He got the full force of fifteen English stone crashing into his lap. *Won't do that again in a hurry, will he?* Shaking with rage, or possibly laughter, the librarian opens her mouth as if to speak, shakes her head, and departs. *It was laughter, I just know it was.*

We are all giggling, quietly, like a group of naughty third-formers, until my wife brings the group to order, no doubt concerned that this latest transgression might turn out to have been a girl-job. 'So what is this say-oss?'

Juan puffs out his cheeks. 'In Espain, we must to pay to drive you car on the street. Every jeer.'

'Road tax!' Chrissie chuckles, no doubt relieved that this is car-related, and therefore a boy-job. 'We call it road tax in Britain, as years ago the money was used to maintain the roads, but nowadays it disappears into a big, black hole!' Then she frowns. 'But why are the town hall involved in this?'

Jose is perplexed. 'Because you must to pay the money to town hall. Every March. You no pay the road tax in Eengland to town hall in March? And it is October. Why you no pay you say-oss to town hall in March?'

'Because we have not had a bill!' she splutters. 'We guessed there would be some form of road tax here, but assumed we would get a bill in the post. Why didn't we get a bill in the post?'

'Because I will have no job!' Amador laughs. He picks up the slip and studies it for the first time. 'Oh my GAAD, I was at your house, YESTERDAY! Castillo street. You no in house, I could have beer, on you TERASSA! I come you house TOMORROW. We have beer on you TERASSA!'

'You are very welcome to have a beer on our terrace, any time you are passing, Amador, providing you do not hit me on the

ASS!' I confirm. 'But why do you need to come tomorrow?'

'Because I bring you beel, of course!'

Now he has me puzzled. I indicate the yellow slip. 'Is this not the beel, sorry, bill?'

'NO! Ees not BEEL! Ees to say you not pay beel, so you must to go town hall, they give to you beel, and you must to pay beel.' And he looks at me as if I have just failed my O-Level stupidity exams.

I narrow my eyes. 'So where do I pay the bill?'

'The town hall, of COURSE!'

'You no have thees system in Eengland?' Teri enquires.

Well let me think… Chrissie beats me to it, however. 'No, we have things like envelopes, and a post office, in the UK. So let me get this straight, the road tax or say-oss is due in March, but they don't send a bill, then Amador walks round your house six months later with a yellow slip to remind you to pay, then you go to the town hall for the actual bill, which you then pay, in the town hall. Correct?'

'Yees!' they chorus, 'ees easy, no?' *Well it is if you have nothing better to do than chase bits of paper around the town.*

'So how much is this say-oss likely to be?' my wife persists.

She clearly failed her O-Level stupidity also, according to Amador. 'You need the beel, the beel will say how much. But it will be much cheaper than Granada.' Which causes further confusion amongst the British participants in this conversation.

'The city is more expensive than, how you say, billage.' Juan states.

'Village?'

'Yees, billage. Say-oss in billage is cheaper.' *Has to be a wind-up, right?*

'Is this a joke?' Chrissie splutters. 'Are you seriously saying the road tax is cheaper here than Granada? Why?'

Amador rolls his eyes. 'Because there ees more roads in Granada. More roads, more say-oss.' *He has to be getting his own back for having his groin put out of action by fifteen English stone.*

I bury my forehead in my hands. 'But I am free to use the roads in Granada, am I not? I can go there, any time I like, and use their roads?' Then a thought strikes me. What if right now, a yellow slip from Granada council is winging its way to us. *Two overnight stays in your favourite hotel opposite the Alhambra Palace. Free sneaky parking in that lay-by. A visit to the oldest ceramics factory in Spain. A stroll around the Arab quarter and a paella outside that restaurant in Plaza Nueva. Plees come town hall for beel.*

Marie giggles. 'But you not live Granada. Go there maybe one time, two time each year. So you not use they roads much. Ees lo-he-cal, no?' *LOGICAL? Is she serious? Then suddenly it dawns on me. Is this road-pricing, in its simplest form? You no use they roads much, so you no pay? Maybe I'll drop Boris a line, although I cannot see this system catching on in the UK, somehow.....*

There endeth the British questions, and now we have a few Spanish ones. 'Amador?' Teri smiles, politely, holding up the yellow slip, 'did you write this? It look like writing of olive-picker!'

'My dow-terr of seex jeer write better than thees!' confirms Marie.

'Writing of booey!' Juan frowns, severely.

'Disgusting!' chimes in Jose.

Very direct, the Spanish. The young man does his best to be offended. He snatches a pen from the table in his left hand, grabs a sheet of paper, and in a crab-claw motion twists his wrist clock-wise and starts to write, face about a foot above the page. He finishes, tosses the pen onto the desk, and shoves the page across, dismissively. The others all glance at the ancient

Greek script. 'Thees writing of olive picker!' Teri grumbles. 'What does it say?'

He leans back and links his hands behind his head. 'Free-end of Juanee teach me thees!' *Oh no, not one of Del-Boy's little gems, please.*

'So what does it say?'

'FOX OFF!'

The following morning I am writing on the laptop on our kitchen terrace, when I become aware of a massive ruckus in the street outside. Which, unusually, cannot be anything to do with Loli, as she is still absent without leave, so it now falls to Juan the soon-to-be-retired dustman, to cause a gigantic hullabaloo in his garden, over the simple task of watering. 'Susanna, Susanna! Turn on the agua. And I want pie and chips today!' I pad through to the dining room and peer around the blind, to see Amador, bag of yellow slips around his neck, being confronted by our new neighbour, Betty Boob. Yes, after years of neglect and gradual deterioration, the house opposite has new occupiers, a Spanish couple, forties I would say, she big, blonde and buxom, with a voice like a fog-horn, he slim, dark, short, with a pronounced limp and a put-upon air generally. Bettina and Javier. Nice couple, very friendly, he drives a beat-up chicken-coop-cum-Renault van, with go-faster stripes, around the town picking up scrap metal and bits of old this-and-that generally, which he than takes to the local scrap yard. Must be quite lucrative, too, as they have a massive cinema-sized telly, regular pizza deliveries about half-eleven at night, and a huge bag of greasy *churros* on a Sunday morning.

Bettina meanwhile seemingly does nothing, apart from gossip, par for the course in this neck of the woods, which she does at regular intervals, in the street, in her nightwear. Now most Spanish women will also don a dressing gown, or a housecoat, just in case, but not our new neighbour. A flimsy cotton nightshirt, bigger than the tent Sir Edmund Hillary and Sherpa Tensing took to the summit of Mount Everest, and long clingy bottoms, which actually cling in all the wrong places, and I'm sorry there is no easy way of telling you this without scaring the horses, no underwear. Which makes conversations with the woman especially difficult, for me. Chrissie however tells me her favourite subject is *Bimbo* bread, that peculiar Spanish brand of white-sliced, which for some curious reason she debates *ad-infinitum* in the street, unless of course she is referring to a family member... or herself.

Betty and her gravity-defying boobs have a terrified-looking Amador backed against the wall, facing certain death by asphyxiation, unless I can ride to the rescue. Quick as a flash I unlock our door and dive into the street, with a cheerful *buena dia*, which causes Betty to heft her ample frame in my direction, whereby my little friend seizes the moment to escape his worst nightmares, calls something over his shoulder, and darts though the door. 'Oh my GAAD! Give me BEER! That woman! I could see her PAW-PAWS! Ees DISGUSTING! I think I DIE! Quickly PLEES. Give me BEER! Fox ME!'

I meanwhile am doubled over laughing, and have to slump in the chair for a few moments. Never like this in Britain, paying the road tax, with some sullen, po-faced woman behind the post office counter, was it? 'Certainly you can have a beer my friend' I giggle, pouring him one, 'but should you be drinking? Aren't you officially at work?'

'I trow-MA! I trow-MA ver badly!'

'You are traumatised?'

'YEES! Oh my GAAD!' He takes a gulp, then another, I proffer the litre-bottle again, and he nods gratefully. Hands trembling, he reaches for his little satchel. 'Now, I have you beel, for sayoss. Seventy-five euros, for jeer. I pay thees for you thees day already. You give me seventy-five euros, but not necessary hooray.'

I chuckle to myself. I know what he means, I think, but decide to play along. 'Hooray? Like HOORAY!' And I pump both arms in the air.

'No no sorree, I mean no quickly. You pay me the money but no need to be quickly.'

'Hurry' I smile, the word is 'hurry'. 'No rush', we say. But I think I have the cash here, just a moment.....' and I delve into my wallet, dig out eighty, and press it into his hand with an air of finality.

'No, no, plees, ees only seventy....'

'Be quiet!' I still have hold of his hand. 'You have had a traumatic morning, with Betty Boob, our neighbour. Thank you very much for your help!'

He swallows the rest of his pint. 'I must to go, I have much work.' And he pokes his head stealthily out of the door. 'She disappear, Betty BOOB! See you the next week? BYEEEE!' And he vanishes, like a phantom in the night.

Still chuckling, I pad back out to the terrace, sit back down in front of my laptop, even though my concentration is shot, after all that, and study the Spanish road tax demand. What an utter drama, like everything in this bonkers country. And am I happy with the amount? Well, I have to say I thought it might be less. I mean, our council tax in the UK was over two thousand, here it is eighty, so I was expecting the road tax to be, what, a fiver? No not really, but twenty-five or thereabouts? Still, we always say if something is less here than the UK equivalent, we are up on the deal, bearing in mind all the free sunshine thrown in. And there it is, look, shining on the olive groves.

Now, what was I writing about?

CHAPTER 8. THE SPANISH HORSE AND THE HOT DOG

Nobody's on the road. It is coming up to half-past two on a baking afternoon, and Spain has closed temporarily for lunch. Extremely regular in their habits, the Spanish. Even in our street, where the immediate neighbours are either unemployed, retired, or in the process of retiring, around two o' clock they will come out onto their patios for a last-minute bellow, windpipes will be evacuated, throats cleared, dietary requirements discussed between Juan and Seve, then it all goes quiet for, ooh, several hours at least, apart from Loli's house, where a number of microscopic specks of dust will be identified on the garden path at around three, which will need to be swept away that absolute instant, after another severe bout of expectorating. Strangely however, Castle Street is enjoying an extended holiday this year, as the three of them are still away, Loli, Isabel and Fernando, no doubt to the horror of their fellow hotel guests, but to the absolute delight of the rest of the street.

We, on the other hand, are far more flexible in our dining habits, seeing as how lunch is usually only a sandwich, which might be enjoyed at any time from say half-twelve, until just before the lung-evacuating period commences. We simply have to eat before that happens, for obvious reasons. Today for instance we have enjoyed a visit to the small town of Priego, buried deep in the Subbetica mountains between Cordoba and

Granada, a captivating mixture of narrow, winding streets, ancient churches, a shopping street devoid of chain-stores, a castle, an historic pub and a picturesque *mirador,* a cliff-edge viewpoint with commanding vistas of the surrounding countryside. And lunch was *pastel de nata,* that Portuguese custard tart which they also sell here, given that Portugal is only just down the road relatively speaking, stuffed with glazed fruit in the Spanish version, purchased from a *pasteleria,* the location of which I refuse to divulge as the next time we go they will have sold out. Oh go on then, it is between the castle and the mirador. Tell them I sent you. So Priego is well worth a visit, I promise you, when next in that area.

Heading homewards in our now entirely legal car, as far as we know, I notice the fuel gauge needle hovering near the lower end of the scale, so decide to pay a visit to Pedro-the-Petrol, our friendly *gasolinera* proprietor. Now I have to tell you I hate the way filling stations in the UK have changed from the roadside type, where you simply drove in, did the business, and sailed out again, to the supermarket ones where you negotiate a roundabout, a slip road, another roundabout, a left turn, then a right, followed by a queue to get onto a pump. And repeat to get out again afterwards. One of the evils of modern life, in my grumpy-old-man opinion. In Spain however there is none of that modern malarkey. Like a throwback to a bygone age, a filling station here usually comprises an excellent cafe-bar, a hunting-knife emporium and a small petrol-retailing enterprise thrown in for good measure. And let me tell you, there are no international coffee brands, chain-store sandwiches or fish & chip franchises anywhere to be seen. A Golden-Arch-free zone, in other words, praise be.

And in a true representation of the Swinging Sixties, they even employ pump attendants, a frankly mixed bunch of individuals who either come scampering across the forecourt, or take all day about sauntering leisurely out of the office, you just never know, which adds a little spice to the filling-up process.

Sadly, this bunch are not known for their collective intelligence, which is why you will never encounter the *Repsol Pump-Attendant Training-College* team on *University Challenge,* for example. I find myself quite regularly harassed, when dragging my aching bones from the car, by the attendant informing me 'you need the key to unlock the fuel cap.' *Well blow me down, I've been driving since I was seventeen, and I never knew that. Where have you been, all my life?* Still, you cannot have it both ways, can you, which is why I have developed my own strategy. If the attendant arrives in time, I unlock the tank, then announce how much I intend spending. 'Benty-thinko euros.' *Benty-thinko euros?* 'Si, benty-thinko euros.' *Benty-thinko?* I usually then nod, feeling that having to pronounce *twenty-five* more than twice is actually a waste of breath. If the attendant fails to arrive however, I fill the tank myself, thus avoiding the words *benty-thinko* entirely. The only deviation from this procedure is on the Harley, when I always insist on doing it myself, thereby avoiding possible fuel spillages on my groin, or having my tank scratched by a badly-aimed nozzle.

Thankfully, we encounter none of these dramas with Pedro-the Petrol, a garage we use regularly when in that area. Slim, middle-aged, greying and smiley, Pedro is keen to practice a few English words, to help his boys who are learning in school, although his vocabulary is extremely limited, comprising a few choice words only, and we usually end up rolling around laughing, something I have never done in a Tesco filling station.

So today we drive onto the forecourt, noticing it has recently been hosed down, as the pumps are still wet, with several large lakes on the concrete. Laying the dust I imagine, although in this heat it will be dry in about thirty seconds, or less. As we pull up to the pump I can see Pedro in the office, and at that moment Rocky the garage Alsatian dog comes strolling leisurely across, bends his head and proceeds to lap luxuriously from the pool. 'Blimey, will you look at that!' Chrissie sniggers. 'He has his own bowl by the shop, in the shade, where he sleeps. Why would he want to drink that polluted puddle? Water, mixed with unleaded, and a hint of diesel. I wouldn't want him licking my face, I can tell you!'

'Well what if he farted, and someone was smoking, behind him!' I chuckle. 'He would go up like a rocket! Imagine the headlines on TV, Andalucia joins the space-race, Alsatian seen racing past the Moon, charting a course for Mars. With all that fuel on board, he'd be there by Monday!'

Pedro joins us, smiling, just as Rocky is licking his lips appreciatively, and I am sure if he were human he would sigh, Ahhhh, and belch noisily. The dog I mean, not Pedro. 'Goo-bye' he grins. Pedro I mean, not the dog. Now this is where it gets confusing. The Spanish often say *Adios* when they greet you, the dictionary translation of which is of course *goodbye*. But what they are actually meaning is *A-dios*, go with God. So Pedro is wishing us a blessing by the Almighty, which he thinks is translated as *goodbye*. With me so far? Complicated business, getting a gallon of four-star, right?

'No' I smile, warmly. 'Hello is *ola*, goodbye is *adios*.' And I mime walking up to him, 'hello!', then I walk away, 'goodbye!'

He grins. 'Ello! Benty-thinko euros? Twenty-fife?'

I nod my head. 'Yes, twenty-five euros, please!'

He inserts the nozzle, glances down at the hound, then puffs out his cheeks. 'Horse.'

Well, he's a big old bugger, is our Rocky, but probably pushing it a bit to describe him in equine proportions. 'Pony' I giggle, which is the same word, more or less, in Spanish. *Ponny*.

Pedro turns serious. 'No, horse.'

I am not really sure what to say next, so I stick out my hand, at shoulder height. 'Horse.' Then I lower it, above our four-legged friend. 'Pony.'

He lets go of the hose, leaving it wedged in the filler pipe, as he clearly needs two hands for his English class. 'No, *perro* no. *CALOR*. Horse.' And he wipes an imaginary bead of sweat from his brow, and points at the sun.

At which I dissolve into laughter. 'HOT! *Calor* is hot! Horse is *caballo!*'

I don't think I've ever seen anyone laughing like this in a filling station. Certainly not in Tesco. People say 'wetting themselves laughing', or worse, well Pedro is in severe danger of wetting us all, with gasoline, and sending us into orbit, along with the dog. He is leaning against the car. '*Calor*, hot, *caballo*, horse! Oh my Gaad!'

Chrissie has just emerged from the Ladies, and has caught the tail-end of the conversation. 'It is very horse today' I inform her, straight-faced, flapping my hand to fan myself.

'No, HOT!' Pedro roars, wiping tears from his eyes. 'Madre mia! HOT! Caballo! I estupid! Horse! No!' Easy mistake to make I suppose, confusing hot with horse, although Rocky looks decidedly unimpressed. He would have better luck on *University Challenge* than his human colleague, that's a sure fact.

Several weeks later we are back in the same garage, but the atmosphere appears to have changed dramatically. There is no sign of Rocky the horse, or Pedro the Petrol, so I perform my own filling-up exercise, then head into the office where Dave the Diesel, another member of staff who speaks no English whatsoever, is on cashier duty, although he processes my card without speaking and barely acknowledges my presence. The cafe-bar meanwhile is empty. Very strange. Chrissie and I both make use of the *facilities*, and when I emerge I spot Pedro deep in conversation with his colleague, although even he barely nods as I pass. I simply have to find out what has happened, nothing we've said or done of course, unless rollicking mirth on a forecourt is a dismissable offence in this country. 'Is everything OK?' I enquire.

Pedro blows out his cheeks, and nods to the far side of the cafe, a huge plate-glass window. 'Robado, last night' he whispers. 'The cigarettes, and the spirits.' I strain my eyes in that direction, but honestly canno.... OH MY GOD, a van-shaped hole in the glass, and my first thought is how the rest of the glass has remained in place, so that the upright rectangle where the vehicle came through is still visible. And the raiders must have come through the shrubbery, as there are steel posts concreted in the forecourt, at the front.

Chrissie then appears at my side. 'Look at that, a ram-raid last night' I murmur, softly.

She glances frantically around, and then at Pedro. 'Where is Rocky?'

He winces, painfully. 'Fuera.' Now the Spanish use this word for a variety of different meanings, usually 'outside', or 'gone away', or... Oh no, no, no. Please, no. I glance at Pedro, and a single tear appears in the corner of his eye, and rolls down his cheek. Quick as a flash I slip my arm around his shoulder, and Chrissie takes both his hands in hers. Poor, poor Rocky, died in the line of duty. Suddenly I cannot ask any more, best to remember him lapping noisily at the puddle, and the simple pleasure he gave to thousands of travellers. Fags and booze can be replaced of course, but the faithful forecourt Alsatian was a one-off. Feeling totally inadequate, we mutter our sympathies as best we can, give Pedro a final squeeze, and drive quietly away.

Visits to that garage will never be the same again.

CHAPTER 9. WHERE'S FERNANDO?

I am getting slightly worried. More than slightly, in fact. On a scale of one-to-ten, a six maybe, or possibly a seven. About what, I hear you ask? Well, my memory. Or not my memory as such, which I've always prided myself as being almost photographic. No, becoming absent-minded, that is it, increasingly absent-minded. In the mornings, getting dressed, I might slip on a sock, only one, then pull a tee-shirt over my head, then hop around trying to locate some underwear, pull the shirt down, locate the other sock, stumble, fall backwards on the bed like some upended turtle, and end up getting into a right tangle, before I've even made a start to the day. This happens more often than I should really admit. Cooking, I might consider the main ingredient, then put some water on to boil, for what purpose I have no idea, start chopping the veggies, some of them, then think about the stock, which might be what the water was for, come to think of it, or the sauce, then whip out *Rick Stein's Spain* to check on the quantities, pour myself a beer, which I should have done to start with, and find myself in a complete fog, staring at nothing in particular. I always get there in the end, as neither of us has died of food poisoning, yet, but I often feel the serving of the dish should be heralded by a fanfare of trumpets. In conversation, I sometimes come to a grinding halt, mid sentence, missing a word, or a name, or…..
And DIY. I could direct you, to the nearest half-inch, to the location of my tools, every single one, in my tool-room, yet when

being used they disappear, I put them down, somewhere ob-
scure, hidden from view, and whole quarter-hours can pass by
before I locate them again, during which time I usually furiously accuse Chrissie, if she is on hand, of spiriting them away.
Which is why she invariably goes out to the garden with her
ear-buds in these days, during my bouts of home improvement, returning periodically to ensure I am not lying maimed
somewhere. In fact I suspect her of taking mental note of the
location of the gauze and sticking plaster whenever I begin
even the simplest tasks, which often result in wounds, and
bloodshed. And just the other day, fitting a new windscreen-
wiper blade to the car, a task I must have performed dozens of
times over a motoring career approaching fifty years, I simply
couldn't get it right. There is a knack, of course, the rubber
blade assembly will only fit to the U-shaped arm one way, but
after half-a-dozen attempts, I had to stand aside, helpless, and
ask Chrissie to come to the rescue, as we were ten miles from
home, and it was raining. Now, in these more enlightened
times there is absolutely no reason why a lady should not
spring into action, although she was muttering about keeping
a dog and barking herself, not to mention getting wet. 'Get the
instructions out!' was another comment. *Instructions? With
wiper blades? Who knew that?* She got it first time, of course.
And has now become the official wiper-blade changer. *She just
doesn't know that yet.*

Concentration. That is it, a loss of concentration. During my
career, firstly with the Inland Revenue, as they were known
then, after which the gamekeeper turned poacher and I joined
the accountancy profession, I needed to devote long periods of
my day to intense concentration, the very thought of which
will undoubtedly cause my former colleagues to dissolve into
fits of laughter, but it was true. So my question is this; is
concentration a finite resource? Are we granted a supply, then
when it's gone, it's gone? Or is the stock unlimited, but requiring regular maintenance, as in, use it or lose it? And there is no

doubt that since retirement, my usage has become irregular, to say the very least.

Or is all this a natural part of getting older? Not a clue, clearly, having never been in my mid-sixties before, although there are phrases, aren't there, like 'senior moment', to explain away the sudden loss of brain function, but maybe I contributed to this decline by retiring early, and switching off my quota, or turning down the dial, certainly.

This was brought into sharp focus this past summer, in the UK, whilst visiting an old family friend, Daniel, a true old-style Cornish countryman, at his snug little cottage in the rolling countryside of the south-east of the county. His beloved wife Mavis had sadly died a couple of years before, although when I last saw him he seemed to be coping admirably, chopping wood and tending his vegetables. This time however we knew something was badly wrong the moment we opened the garden gate, as his plot was lying fallow. Superficially however he seemed perfectly normal, although I detected a vagueness behind his smile. I asked him how he was managing, for meals. 'All right, boy' he assured us. 'I got one of these, look' indicating a microwave oven, 'and a load of these 'ere, see' opening a freezer door to reveal several dozen frozen ready-meals neatly stacked inside. 'The maid up the road does me shopping, forget 'er name but 'er's very good, and what I d'do is break 'im like this', mimicking stabbing a fork through the cellophane, 'then I puts 'im in this 'ere, and turns 'im up to the red mark' gesturing at a hand-painted dot and the dial, 'then the bell pings and 'ee's done.' The entire sentence without actually naming a single item.

'So do you still sell the sawing-horses, Dan?' Years ago he used to take delivery of a stack of wooden pallets from a shadowy figure who for some reason seemed to arrange the drop-off during the cover of darkness, then fashion the planks into maybe a half-dozen rustic work-benches, which he would proceed to advertise in the small-ads section of the *Cornish Times*.

'I only advertises one, boy, keep they nosey beggars in Caradon Council out o' me business. Advertise one, sell all six, see? People thinks I only got the one to sell, just private, like.' he used to grin, tapping his nose, and winking.

Forty years on he looked suitably vague. 'I got a sawing horse out in the shed, boy, what I made, years ago, but I never used to sell 'em.'

Perhaps he thinks I'm a nosey beggar from Caradon Council. Only one way to find out. Take the bull by the horns. 'You do know who we are, Dan, don't you?'

My old friend looked me straight in the eye. 'I got be honest, boy, no I don't.'

My heart sank as a part of my world crumbled away, although I ploughed on, attempting to jog his memory. 'You remember us, Dan. Chrissie and John, we used to live in the village, opposite the pub, next to Mrs Scawen, near Jim Treloar who swept the streets in Looe, remember? By Bob Rowe, who played in the band, worked for SWEB? I used to come out here on a Saturday morning, have cup-tea, bit-cake, a good ole yarn?' I persisted, reverting to the vernacular. 'Then we moved away, down west, when I changed my job, and you and Mave used to visit me on your way down Helston to see auntie, you used to bring a great box of onions into the office, in Truro, remember?'

'He was gazing into space. 'No, boy, I don't remember you at all. Mave's gone now, you know? 'Er's in a better place, now.'

We drove away in abject silence, I remember, that morning. We stopped in the village of course, had a look at the old place, which on the face of it was the same, yet in reality was utterly changed. No old men leaned on the railings outside the post office, or sat slumped on the stone benches in the lych-gate. Shiny new cars had replaced the ratty, sagging old bangers, the pub was advertising a seven-course tasting menu instead of the formerly ubiquitous pasty in a paper bag, and the whole place had that freshly-painted but deserted feel of a commuter village, compared with the slightly scruffy yet vibrant community of old.

So is this what I have to look forward to? I really am starting to feel this. Maybe I'm actually an eight, on the dial. Take this evening, for instance. We needed a few things, in the supermarket, so I decided to accompany Chrissie on her walk down to her student Anna, or *Anna-but-don't-ask-me-which-Anna* as they're all known by me, these days, then veer off and do the shopping, before returning home in time for my student Alberto, at seven. What could be simpler? What indeed. All went well until I was delving in my pocket for the money, suddenly realising I'd forgotten my key, as Chrissie had locked the front door, making it her fault actually as you'd have thought she'd have reminded me, surely? And I'd also forgotten my mobile phone, making it doubly her fault. *'Got your phone and your key?'* What would have been wrong with that?

So here I am, at the check-out, staring at the ceiling, holding everyone up, in my *'what is that dozy old man doing?'* mode. I pay, realising I've forgotten the club-card, stuff everything into my pockets, as I've forgotten the bag-for-life, then move away, and ponder my next move. And my options are limited. I don't know which Anna Chrissie is visiting, and I have no idea where any of these Annas live in any case, I cannot phone her to ask me to meet me with the key, so I am well and truly stuffed. Along with my pockets, unless I pay for a plastic carrier, which I hate doing as there's far too much plastic in the world already. Now, I have actually made plans for just this eventuality, as I've been feeling for quite some while that it was only a matter of time before I forgot my key, or even lost it somewhere. I could knock on Loli's door, ask to go out into her garden, and hop over the wall into ours. Our back door is usually only latched, not bolted, unless we go away, so two minutes and I would be inside. Simple? Er, no. One major flaw in that cunning scheme. Loli is away. As are sister Isabel, and brother Fernando. Which means the next inhabited house going up the street would be

Mercedes, but that would involve scaling her wall, Fernando's chain-link fence, Isabel's wall then Loli's. It could be done, but only if I were half-man, half-chimpanzee.

Never fear. Cunning plan number two. Heading down the street, next door is currently uninhabited, as the dungaree-clad Waltons, plus Luna Guapa Chica are safely tucked away in Bilbao, presumably, but Juan the-soon-to-be-retired dustman should be there, so leap over his crumbling rampart, then the Waltons' equally decrepit bulwark, and into ours that way. The major stumbling block with that strategy is that those two obstacles are much higher, around six feet I would imagine, and I am wearing shorts, so my knees and shins are going to get cut to ribbons. Still, this should teach me a valuable lesson, shouldn't it? And if Juan happens to be out, Alberto and I will have to stage the class in the street. And I cannot phone him to postpone.... Grrrr. Need to get a move on too, as I have no way of telling the time, but it must be half-six already. As I puff my way up our road, I mentally curse, as Cruzojo is standing by his front door. Brother-in-law of Juan. Just standing. Staring. Doing nothing. The national pastime. And there is no way he will disappear until he has seen what I am up to. Even though as far as he is concerned I will simply unlock my door and step inside. Fascinating, watching British people unlock their front doors. How utterly bored does someone have to be? But that is the reality, in this country. Fair enough, if there's nothing better on telly.... One slight complication, however. Last week, the brothers-in-law had a massive row, outside Juan's front door, so loud, so aggressive, it seemed at one stage they would come to blows. Cruzojo, the taller, fitter, younger of the pair was the accuser, Juan, five-foot-nothing in his socks the accused, what he was supposed to have done completely passed us by, but it went on fully five minutes. Made a nice change actually, to witness a blokey conflict, as usually it is Loli providing the entertainment.

I call a cheerful 'good afternoon' as I pass, even though it is strictly the evening, although there is no such time of day in this country, so afternoon it is, and his patience is finally rewarded after all these years as I knock on his relative's door. *What could the Englishman be up to?* I am greeted by a cacophony of barking, which comes as somewhat of a surprise, because as far as I'm aware they only have the one dog, the little white Bichon, invariably found clamped around the bosom of wife Susanna as it accompanies her on window-cleaning excursions. This sounds like a small pack, however. Eventually, the door is pulled open a crack and about half of Juan's head appears, no doubt wary of incoming fists, until he spots who I am and flashes me his toothless grin, opening the door fully. Not gonna get walloped in front of witnesses, is he? Now, I've been rehearsing my little speech, my explanation, as to why I would like to climb his garden wall, but do you think I can remember the Spanish for 'forgotten'? Or 'climb'? 'I've lost my key, Juan. Could I possibly jump your wall, please?' *Saltar.* To jump, or to dive. Not that there will much jumping, or diving in evidence, trust me on that. Arthritic scrambling, or falling off into the bushes, more like. And I accompany my words with an up and over gesture.

Suddenly, a fox comes hurtling down his hallway, making a desperate bid for freedom, and my frail-looking neighbour appears in real danger of being trampled by escaping wildlife. Displaying surprising dexterity for one his age, however, Juan sticks out a boot, the ginger fugitive cannons into his leg, whimpers, and retreats. So where has it come from? And is it actually Foxy Loxey? Did it come in through the garden? In which case why didn't our neighbour simply usher it out? It is certainly fox-colour, fox-shape, fox-size, and you know what they say, if it looks like a fox.... I smile, Juan smiles, although only I know I'm imagining a huntsman in a red coat, blowing a horn, galloping through the kitchen, followed by a pack of baying hounds. 'Zorro?' I giggle. Thorro. Spanish for fox. And please don't ask me how I know this. Oh, all right, then, Alicia

at the library group taught me it, OK? Whether she was implying she was a bit of a fox, I'd prefer not to think about, if it's all
the same to you.

He throws back his head, and roars with laughter. 'Claro!' he
slobbers, and I take a step backwards, in case of scattered spittle showers. 'Gray-Donn.' Is that what he said? Something like
that. I struggle with this language, at times. Chrissie is far better at picking out words, and meanings, whereas to me it often
sounds like unintelligible shouting. And she's not here right
now, as we all know.... Anyway. Never heard that particular
word. Is this the species, or the creature's name? Perhaps the
generic term for a mutt, like Lassie, Spike, Prince, Rex, or
Rover? And suddenly I cannot help smiling, nostalgically, recalling the great Ray Graydon, mercurial winger in the sixties
for the vastly under-rated and serial underachieving football
team, Bristol Rovers. So is this actually a pet? The fox I mean,
not Ray Graydon. It does look surprisingly well groomed, for a
wild animal, and it seems very much at home, sprawled across
the hall floor, licking something horrid. Now, how can he possibly not know about his neighbours' pets, I hear you ask. Well,
not the most enthusiastic dog-walkers, the Spanish, I have to
say, and that is being kind. The Bichon has never once been
seen, on its own four legs, trotting happily down the street on
the end of a lead. Cruzojo has a yappy terrier which he lets into
the road, then stands idly by whist the creature cavorts
around, dodging the odd moped. Campo Pete, Leopard-skin
Woman's husband, ties his pair of greyhounds to his ancient
pop-pop and rides up and down, a depressing spectacle of abject laziness which goes a long way to explaining his massive
gut. Back in the spring, Fernando acquired a dog of sorts, and
we only know this because it made the occasional doggy noise,
which he kept in an old chicken run, or aviary, at the back of his
house, of which we can only see the top, due to the configuration of the garden walls and outbuildings. I asked Isabel if her
brother had a dog. 'Yes, neighbour' she confirmed, and then ut-

tered some other word which I didn't understand. Could have been Gray-Donn, now I come to think about it. So what about this, given that Fernando's pet suddenly fell silent. Did he donate it to Juan? Was the task of topping up the water bowl and throwing down a few Meaty Chunks proving too onerous? We had speculated whether the animal had died of boredom, but perhaps this is the answer? He passed it on to Juan? Consider also the casual attitude of the Waltons, returning to Bilbao and leaving Luna Guapa Chica to make her own arrangements. Sad, isn't it? We considered it one of life's joys, walking our retriever Nelson, even in the pouring Cornish rain, and would give anything to have him with us here, now. And it's not as if these people have anything particular to do. Would benefit from the exercise, many of them.

Juan beckons me inside, and there is Susanna, as predicted, fluffy one welded securely in place. 'He's lost his key, wants to dive over our wall' he confirms, and I swear the dog nods, or maybe it was the natural heave of her chest. 'Here is our *salon*, neighbour' he grins, which seeing as how it contains a sofa and two armchairs, I'd managed to figure out for myself, bearing as it does a striking resemblance to our place. Not always the case, of course, and I do always say these houses are all the same, yet all different, being of varying heights, widths and internal configurations, but this one has the stairs down to the garden on the left of the hall, same as us, somewhere I'm keen to get at the earliest, as I have a total of twelve feet of climbing, and the same of descending, or falling, still to perform.

'I have my student coming at seven' I smile, politely, hoping we can maybe postpone the grand tour until another occasion. 'What is the time now?'

He consults his watch. 'Seven minus twenty' he confirms, in the Spanish style. Twenty-to-seven in old money. 'Plenty of time. Here's the kitchen, look.'

Yeah, plenty of time for you, maybe, but I'm the one who is

going to be cleaning up blood, before Alberto arrives. This is turning into an episode of *Escape to the Country*.

'What is that in your pocket, neighbour?' Susanna enquires, gesturing at my bulging shorts. Typical, isn't it? For decades I've been itching to use the line 'It's a banana and I'm pleased to see you!' Not appropriate here, of course, and anyway, that needs an instant riposte, and I'm not sure my Spanish is up to it. *Banana* is banana of course, but *pleased to see you* will need a little thought. Too late already. 'Would you like a *bolsa*?' she continues, helpfully, pulling a plastic carrier out of a kitchen drawer. Well, this one already exists, and we can always recycle it of course. Plus, it was free.

A jar of pesto, a three-pack of tuna and a tin of sweetcorn emerge from my pockets, and I stare, intensely, wracking my brain. *I am sure there was something else I was supposed to get....* Speaking of Fernando, as we were, just a while ago, I have a question. *I am sure there was something else....* 'Do you know what has happened to Loli, Isabel and Fernando?'

Juan grins, widely. 'Hospital, neighbour.

What, all of them? 'Who is in hospital?' *Positive there was something....*

'Fernando, neighbour.' And I swear he looks pleased about it. Like pulling teeth, though, isn't it? Must be something serious, they've been gone two months at least. Not having an ingrowing toenail removed, is he?

'What is wrong with Fernando?'

He taps the side of his head, and winks. 'Cerebro, neighbour.'

Cerebro. Cerebral? Brain? Blimey. Poor fellow. Again, this is the problem, living a foreign country. I feel I should ask more, but I don't know if I should. The Spanish are usually forthright, so I don't suppose it will be seen as intrusive. It sounds serious, but why did Juan wink? Has Fernando finally flipped, after all those years of living with Loli? OK, here goes. 'Que problemo?'

Our diminutive neighbour puffs out his cheeks, and shrugs dismissively. 'No say.'

He doesn't know, and by the seem of it, doesn't care either. Right, one last go. 'Which hospital?'

He shoots me a *bugger Fernando, wasted enough time talking about him* look, still puffing, still shrugging, and there endeth the questions. 'Follow me, neighbour' and he opens the door down to the basement, and disappears. 'Take care of your head.'

Clutching my shopping, I descend the uneven stone steps into what appears to be a dungeon, complete with damp, musty aroma and flaky whitewash, but thankfully no chains or other means of restraint, and I cannot resist a feeling of pride, recalling how our place was originally like this on the lower ground floor, yet is now a cool, light, rustic summer bedroom of great charm, freshly painted exposed beams and stone walls, complete with walk-in fireplace, adorned by Chrissie's collection of ceramics, all achieved at very little cost at all. Scraping the walls was the biggest job. I don't understand how people can live like this, quite frankly. Still, at least there is none of that horrible plastic, flexible, imitation tongue-and-groove planking nailed crookedly, anywhere to be seen, which is always a bonus. I duck to avoid a naked forty-watt light-bulb hanging forlornly from a scruffy length of yellowing bell-wire looped alarmingly around a rusty nail hammered haphazardly into the beam, giving thanks and praise that there is sufficient natural light, just about, to enable us to locate the back door, thereby avoiding severe risk of electrocution.

Pride of place in this depressing cell is a hand-painted plywood dresser with double frosted-glass doors and a pull-down worktop, such as graced our family *scullery* in the late nineteen-fifties. Fully restored, such an item would undoubtedly fetch a small fortune in the trendier antique emporia just about anywhere in the UK, this one however appears to have been colonized by mice, at least on the lower levels, although the worktop does display a pleasing collection of miniature liquor bottles, which are also spread across just about every available flat surface around the room. *Well well well, I never had Juan down as a boozer.* 'Wicky?' I enquire, even though a cursory glance fails to reveal a single recognisable label from Bonnie Scotland.

'HA HA HA NEIGHBOUR!' he bellows. 'Wicky no! Assy-etty!' Olive oil miniatures? Who knew that was a thing? Although actually, come to think of it, we have occasionally been presented with similar to these in restaurants, as opposed to the more usual tapered glass jar with a cork and built-in spout, for drizzling over our morning *tostada*. So, has he been going round nicking souvenirs? He was the street sweeper, of course, so could easily slink past a pavement table and slip a little momento into his pocket. What a delightful collection. I think personally I would prefer single malts, and actually could do with a wee dram right about now bearing in mind what is lying in wait outside the back door, but this is lovely. Were we in the more touristy, cobbled back-streets of Cordoba or Granada, he could open this as a quaint little cave, with tastings, and Susanna in a wenches costume behind a stall dispensing souvenirs. Who knows, they could even incorporate the fox into the experience somehow, although perhaps that needs a little more thought…. Juan notices my interest. 'Phenomino, no?' *Oh, if only he knew what was running through my mind….*

Suddenly I am transported back in time to the *anise* factory on the chocolate Nativity trip with crazy mad-woman Elena, last Christmas. 'Si. Estupendo!' *I need to get over that damned wall.* This only serves to encourage him, however, and I get the full tour, every bottle. 'Que bonito.' Every label. 'Pressy-osa.' Every factory. 'Que mono.' Right, that is it, I've run out of superlatives. The wall.

Mercifully, Susanna comes stumping down the stairs, tapping her wrist with a *mind the time* gesture, minus her menagerie, and conventionally dressed, thank heavens. 'Do you want the *ekky-lera* neighbour?' she enquires. Ah yes, the *ekky-lera*. Actually spelt *escalera*, this is the Spanish word for stairs, steps, a pair of steps or a ladder, all four, same word, as mangled by the Andalucian dialect. Might be handy to scale their wall, actually, save stripping my skin, but then I still have the Waltons' to conquer. Still, nice of her to ask.

'Si, por favor' I smile, gratefully. For a second or two, nothing happens. I grin at Juan, assuming, I don't know, he will produce an *ekky-lera* from somewhere. He grins at his wife. Then she grins at me. What? Is this pair of steps, or ladder, expected to arrive here by magic? I am assuming it, in whatever form it takes, is tucked away in a nearby cupboard, or maybe stowed neatly alongside the garden wall?

Nope. Juan scratches his head, and looks me straight in the eye. 'You have an *ekky-lera* in your garden, neighbour' he asserts. I do. I really do. I am a man of many *ekky-leras* actually, all four varieties, but annoyingly, like policemen, there is never one around when you need one. And I can hardly go grubbing around in his *assy-etty* collection searching for one, can I? Or rise, vertically, like an RAF jump-jet from the deck of the *Ark Royal*, glide majestically across to my garden, swoop down and snatch my ladder from where it resides under the fig tree, and effect the perfect landing, outside Juan's back door.

'Er. Ah. No problem.' I jabber, partly in confusion, but mainly in fear. Because I know what lies in wait, outside the back door. A garden wall, for me to climb, obviously, but not any old garden wall. Oh dear me no. Any old garden wall would be too easy, wouldn't it? I could simply scramble over any old garden wall, couldn't I? But this is Spain, where nothing is straightforward. No, what is out there, in the gathering dusk, is a small earthquake zone, with accompanying subsidence. Now do not laugh. There are regular earth tremors in Granada, most of them quite low on the Richter Scale admittedly, but occasionally there is damage caused, as occurred across the border in Murcia a few years ago when the small town of Lorca suffered considerably. And what else could have caused the whole of the support pillar holding up the Waltons' kitchen patio to separate alarmingly from the back of the house? Or the garden wall between the two properties, the same wall I am about to climb, to lean worse than the fabled Tower of Pisa? This is not something a bucket of mortar would fix, slap it in the crack, in the Spanish way, then head off to the nearest cafe. This is serious structural damage. And quite honestly I'm not sure Juan appreciates quite how serious, given that this crevice, this fissure, is getting wider, a vertical split the entire height of the lower ground floor, from the weeds at the bottom to the patio lintel at the top, is directly outside his back door. I've been watching it, from the safety of our garden, for the past year, and it is becoming visibly worse, no doubt about it, especially after the long hot summer. In lighter moments, Chrissie and I speculate humourously about the breakfasting Waltons, Papa, Tonio, Sonia and Luna Guapa Chica, crashing spectacularly into Juan's garden one morning, Corn Flakes flying everywhere like a shower of confetti, but this is not funny. To me, the patio lintel needs propping, the offending column put out of it's misery, a new footing constructed and the pillar rebuilt. Sooner rather than later. But what can Juan do, given the fact that the Waltons live at the other side of the country? Did he speak to Papa, on their last visit? Is the old man even aware of the potential collapse, bearing in mind he never even visits the depressing collection of rubble which comprises his outside 'rockery'. Sonia occasionally stands inside the back door when Luna is allowed a brief scamper around the bomb-site, but has she ever said *'here Dad, have you seen that dirty great crack outside the back door?'* Seems unlikely.

But never fear. Juan has spoken to the Gingerbread men. The key-holders, who live next door to each other at the top of the street, near the hairpin bend. Father and son, diminutive, cheery little fellows, round shiny faces, button eyes, high, piercing voices, chat the hind legs off a donkey. The first time we encountered the pair, I remarked how they reminded me of the confectionery figures in a cake shop window, and the name stuck. Father and his wife must be well into their sixties, their boy and his family, wife and two young kids, live next door. Now, are these people family of the Waltons? Are they merely friends? Or simply professional key-holders for visiting holiday-home owners? Have they even passed the message on? Is a delivery of sand, cement, concrete blocks and a couple of Acro props, accompanied by a team of beefy labourers, imminent? Well, not according to Juan. Every time he bellows 'LOOK AT ANTONIO'S CRACK, NEIGHBOUR' across two garden walls at me, which must be at least once a week, I always reply 'QUE ESTAN HACIENDO?', what are they doing, whereupon he will shrug, raise his arms and holler 'NO SAY'. I feel really sorry for him actually, having this Sword of Damocles greeting him every time he gazes out from behind his patio 'curtains.' Not strictly his problem, is it, although one fine day, when the inevitable happens, the domino effect will surely take Juan's *assy-etty* collection with it. So could he take unilateral action by complaining to the local council? Is there some municipal engineer who could order the repairs, on the grounds of an imminent threat to life and limb, then bill the Waltons direct? And could the domino effect, instead of running left to right, as seems most likely, instead collapse right to left, and flatten our pool changing room? Is there the possibility of Tonio Walton crashing through the roof as I struggle into my trunks? Questions, questions, none of which are getting me over this cursed wall.

I hand Juan my carrier then place both hands on the top of the obstacle, attempting to rock it backwards and forwards, just in case, although mercifully it seems steady enough, which is a shame actually as if it collapsed now I could simply walk across. Now, in the days of my youth I could have vaulted the crumbling structure, easily, yet in my mid-sixties it resembles the Matterhorn, the Eiger and that other big one all rolled into one. All five-foot-plus of it. And it is leaning towards me. And there is no brawny Kiwi standing at the top, to haul me up. I know what it was I forgot, earlier. My ice-axe. About half way up is a large rock protruding enticingly through the disintegrating plaster, so throwing caution to the wind I jab my right foot onto it and haul myself up, ignoring the pain emanating from just about everywhere, particularly my groin, and suddenly I am there, spreadeagled on my front, eyes watering, at the summit. Jonno one, Spanish wall nil.

A small round of respectful applause would have been nice, in the circumstances, whereupon I could have offered to sign autographs, modestly. Instead, I get hollered at. 'LOOK AT ANTONIO'S CRACK, NEIGHBOUR.' Look at it? I'm so close I can taste it, almost. Shakily, I haul myself to my feet, then arms outstretched like a veteran tightrope walker in a second-rate circus, I approach the gaping chasm. Oh. My. God. Up close and personal it looks absolutely enormous, and gingerly I place my arms around the pillar and insert my hands, either side. All the way in, up to my wrists, almost. A world first. Forget the Mars Explorer, this is history being made, right here. One small step... yet still the crowd refuses to clap.

Now of course I have the unenviable task of climbing down the other side, and for a split second I consider emulating my schoolboy self and executing a perfect vaulting-horse dismount, feet neatly together, then dismiss this ridiculous notion as you never know what is lurking in the Waltons' weeds down below. And a twisted ankle is not on my wish-list. There is nothing else for it, I will have to slide down, feet first, on my belly, and maybe jump the last couple of feet. Realising, too late, that standing up to examine Antonio's ravine was a bad idea, I slump onto my back-side, then execute a perfect roll, positioning my feet exactly where they need to be, half way down the other side, pivoting on my gut, regretting, perhaps, that second beer last night. I smile serenely at my unappreciative audience, as if this were an everyday occurrence in the life of a British expat, then gesture for Juan to place my car-rier where I will be able to reach it, after I've disappeared from view. 'Thank you very much for all your help' I grin, then like the *Queen Mary* launching gracefully into the Clyde, thankfully minus a magnum of champagne smashed across my bows, I glide gracefully into the rocky undergrowth.

I take a moment to regain my breath, staring in disbelief at the rear of the Waltons' house, whimpering all the while in the realisation that a cheap polyester Primark polo shirt offers scant protection from wall-rash, and shredded skin. I have a confession to make, however. I have been here before. Back last spring, a vicious gust of wind tore my swimming shorts from where they lay, peacefully drying, and deposited them in the middle of this squalor. So I know the best route to scale this wall from our 'cactus-garden' patio, in front of the pool house, by standing on a garden chair, neatly avoiding evil prickles, along the changing-room roof gully, and down again in the corner of their yard, using a ridge on their all-steel, battleship grey, solid, prison-style back-door as a foothold. Why would anyone want to spend the whole of August amid this dilapida-tion? And how bad must it be in Bilbao? Not this bad, surely? No wonder Luna Guapa Chica escaped. Either side of the rear entrance, the back wall features a series of horizontal cracks, none of them knuckle-sized, like the pillar, but fingers, cer-tainly. The window is barred, emphasising the jail theme, al-though whether to prevent intruders, or escapees, is not im-mediately clear. There is no glass, a sheet of metal gauze hav-ing been nailed crookedly across the opening to forestall insect ingress, although no self-respecting meat-fly would be seen dead in this hovel, trust me. Through a foot-square opening in the back wall, a venerable grape-vine the thickness of an ele-phant's trunk snakes optimistically across a rusting trellis, the fruit dangling forlornly, withered and rotting. Decay and neg-lect. Such a crying shame, to my mind. This could be a lovely area, with minimal outlay. A retaining wall across the garden, back-fill with rubble, tile over the top, and with a little scraping and painting of the walls, the perfect spot for a patio set and al-fresco living, shaded by the vines. Plus, if they shared the materials and labour with Juan, he could also benefit from what could only be an improvement to this little corner of Spain. Providing they got the subsidence sorted first, of course. Function over form, however, is the motto of many of the locals. These nasty, dangerous, cracked concrete slopes serve as the access to the gardens, they do the job, so who cares what it looks like? They've all seen what we have achieved, all commented how lovely it looks, yet so far at least we have failed to provide inspiration. Maybe they were just being kind? Who knows, perhaps one of them has written a book, a Spanish *Sunsets and Olives* if you like, about what happens when nutty Brits move in next door?

Grinning to myself at this intriguing prospect, I nimbly place my foot on the thoughtfully-provided toe-hold on the back door, and with a heave I launch myself gratefully through the looking glass into our little world of riotous colour, and order, Chrissie's plant collection providing the perfect backdrop to the rippling, enticing waters of the pool, where I am about to throw myself…. oh damn and blast. The town clock is chiming seven. There isn't time. Alberto will be knocking, any moment now. I grab my shopping and dash upstairs, a quick swill of hands and face, throw on a clean shirt, and here he is, almost bang on time, grinning widely. 'Jonneee, you face, ess so red! And why have you blooodth, on you k-nee?'

Ninety minutes later I am preparing a culinary masterpiece, as always, when Chrissie arrives home, with a somewhat strange look in her eye. I usually time the serving of the meal to around fifteen minutes later, to give her chance to freshen up, but tonight she is crouching, in front of me, on the kitchen floor. Which is strictly *verboten*. Us maestros need the space to work, uninterrupted, you know. And for some reason, she is examining my legs, peering up my shorts even. 'Hmm, just a couple of scrapes and wounds' she comments, like some stony-faced A&E triage nurse. 'You got away with that, didn't you?' What the hell? I haven't even told her of my escapades, yet. Thought I would save that saga until we are sitting down. And she knows I hate being disturbed when I am creating. Sometimes I suspect the woman of possessing psychic powers, or cameras. 'Lucky for you that Juan and Susanna were home, wasn't it? That will teach you, won't it? I don't think you'll be forgetting your key and your phone again, do you?'

You can hear the penny dropping from the end of the street. 'You swine! You absolute bloo… you knew, didn't you? You let me go out, without them, and you didn't remind me, did you? I've had my hands inside the Waltons' crack, all because of you! Thank you very bloody much!'

She smiles, victoriously. 'Well maybe that will teach you to get your brain in gear, before you leave home.' She rustles through the carrier bag, which is still on the armchair where I threw it, when answering the door to Alberto. 'And where is the tin of baked beans I asked you to get?'

Around a week later Chrissie comes trotting down the steps to the garden, bearing a pair of choc-ices, for our mid-afternoon treat. 'They're back' she grins. 'Prepare for the peace to be shattered!'

I have only just woken up from my pre-choc-ice nap. 'Who is back? What?'

'Next door. Not Loli, as I cannot hear her shouting, but someone is in there, I can hear furniture being shifted around. I imagine Fernando is in the process of being discharged, so perhaps the niece, Sabrina, is giving it a jolly good clean. Can you imagine how Loli and Isabel must be feeling, not having dusted and swept for the past two and a half months? Withdrawal symptoms. Anticipate a barrage of housework, any day now!'

We have been speculating, Chrissie and I, this past week, after I managed to wring the barest details from Juan, over the whereabouts and well-being of our corpulent neighbour. Now clearly there is no specialist brain-injury department in our local cottage hospital, so Fernando could be in any one of a number of different locations, Granada possibly, Malaga, or, who knows, even Madrid. Neither Loli or Isabel can drive, so they must be staying, either in a local hotel, or quite possibly in a relatives room within the hospital. Or, as we saw when Chrissie had her small operation earlier this year, on a put-me-up bed in the ward. This is curious to us Brits, more used to getting booted out at the end of visiting-time, that family are permitted to stay around the bedside, twenty-four-seven, offering makeshift nursing cover during the night. Our friend Tony, the Geordie fellow for whom Del and I did a little pig-sty removing a while ago, had a brief stay in a local hospital recently, and reported that whilst the treatment he received was exemplary, the relatives of the other patients were a complete nightmare, crowding around the beds, shouting and bawling excitedly as Spaniards occasionally do, waking him up in the early hours at regular intervals.

Even with daytime appointments, doctor, dentist, physio and the like, a whole troop of relations will invariably accompany the patient, even for, ahem, highly personal, *below-the-waistline* complaints. One of Chrissie's pupils had such an outpatient visit in Seville a while ago, and was accompanied not only by her partner, but her father, and aunt. Now much as I love my auntie Ann, never in a million years would I ask her to join me on a hospital visit, particularly of a *downstairs undercarriage* nature, and I'm damned sure she would refuse, if I did....

A few more days pass peacefully before our period of tranquility is shattered one morning, by truculent bellowing. Isabel must be possessed of saintly qualities, is all I can say, to even begin to tolerate being shouted at in this manner. Suffered a lifetime of it, no doubt, but the way her sister carries on takes some believing, to our British ears. The Spanish language can sound fairly aggressive at times, especially the local variety, the intonation, the manner of delivery, but Loli's machine-gun, scrapyard-Alsatian expressive style goes way beyond that. Particularly when the medication wears off. 'I'd leave it if I were you!' my wife giggles. 'Ask about Fernando some other time, when she's calmed down. Next week, possibly!'

Then, as is so often the case, the storm blows itself out, and peace, in the form of aggressive path-sweeping accompanied by tutting and muttering, reigns. Someone no doubt slipped something soothing into her lunchtime cuppa. I close my eyes and slip gracefully into the cooling waters of the pool, resurfacing a few seconds later to find our nutty neighbour gurning over the wall. 'Oh, how is Fernando?' I enquire, inadequately, bearing in mind the length of his hospitalisation, and presumed seriousness of his condition. It is times like this when the limitations of my conversation skills become woefully apparent.

'Going well, neighbour' she confirms, disinterestedly. 'He has to stay inside the house a few days. Isn't that water cold?' And she returns to brushing her blessed concrete. Incredible, her dismissive reply. Is she heartily sick of her brother, the sole topic of conversation, keeping her away from her beloved housework, all these weeks? Was she gathered around his bedside, helping herself to his grapes, fretting all the while about imaginary dust? Or was his condition so serious that she is reluctant to dwell on how close they came to losing him?

I towel myself off, then return to my sunbed. Chrissie of course, from her vantage point, overheard the conversation, if it could be so described. 'So was the water cold, neighbour?' she chuckles. 'I'm surprised you didn't enquire about her brother. Still, never mind. Were her steps terribly soiled, could you see?'

Another week of alternate yelling and blessed silence ensues, then one afternoon, just as we are carrying the pillows and sunbed mattresses up to the pool house, the sum total of our afternoon exertions, both Loli and Isabel appear on their side of the wall, smiling. Isabel nods her head towards a spot further down the path, and there, emerging through the undergrowth, is.... Jonathan Ross. For a few seconds I am dumbfounded. Brown, collar-length hair, centre parting, smug grin, fitted tee-shirt, tailored trousers. Who the hell is this? 'Ola' he smiles. FERNANDO? Good God. I've never seen someone so utterly transformed, it truly is difficult to imagine this is the same bloke. What did they do to him, in that hospital? He must have lost five stone, easily, his hair grown several inches, at least. He looks fit, and glowing. Unbelievable. Chrissie, of course, recognises him immediately. 'You look well, Fernando' she smiles.

'You look like one of Los Beatles!' I confirm, as the Fab Four are known in this country. Well, he's not going to have a clue who Jonathan Ross is, clearly. I hope. 'I like your hair!' And I do. It suits him, actually, makes him look younger. Of course, the weight makes a huge difference, too, and the clothes, but the whole effect is stunning.

Isabel slips a sisterly arm around his shoulder. 'Come on, enough now. More tomorrow. *Bamos arriba.*' And the trio make their way up the path, towards the house. Before they have gone more than five yards however, a rumbling, grumbling row breaks out, and as they disappear inside it turns into a full-scale shouting match.

Chrissie is slumped against the wall, hand over her mouth, tittering helplessly. 'Welcome back, Fernando. Normal service has been resumed!'

CHAPTER 10.
THERE GOES THE
NEIGHBOURHOOD.

NB; This chapter has it's origins over a year ago.

You know sometimes when a new family moves in, the whole dynamic of the locality can change? The atmosphere, the camaraderie, the feelings of goodwill in the community? The new lot cast a shadow somehow, an alien presence. At first, they seem friendly enough, then gradually, things change. Noise, disruptive behaviour, damage even, disturbed nights, turning what was once a peaceful street into a neighbourhood of turmoil, neighbour against neighbour, resentment and mistrust. And it has happened here. Where this bunch came from nobody seems to know, they simply arrived one day, and immediately took over. We call them the Shaggies, due to their propensity to engage in acts of rumbustious sex, at any hour of the day or night, seemingly without regard to the norms of public decency.

Mind you, they are an attractive group. Mister Shaggy has a beautiful coat, like that triple-chocolate you used to be able to buy, white, plain and milk. A long-hair too, in beautiful condition, considering all the, ahem, action in which he engages. What? You knew I was talking about cats, right? Mrs Shaggy is all-black, sleek, slinky, Mrs Shaggy-one-eye the same, minus her left eyeball, and finally an optically-challenged black-and-white, unimaginatively titled Mrs-one-eye-Shaggy, minus her

right. Look, let me make this clear, I didn't name these creatures, OK? And we're not even sure of the genders. Mister
Shaggy is definitely a bloke, as he does that little wiggly spray-
ing thing with his rear end, but the others, who knows? This
was brought home to us recently when Chrissie, gazing out
of the bathroom window, uttered the immortal line 'ooh look,
Mrs Shaggy is shagging Mrs-one-eye-Shaggy, on Loli's wall.'

And therein lies the problem; neither Loli, Isabel, Fernando or
Juan like cats, despite the fact that when we moved here Loli
had a large black-and-white named *Peeky*. And I say *had* in the
loosest sense of the word. She fed it, on table scraps, presumably, it resided in the lower level of her basement, but was not
allowed into the main house, which we found strange, initially,
coming from a country where our four-legged-friends are a
part of the family. An amiable creature, Peeky I mean not Loli,
we used to love watching her coming across the rooftops in the
mornings, after breakfast, from our patio, heading homeward
from her nocturnal ramblings, no doubt, disappearing from
view, into the gardens, then re-emerging suddenly in a different location, as only cats can do. Incredible where they get, and
how they get there, and this locality must be feline heaven,
empty and abandoned houses and gardens, little nooks and
crannies to explore, and, I imagine, an abundance of wildlife
on which to feast. One of the delights of our morning, watching the cat come home.

Then suddenly, no more Peeky. And in her place, the Shaggies. I
asked Loli what had happened to her pet, thinking perhaps she
had developed an ailment, requiring multiple visits to the vet,
which had finally proved sadly fatal. She shrugged, disinterestedly, with a *don't ask me* gesture. *'No say.'* And that was that. A
complete lack of concern, or sentiment, at her pet's presumed
demise. And now this outright hostility. Should a wayward feline encroach on her property, or that of her siblings, a whole
range of hissing and other throaty noises, of a human variety,
ensue, followed by a sheet of water inaccurately hurled from

a balcony, falling well short of the intended target, provoking much silent mirth on our side of the wall. OK, we get it. Many people dislike moggies, for whatever reason, we understand this. But what we cannot fathom is that our neighbours used to keep one. Once a cat-lover, always a cat-lover, surely?

When we moved to this country, we were intrigued to see litre and two-litre bottles of water placed strategically on various doorsteps. Was this an additional delivery service, like the gas, the bread, the fruit and veg? Not so, according to our friends at the library group. It was a cat repellent, the idea being that the unsuspecting feline, out for his morning constitutional, would be suddenly confronted by a multifaceted prism of reflections of his own image and, convinced that a massive six-headed lion was on the prowl, run hike hell. I can probably think of stupider theories.... no actually I cannot. In fact it amuses me to picture Mister Shaggy, sauntering carelessly along the street, spotting a bottle of *Highland Spring* balanced precariously, chuckling to himself wickedly *'how unintelligent do these humans think I am?'*, unsheathing a furtive claw and puncturing the plastic, causing a dribble of water to spread across the step. Either that or performing that *Tom-Cat Shuffle*, and imbibing said bottle with his personal, pungent aroma.

There are many feral cats, and dogs, in Spain, living in parks, gardens and around waste bins, and I've heard it said one can judge the humanity of a particular country by the number of abandoned and wild 'domestic' creatures running free. If that is the case, this country comes well down the list, although it has to be said the vast majority of these animals seem in good condition, the cats in particular, considering they must be scavenging for their food. The Shaggies for example could be someone's pets such is their excellent, groomed condition, Mister in particular, with his long fur, looks as if he is on his way to a village pet show. Perhaps they are, who knows, but quite why they have all of a sudden found shelter on our covered *El Sombrero* patio will forever remain a mystery. Were they born wild? Have they been turned out of somewhere? Whatever the reason, they cause us no harm. A great deal of joy, in fact, finding the three 'ladies' snuggled together on a patio chair, or Mister performing his ablutions, beside the pool. They are most welcome, and if I am honest, provide a little *frisson* of pleasure, providing them with a haven from the persecution emanating from next door.

Chrissie and I have always been cat-people, despite receiving a rollicking retriever for my fortieth birthday, whom our cats at the time, George and Prudence, soon learned to ignore. As a boy, my Mother would not allow animals in the house, although I was permitted a tortoise, who stalked around the garden feasting on Dad's dahlias. My Nan, however had a black-and-white mouser called Frisky, and bearing in mind I spent most of my spare time there, she became 'my' pet. Chrissie similarly reported a succession of moggies throughout her formative years, and soon after our marriage we acquired the first of an unbroken run of felines, which continued until just before we came here, when George and Prudence sadly succumbed to old age.

Several weeks after the Shaggies' arrival, I am performing a minor DIY task in the downstairs summer kitchen, near the back door, when I clumsily knock my box of screws across the floor. Cursing mildly, I drop to my knees to begin gathering them up, when suddenly, under the bed, hidden from view, I spot a small sack of dry cat-food. Salmon flavour, no less. I confront my wife with the irrefutable evidence. 'Look, we agreed we wouldn't feed them, didn't we? We agreed that if we did start feeding them, we would have to continue, didn't we? That it would be cruel, when we went away to the caravan for a long weekend, they would go hungry? We agreed to put a pail of water out for them, but that was it. And just about every other day Loli bellows 'don't you go feeding those cats, neighbour." She bursts out laughing, and I likewise. 'Well done' I snigger, 'but seriously, what are we going to do, this weekend coming?

Are you planning on putting four dishes down, with strict instructions, you know, Friday, Saturday…? And are you sure Mrs Shaggy-one-eye really likes salmon? She looks like more of a beef-and-gravy girl, actually!'

She is grinning mightily. 'Don't worry, everything is in hand. Your student Lydia loves cats, I have been speaking to her on Facebook, and she has agreed to pop in over the weekend. In fact, she said that things were impossible at home, as her father was caught having an affair, and the atmosphere is terrible at the moment between her parents. So, I said she is welcome to stay the night here, while we're away, to get some studying done, if things get too bad, just to give her a break. And besides, Mrs-one-eye-Shaggy looks pregnant to me, so she has to keep her strength up! I've been meaning to tell you about it, but I somehow forgot….'

A few weeks later we are lazing the afternoon away, under the fig tree, which is slowly shedding its leaves, when suddenly Chrissie sits bolt upright. 'Do you hear what I hear?'

I drag my eyes away from my Kindle. 'Is that a question, or are you singing me an early Christmas song? *Said the little lamb to the shepherd boy, 'do you hear what I hear?'*"

She flaps her hand. 'Shhh! There it is again. Mewing. Very faint, but definitely mewing. Sounds like only one, but I reckon there is a kitten around here somewhere. Something is happening in Shaggy-world, isn't it? We haven't seen the rest of them for about a week, Mister and Mrs, plus Mrs Shaggy-one-eye have vanished, completely, and now I reckon Mrs-one-eye Shaggy has had her litter, but where? In the undergrowth below the fig, or in the Waltons' weeds? Or some other hideaway we don't know about? Of course, we have no experience of wild cats, do we? Daisy was a rescue, George came from a pet-shop, Prudence from that woman in work, Henry just turned up on our sofa one morning. We got them all inoculated and spayed, like proper house-cats. This lot you'd never get near!'

I am sitting up now, but, unsurprisingly, am unable to detect these alleged sounds. Hardly surprising really. My mother always warned me 'that damned rock n roll' would damage my hearing. 'Well, we just have to let nature take its course, won't we? Nothing we can do to help, and we'd probably be doing more harm than good, interfering. She must be feeding them, somewhere, and we've never seen new-born kittens before, or a nursing mother. Quite exciting, isn't it? Things are gonna get quite lively, around here, pretty soon!' And I nod towards Loli's wall. *Famous last words....*

A couple of days later I am sprawling on the patio after breakfast, pouring my third coffee, when Chrissie arrives breathlessly, having been downstairs, checking on her charges, most of whom have still not returned. 'Come and see this, you have to see this' she gushes. 'Be very quiet, and follow me.' Down through the summer kitchen and out through the back door, where she puts her finger to her lips. She nods towards the laundry area, the ancient stone sink with corrugated washboard, and the slightly more modern cousin, our washing-machine. 'There is Mrs-one-eye-Shaggy, under the table, the proud Mum,' she whispers, 'but look behind the machine. Quietly.'

I crane my neck forward, slowly, as Mrs-one-eye starts to hiss, menacingly, and there, crowded into the three-inch gap between the machine and the wall, is a little miracle, a litter of tiny kittens, smaller than the palm of my hand, a jumble of bodies, shivering, some of them, impossible to count, but a tabby, certainly, one, maybe two black-and-white, just like mum, and a tortoiseshell. Breathtaking. Mother nature, in all her glory. And it all happened without any human intervention whatsoever, just as it has since the dawn of cat. Not wishing to disturb the family, or antagonise *madre* further, I step away, and with a tear of joy in my eye, but grinning widely, offer her my warmest praise, which I am sure she appreciates, deep down.

My wife seems concerned about something, however. 'All very well you cooing at Mrs-one-eye, but what about me?'

'Of course, the proud granny' I chuckle, 'many congratulations! Does this make me a grandpa?'

'Oh you complete idiot' she snaps. 'I wonder about your sanity, sometimes. What I mean is that I will not be able to use the washing machine, will I, for the foreseeable? Imagine the spin cycle, hammering away, with those poor mites crammed down the back? So I am going to have to wash your underpants by hand, aren't I? Can you imagine anything worse?'

Over the next week or so we embark on a voyage of enchantment, of feline discovery, the highlight of which is witnessing Mrs-one-eye squeezing herself into the gap in order to perform her motherly feeding duties, seemingly walking across her bundles of joy, who are scrambling over themselves to gain a foothold, and access to nature's bounty. She then emerges from the other side of the machine and strolls casually to the rose garden, where she curls up to sleep off her exertions. Chrissie usually then winces. 'Are kittens born with milk teeth, do you know?'

One day however, tragedy strikes. The whole family has disappeared. Vanished, completely. The little dish of biscuits, untouched. A frantic search behind plant-pots, under patio chairs, in amongst the vines, reveals nothing. The door of El Woodshed remains firmly closed. And the steps down to the pool patio and the wider garden are quite high, far too difficult, surely, for a three-inch kitten? I naturally suspect the worst. 'When I was working at Tony and Jo's place, every morning there was poo on the roof, in exactly the same spot. Every day I would sweep it off, and every morning it was back again. Too small to be a dog, but bigger than a cat. At first I thought their neighbours were playing tricks and throwing it up there, as why else would there be poo on a tiled, sloping roof? But it was always in exactly the same location, which you wouldn't get if someone was flinging it. So I mentioned it to Tony. 'Ah that's the polecats' he murmured, 'nothing you can do about them. They try to burrow under the tiles. Forget about it.' Polecats. Who knew that? Mind you, Tony did think there was a land border between Spain and Mexico, remember? That Spanish TV programme he loved to watch, in the bar? I wasn't sure whether to believe him or not, but maybe that is what happened here. Do cats have natural predators? Has something attacked and eaten the kittens, scared away the rest of the Shaggies? We have no idea what goes on out here, during the night, and don't forget we are sleeping in the front bedroom, above the street, so we wouldn't hear any commotion going on down here.'

Chrissie shivers. 'Oh, be quiet. What does a polecat look like, anyway?'

'No idea' I shrug. 'Like a ferret, I imagine, or a mink, maybe? Long and thin, easily able to squeeze into that gap behind the machine.'

She has her hands over her eyes. 'Just shut up, will you? I expect mum has carried them off somewhere. Maybe the space behind the machine was getting too cramped.' She surveys the garden. 'They are here, somewhere, I know they are. We just have to wait for them to show themselves.'

This is turning into a right roller-coaster, quite honestly. First the original Shaggies, and now the offspring. It's almost as if some malevolent hand is at work. *No, I mustn't think that. Put it away. Don't go down that slippery slope.* Chrissie is correct, they will turn up, in the fullness of time, hopefully. Our lunch is tinged with sadness, however, and it is with heavy heart that I lay my sunbed flat, and attempt to doze, in the pleasant afternoon sunshine. For once, sleep will not overtake me. I lie, open-eyed, gazing vacantly at the yellowing leaves of the fig, at this tail-end of the year. The box is open, the lid is off, just a crack, but I don't know if it will ever go back as it was. Mister Shaggy in particular was such a beautiful cat, he had this vacant, *dim as ditchwater* expression on his face, as if he was never quite sure what was happening, yet so endearing, the way he always made sure his 'ladies' were fed, before strolling across for his share.

Suddenly, I become aware of faint rustling noises, and Chrissie stirring on her sunbed. 'Shhh, don't make a sound, but look behind you, under the tree,' she whispers, softly. 'Here they come!' I swivel my body around, so that I am lying on my front, and there, emerging through the fallen leaves, are five kittens, wide-eyed, on their very first voyage of discovery. In the lead is an all-black, with just a thin white stripe on his nose, next to him a tabby with white face and bib. Then a black-and-white with a broad face and much wider white stripe, a fluffier coat than the others, seemingly, then a calico, mostly white with ginger and black splodges, and bringing up the rear, timider than the rest, a tortie, her coat the rich shades of autumn. Each one is alert to the dangers, glancing furtively all around, testing, sniffing the air, sometimes advancing, sometimes darting back under cover, and I lie, transfixed, gazing in wonder at this special moment. Suddenly, the all-black leaps spectacularly onto his sister the calico, and the pair roll across the gravel, then regain their footings, covered in leaf fragments, as if nothing had happened. 'He's going to be trouble!' she smiles. 'I think his name is Sam. The tabby is Fred, the black-and-white is Ern, and the tortie is Floss.'

'Is there any particular reason why they are named after your uncles, and your granny?' I enquire, not unreasonably. 'I'm naming the calico, in that case. The obvious one is Patch, but I think she should be called after our first cat, Daisy, don't you? She looks like a Daisy, I reckon.' At that moment comes a loud miaowing, and Mrs-one-eye jumps down from the wall under the bay-tree, where she must have been observing her off-spring, and I swear she glances at us, proudly, *aren't my babies beautiful*, signaling perhaps her approval of the names. She then flops onto her side, and the youngsters need no second invitation. They are on her in a flash, scrabbling one over the other for the best places, their favoured spots, each suspicious of his twin, that he might have made a better choice. They needn't have worried, of course, there is plenty for all, although we do giggle at Sam, finishing first, then after a quick lick of his lips, returning for seconds. Their personalities developing, already. This is such a privilege, quite honestly. All baby animals are enchanting, of course, but there seems to be an additional cuteness about a kitten, and to witness them 'in the wild' like this is a moment to treasure. David Attenborough should be here, providing the commentary.

All too soon the show is over. Mother stands, shaking off the stragglers, then one-by-one gathers them in her mouth, like a lioness in the Serengeti, and deposits them into the undergrowth, safe from predatory eyes. We gaze warmly at each other. Wasn't that incredible?' my wife breathes.' And I'm glad she has hidden them away like that, I was worried about those eagles, or whatever they are, who soar around the mountain, searching for prey, they could easily swoop down here and snatch one up.' She shivers. 'We will have to be on our guard, for birds of prey. And polecats.'

Now I can sleep. I turn onto my side, and stretch, luxuriously. 'Never mind being on guard, you have work to do, don't you?'

She narrows her eyes. 'I beg your pardon?'

I plump up my pillow. 'Well, you've got your machine back, haven't you? I have some underpants, which need washing!'

And then there was Billy.

He came to us in unusual circumstances, to say the least. Walking home one morning, along the street outside Jade's house, before she bought it, we were suddenly aware of a loud, plaintive mewing, coming from above, somewhere. Glancing upwards, I suddenly burst out laughing, for there, clinging precariously to the electricity cables which adorn the fronts of these old houses, like an explosion in a spaghetti factory, was a tiny tabby kitten. Unable to dig a simple trench in the street, seemingly, the Spanish simply tack their wires, electricity, telephone, TV aerial and other assorted, unrelated, tattered lengths of flex to the cottage walls, to dangle forlornly and depressingly in the breeze. The fourteen different examples which cross the front of our premises, I'll have you know, are zip-tied neatly together, as we are British and therefore take pride in the appearance of our frontage, which incidentally took me less than sixty seconds, but the majority of the locals don't bother, which presents two major problems, as I see it. Firstly, it looks appalling, another example of function over form, and secondly, new-born cats have a hell of a job traversing this hideous mess. How in the name of all things holy did he get there, where does he think he is going, where is his mother, and most importantly, how will he get down before he loses his grip and tumbles painfully to the ground? I say he, because he reminds me of a mischievous little boy, and besides, a girl-kitten would surely have more sense. A determined little fellow, certainly, I imagined him as a *Dennis the Menace*-like character, full of mischief, with a pocket-full of worms, but quite honestly he needed to get down. Pronto.

Chrissie had her hand to her mouth. 'Oh no, poor little fellow, he's going to fall. Quick, grab him.' And suddenly, as if to emphasise her point, his beck legs slipped and he was left scrabbling frantically in mid-air, and I had visions of a claw piercing the outer casing of the wiring, and connecting himself to the National Grid. Not that Spanish electricity is powerful enough to give him anything but the merest jolt, but I was not keen to witness his fur standing on end, like a scene from a *Tom & Jerry* cartoon. The problem was, these cables are over head height, and I didn't want to make a sudden lunge, miss, alarm the creature and inflame the situation.

Luckily, earlier that morning I had been spring-cleaning the hall light-shade, and my pair of steps, my *escalera*, was standing just inside the front door. 'You stay there, underneath, like a wicket-keeper' I grinned, 'Catch him if he falls. I'll just pop back for the steps.' Moments later I returned, and as unobtrusively as possible, climbed up so that we were face to face, eye to eye. Blue eyes, just like me. 'Hello kitty' I smiled, reassuringly, wobbling slightly despite my wife supposedly holding on, 'come on, hold still, I'll just get you down, carefully....'

'Never mind having a chat, get hold of him, before the pair of you crash to the ground' she hissed. 'You're not fire and rescue, or the Samaritans. Get him, and get down.'

Not as simple as it sounded, I have to say. They grip on, don't they, cats, when you pick them up? Dig their claws in, to whatever they're standing on. And this ropey rubber looked like it had been there since electric was invented in this neck of the woods, which might have only been about 1979, but it's been baking in the sun every day since. And if the kitten connects himself to the mains, then I grab the kitten, will we both light up like Oxford Street on a Boxing Day morning? I extended my right hand, slowly, then with my forefinger gently stroked the top of his head, which he enjoyed, I know he did, then quick as a flash I grabbed his front with my left and lifted him clear of the wires, wobbled again, then took the three steps back to terra-firma. And he didn't bat an eyelid. No wriggling or struggling, I handed him gently to a cooing Chrissie, who cradled him in her palm and ruffled his back, causing him to roll over and expose his belly, for the same treatment. 'He loves that, don't you Billy?' she giggled.

'Billy?' I smiled, because he did look exactly like a Billy. 'Is this another one of your uncles? Whoa. Hold on a minute. Giving him a name implies we are keeping him, and we cannot keep him, can we? He needs his mother, wherever she is. He has barely opened his eyes, let alone weaned. He needs her milk, the nutrients it contains, the antibodies against disease, and all that. What milk do we have at home?'

My wife, and Billy, eyed me defiantly. 'Mercadonna, full-fat' she growled.

'There you go then. UHT. Long-life. Sterilised. Contains bugger-all in the way of nutrients. All right for pouring on your Corn Flakes, useless for kittens. He should have the protection of mum, and the security of his family. He's too young, and he won't survive. Besides, he's probably a pet, who's escaped. Some little kid is no doubt heartbroken, as we speak. 'Lost-kitten' notices are probably being drawn, right now.'

'So what do you suggest we do, Mister Veterinary expert, just leave him here?' she hissed. 'You can run down the chemist and get him a box of Cow & Gate formula, if you like. Me and Billy are going home. I will make up a little bed on the Sombrero, and he can stay there for now. I will put down a saucer of milk, with some bread in it, some water too, and if his mother comes calling, then fine. If we see any distraught kids, or lost-kitten notices, fine again. If not, he can stay with us. Can't you, little Billy boy?' And he writhes with pleasure as she tickles his fluffy white tummy.

'Bread and milk?' I echoed. 'What do you think he is, a hedgehog? What about Mrs-one-eye, and her teenagers? They might attack him. What about these alleged polecats? Or those damned great hawks, swooping in. No, of course we cannot leave him here, just don't get your hopes up, OK? Don't become too attached' I warned, tickling behind his ears. *I'm a fine one to talk....*

We managed to reach home without attracting attention from circling birds of prey, or the hawk-eyed neighbours, and Chrissie quickly cut down a cardboard box, which she stuffed with some material which looked suspiciously like one of my old rugby shirts, and our latest feline acquisition took up residence in the corner of the patio. Wolfed down a dish of bread and milk, then proceeded to terrorize the other inhabitants mercilessly. We watched, transfixed, as he crept up on the sleeping Ern and tapped him on the back, causing the almost fully-grown, cuddly, fluffy, black-and-white to leap spectacularly into the air, as if electrocuted. Then as Sam, crouching, pounced on the little one, knocking him flying with a sheathed paw, then actually ran away as Billy, seeking vengeance, chased after him. But undoubtedly the most heart-warming scene was finding the big tabby Fred curled up on a patio chair with the kitten under his arm, a two-headed version of fifty shades of grey stripes, with eight white socks. It seemed as if the newbie was settling in just fine.

And so it proved. Over the next few months he grew mightily, confounding my fears, and a testament to the life-enhancing properties of Mercadonna full-fat. Within half a year he was bigger than any of Mrs-one-eye's offspring, both in height and length, and would stalk regally around his territory, benign expression on his face, soon learning to ignore the hissing and booing emanating from next door, but remembering to urinate copiously amongst their shrubbery, during the hours of darkness. Afternoons would find him in pole position for a place on Chrissie's chest, as she lay on her sunbed, thereby earning first dibs at any fallen fragments of choc-ice, of which there were many. 'Well you try eating an ice-cream with a damn great cat on your boobs' she used to giggle. Thankfully not something I had to worry about. He even received plaudits from Sonia Walton, on her last visit, as we were reading on the mountain patio one evening, shaded from the harsh rays of the setting sun by the bay tree, on one of her rare excursions to their back door, with Luna Guapa Chica. 'What a beautiful cat, neighbour. I love his paint.' I looked at Billy. Billy looked at me. He then looked at Sonia. 'Paint?' I could imagine him thinking. 'I am not painted, you stupid woman. Unlike you. I am natural.

I was born this way. I am descended from Royalty, I'll have you know.' I merely smiled, warmly. She was no doubt referring to his markings, unless she was proposing to get her easel and palette out.

Then, one morning, he simply vanished. He did not return, that evening, not an unusual event with an adult cat, of course, although he rarely seemed to roam terribly far. By the end of day two we were starting to become concerned, and by the third it was clear something serious had happened. But what? Had he gone exploring, and become trapped somewhere? Certainly possible, with all the hidey-holes around here. Had he met a lady-friend, and eloped together? Well I'd spoken to the local vet about the best time for separating him from his *cojones*, although we'd demurred, for the time being, feeling that such action might alter his personality. Had someone else nearby simply claimed him? This happened to us many years ago when Henry, a large black-and-white, simply moved in, and took up residence on our sofa, although I did track down the owners and offered to return him, which they declined. Or is this malevolent hand is at work again? *No, I mustn't think that. Put it away. Don't go down that slippery slope.* He was inoculated, of course, but could have fallen prey to some unspecified ailment, or be lying injured and alone, the thought of which was too horrible to contemplate. But by the end of the week we had resigned ourselves to the fact that he was not returning, which left a huge hole in our lives. We still had Mrs-one-eye and her almost fully-grown family, who gave us great joy, watching them growing up, their personalities developing, the way Daisy took over the role of choc-ice cleaner-upper, how Sam developed a taste for the huge locusty insects which seemed determined to feast on Chrissie's plants, Floss forever getting stuck in the trees, and Ern sitting provocatively on Loli's wall, with a *who, me?* expression on his face. Fred the tabby meanwhile seemed bereft without his lookalike buddy. As were we, of course.

So now the story resumes, in real time, about which I am writing. Late September, 2019.

I am leaning patiently on the garden wall between us and the Waltons, three feet high maybe on our side, double that on theirs due to the geography of the location, awaiting with anticipation the delivery of our afternoon ice-creams. Sam, having deferred the consumption of his first locust of the day to enhance its flavour, is circling, intending no doubt to leap ahead of his sister in the scramble for chocolate fragments, and I am merely contemplating. Nothing in particular, mark you, my brain in its resting mode, as it is too sunny to think, I am merely stretching my spine in preparation for several more hours lying prone, with my Kindle. The Waltons' weeds have died back since the summer, I notice, vaguely, and several bare patches of soil are visible through the undergrowth, including one in particular which is an unusual shade of grey, about a foot long, maybe more, four inches across, probably. My eyes focus on the substance, whatever it is, and I lean further across, to get a closer view.... *Oh my God.*

Chrissie returns with our refreshments, hands me mine, and I sit on my bed to consume it, as always, being totally unable to prevent spillages in the prone position, even without a belly-full of felines to fend off, and better able to observe the fun and games opposite. Besides, I have news to impart. We finish our delicacies, and I gather up the sticks, and the cellophane, then turn serious. 'Look, there is no easy way to tell you this, but I have located Billy's remains. He is down there, below the Waltons' wall, where he must have been all along, I imagine, which is really annoying as we looked over there when he first went missing, didn't we? If we'd found him in time we could have taken him to the vet, of course.'

Her face is a picture of sadness. 'Oh, no, poor Billy. All this time he was just a few yards from us. If only the Gingerbread man had maintained the garden this year, we would have spotted him.'

'Anyway' I continue. 'I wanted to know if you would like me to climb over, gather him up and bury him properly in our garden, there possibly, under the fig tree? I thought maybe if you had a cardboard box, with a lid, I could place him in that, and he could find his final resting-place with us, where he belongs. I cannot bear to think of him lying there, uncovered, prey to scavengers.'

She closes her eyes, partly in sadness, partly in concentration. 'Yes, please, that would be a fitting spot for him. And I do have a box, from that delivery a few weeks ago. I was keeping it for something, no idea what particularly, but it must have been fate. So when do you want to do this? And you know what you are like, a little squeamish, will you actually be able to do it?'

I take a deep breath. 'Well, it's Billy, isn't it? I have to overcome those feelings. And I think we should do it now, while it is quiet. My folding ladder is propped against Loli's wall, there, if I can extend it, quietly, place it over the wall, I should be able to climb down without attracting an audience. If you can get the box now, I will use the Iron-Age implement to chop out a hole under the tree, then I climb over, you pass me the box, I will scoop him up, pass him back, retract the ladder, and we can get the whole thing done with dignity, and without any Spanish shouting.'

It's not really a pre-Roman relic, of course, simply something we discovered in a rickety shed in the garden, an L-shaped tool with a wooden handle about two feet long and a steel hoe-like end running at right-angles, perfect for digging trenches. By the time Chrissie returns from her craft room at the top of the house, I have a rectangular grave dug, a couple of feet deep, in the loamy soil, which hopefully should be sufficient. Together we lower the ladder, silently, into the Waltons' jungle, and I concentrate on the undertaking in hand, scaling this cursed wall, although hopefully with less bloodshed than my last visit. She was correct of course, I am extremely squeamish, and up close I am ashamed to discover I simply cannot contemplate touching the skin and bones which constitute the remains of our old friend. 'Can you hand me down that old shovel please?' I whisper. Another antiquity of bygone times, the shield-shaped head of this implement will be perfect for the task, and now I am easily able to slide it under the corpse, and deposit him gently into the box.

Replacing the lid, I pass him to the waiting Chrissie, climb back over and replace the ladder in its former position, without a Spanish inquisition. Perfect. She places him gently in the trench, then uses the hoe to replace the soil, patting down the mound, gently, then casts around under the tree for a suitable marker stone, which she places at the top end of the grave. 'Good night, Billy' she whispers, 'sleep tight.' Silently, I squeeze her hand, and we return to our individual beds. Suddenly, down the steps comes Fred the tabby, who spots the freshly-dug soil, sniffs out a suitable spot, loosens the earth with his paw and squats over the hole. 'Seems like we will have to try that old Spanish trick, and place bottles of water around the site' she smiles. 'What are you like, Fred?'

I lay back down, and settle in for the remainder of the afternoon. 'Cats, eh? No wonder Loli is always moaning. Just be thankful he only did a number-one!'

CHAPTER 11. THE HEAD VIRGIN

I don't know about you, but I loathe graffiti. The wanton, mindless desecration of public and private property is an abomination, I believe, and the perpetrators should be made to stand there and clean it off, and publicly humiliated. I am talking gang 'tags', 'Pete loves Jane', 'Up the Rovers' and other moronic utterances. Nothing is as indicative of a locality in decline, in my opinion. I have no objection to street art, if done correctly it can enhance a drab, ugly surface, and political and social commentators, like Banksy in Bristol for example, produce thought-provoking work with great humour.

But I tell you what. Whoever painted the cat's face on this road-sign did an absolutely fantastic job. Yes, a regular, official, triangular warning sign, edged in red as usual, with a tabby's head superimposed where the official hazard symbol would usually go, the bend or the tee-junction, or whatever. I say tabby, and certainly the markings are of that ilk, grey, tinged with yellow and orange, more like, dare I say it, a tiger, but with an enigmatic look on his face, as if he knows we are surprised and delighted at his apparition, and is pleased about it. And I say 'he' despite the fact that determining the sex of a feline is notoriously difficult, without checking underneath, although if the body of the creature is in proportion to the head, and these animals actually exist, roaming around these hills, I am leaving it as that. He is a Tom, believe me.

We are in the border region of Andalucia and Castilla, the range of mountains known as the *Sierra Morena,* in search of a dot on the *Michelin* map entitled *Santuario Virgen de la Cabeza,* accessed along country lanes lined with green ink, which I assume signifies an area of outstanding natural beauty, although perhaps also warns of the presence of tigers, who knows? Juan at the library swears there are wolves in this wilderness, so can wild canines and felines peacefully co-exist? The sierras run east to west for fifty miles, so perhaps they each have their own turf? Maybe we are looking at a gang tag after all? *Cats rule OK?* There is a mountain range to the north-east of here called Despenarperros, which must be something to do with dogs I assume. Maybe the different species carved up the territory, back in the mists of time?

Now with our limited Spanish, we assume we are headed to the sanctuary, or church, of the Virgin of the Head, the literal meaning of *Cabeza,* and believe me I am not trying to be flippant about a religious figure, but that is how it translates. And this is what we love about living here most of all, not only discovering different locations, and these hills are way bigger than Exmoor let me tell you, but alternative cultures too. A voyage of discovery.

With this in mind we spent a couple of hours this Saturday morning exploring the small town of Andujar, notable for a delightful selection of pedestrianised streets, in their original form, not some ugly concrete mall, containing a range of independent shops, most of which appeared to be open for business. Now don't laugh. In many towns around this area, the shops seemingly refuse to invest in anything more than a single sixty-watt bulb, as if there is a war on somewhere, and a blackout imposed, so that it is almost impossible to tell if it actually is a shop, given the lack of signage, or lighting, and whether they are open for business. Not so Andujar. Well worth a stroll round, and if you find that tiny cake shop up the main drag, well, welcome to a little piece of Heaven.

So this sign of the feline. I brake suddenly, having checked my mirrors for following traffic, then ignoring it, pull in and take a photo. Then jump back in the car, just in case. We have seen home-made signs down country lanes in the UK of course, warning of ducks, or free-range kids, but this one is most definitely official, or it certainly was at one time, before the artist got hold of it, and presumably painted it in situ, with great skill. Delightful. Even Michelangelo couldn't paint cats, did you know that? Chrissie is giggling. 'He has a look in his eye, that cat. I wouldn't like to meet him on a dark night!'

'Ahh you're safe enough with me!' I smile, pulling away. 'Just keep your window done up, and if you see any giant pussies, look the other way!' About a mile down the road, or up the road I should say as it is climbing all the while, we encounter another feline road sign, slightly different this one as the colouring of the face is more yellow. Perhaps it has faded in the sun, or maybe the artist bought the paint in the Chinese bazaar, a big no-no if you want my opinion. Fascinated, I pull in again. 'Who can be doing this, and for what purpose?' I ask my wife, who is really laughing now. 'Climate-change protesters, anarchists of some sort?'

She rolls her eyes. 'What if it actually means *look out for wild cats?*'

'WHAT? An official sign? So you think some Spaniard is locked away in a traffic office painting multicoloured moggies? Why? I thought road signs in the EU were supposed to be standardised, and isn't the one for *wild animals* supposed to be a leaping stag, with antlers? And think about that sign they do actually use here, where you cannot tell if it's supposed to be a horse, cow, donkey or bull. Painted by a three-year-old, seemingly. No, I reckon these are guerrilla tactics of some sort.'

She has her head in her hands now. 'Oh, what, a declaration of independence for the Sierra Morena, you mean, like Catalonia? Have there been elections here? Did you bring the passports? Just drive on, you buffoon.'

So onwards we go, laughing to ourselves, until we reach a *mirador*, an official viewpoint, with a pull-in, so we do. A stunning vista of steeply wooded valleys, lined with the ubiquitous Mediterranean pine and holm oaks of the deepest green, with a life-size statue of a man, standing next to a little boy, pointing towards what appears to be a Tibetan monastery on the crest of a hill, some five or more miles distant. The inscription on the plinth had faded badly, so the significance of the sculpture is indecipherable, and unfortunately the effect of this delightful tableau is diminished somewhat as the main figure has lost his hand, unless he is about to perform a conjuring trick. My money is on vandalism, however. There is also an information board depicting various landmarks on the horizon, although curiously it fails to mention the monastery, together with notes on the flora and fauna of the forest. My attention is drawn to the final couple of paragraphs, and I attempt a clumsy translation. 'Listen to this. At the commencement of autumn the mountains are inundated with deer, and towards the end of the year you might be lucky to hear the mating call of wild boar.'

My wife sniggers, clearly unimpressed at my efforts. 'Lynx.'

I narrow my eyes, suspiciously. 'What are you talking about? What lynx? It says *Iberico*, doesn't it? That is the Spanish ham. *Jamon Iberico.* I should know, I've eaten enough of it. *Serrano* is the cheaper one, *Iberico* the expensive stuff. The pigs, or boar, with the black feet. And I tell you what, I wouldn't want to be out here at Christmas when they're all having it off. Seen the size of them?'

She rolls her eyes. 'Lynx, you pillock! Iberian lynx. The throaty meow of the Iberian lynx. That's what it says. *Maullido* means meow. *Ronco* is throaty, or hoarse. Ever heard pigs meowing, have you?'

I am rolling with laughter. 'Perhaps they do when they get excited, who knows? Hoarse meowing? What a complete load of cra....'

'LYNX! You have missed out the word *lince*. Which means lynx. Which is what the road signs were all about, of course. *Beware lynx.* Especially at Christmas, when they're having throaty sex!'

I am not having it, however. 'Those road signs are not lynx. Those signs are a tabby, most definitely not a lynx. And I will tell you how I know. Do you remember the magazine *Look and Learn*, when we were kids? I can't remember if it was weekly, or monthly, but Dad used to get it for me, and I specifically recall an article on wild European animals. There was a picture of a Scottish wild cat, which scared the hell out of me, together with a lynx, which had hairy ears. Really hairy ears. And are there hairy ears on those signs? No.'

Still bickering good-naturedly, we continue along the winding lane, past huge prehistoric granite outcrops, reminiscent perhaps of Dartmoor, with pine trees. Suddenly, we reach a clearing, a pull-in, another lookout it seems, complete with a sculpture.... of a pig. *He shoots, he scores, one-nil to the boys!* I leap out of the car. 'Ooh looky here. What do I see? Could it be a boar? An Iberico boar? And hark. Do I hear a throaty meow? Is there a lynx statue anywhere? And what is that you are saying? You were correct, husband dear? Stand there, in front of the pig, while I take a photo. As evidence.'

Silently, which I take as a little victory, we reach the summit, with what appears to be a little village away to our left, the monastery standing proudly on a rocky pinnacle some fifty or more feet above us. 'STOP THE CAR!' She is grinning, widely. 'Back up a few yards, if you wouldn't mind. Bit more. Bit more. There. See that sign? With that picture of a hairy-eared beast? And what does it say? Would you like me to translate? *Restoration of the habitat of the Lince Iberico.* And what is a *Lince Iberico* do we know? Meow meow!'

Sheepishly, I park up, and we set out to explore what at first glance appears to be a wild-west town, wide main street and large hacienda-style houses lining the road, two-storey with brick arches and stucco walls, ornamental wrought iron balconies and Mexican-style bell towers, each bearing the name of an Andalucian town. On the right is a row of plain wooden kiosks, maybe half a dozen, like unpainted beach huts on a drizzly sea-front, out of season, and ahead a straggle of market stalls selling various religious articles, crosses, crucifixes, candles, and cheap Chinese toys. Resisting the urge to acquire a plastic drum or an assault rifle, we turn left off the street up a delightful if steep rocky causeway, through a plain stone arch, winding our way breathlessly past what at first glance appears to be the Stations of the Cross, each one mounted on a plinth, complete with a religious scene etched onto lead plaques. Unbelievably however, some unspeakable imbecile has sprayed graffiti on a number of the bases, and we stare, wordlessly, in dismay at this vile desecration. Unless the cafe-bar at the foot of the causeway sells paint, which seems highly unlikely, this so-called 'person' has specifically driven up here, all of twenty miles from the nearest shops, armed with a spray-can, to commit this vandalism. And why hasn't the local authority done anything about it? Industrial solvents are commercially available, for this precise purpose. I shake my head and glance at Chrissie, similarly dumbfounded, in silence and disbelief.

None of our fellow travellers appear bothered in the slightest, sadly, as a number of family groups are puffing their way up the slope, including a barefoot duo clearly on a pilgrimage to the summit. People who have already made it to the top are joyfully descending, laughing, joking, shouting at their friends, kids swinging on the crosses and jumping off the plinths, treating the whole scene as if it were a beer-garden, as opposed to a religious experience. Maybe I am overly sensitive, I don't know, but this behaviour seems disrespectful, somehow. We have often admired the natural exuberance of the Spanish, particularly compared to us reticent Brits, but there is a time and a place, surely? Would our kids have climbed a cross in the grounds of a monastery?

Away to our right, a tall, slim white structure, which from down in the valley we had thought might be a chimney of some sort, reveals itself as a statue of a female saint, forty feet tall, I am guessing, head bowed slightly, wearing a hooded cloak, her hands clasping what I can only describe as a ship's wheel, with a winged angel affixed near her feet. The cars parked around the base do nothing to enhance the scene, attended by three yellow-jacketed wardens waving their arms ineffectually at passing motorists, who themselves feel unable, or unwilling, to attain the summit on foot. Fair enough, I am panting, myself. And thankfully no-one has found it necessary to 'decorate' the structure.

A short flight of steps takes us to the *plaza* of the basilica itself, the Tibetan monastery as we thought, constructed from plain, unadorned, creamy-grey stone blocks, with a triple bell-tower to the front. Unlike many religious structures in Spain, there is little decoration to the facade, reflecting its function as a hermitage, or sanctuary, as opposed to a regular church, perhaps. A formidable, unappealing building, it reminds me in may ways of Dartmoor prison in the way it dominates the landscape, constructed, to my mind, without regard for the surrounding hillside. Inside, rows of pews are laid out either side of a central aisle, and at the far end a massive stone arch, twenty feet high maybe, adorned with decorated wrought iron, containing the figure of the Virgin. Annoyingly, I have left my specs in the car so am unable to make out much of the detail, and the glare from the spotlights within the arch, together with the press of people crowding around, taking selfies, means that unless we are prepared to fight our way to the front, we will have to be content with a distant vista. We find a seat on the left, content to simply absorb the ambiance of the location, which is more akin to that of a market than a place of tranquility. Groups of people are standing around, gossiping, checking their phones, laughing, joking, disrespecting, and getting in the way generally of the small group of barefoot pilgrims seeking, in vain, to actually view the statue and to maybe offer up a brief prayer.

Slumped in the pew in front of us is a young woman, in her thirties possibly, crying uncontrollably. Her female companion is doing her best to console her friend, who appears to have lost her hair, recently, the result of chemotherapy I imagine. I bow my head and blink away a tear at this achingly moving scene, although it does appear her hair is starting to regrow, a sign she has beaten the disease, and is shedding tears of joy, not sorrow. Please, let it be so.

'WAHEY!' Suddenly, a coarse, uneducated shout echoes around the basilica, and I turn my head in sheer utter disbelief to see a middle-aged man, scruffily dressed in a cheap nylon tracksuit, waving at a friend across the aisle, as if the pair of them are trying to locate each other in a packed bar at a football stadium. Chrissie nudges my arm. 'Come on' she whispers, 'I cannot stand any more of this.' We edge our way into the aisle, and as I pass tracksuit-man I shoot him a contemptuous glare, curling my lip as I might at the sight of a shoe-scraping. Water off a duck's back, of course. He is pushing his way along the pew, rudely, towards his buddy, totally without regard for those enjoying a brief moment of quiet contemplation, if such a thing exists in this place.

Back outside, blinking in the strong sunshine, people are filing into a smaller doorway, so we follow, down a corridor, the walls of which are adorned with yellowing, sepia-tinged framed photographs, all of which depict a similar image, literally thousands of people crowded together, down the stone causeway, along the road below, out of the village and into the trees, passing, above their heads, the figure of the Virgin on a small oblong plinth. So far in this country, every religious event we have witnessed has featured the orderly procession of the figure, borne regally by the hooded *costeleros*, followed maybe by the town band, the civic dignitaries, the officers of the *cofradia*, the brotherhood, and at a respectable distance, the congregation. This event however seems to be the exact opposite, a riot and a bun-fight all rolled into one. Like a ship tossed by a winter gale around Cape Horn, the plinth with the hopefully securely-attached saint is rolling alarmingly down the hillside, and several close-up shots show the crowd, arms aloft, heaving and straining as the throne passes overhead, like naked body-surfers at a chemically-enhanced all-night rave, albeit dressed as if it is 1928. Which it probably was, judging by the age of the pictures. Disorganised Spanish chaos, it seems as if a mass stampede was inevitable, with the plinth pitched unceremoniously into the undergrowth, although mercifully there appear to be no wild bulls charging around. We are both grinning widely at these images of utter lunacy. 'Would you like to come here for this, next year, whenever it is?' Chrissie giggles.

'If I was thirty years younger!' I giggle. 'I always thought trying to get a pint in the *Cabbage Patch* pub outside Twickenham for an England-Ireland game was bad enough, but this? Can you even begin to imagine the noise? If we could bag a room in one of those guest houses with a balcony than yes, otherwise, forget it! Our life insurance policy would be invalidated, for sure!'

Moving along the corridor, our mood having improved considerably at the sight of this insanity, we emerge into a delightful walled courtyard with stone-tiled floor and covered arched walkways, dotted with potted plants, but the undoubted star of the show is a large display of rocks piled one on the other, with a Virgin, maybe two feet high, perched under a granite dolmen at the summit, and nearby a frieze of richly glazed ceramic tiles depicting her appearance before a kneeling shepherd, tending a small flock of sheep.

Back outside, the vista from the plaza in front of the sanctuary is astounding, a full three-sixty degree panorama, on one side overlooking the holiday village and the forest beyond, the other stretching to a range of distant mountains, shimmering in the haze, all of forty miles away, I would guess. To one side is a statue, fully life size, of a kneeling shepherd, crook in one hand, a small flock of lambs gathered around him, a dedication on the side of the wedge-shaped plinth bearing the legend *A JUAN DE RIVAS PASTOR DE,* the name of the shepherd presumably, then on the front edge *COLOMERA,* as if the sculptor ran out of space unexpectedly. Juan de Rivas, shepherd from Colomera, wherever that is, a nearby village, presumably. We are smiling to ourselves at the absurdity of not having the inscription together on one line, when suddenly a diminutive old man in a pair of jeans that would surely fit me and trainers several sizes too large comes shuffling by, puffing on a Winston Churchill-sized cigar, and notices our interest in the lone word *Colomera.* 'Granada' he rasps, brushing flakes of chewed, spittle-encrusted tobacco from his lips.

'Granada province, or Granada city?' I smile, disbelievingly, although only I know that.

He draws luxuriously on his battered cheroot. 'Province of Granada', sweeping his hand in a northerly direction, entirely the wrong way, unless he is attempting to disperse the billowing smoke, before continuing his promenade.

'Awww, bless him' Chrissie beams. 'Shame his sense of direction is slightly awry!'

I adopt my best ironical face. 'Oh, really?'

She narrows her eyes. 'OK, Mister Geography O-Level, I might be a simple woman who sometimes gets the map the wrong way up, but come here a minute.' And she leads the way back across the *plaza,* past the gossiping throng, to the side with the expansive view. 'Listen up, you might learn something. Right to left, those flat-topped mountains on the horizon, which look like a pair of beanie hats. That is Cordoba province, you pass them on the way to Rute, and the chocolate Nativity. Moving to the left, those saddleback hills are near Alcaudete, which is

Jaen province. The mountain with the crest is *Jabalcuz*, above Jaen city, which has a monument on the top but you cannot see that today because of the distance, and on the far left those huge lumps are *Sierra Magina*, the magic mountains, to the east. Now, the Madrid to Granada motorway passes the magic mountains, before you even get to Granada province. So tell me, Mister *Look and Learn*, how far away are the magic mountains?' And she leans on the railings, and smirks.

'I stroke my chin, thoughtfully. 'Well, actually, it *was* in *Look and Learn*, about the curvature of the earth. Apparently, a six-foot person, standing on a beach at mean sea level, can see twenty miles. Or was it twelve miles, I forget now. Of course, we are much higher elevation here, a couple of thousand feet up, I imagine, it has to be twenty miles back to Andujar, so the magic mountains have to be, what, forty miles away? I'm only guessing, quite honestly. If we had a decent smart-phone between us we could look it up, but what is your point?'

'Well, let us imagine you are right, which you generally are of course' and she rolls her eyes, dramatically, 'and it is forty miles. Than you have to go another twenty, or thereabouts, before you even come to the boundary of Granada province. So sixty miles? Let us be kind and say fifty. So my point is what was that shepherd, Juan de Rivas, doing up here with his sheep? How far do those goatherds we see around our mountains travel each day? Five miles? Cannot be much more. And for what? Can you spot any special vegetation up here? We've barely seen a blade of grass all day. So he's going to travel for, say, ten solid days, to come up here with all these lynx running about? Doesn't make sense. I can understand the story of the Visitation, but why was he actually here in the first place?'

I smile at her topographical knowledge, which is spot-on, as far as I am concerned. 'Well, who knows? Maybe he rammed his meagre flock into the back of a long-wheelbase Landrover, and drove up here, in a couple of hours. I mean, how long ago was this apparition? I always thought they were supposed to have occurred hundreds of years ago, but for sure, this basilica is modern, isn't it? What, fifty, sixty years old? That tall white statue looks Art Deco to me. When was that, between the wars? Anyway, who cares? This place is giving me the gripe. Look at these people, what are they doing here? Not a single soul is admiring the view, and apart from those few pilgrims on their knees, and that poor lady in front of us, I've never seen such disrespect for a religious site in my life. Contrast this with the Virgen de Araceli, that hilltop chapel just off the Cordoba to Malaga motorway. That was stunning, wasn't it, the entire interior of the chapel adorned with exquisitely painted, molded cherubs and figures, people behaving with decorum. Come on, I've had enough, let's get out of here.'

We wend our way back down the causeway, and are intrigued to see two couples checking-in to one of the holiday cottages, bearing the name *Baena*, their cars backed up as close as possible, unloading their luggage.... *in black plastic bin-bags.* Now I don't want to appear sniffy, not everyone can afford Ryanair-approved cabin bags, least of all me, and I will admit to attending biker rallies with my possessions in black sacks, bungeed to the back of the bike, for waterproofing purposes you understand. But a weekend away with friends? I can imagine the smiling receptionist. 'We've put you in Baena House this year, flats one and two. Here are the keys. Do you need a hand with your luggage?'

'Naoooo.'

Chrissie is on the same wavelength. 'Damn it, I forgot the Tesco carriers!'

We head back to the car, past the stallholders who appear to be packing up the plastic Kalashnikovs ready for the siesta, and the beach huts which are still barred and shuttered, then back down the mountain, the way we came, keeping a wary eye out for wildlife, both feline and porcine. 'So what did you think?' I enquire.

She screws up her face. 'Well, Andujar was lovely, we will certainly go there again some time, and the views out here are stunning, from the summit, particularly. But the people, in general, were horrible. I cannot understand it, there was something wrong about the entire place, I don't know, I cannot put my finger on it, but the whole atmosphere was unpleasant. And like you say, such a contrast to Araceli. Very strange. And sadly we didn't get to see any lynx, not even a hoarse throaty meow!'

I have to be careful not to laugh too much, steering around all these hairpins. 'Well I feel like those people you see in the UK, 'Mum went to London and all I got was this lousy tee-shirt!' I feel like getting one printed. 'I went to Lynx Country and all I got was a photo of a lousy road sign!'

A couple of days later we are with the library group, showing off our photos which I have skilfully downloaded to my Kindle Fire, in particular the one of the cat's head inside the red triangle, which is causing much merriment. Came out well, that picture, the enigmatic smile on his face like a feline Mona Lisa, eyes focused into the distance, contemplating a spot of conjugal purring, perhaps. Incredibly, however, none of the Spaniards has the faintest idea what the sign is all about. Until Amador bounds into the room, like a playful puppy, late again, as usual, and spots the picture. 'Oh my GAAD! You visit LA MORENITA! I fockeen hate thees PLACE!'

Chrissie frowns, although maybe light is about to be shed. Possibly. 'Why?'

'I bored een Andujar. HODAR! Sorree, I BORN! All person Andujar hate thees PLACE. Thee Santuario. Thees Romeria, een April, when come out La Morenita, we no like. Ees people from MADREED! Thees Santuario, ees from War Civil. Santuario original destroyed by Republicans, een War Civil. After finish War, Franco he rebuild, he say you must to have new Santuario, as symbol of power of he. He build with architecture broo, broo, HODER! How you say, oogly?'

'Brutal?'

'YEES! Brutal. And statue of Vergen, look out over village, power of Dictator. I HATE THEES!'

Oh my God. I usually tend to avoid references to the Spanish Civil War, as quite simply I do not know enough about it, the background, the sensibilities. Also, since my fox-paw with Jesus and his rivers of blue, I am frightened of saying the wrong thing. Or singing any football songs. Additionally, I am wary of commenting on what we regard as adverse behaviour, such as occurred last Saturday. I'd be interested in their thoughts of course, but only if they raise it first. And a bit of a conflab has broken out around the table, to say the least, although whether this relates to the Virgin, the Civil War, Franco or Amador's language is impossible to say.

As always, however, Chrissie is one jump ahead of me. 'So if the locals dislike that place, is that why they were behaving, er, slightly disrespectfully?' *Well that is putting it mildly.*

'YEES!

I turn to Marie, for some serious comment, hopefully. 'So the name, Virgin of the Cabeza, the head, what does that actually mean?' And I tap my forehead, to emphasise the point.

She giggles. 'No. Yees! No. Yees! Cabeza is head, een Eengliss, but this sanctuary no mean head, you head.' And she taps her own. 'No mean thees. It mean, head of mountain, like thees.' And she places the fingers of both hands together, and forms a triangular shape. 'Head of heel.'

Finally. The answer. 'The summit' Chrissie chimes in. 'The top of the mountain, the peak, the Virgin of the summit?'

'YEES!'

Amador is off again. He takes my hand, and it takes all my

willpower not to flinch. 'Ow-goose. Een Ow-goose ees Romeria for people Andujar. Ees secret. We no tell people of Madreed. Secret Romeria for we. You must to come my house, house of my Mother, in Ow-goose. Pass the night weeth we. Eaty, much drinky. No ees Romeria fockeen Franco!' And he taps the side of his nose, and winks.

Suddenly another massive conflict breaks out across the table. Everyone is shouting, all at the same time, in that aggressive manner Spaniards often employ, which often sounds worse than it actually is, to our ears. Or maybe not. This is getting serious. They are behaving as if we are not here, superfluous to requirements. English lessons have been suspended. I glance at Chrissie across the table. 'Look what you have started!' she whispers, although why she is bothering to lower her voice I have no idea, given the ranting and raving going on.

'What do you mean?' I giggle. 'What does this have to do with me?'

'It's all your fault!' she laughs. 'All this, because of your photo of that stupid cat!'

I'm off. I'm out of here. None of this Franco stuff means anything to me. If they want to argue about it, fine, but there are better things I can be doing with my time, like lying in the garden. The sun is out. Stuff this. I nod towards the door and the pair of us stand, un-noticed, and stride across the room. Suddenly, the voice of Juan calls out amid the shouting. 'Where you go, plees?'

I half-turn my head, and grin. 'Meow!'

CHAPTER 12. THE SPANISH ACCIDENT

'There are no coincidences.'

Harry Bosch, detective third-grade, Los Angeles Police Department.

Well sorry Harry, but I think you're wrong. Much as I love the writing of Michael Connelly, the adventures of Harry and his step-brother Mickey Haller, the *Lincoln Lawyer*, I know he is wrong. And I'll tell you why. In my last book, *Sunsets and Olives 2*, in the chapter where we bought the car, I told you about how we had discovered a quiet street where we could park, where we wouldn't be blocking anyone's entrance, or causing a nuisance generally, a respectable area, an absence of inattentive, myopic Spaniards, with relative piece of mind. And I recommended that anyone considering buying an old cottage on a zigzag street with hairpin bends to seek out such a location, beforehand.

So here's the coincidence. On the day that book was published, the very day mark you, the actual day it went live on Amazon, we arrive at the car, on our way to Baena to discover this plastic Disneyland castle, to find the side bashed in. Me and my big mouth. *So was that a coincidence, Harry?*

Chrissie, being wider awake than me, always, is the first to spot the damage. 'Oh no, no, no. Look what some swine has done to our car.'

My heart sinks to my boots as I survey the carnage, and my first thought is; Write-off. Has to be. And my second thought;

Thank Heaven we got the car taxed and MOTd. And my third thought; Bang goes the no-claims, and up goes the premium next year.

My wife rides to the rescue, partially. She is crouched down, inspecting the crumpled dent. 'Actually, it's not too bad. Could be a lot worse. Look, the door is straight, not been twisted, it opens perfectly, the lock works, the window goes up and down, the door pillars on the body-shell are untouched, as is the sill. It is only the door panel itself.' She straightens up, and demonstrates the opening and closing, and the complete absence of horrible grinding noises. 'There you go, four hundred quid, tops.'

I fold my arms, puff out my cheeks and make a face like a body-shop guy. 'No way. Double that. I can remember people 'in the know' years ago, in the UK, saying *new door skin, eight hundred.* And how much did we pay for the car? I mean, I don't know the rule of thumb here but in Britain it is seventy percent or something, if the repairs exceed that it is hello scrapyard. Plus, it's a two-door car, so they are wider than a four-door, to allow the back seat passengers in and out. That is a big panel. Write-off, for sure.'

She is not having it however. 'That is the UK, this is Spain, where labour costs are much lower. Lucia my student had a similar bang in her car, and it was four hundred to fix. Have a bet with me if you.... hang on, what's this on the windscreen?' And she steps around and unhooks a slip of paper from under the wiper-blade. 'Look, a phone number!'

I am unimpressed. 'Yeah, a false one I bet you. People do that, don't they, in case anyone is watching. Janie and Nigel had it done to them, in England, didn't they? Some bastard stuck a bit of paper with a false number on it under their wiper, but luckily an off-duty copper witnessed the whole thing, and took their registration number, so they got the bloke in the end.'

Her turn to fold her arms. 'Why must you always be so damned negative? Write-off. False phone number. Just get the Spanish phone out, and call it up, for pity's sake.'

'No way!' I gulp. 'It's your car! No, seriously, you know how difficult it is speaking Spanish on the phone, if the person starts babbling away I will be totally stuffed. Alberto is coming round on Monday evening for a lesson, he will call them for us, I am sure, tell us what we have to do and all that. Leave it to him. Anyway, come on, no point hanging around here, it'll be too late to go anywhere in a minute.'

We head out of town, my mind racing with the possibilities and permutations of the problem. I am a Capricorn, so I am good at this, apparently... Chrissie breaks the silence, and my train of thought. 'So will you phone the insurance company, when we get home?'

I frown. 'Right, look, I am just turning this over in my mind, so these are just random thoughts, but I'd prefer to see if the number is genuine first, and if it is, whether the other driver admits it. Now if he left a number he must be admitting it, but until we know for sure, I don't want to contact the insurance. We don't know the procedure here, he might not have any insurance, who knows? But if we contact our lot, and they are anything like UK insurance companies, you know they will jack the premiums up next year, even though it wasn't our fault. You know what those bastards are like, it was in the paper about a year ago, remember, people were getting huge increases in premiums simply for phoning the company, even though there was no payout. The companies were justifying that by claiming that because the accident had happened, it was a statistic, regardless of who was at fault. The Government were supposed to be doing something about it, I think, but it's all gone quiet. Of course it could be different over here, but don't forget our insurance is a Spanish subsidiary of a UK company, so it could be the same here. So let's wait until Monday, OK? And do you mind if we forget Baena today, just go through the olives for a walk? My mind is a jumble so I'm not in the mood for castles, even plastic ones!

Ah yes, our Spanish insurance company. Now, among the first items new arrivals to these shores will discover are three English-language 'newspapers', available free in various locations along the coast. I use the term 'newspapers' advisedly, as it seemed to me they contained very little actual 'news', apart from that new one-way system in Torre del Mar, which is worth bearing in mind actually as you wouldn't want to drive up the wrong way, past the tobacconist, but a plethora of 'advertorials' detailing myriad catastrophic financial, medical and legal pitfalls the unsuspecting Briton is likely to encounter, and offering tailor-made solutions. At a price of course. Or you could follow our advice, and just wing it.

Nestling within these publications was one little gem, however. An advert for an insurance company, an offshoot of a British one, you know, with the red telephone, dating from an earlier century, updated by the addition of a computer mouse, both with big fat tyres. Motor and household, the announcement promised, with English-speaking staff. What more could you want? Now we tried, we really did, in the spirit of 'winging it', finding this stuff ourselves without recourse to British helplines, but like so many aspects of life here, the Spanish don't make things particularly easy, for non-natives. We simply couldn't find any independent insurance brokers, who could compare a range of companies, and prices, and recommend the best for our situation. The cheapest, obviously. Sure, there were offices of individual companies, including one featuring an image of a tall, blond, blue-eyed Scandinavian in hiking gear, standing next to an immaculately-coiffured lion, who looked as if he'd just stepped out of a salon. The lion I mean, not the Scandinavian. A blow-dry and a manicure, maybe a light massage. And the bloke had a satisfied grin on his face, too. The lion meanwhile possessed an enigmatic look, rather like the Mona Lisa, with claws, knowing perhaps, as all lions surely do, that under a thin layer of Gore-Tex was lunch.

Balking at the prospect of conducting business with such obvious fakery, we turned out attention to adverts on Spanish television, a dispiriting prospect if ever there was one, and in particular, a price-comparison website, rather like the meer-kat, only without any cinema tickets, cut-price meals, two-minute animated slots after Coronation Street, or actual meer-kats. So nothing like it really, merely a cartoon dog, at which some throaty Spaniard barked *woof woof*. Not that big on sell-ing stuff, the Spanish. I did in fact pay a visit to the site, but soon discovered there was a huge difference between winging it, and not having a clue, given that I didn't understand about half the questions, particularly whether my twenty-plus years motorcycle no-claims was more valuable than Chrissie's ten years in a car.

In the end we went with *Linea Directa* after all, and I have to say they were excellent, so far, although we haven't made any claims yet....

Come Monday evening Alberto expresses his delight at becom-ing our bespoke claims-handler, no doubt the prospect of extra free English conversation classes, in a real-world situation, influencing his decision. He phones the number left on our windscreen, and after a few anxious moments it is answered, and a rapid-fire conversation ensues. 'Thees man say he know you' he smiles, ringing off. 'Plees, we go to his house, now. He give you friendly declaration. He is Percy-Anna.'

Now don't laugh. Having both male and female names here is not uncommon. Marie at the library is actually Marie-Jose for instance, and who could forget that champion Spanish golfer of a few years back, Jose-Maria Olazabal? After the lesson we stroll down to the car, with me explaining the joys of third party, fire and theft, to find *'that bloke with the trousers who lives with his mother'*, as Chrissie and I know him, waiting for us. So this is Percy. Not a particularly Spanish-sounding name, I grant you, but he does look exactly like a Percy. Not in the rude connotation of the expression, I don't mean, you know, *point Percy at the porcelain*, but a *Percy*, a rotund old bloke in heavy twill trousers up to his armpits, fastened by a wide leather belt, like my Grandpa in about 1963, a style still hugely popular in this neck of the woods. A bachelor, almost certainly, is our Percy, and we often see him ferrying his frail old *madre* to the supermarket, hence his Anglicised nickname.

He covers his eyes with his hands, then gestures at our little white SEAT. 'I am sorry!'

Awww, poor old chap, he seems really embarrassed. And I've just realised there was a small ding on that particular door, so can afford to feel magnanimous, with the prospect opening up of his insurance company paying for it. 'Don't worry Percy' I smile. 'It was an accident.' I can see Alberto frowning, but decide to ignore him. This is what we are like, us Brits. He is learning a culture, as well as a language.

The front of Percy's 'house' consists of a huge up-and-over garage door, with a smaller access opening cut into it, and into this he disappears, returning seconds later with an A4-sized form, printed in yellow, but thankfully a different shade than the one used by the council, which still gives me the willies. 'Thees your friendly declaration' smiles Alberto, and hands it to me. 'You must to plees put you name, and you knee.'

The thing seems to be a questionnaire, an accident report I am assuming as there is a hand-drawn plan at the bottom, although a plan of what is impossible to say, certainly not the scene of the crime as we are standing next to it, and I don't recognise a single feature. There is a rectangle which may or may not represent a little white SEAT, but if so it's no wonder Percy hit us, as we are wider than the actual road. Do all Spaniards write like this? I turn the page to a different angle but I'm just not getting it, and quite honestly the whole thing is making my eyes ache. I hand it back to Alberto. 'Where do I put my name, and sorry but I don't know my knee.'

My student is astounded. 'Why you not know you knee? Where is you wally, weeth you knee inside?'

Wally? 'Wallet' I giggle. 'Wallet. T.T.T. At home. And my knee is in a pile of papers, upstairs in a drawer.'

He shakes his head. 'Oh my God you Eengliss people. Een Es-pain ees mandatory to carry you knee, at all times.'

Yeah well we don't, but the reasons why not are a subject for another lesson, as I imagine Percy will want to be toddling off to bed with a mug of Ovaltine, very soon. 'Can you show me where to put Cristina's name, because it's her car, and we can enter her knee later.' So we all file inside, into what appears to be a workshop of some sort, with dozens of crappy exterior window blinds hanging on the walls, like the Venetian style only far less sophisticated, hauled up and down by lengths of fraying baler-twine, as if it were still 1949. We had them outside our windows, hanging drunkenly on different sized hooks, painted barrack-room grey back when Mick Jagger was a boy, now a flaking, depressing relic of a bygone era. The blinds I mean not Mick Jagger. We had them down in about week-two of our existence here. I cannot help giggling dismissively. 'We had this *basura* on our windows!' I announce.

Percy hands me a pen, Alberto indicates the box, and I enter Chrissie's name, and for some reason which escapes me now, our daughter Charlotte's UK address, which we use for official correspondence. 'I'll have to put our Spanish phone number later, because I don't know it. And her knee number. Please explain to Percy, will you?'

My pupil frowns. 'Who?'

I wave the form in the direction of old twill-trousers. 'Percy. Percy-Anna.' *Duh!*

He bursts out laughing, leaning on the workbench for support, then fires off a rapid burst to his compatriot. 'He name not Percy-Anna! He name Juan-Antonio Dominguez Montella.

Percy-Anna he job.' And he sweeps his hand towards the collection of seventeenth-century window coverings on the wall. 'He make thees. Percy-Anna.'

I grin sheepishly. With any luck they didn't understand my rudimentary Spanish about having that rubbish on our windows…. Juan-Antonio Dominguez Montella indeed. So good they named him four times. 'So what actually is this friendly declaration, Alberto? What does it mean?'

He rubs his hand across his forehead. 'Ees mi culpa. It mean sorry I hit you car. It say to he company of seguros, how you say, insurance, he did thees thing. Ees copy for he, for you, and for insurance.' And he takes the form from me, licks his thumb, and attempts to pull apart the three carbonated pages. Which turn out not to be carbonated at all, as sheets two and three are completely blank. He turns to Percy, sorry Juan-Antonio, but typing 'Percy' is quicker, and waves his arms in the air in a 'what the hell' gesture, although where some old man is supposed to get two sheets of carbon paper is not clear. 'Not to worry, we take photo, you have mobile telephone weeth camera, Juan-Antonio? To send to your insurance?'

The poor old fellow seems confused by the words 'camera' and 'telephone', and no surprise really, as anyone commissioning this antique style of blind would be unlikely to possess such modern technology themselves. Percy would no doubt send a carrier pigeon, or a horseman, when the thing was ready for collection. 'OK ees no problem, I take photo.' And he whips out the obligatory Chinese smart-phone which all young Spaniards seem to carry. *Ees cheaper than iPhone.* He fires off a few shots, barks some instructions at Percy, we all shake hands, I again tell the old fellow not to worry, and my student and I file out into the street.

I fold the intelligible form and stuff it into my pocket. 'This is a very good system, Alberto. He has admitted liability. To admit. He did it. They tell us not to admit anything in the UK, the insurance companies work it all out. So what happens now with the repairs to our car?'

He smiles knowingly. 'Thees ees Espain. We wait. Always we must to wait!'

Three weeks pass, and we are still to be waiting, when out of the blue comes a phone call, around one in the afternoon, just as we are settling town to lunch under the fig tree. Alberto. 'Plees to come to Asha, now. In front of Vodaphone shop. I wait for you there. We speak weeth Begonia. You come now plees?' We know the Vodaphone shop of course, despite never having set foot inside, but no idea about Asha or Begonia, although doubtless something to do with our insurance claim, although why they cannot simply send an assessor to look at the damage I cannot imagine. The car is parked in exactly the same spot as described by Juan-Antonio, although perhaps they are confused by a twenty-foot-long SEAT, who knows. But a five-minute job, tops, surely? I could meet him there with the key, but he really doesn't need to get out of his car to see the thing is a write-off. A couple of snaps on his Chinese smart-phone, and job done. Cheque in the post. *Famous last words....*

We hurry down the cobbled streets to find Alberto waiting outside a shop entitled *AXA*. A small shop-cum-office. A small, crowded shop-cum-office, containing a woman in her late-thirties behind a desk, a younger lady on a smaller desk in the corner, and two little girls in school uniforms playing with a pile of zoo animals. With me, Chrissie and Alberto squeezed inside, the place is heaving. The older woman is Begonia, I know that because she has a small plaque on her desk bearing the legend 'Begonia', together with a picture frame containing the complaint-form legend, which is always good to know in case this turns ugly. Asha is no doubt AXA, an insurance company, in the local dialect, so that is two little mysteries solved. Progress is being made. Grinning, I pick up a plastic lion, and wave it at the girls. 'What is this in English?'

'Lion' sneers the elder, snatching it back without even looking up. *Fair enough, I won't bother with the crocodile, in that case.*

Begonia is jabbering away on the phone, about us I assume as I pick up the occasional 'Eengliss', when suddenly she places her hand across the receiver. 'What is the name of your insurance company?' she demands, sourly I feel, bearing in mind we haven't even been introduced yet.

I glance at the picture-frame. *You just never know, do you?* 'Well' I smile pleasantly, 'in English they are Direct Line, but...' She cuts me off mid-sentence, and resumes her conversation. *Blimey. No doubt who those kids belong to, is there? Chips off the old block.*

'She is speaking to the senior office about you' Alberto confirms, as if we hadn't come to that conclusion ourselves. 'Ees ver strange situation.'

'Head office?' I gently correct. 'We say head....'

Begonia replaces the receiver, loudly, and sighs, and frowns, as if dealing with insurance claims is all getting a bit much for her. And I am suddenly transported wistfully back to my insurance broker in Perranporth, where smiling is the default facial expression, and there is certainly no need of complaint forms. 'You must to write a letter, asking for company insurance of Juan-Antonio Dominguez Montella to pay for you car' she huffs, switching her gaze between Chrissie and me.

I can almost feel the agitation radiating from my wife. 'Well give me a sheet of paper and I will write it now' she growls.

'No' bellows the inappropriately-named broker. *'Thistle,' or 'Deadly Nightshade' might be more apt.* 'The office is closing. Return tomorrow, with letter, you passa-porty, knee, and eskytoora.' And she scrapes back her chair and reaches under her desk to switch off the electrical equipment. Interview terminated. Failed her charm-school exams, our Begonia.

Now our natural reaction would be to say something like *'well how long will it take to write a single paragraph, and you can tell us what you want us to put'* but Alberto has already turned to leave, and they do need to see Chrissie's ID, and house deeds, as proof of address. Money Laundering regulations, no doubt, *and we wouldn't want to fall foul of those now, would we?* But this aggressive irritation displayed by these officials here gets so wearing, and is totally unnecessary. Yes, abroad is different, we accept that, but these people wouldn't get past the first interview in the UK and it's not as if there is a labour shortage in this country. I am really struggling with this, as you might have gathered.

Nevertheless I can display some British politeness, so I smile at the ladies and girls as I stand up, but they are all occupied with gathering their various belongings, and studiously avoid any eye contact whatsoever. Deep breath... Out in the street we shake hands with Alberto and thank him for his efforts on our behalf. 'What were you saying about a strange situation?' I ask.

He grimaces in concentration. 'Well, here in Espain it is usual that you company insurance pay for the danyo, how you say, damage, and then ask company insurance of Juan-Antonio to pay they. But you live in Eengland and have Eengliss insurance, so Begonia speak to her senior, sorree head office and agree that Asha will to pay.'

'But we don't have English insurance' I splutter. 'She interrupted me mid-sentence. I was explaining they were called Direct Line in the UK, and she cut me off. And we don't live in England of course!'

'But you put you Eengliss address on friendly declaration' he correctly points out.

'Well, I'm not really sure why I did that' I confess. 'Force of habit, with official forms, I suppose. I am sorry if I left you in a difficult position.'

'Ah ees no problem. Ees crazy here in Espain, Juan-Antonio give you friendly declaration, he admitted liability, as you say, so is estupid you company to pay, then ask company of he to pay they. We make work, in thees countree!'

The following morning I am writing on the patio, so in pole position to hear my wife crash through the front door, stamp across the lounge and throw her bag on the chair. She appears agitated about something. 'Grrrr! Grrrr! That bloody useless Begonia! They are supposed to open at nine-thirty, it says so on the door. So I went down there at five-to-ten and were they open? Were they hell! Closed. Nothing on the door, you know, *'back in ten minutes'*, I had a few other things to do so I thought I would come back in half an hour, I mean she told me to return today with the letter, didn't she? So walking past the cafe on the corner I happened to look inside and who should I see? Begonia, and that other woman, having a leisurely *tostada* with coffee, not a care in the world, sod the customers, together, the pair of them. I mean, surely the whole point of having two of them is so they can keep the office open? *'You have your break now and I will go when you get back.'* And they are only open nine-thirty to one-thirty so I don't see why they need a break anyway, AND WHY DON'T THEY HAVE THEIR BLOODY BREAKFAST BEFORE THEY START WORK, LIKE THEY DO IN NORMAL COUNTRIES?'

I shake my head in sympathy. 'Pathetic service, isn't it? I think I would have gone inside the cafe, interrupted them, looked pointedly at my imaginary watch, said 'why isn't the office open, it's ten o-clock', something like that, see if you could have shamed the pair of them.'

'Water off a duck's back' she sneers. 'And listen to this, I went back to the office about twenty minutes later and there was a bloke parked outside, on the pavement, her husband or partner I assume, with those two girls in the car, and she is fishing around for their school satchels, and their packed lunches, then she got her husband's sandwiches, so it was half-ten before she actually got the place open and started doing some work. Anyway, when she finally decided to tap the keyboard with her tarty pink fingernails and open our file, she simply copied the documents, and my letter, and gave it all back. So now we have to wait. Again.'

Two more weeks pass and my wife is just about at the end of her tether. 'Every day more or less I've been past that damned office, and she's either closed, or the place is packed with people shouting. Anyway, today I'd had just about enough so I took a leaf out of your book and interrupted the pair of them in the cafe. They didn't like it I have to say, but I was beyond caring. So, we have to go there tomorrow, at one o-clock again, and she will give us instructions about the engineer.'

I bury my face in my hands. 'Engineer? What, Isambard Kingdom Brunel you mean? She cannot tell me anything about Brunel let me tell you, I studied him at....'

'Oh be quiet will you. Engineer. The assessor, I assume. Although why we have to keep trooping down there I really don't know. Punishment I suppose. The cross I have to bear, being married to you. I couldn't care less about the assessor, as long as he agrees to pay for the damage.'

'The write-off you mean!' I chuckle.

'No, I mean the damage. That bet is still live, and you will owe me big time, Sonny Jim, you mark my words!

The following day we all schlep down there again, Alberto insisting on coming even though we assured him we could probably handle it ourselves from here on. 'No, I enjoy thees, practical Eengliss lessons!' The usual crew are packed inside, but I make a beeline for the picture frame containing the complaint form instructions, avoiding a couple of polar bears and a giant tortoise. 'Hmmmm, look at this, darling! A complaint form!'

Deadly nightshade ignores the barb and taps away with her

tarty fingernails, which I have to say I thought were more orangey than pink, although what do I know? 'OK, you must to take the car to *Taller Alonzo Diez*, at nine hours next Monday. Here is the direction, and the Google map.' And she swivels her screen around.

And I almost fall off my chair with shock and rage. 'Granada? We have to take the car to Granada? Why doesn't the engineer come to us? None of this was our fault, and you expect me to take time off and drive all that way? Percy-Anna caused the damage but we are having to do all this, wasting time coming down here, then driving to GRANADA?'

Alberto does his best to look sympathetic, while Nightshade looks at her tarty fingernails. 'You say in Eengland the en-hen-arryo come to you?'

'Engineer. We say 'assessor' in English. To assess the damage. Yes he bloo.. sorry yes he does! Or they did, certainly. The last minor accident I had was ten years ago, so it might have changed, but yes, I told him where the car was, outside our house, he visited, then called me afterwards. I was in my office the whole time.'

'Will they give us a courtesy car?' Chrissie glowers, through her teeth.

Alberto fires a ten-second burst of excitable Spanish to Nightshade, then turns to us. 'No. On the first occasion, no. Ees only for en-hen...sorree, assessy to look at car, he make decide, speak to Asha, Asha call you, and you again take car to *Taller Alonzo Diez*. Then they give you car of cor-tessya.'

And then we have to go to Granada to collect it afterwards. So three visits. Deep joy. Still, it's gonna be a write-off....

The following Monday we are up well before the crack of dawn, yawning and stretching, bleary-eyed, on our way to this cursed *Taller Alonzo Diez* place, before nine hours. Or nine o-clock in real money. Now I have to tell you that Granada is my favourite city in Spain, of the ones we've seen so far, and the Alhambra Palace deservedly the number one heritage site in the whole country. Probably at its best in May when the roses are in bloom, but such is the skill of the gardeners that there are flowers out whatever the season. And at this time of year, the autumn, the pomegranates are ripe, a beautiful dark red, seeds bursting spectacularly from the succulent fruit. And the Spanish call pomegranates *granadas*, the emblem of the city, a joy to witness the trees groaning under the weight of the crop, and we usually return from our October visits with pockets bulging. Just don't let the palace groundsmen catch you.

No such luck today however as this body-shop is located on an industrial estate of unspeakable ugliness, of which I have drawn a pen and ink map, entrusted to the skills of the navigator, in whom I have complete confidence. It's usually me who gets us lost, incapable as I am of following simple directions. And I hate driving round industrial estates I have to tell you, lorries and vans wedged into every conceivable space, people pulling in and out, total confusion and chaos. So it is with great relief that we reach the premises unscathed, I swing onto the forecourt past a row of dented cars, and peel my sweaty fingers from the steering wheel. Made it! One side of the building is a glass-fronted office containing around half a dozen workstations, behind which are seated four members of staff, two male, two female, all of whom studiously avoid any eye contact whatsoever. So far so par for the course. There is however a large bowl of boiled sweets on a side table, so I grab two, unwrap mine noisily and begin chewing, like a camel. Always been a cruncher, cannot suck a sweet to save my life, but hopefully my dromedary impressions will attract a modicum of attention. Nope. Chrissie meanwhile coughs theatrically, attracting the attention of one of the ladies, who without looking up, mumbles 'dee-may?' Literally *'tell me'*. Translation? *'Good morning how may I help you?'*

She is, I have to say, an unusual-looking receptionist. Heavily tattooed forearms, long hair on one side of her head, the other half shaved, as if she dozed off in a cornfield during the harvest, and a bullet hole in her exposed ear-lobe. Were she to slap a plate of watery cabbage accompanied by unidentifiable gristle, together with a bread roll the consistency of a cannon-ball, onto the table, we could be in Wormwood Scrubs. As pre-arranged, I let Chrissie do the talking, as it is her car, and her documentation, so spotting a waiting area with an occasional table on one side of the room, I take a seat. On the table is a single car magazine of dubious vintage, dog-eared and stained like an Easy-jet in-flight publication, which I decide to avoid on health grounds, and I find myself wondering why there is never a copy of *Country Life* when you need one. Who was Miss September this year? I guess I will never get to find out.

Having eaten my sweet, there is nothing else to do other than gaze at the ceiling, which wastes all of six seconds, then turn my attention to half-shaven head. Who, despite an indifferent start, appears to be taking a shine to my wife, laughing together as she processes the documents, which is always a good sign, I always feel. Suddenly my wife's new friend jumps up, exposing a tartan mini-skirt, pale, skinny, white legs, like a schoolboy's, black patent Doctor Martens-lookalike boots, and pink ankle socks. She strides purposefully into the workshop, whips out a smart-phone and proceeds to take about twenty photos of the car, not simply the damaged door but from every conceivable angle, including under the front and rear bumpers. 'That was fairly painless' I giggle. 'She seemed a nice girl! With a bit of a twinkle in her eye, didn't you think?'

'Shut up!' she whispers, smiling. 'Look, she is driving the car out for us. Isn't that good of her? She obviously saw you pulling up, like a little old lady with a basket of eggs on the passenger seat!' And I turn to see the little white SEAT disappearing towards the end of the workshop, then turning sharp left down an alleyway, back towards the street.

The Punk-cum-Gothic receptionist returns, ignores me completely and addresses Chrissie. 'OK, you must to wait now for the en-hen-arryo. He coming.'

WHAT? So not fairly painless, then. And there was me thinking we were free to go. Our appointment was nine o-clock after all, and, silly me, I'd assumed we'd be meeting the assessor at that time, not enjoying a fashion show from the nineteen-eighties. 'When is the engineer coming?' Chrissie wonders. 'How long?'

Her friend shrugs, frowning. 'Don't know. One hour maybe, one hour and half.'

For pity's sake. 'So is there a cafe around here?' I enquire.

'No.'

Dejectedly, we file out into the street, into the blazing sunshine, glancing both ways at rows of featureless industrial warehouses. 'What a complete waste of time' my wife groans. 'Why did they get us here at nine if the cursed assessor wasn't coming until eleven? What the hell are we going to do for an hour and a half, in this dump? You wait till I see that Percy Anna bloke. How far is the Granada ceramics factory from here? I'm in need of some retail therapy!'

'Miles away' I lie, not really having a clue. 'There is a DIY warehouse round here somewhere, the one I went in with Dutch Dick a few years ago when he got wet and reckoned he smelled of cat piddle, but I'm reluctant to go too far in case we get lost and cannot find the garage again. But look, is that a Mercadonna supermarket sign I can see at the end of the road? Why don't we wander slowly round there? At least it will be air conditioned! Come on, let's have a look at the cheese, far more exciting than the ceramics factory!' *And far cheaper of course, given that we don't actually need any cheese...*

The next ninety minutes pass excruciatingly slowly before we find ourselves back at the workshop, and spot a fellow with a clipboard wandering about who might possibly be an insurance assessor. There is no sign of shaved-head, but her male colleague, an ordinary bloke with an ordinary haircut and no holes in his ears wearing a boring *Taller Alonzo Diez* tee-shirt, who was just sitting doing absolutely nothing, seemingly, all the time we were there earlier, now addresses us in almost perfect English. 'OK, the engineer has agreed your claim, so can you please return next Thursday with your car, for the repair. We will need it until the following Tuesday, probably, and we give you a car of courtesy.'

Driving home later, Chrissie has a large grin on her face, so having navigated our way out of the industrial estate, I reluctantly enquire the reason for her mirth, given that it is likely to involve me, in some way. 'Come on then. Out with it.'

'Out with what?'

'With whatever is amusing you. Let's have it.'

'Ooh, I don't know' she grins, 'I was simply basking in that certain glow a woman feels when she has won her bet against a know-it-all bloke.'

'What bet?' I query. 'And what know-it all bloke?'

'About the repairs to the door.' she replies, all serious-face. 'Which some know-it-all bloke swore would be a write off.'

I remove my left hand from the wheel and rub my nose. 'All right, all right, you got me there, but I seem to recall the actual bet was about the costs of the repair, which you predicted as four hundred. I said double that, but bearing in mind they haven't actually done anything yet, you ain't won Jack Diddly.'

She maintains her serious look, although I detect a slight turn in the corner of her mouth. 'Au contraire, Mister Know-It-All. I have won the first part of the bet, the prize for which is one of those *Radley* bags I've been looking at, online, in a fetching shade of navy blue. I don't have one that colour, as you are aware. The second part of the bet I will let you know, in the fullness of time, after I've won.'

Did I know she didn't have a navy blue bag? Search me. 'I don't know why you're finding this so damn funny. Six weeks already we've been waiting for this repair, and by the time we get the car back it will be eight weeks. And every time we have to come here we are losing money, with the petrol and my lost wages at Miguel's. Three trips, three lost mornings, you are looking at around a hundred and fifty quid. Which is what one of those over-priced bags costs. So you can whistle for it!' And I purse my lips and start humming the theme tune to *The Great Escape*. 'And besides, it might have escaped your notice that we will have a hire car that weekend you are flying to Bristol to see your Mum.'

'So what?'

'So I have to drive round Malaga airport to the drop-off zone, and you know what a nightmare that will be, in a strange car, especially if they give us a damn great big thing, trying to avoid those idiots kissing and flopping in the parking zone while having kittens about the thousand-quid excess, or whatever it is. Hundreds for sure. So while you are dreaming about ruddy handbags, I am applying my know-it-all man-brains to more serious issues.'

She will have the last word, for sure, although she is silent for a few moments. 'Right, I have just decided what the prize will be when I win the second part of my bet.'

'And what is that, pray?'

She narrows her eyes, and grins wickedly. 'Oh, you will find out, in the fullness of time.'

The following Thursday we present ourselves at *Taller Alonzo Diez* at the appointed hour, and are seen without delay by Ordinary Bloke in his ordinary tee-shirt, which does appear to be a different shade of ordinary black from last week, thankfully. He produces two sheets of paper which he painstakingly explains relate to a receipt for our car, and detailing what they are proposing to do to it, then he rises from his chair. 'OK, I will collect your car of courtesy. Wait here plees. It is a Fiat Cinquecento.'

Ooh, fantastic! A Fiat Five-hundred. We both love those little cars, and Fiat have done a wonderful job of re-creating the original nineteen-sixties original, we believe. I have always fancied driving one, so this is a huge result, and there is no way I will be mowing down any kissers and floppers outside the airport, that's for sure. Chrissie gives a little skip, and squeezes my arm. Suddenly Ordinary Bloke turns onto the forecourt in a white car, a large white car, bearing the Fiat badge certainly, but it sure as hell ain't a five-hundred. My heart sinks. He opens the door, and jumps out, beaming. 'Here is your car of courtesy, come and look, plees.'

I don't want to appear ungrateful, as this thing is free, we assume, but this is not what he promised. It actually looks like one of those 'crossover' models, I think they are called, something between a four-wheel-drive and an ordinary hatchback, but I have to be honest and say I actually don't know, having lost all interest in new cars around the time the kids were born, in the eighties. It seems so high off the ground for one thing, and so wide, and straight away I decide I hate it. *Do I really have to drive around Malaga airport tomorrow in this?* He senses my confusion, I guess, as he beckons me round to the tailgate. 'Cinquecento ekky' he smiles, proudly, indicating the badge, which comprises the legend *500x.*

'I thought the Cinquecento was a small car' I smile, trying my best to hide the crushing disappointment, and yes a certain amount of anxiety, as I'm not sure I will be able to get this beast into the road, let alone off the industrial estate.

He laughs. 'Yes, but this the model ekky. Ees much better.' *Bigger, yes. Better? Nah.* Chrissie meanwhile has visibly deflated. 'Here is the radio' he grins, switching on the ignition, and, pressing a button, the top of my head almost blows off as a blast of crappy Spanish pop invades my eardrums. Whoever had this thing before us must have been brain dead, as well as stone deaf and completely lacking in taste. 'And here is the freno de mano, how do you say, handbrake?' And he pushes a button at the bottom of the dashboard. A *button*? Since when has that been a thing? And what was wrong with how you did it for the past hundred years, by pulling a lever? 'OK' he continues, see you the next week, Tuesday I think, but we will call you.' I am seriously considering telling him to forget it, Chrissie can get the bus to the airport, but he has vanished, leaving us alone with this tank-like vehicle. I mean, our last car before the little white SEAT was a Volvo 740, but to me it didn't look as big as this ekky, not as high for sure, and I regularly hit walls in that, to the amusement of the boss one time when I almost took out the side of the office.

Still, gift horses and all that. 'You'd better see me out, but make sure you stand well back!' I tell my bemused wife, so climbing aboard I start the engine, then promptly stall, grappling around for the non-existent handbrake. And stall again. And again. Some message in Spanish appears on the dashboard, *Stop Stalling You Bloody Idiot* possibly but it disappears before I can translate. Quite honestly it would have been quicker to contract a mobile crane to lift me out, but eventually I manoeuvre the thing onto the street, facing in the general direction we wish to travel, I press the button, stall yet again, and Chrissie takes the opportunity of climbing in. And I do mean climb, as ideally she could do with a ladder, or a hoist, to get her aboard. Gingerly, I set off down the street, although slower than back in the days when a bloke with a red flag walked in front of a car, reach a T-junction, turn right and pull into the kerb. And stall.

'Nice driving' my wife smirks, in her best Bruce Forsyth voice. 'Didn't you do well!'

'Well you can always take over, if you want' I hiss. 'But this is ridiculous. I need to familiarise myself with the controls, before we go any further. Where are the wipers, for instance?'

She gazes theatrically into the clear blue sky. 'What, expecting rain, are you?'

But I am too busy fiddling to be insulted, and soon the wipers are going double speed, plus the rear, the hazard lights are clicking and the headlights functioning as advertised, judging by the fellow who gives me the finger as he passes, pointing to his eyes. *That must be full-beam then.* 'So are we satisfied with everything?, she moans, sarcastically. 'Is there any chance of getting on the move, before my flight leaves in the morning? Or do you need to check where the spare tyre is?'

'I'm going to have a walk round outside, if you don't mind, before we get going' I harrumph.

'I thought you said the ceramics factory was too far....' But I've slammed the door already.

My inspection complete, I climb back inside, and fold my arms. 'Right, please listen. This is serious. We have no papers for this car, no proof of where it came from, if we get stopped. I cannot even remember the name of the garage, can you, or the address? Taller-something. *'Oh sorry officer it is a courtesy car from somewhere in Granada called Taller.'* We have no insurance details, we don't even know if I'm allowed to drive. Everything is in your name, presumably, but he didn't ask to see your license, did he? Is there any breakdown cover? Have a look in the glove compartment a minute, will you?' She does, and comes out with a user manual for the radio only. 'See what I mean? Nothing. Usually, when you hire a car, the person walks round it noting all the dings and dents, then offers collision damage waver at twenty quid a day or whatever, otherwise you have to pay the first eight hundred of any damage, and they hold that amount on your credit card. Remember when we hired that car in Bodmin and they did that, took two weeks to get it off the card I recall? Now legally he doesn't have a leg to stand on as he didn't take us round the car, but you know that car-hire rip-offs are the biggest sources of complaints in the travel industry, in the Sunday papers every week almost, especially here in Spain. Now this is slightly different as it's a courtesy car but they're not gonna be very pleased if it comes back with a bloody great dent in the side, are they? Insurance and car-rental companies. The two biggest villains in the....'

'Well you'll just have to drive carefully, won't you?' she growls. 'Either that or go back with the car and ask about all this.'

'No way am I driving around that maze of streets again!' I chuckle, fastening my seat-belt, starting the engine, engaging first gear, checking my mirror, glancing over my left shoulder, pressing the handbrake, mirror again, and pulling gently away, like a text-book move from my driving test. 'Besides, I don't know the Spanish for 'bloody great dent' do I?'

Next morning we are up and away at four, as Chrissie needs to check-in by six or thereabouts, for her flight at eight. The Fiat Ekky survived the night parked outside Percy-Anna's, although sadly the man himself was tucked up soundly between the sheets, as I felt like hollering 'look what we've been lumbered with' at him. Still, there's always next week. After several close shaves, we make it out of town and I start to settle into the drive. Or not. 'You're getting awfully close to the edge of the road, on my side' my wife keeps grumbling.

'Well I'm trying to work out the fuel gauge' I keep telling her. 'One of these days some bright spark will invent a little pointer which goes up and down, with 'E' at the bottom and 'F' at the top, and a little red zone. Wouldn't that be an improvement on this digital LCD or whatever they call it. All the way back from Granada yesterday, and half way to Malaga this morning, and we don't seem to have used a drop.'

'And why are you doing sixty miles-per-hour?' she continues.

'Because that is the speed limit on these roads?' I chuckle. 'Hundred kilometres an hour. Sixty, in real money. Hundred and twenty on the motorway, seventy or thereabouts. And you know what a law-abiding....'

'But you're now doing sixty-two, look!'

'Oh what a naughty boy....'

'NO, LOOK AT THE DISPLAY' she cries, irritably. *Well it is five in the morning, after all.* 'Look, it says 60 MPH. *MPH.* See what I mean? This is a Spanish car, last time I checked. Surely it should read KPH? Kilometres per hour? So why is it reading miles per hour?'

I shift my gaze from the immovable fuel gauge to the speedo. 'Blimey, so it does. D'you know, I didn't spot that. Perhaps the car knows we're British, and therefore prefer miles to that foreign rubbish. Good job I was an accountant and can do the conversion in my head then, isn't it? Maybe there is a sensor in the cabin which detects I am not waving my arms about, turning my head sideways to gossip loudly, and playing with my phone at the same time, so I'm clearly not a Spaniard. Whatever will they think of next?'

'But you're still getting awfully close to the edge of the road, on my side!'

So here's a plan. See what you think of this. How I see my day panning out. One, drop my wife at departures. Two, drive a couple of miles, not kilometres, to Torremolinos, and that hotel where we spent our first night in Andalucia, you may remember, in my first book, the one with the lumpy Germans, seven-foot Scandinavians, the orange-haired woman, the knitters and Los Paraguayos. Three, partake of their all-you-can-eat buffet breakfast. Four, cross the road and crash on the beach, and five, head back to the caravan in the evening. And the following day, repeat. Sound good?

Well, just a couple of flies in the ointment. Firstly, Malaga airport has recently got wise and monetized the airport drop-off, so you now need to take a ticket, pass through a barrier, and negotiate not only the kissers and floppers, but the labyrinth that is the short-stay car park, designed back when cars were a lot smaller than they are today. As evidenced by this *Ekky*. To my mind, the parking bays are simply too small, and I used to have nightmares about driving the little white SEAT through there, let alone this thing. The first fifteen minutes are free mind you, so providing I give Chrissie just the one peck on the cheek, and a quick hug, I can usually get away without paying, unless there is more than the usual quota of kissers and floppers blocking the exit.

And secondly, the breakfast is not what you might call the real McCoy. The bacon is that thin, streaky stuff, the mushrooms are out of a tin, as are the cocktail 'sausages', there are no hash browns, fried bread or black pudding, and the eggs are scrambled, not fried. So nothing like the Full Monty. They do however have great cold meat, smoked salmon and cheese platters, plus sticky pastries, several different styles of bread, real orange juice and bottomless coffee, and there might even be fruit, come to think of it, although don't quote me on that as I've never had any on my previous visits, being a dyed-in-the-wool fry-up man. Anyway, it is perfectly possible to fill up for the day, before the arduous task of sunbathing commences. *Need plenty of protein for that, right?*

Approaching the airport along the new elevated section of highway, I manage to place the passenger-side wheels on the rumble-strip at the side of the road, which is a skill in itself, causing Chrissie's teeth to rattle. 'Y-you're s-still g-getting a-awfully c-c-close to the e-edge of the -r-r-road!' I then avoid, narrowly, demolishing the ticket machine, before a sharp left turn into the multi-storey, an even sharper right causing half a dozen Japanese tourists to scatter like mice who've just spotted a Tom-cat, then execute a text-book parking manoeuvre in the middle aisle. Made it! By my reckoning, I still have twelve of my allotted fifteen minutes, time for a peck on both cheeks and maybe a big hug, if she's lucky, so hauling her carry-on from the back seat, as I still haven't worked out how the hatch-back opens, we step smartly around the shell-shocked Orientals and into the terminal building. Now, had we possessed a smart-phone between us we could have checked the online departures board on the road coming in, although whether she could have pressed all those little buttons whilst having her teeth shaken is open to doubt. Say what you like about new-fangled technology but it's not infallible, is it? But we haven't, so we can't. Instead we have to do it the old-fashioned way by walking up to an electric screen and using our neck muscles to gaze up at the legend, thereby burning up enough calories to ensure I need feel no guilt about that third scoop of those little sausages. It's like I've always said. Getting a smart-phone would make me fat. Plus, with a whole eight minutes left, we can do our kissing and flopping without the threat of being mown down by nervous drivers in humungous cars, which is what terminal buildings were designed for, surely?

I watch her disappear down the concourse towards security, then with over five free minutes still available, and wishing to savour them fully, I saunter leisurely back to the car park......... and my heart sinks to my boots. OH NO NO, please NO, some BASTARD has hit the side of car, and left an ugly black stripe, from the rear bumper, managing to catch the front bumper also, BREAKING A SIDE-LIGHT LENS INTO THE BARGAIN. This bloody car is jinxed. This bloody car which I'm not even certain is insured. Furiously, with a sick feeling in the pit of my stomach, I glance around for CCTV, witnesses, or a note on the windscreen, of which there are none. Christ, I was only gone less than five minutes, the myopic swine must have done the dirty deed as we were walking into the terminal, and is more than likely still on the premises somewhere.

With mounting anger and frustration, not to mention the real fear that this episode will cost me big-time in repairs, I leap into the car, slam the door loudly in a fit of rage, and head for the exit, around the chicanes and twists and turns, clearing the barrier with seconds to go. All thoughts of breakfasts and beaches and sunbathing gone from my mind I head straight to the caravan, grab my Kindle from the car, fling myself onto the bed, download today's paper and immerse myself in yesterday's news, in a vain attempt to clear my mind of the million thoughts all racing around. The problem is that every time I glance out the window, the cursed vehicle is staring back at me, taunting me, black stripe and broken side-light all I can see, so I grab the car keys intending to turn the thing around, so that the damage is on the opposite side, hopefully allowing me to forget.... Suddenly realising I haven't actually examined the paintwork, I crouch down, I run my fingers along the black marks.... Hmm, I wonder... there is a tube of car polish in the cupboard under the caravan sink, surely? Yes, it is still there, so grabbing a cloth I apply a generous blob, and start rubbing. And by some miracle, the ugly black mark starts to disappear. There is a small crack in the paintwork on the rear bumper, but it hardly notices, and the faintest of creases on the front wing, which disappears depending which angle you look at it, but the main problem is the broken lens, about which I can do nothing as it appears to be fitted from the inside, and integral with the front bumper in some way, so that even if I could find the nearest Fiat dealer and buy another lens, I doubt very much if I have the tools, or skills, to repair. The indicator lenses on my 1964 Ford Anglia just screwed on, why must everything be so damned complicated, these days? Suddenly I remember there is a multi-tool in the van, with the thing for removing the stones from your horse's hooves, but also a pair of pliers, so carefully I pick the remaining shards of plastic from around the light. Looks a lot better actually, and if you didn't know there was supposed to be a lens cover, you'd never guess. *Mister Normal in the body-shop will know though, won't he?*

Sick with worry, I head to the campsite pool, where I chat to a lovely Dutch lady and her husband, who are here for a couple of weeks, while bobbing about in the cooling water, about Brexit, the forthcoming election, Brexit, the weather in Spain, Brexit, the best time to visit the Alhambra Palace and the finer points of Brexit. Still, it takes my thoughts away from insurance excesses. Luckily she is fluent in English, bearing in mind the only Dutch words I know are *Ajax, Feyenoord, Johan Cruyff* and the lyrics to *A Mouse Lived in a Windmill* by Ronnie Hilton, and the only Dutch word in that song is *Amsterdam*. Trouble is, every time I return to the van I am confronted by that hateful car.... But decision made, I am staying put, here, I can get whatever food I need from the site shop, not using the thing until Sunday evening when I have to collect Chrissie, then home, where it can stay outside Percy Anna's until we can collect our little white SEAT. After that, if I never see another Ekky until Kingdom Come, that will be too soon for me.

Now, let me tell you a secret. You must promise to keep this to yourself, otherwise there will be consequences, because we don't want everyone party to this, but I know how to obtain free long-term parking at Malaga airport. What about that, then? Coming from the direction of the city, the motorway divides, and the new signs direct you to the left, and across the elevated section, complete with rumble strip, as outlined above. If you fork right however, as we did in the old days, you approach the airport at ground level, past the San Miguel brewery, opposite which are the offices of various car-rental businesses, together with airport parking, from three euros a day, allegedly, although best of luck getting it for that price, unless you book about eight years in advance. But here's the secret. The street in front of those enterprises, and those surrounding, offer free parking, and if you are unable to squeeze in there, a dirt road leads under a motorway bridge where you are almost guaranteed to find a spot. OK so I wouldn't leave my Rolls Royce there, if I had one, but we have taken advantage of this largesse on many occasions, and come to no harm, plus there is always a certain frisson in parking free outside a place advertising it from three euros a day. And don't go thinking that secure parking would be safer, as, if you drive around this location at nine in the evening when the parking jockeys are packing in for the day, you would have a fit. Just like the dodgems on the end of the pier, with added road-rage, it is. I sure as hell wouldn't leave my Rolls Royce with those maniacs, either.

Of course, there is a down-side to getting something for nothing, which in this case is having to cross a dual-carriageway, although it's hardly the M6, then walk five-hundred yards or so into the terminal. Done it many times, so what we do now is that I drop Chrissie, and the luggage, outside departures, take the car back to the free zone, then grinning smugly at the parking garages, I walk briskly into the terminal.

So there you go, you pays your money and takes your choice, as they say. Or you pays no money, if you takes my advice.

So this particular Sunday evening, nerves shot to pieces, my stomach in knots, and my mind a jumble of negativity, there is no way on earth I am taking the Ekky into the multi-storey, so I locate a free slot, easy at that time of the day, and stroll leisurely into arrivals. No ticket barriers, time constraints or kissers and floppers to negotiate means we have time for our own kissing and flopping, when Chrissie eventually appears, although I do face a dilemma; should I mention the damage to the side-light? Now, I am a nineteen-fifties model, and was brought up in a household where the menfolk took care of this stuff. Times are different now of course but Chrissie operates within a much wider bandwidth than me, she worries about stuff I don't even know exists, and I don't want to add to her concerns. So rightly or wrongly, I have decided to say nothing at this stage, she will have to know eventually of course, but I thought I would casually mention it on the way to the body-shop, on Tuesday. Or maybe not even then. She is all smiles as she passes through the barrier, she gets her big hug, the lucky girl, and we head outside. 'I hope you don't mind but I've parked in the free zone. It's a lovely evening and I thought you might like to stretch your legs, after being cooped up on Paddyair!', I tell her, truthfully.

As we approach the car, I realise suddenly I have boobed and left the damaged light facing outwards, I can see her looking vaguely at it but she says nothing, so with any luck she hasn't noticed. Along the motorway towards Malaga, then inland on the Granada-Cordoba road, she describes her weekend, how her Mum is feeling much better, her brother's escapades working for British Rail or whatever they're called these days, Railcrap, that's it, and of course her day out with our daughter Charlie. Then she folds her arms. 'So are you going to tell be about the car?'

'What car?' I ask, innocently.

'Er, this car, obviously.'

'What about it?' I frown.

'Er, the broken side-light lens, and the extra-shiny paintwork, all down the side. You've had an accident, haven't you? You've had the polish out. Did you think I was some little woman who wouldn't notice?'

My resolution breaks down completely, and I confess, the whole story. 'I've been so worried about this damned insurance excess' I conclude. I haven't been outside the campsite all weekend, haven't used the car, in fact I was too scared to use it. I didn't get my cooked breakfast as my stomach was tied up in knots, my appetite disappeared, and I've just been killing time for three days. I've been waking up in the night, my mind churning, and I cannot wait to get rid of this cursed car on Tuesday.'

She smiles, sympathetically. 'I wouldn't worry about it, but do me a favour would you, you're still getting awfully close to the edge of the road, on my side!' And she has her little giggle. No doubt spending a few days away from me did her good. 'But look' she continues, 'this is a courtesy car, not a rental, the bonnet is peppered with tiny stone chips, and there are little scratches here and there too. They obviously aren't worried about it. No paperwork, nothing to sign. Blimey, they gave me two sheets of A4 just to hand our car over. You know the Spanish, obsessed with paperwork, aren't they? They gave us none, because there was none. Seriously' and she squeezes my knee, ' stop worrying!'

I am astonished. 'Stone chips, scratches? I didn't see those. The bodywork looks perfect to me!'

'Well you should have gone to Spec-Savers then, shouldn't you! But you've been obsessed about how much you hate this car, not hitting anything, you probably didn't notice. But have a look when we get home.'

Unsurprisingly, we hear nothing on the Monday, but on Tuesday, just as we are resigning ourselves to yet more delays, we receive a call in the evening summoning us to Taller-something the following morning, at the slightly more civilised hour of eleven, for the big hand-over. Praise be! We don't as a rule use the car during the week, the Ekky remains parked outside Percy-Anna's, as far as we know, and quite frankly I am past caring, but this damage has been hanging over me like the Sword of Damocles, despite what Chrissie says. I just know something will go wrong. I can feel my wallet twitching. So at the allotted hour we pull up outside the body-shop, for the third and final time, fingers crossed, I extract the keys, step onto the pavement, and feel the tension draining away. Never in my life have I been so glad to see the back of something. Well, I was quite pleased to get rid of that Triumph Toledo with the dodgy gearbox in about 1978, but you know what I mean. And I will be quite happy to never have to negotiate this vile industrial estate for another hundred years, I can tell you. Turning our backs on the Ekky for the final time, we stroll into the office, to be greeted by a beaming Mister Ordinary, brandishing a clipboard. 'Just one moment plees, I must to check...' and he disappears into the street. 'I cannot look. He is going to spot the lens.' I whisper. 'And look, he is coming back... he's wagging his finger...' *Heart. Boots. All over again.*

He strides purposefully across the forecourt. 'Foo-ell.' *I know I am mate, I'm a complete fool, getting into this state about a bit of plastic.* 'Foo-ell' he continues, 'you must to put foo-ell, in thee car!'

PETROL! FUEL! Jeez, I completely forgot. I never did manage to figure out the gauge, but conducted a thorough search the inside of the car, last weekend, for a lever, or switch, to open the flap, but couldn't find anything remotely like it, and in the absence of a handbook I gave up, and haven't given it a moment's thought since. I want to give him a hug, but decide to tell the truth, instead. 'SORRY! But I cannot open the little door! It does not open!' And I waggle my hand from side to side like a haddock on the deck of a fishing trawler, to hopefully imitate a fuel flap opening, as I don't know the Spanish for 'fuel flap.' He frowns, then leads the way back to the street to the car I'd hoped never again to clap eyes upon. The fuel door has a little indent, which of course I'd tried pressing, a number of times, in vain, over the weekend. He presses it. *If it opens, I swear I will curl up and die.* Nothing happens. He presses again, slightly harder. Still nothing. *I am grinning like that meat-fly.* He pauses, then opens the driver's door, pauses again, closes the door, scratches his head, then gives the flap a hefty jab, and hey presto, *open sesame,* as Ali Baba used to say.

He does a double-take, then steps back, abruptly. 'Where is the tapas?' I could murder a tapas, actually, a thick, warm slice of that Spanish omelette with a cold beer would go down a treat, but not until I'm about fifty miles away from this hell-hole. 'Look' he continues, 'where is the tapas?' And he points inside the flap. I bend my head, disinterestedly. What am I supposed to be looking… oh bloody hell, some thieving oik has swiped the filler cap! I shrug unhelpfully, like a Spaniard behind a customer-service desk. *Don't look at me, pal, I just told you I couldn't get the flap open. Don't even think of trying to pin this one on me.* 'MANOLO, BEN AKEE!' he bellows at a spotty youth in a pair of greasy overalls, and I step smartly back against the wall, to avoid further loss of hearing, where Chrissie is tittering helplessly.

'Oh that was so funny! How many men does it take to figure out a petrol cap? Look, another one is coming now. That is three of you!' And sure enough, Manolo crosses the road, and a Spanish conversation ensues, featuring hand waving, and shouting, and elaborate gestures. Talk about making a drama out of a crisis, but it is always thus, in this country. I am standing against the wall still, enjoying this piece of impromptu theatre, when suddenly the situation resolves itself. Manolo stalks off, still flapping his arms like some crazy bee-keeper, and Ordinary Bloke closes the flap, sheepishly.

'There is no tapas, with thees model" he grins. 'Now plees, you go to gasolinera. End of street, turn left. Fool, plees. Foo-ell fool.' *I certainly am, my friend.*

Gritting my teeth, having sworn to never again drive another Ekky, in this lifetime, I leap into the thing, start the engine and tear off down the road like we are in an episode of Starsky & Hutch, with Chrissie still scrabbling with her seat belt. I take the left-hander on two wheels, almost, and screech onto the forecourt, cutting up some doddery old man in a beat-up Landrover. Jabbing furiously at the petrol flap, I get it open at the fifth attempt, and ignoring the attendant making his leisurely way from the hut I stab the nozzle aggressively into the pipe and snatch the handle. As the pump is running I take a deep breath, uncross my eyes and turn my head in a full circle to stretch my neck, jumping back smartly to avoid the slosh of fuel, from the filler pipe, indicating the car is fool. Forty-six euros.

At a more sedate pace this time, we head back to the body-shop, where a gleaming little white SEAT is standing proudly on the forecourt. Oh my word, what a beautiful job they've done, actually managing to match the new paintwork with the rest of the car, seemingly. They've even given the whole thing a polish. Suddenly, the strife of the past six weeks, or was it eight, I forget now, and frankly who cares, fades away. I shake Ordinary Bloke warmly by the hand, as does Chrissie, congratulating him on a superb job, but she has one last question. 'Do you know how much the repairs cost, please?'

He consults his clipboard. 'Yees, four-hundred and forty euros' he smiles. 'You are happy weeth you car, no? Sign here, plees.'

Back out on the road home, I can feel the tension draining away. 'Can you believe that?' I giggle, 'no filler cap. A flap with no lock, and no filler cap. There must be some other anti-theft device to stop some tea-leaf siphoning the petrol away, but what a strange car that was, a button for a handbrake, and no fuel cap. And we never did get to see what the boot was like!'

She is grinning widely. Just like that meat-fly. 'I tell you what, though, forty-six euros, for all that way, is blooming good, I reckon. Home to Granada and back, then Malaga and back, airport, and the caravan.' She is still smiling, about something. 'And do you know what, I really liked that car, in the end. I'm going to miss it!

'Me too, actually' I admit. 'Once I got used to the size, the width, it was fine, it went along really well, drove superbly, one or two quirks, but by the end I was starting to enjoy it. If I was buying one I'd get the smaller model, as we don't need anything that big, but yeah, on that dash to the garage I felt totally in control! What? What are you laughing at?'

She smiles, contentedly. 'Oh, you know.'

'What? What do I know?'

She stretches out, luxuriously, like that cat who got the cream.

'Winning the second part of my bet, of course, with some know-it all-bloke, just enjoying the feel...

'OH NO YOU DIDN'T' I splutter. You didn't win any damned bet. Four hundred you said. This car cost four hundred and forty. You were close, but no cigar. Sorry!'

She throws back her head and roars with laughter. 'Oh yes I did win, Sonny Jim. I said four hundred QUID, remember? And how much is four-forty euros? Eh? Come on, out with it. Four-forty euros is, as near as damn-it, four hundred English quids. Right? And I've just decided my prize will be a tropical holiday, I think I deserve one, putting up with you these past two months. Sorry, these past forty-two years.'

I consider the implications for a few seconds. *Yeah, why not? Couple of days on the coast will do us good.* 'OK, we could do that, the Costa Tropical, south of Granada. Where do you fancy, Almunecar or Salobrena? What was the name of that hotel where I got the half-board deal last year?'

She rolls her eyes and sighs at the same time. 'That is so wrong, on every level. First of all, what is this 'we' business? Did I say you were coming? And secondly, I didn't mean the Costa Tropical, down the road, I meant the tropics, you know, either side of the equator. Somewhere exotic. So when we get home, fire up the laptop and get searching!'

CHAPTER 13.
THE MOON AND
THE WHAT?

'I must to go to buy a dolly.' We are having a relaxing coffee with our good friend and student Rosa. Like the vast majority of our Spanish amigas, or amigos for the fellows, we first encountered Rosa at the conversation group in the library, where she very soon tired at the antics of Alicia, she of tight blouses and fishnet stockings fame, and begged Chrissie to take her on for one-to-one classes. Late thirties maybe, single, tall for a Spaniard with dark brown hair and eyes, and a mouth which curls up up at the corners as if she is about to crack one of her wicked jokes. Originating from the north of Spain somewhere, Rosa flat-shares with An-hella, Angela, one of her colleagues in the local factory, and we have spent some hilarious nights watching Real Madrid on their pay-TV package, where we taught the pair of them a few British football songs, as you do. Including the one directed at opposing managers. 'Fat Spanish waiter, you're just a fat Spanish waiter, sacked in the morning, you're getting sacked in the morning!' Everything had to be translated for the benefit of Angela, so whilst I was confident that 'fat Spanish waiter' was *camerero Espanol gordo*, 'waiter Spanish fat' in this arse-about-face Continental lingo, I struggled mightily with 'sacked in the morning.' You had to be there I suppose, but we all creased up laughing.

We even took advantage, one roasting hot Saturday afternoon, of the communal swimming pool thoughtfully provided in the private garden at the rear of the apartment block, although for some reason Rosa seemed reluctant to dip her toes in the water. 'Thees woman ees sex-worker' she hissed, indicating one of the other residents, 'I not get in same water as she!' Priceless.

So this dolly. Rosa has a brother, I'm fairly sure, with a couple of kids, I think. My wife of course knows the genders, names and ages of his offspring. 'So is the dolly for your niece, Marta?' she enquires.

Rosa's mouth curls up, then back down, and turns into a frown. 'Sorree?'

'You said you were going to buy a dolly' Chrissie repeats, patiently. 'Is the dolly for Marta?'

'Sorree, yees, I go to buy a dolly. And yees, my niece ees Marta. My neff-ooo Javier.'

'But I thought Marta's birthday was in August? So is the dolly for some other occasion?' Remarkable, isn't it, not only knowing the names of the brother's kids, but when their birthdays are.

'Sorree?'

Something is slightly off here. I'm beginning to suspect we might be talking at cross purposes. Chrissie tries again, this time in Spanish. 'Comprando una muneca?'

Our friend's frown grows deeper. 'Buying a … muneca? What is muneca in Eenglees, plees?'

'Dolly!'

Up go the corners of her mouth, and our friend bursts out laughing. 'Sorree, I not buying a dolly, muneca, I say I must to go to buy a dolly. My cit-ee, in nort of Espain. My cit-ee, buy a dolly. I have new jov in buy a dolly!'

'So how do you spell this buy a dolly place?' I grin, then am suddenly gripped by apprehension. Is she moving away? I have never heard of anywhere called buy a dolly, in this neck of the woods.

She scrabbles around in her bag and comes out with a pen, and the back of an envelope, on which she scribbles *VALLADOLID.* Oh hell, that is about four-hundred miles away, I rode past it once, on the motorway, coming back from the ferry-port. Pronounced it how it is spelt, in English, of course. Chrissie studies the envelope. I don't suppose she has even heard of the place, and why should she, geography not being her strongest point. Birthdays yes, maps no. 'Valla.. is that how it is pronounced?' she smiles. 'That is on the road to Santander, isn't it? So you have a new job in buy a dolly. Congratulations! What fantastic news, I'm so pleased for you!' And she steps around the table and gives her friend a big hug.

I reach across and squeeze her hands. So sad for us of course, especially Chrissie, losing intelligent female company, which she still suffers from a lack of here, and causes her more pain than she lets on, but great news for Rosa in this current economic situation in Spain. 'So tell us all about this new job, you must be so excited!' And I order another round of drinks, as this could drag on a bit...

'Well, I will try!' she smiles, taking a deep breath, and up go the corners. 'Een Espain we have Opposition, which is to get jov in Gobby-Enry. You want jov in Gobby-Enry, you must to study for Opposition. Two years. Study all laws, and Constitution of Espain. Then you take exam, and win points. I study Opposition for Ministerio of Forest, but not to get sufficient points, so I go in bag, how you say, waiting list, for temporary jov. So one year later I get temporary jov, in department feeshing, permissions for feeshing, in forest, but in creesis I lose jov, and so I come here. Santa Marta. Then thees week my old boss call me, and say there is temporary jov now in forest, so plees to return to buy a dolly. Now ees a problem for me, if I do not return I lose my position on list. I love Santa Marta but do not want to lose my position, I can to study new Opposition for permanent jov, and win extra points also because I have my old Opposition points. You understand?'

We do indeed. Well more or less anyway, and have heard of many other instances of the inhuman, bureaucratic rigmarole surrounding local and national government jobs in this country. Inhuman, I hear you ask? Isn't that a bit strong? Over the top? Well listen to this, if you don't believe me. I swear this is true. One of Chrissie's other students applied, before we met her, together with thousands of others, for the Opposition to become a primary school teacher. Paid the fees, which were substantial, studied like crazy, took the exam, but failed by just a few points, and was therefore placed on the waiting list, or bag. Heard nothing for over a year, then suddenly, out of the blue, was called by the education department late one Friday afternoon, and instructed to get herself to the *Canary Islands* ready to start work on the *Monday morning.* The Canaries, in the Atlantic ocean, off the coast of Africa, in under sixty hours. Failing which she would forfeit her entire place on the waiting list and be forced to start again. No flights or accommodation provided, no meeting or interview with the headmaster or senior colleagues, no idea where the school was, the location, the demographics, and no clue as to the length of the engagement, be it three days, three weeks, three months or three years. Get there, or else. And from the school's point of view, they had no notion of what this young woman was like, her qualities, her personality, whether or not she was capable of actually teaching the year-group, bearing in mind it was her first appointment.

We mentioned this situation, without divulging personal details of course, to our other educated Spanish friends, all of whom expressed no surprise whatsoever, and had similar stories of their own to tell. They all despised the system, a huge money-spinner for the Government, but with literally hundreds applying for each post, had little option but to comply.

Can you imagine paying the best part of two thousand euros and studying the Constitution and other rules and regulations for two years simply for the privilege of a one-in-two-hundred chance of a lowly job behind a desk? 'Your free-end was lucky' was the general consensus.

Now I have to tell you that it has all worked out just fine, for our free-end, so far. She has been on the Canaries for five weeks now, at time of writing, her contract has been extended to the end of the academic year, and the formerly shy, retiring, nervous little girl, who spent most of that first weekend weeping at the prospect of her first ever flight, leaving her family and fiance behind, has blossomed overnight into a striking, confident young woman. Chrissie speaks to her on Skype each week, her English has come on in leaps and bounds, and the transformation is remarkable.

At least Rosa won't have such problems, with a whole six days to resign her job here, say goodbye to Angela, load up her car, phone her Mother to get the spare room ready, *keep the room above Joe's,* at least until she can rent a place of her own, but for how long she has no idea as the current occupier of her new position fancies trying a different task within the forest department, but retaining the right to return to his old job any time he chooses, in which case Rosa will be out on her ear again. And will the factory here want her back again, with a waiting list half way down the street?

Anyway. Rosa has been in buy a dolly for over six months now, is renting her own apartment, is settling into her new jov despite being totally confused by the myriad rules and regulations concerning fishing locations, the type of fish you are attempting to catch, and the size of your tackle, I kid you not. We both speak to her each week on Skype as *there are no Eenglees persons in buy a dolly*, and she has been pressuring us to pay her a visit. And it didn't take much pressure, I have to tell you. I remember the conversation well. 'I suggest you stay weeth me the night of Friday, ees not much een buy a dolly, but cat-ed-ral and old buildings are very nice. Salamanca ees old university cit-ee, but maybe to visit next time as two days there are best. So on Sat-oor-day you can travel to Abbey-la, ees fa-moos for wall of stones outside of cit-ee and you must to eat chooly-tonn. Then Sunday you can to travel to Se-go-bia, has bridge of stones, castle of Disney and must to eat coachy-knee-o. Ees delicioso!'

Did she mention eating? Stuff the old stones, and we've been to Disneyland. 'Chooly-what did you say, in Abbey-la?' I giggle. 'Is Abbey-la a place, and chooly-something to eat? How do you spell Abbey-la please?' *We got caught out with the buy a dolly place, didn't we?*

She types away on the conversation side of the screen, which I always keep open for translations. Getting good with this modern technology, I am. 'AVILA. SEGOVIA.' Well, I've been to Avila before, on the motorbike, same trip as buy a dolly, but I certainly didn't get to eat any chooly, or see any wall of stones come to that, as the heavens absolutely opened just as I was entering the town, so, cold, wet and thoroughly miserable, I decided to press on, and see if I could outrun the rain. Pronounced the name as it is spelt, of course, A villa, which reminded me of the football team, from Birmingham, European Cup winners, ooh, must be getting on for thirty years ago now. Peter Withe snatched a great goal to defeat Bayern Munich, as I recall. Se-go-bia I know nothing about, however, which is surprising, if there really is a Disney castle there.

'So what are these things to eat, Rosa?' Chrissie enquires, from her seat next to me, elbowing me off the screen.

'Well, een Abbey-la, ees much famooos for chooly-tonn, ees the best een Espain!' she giggles. 'You must to try!'

'Yes but what actually is it?'

'Our student's mouth comes up at the corners. 'Moooo! How you say, ste-ack? Boff?'

I regain my place in front of the camera. 'And what is this coachy thing, in Se-go-bia?'

The corners stay up, and she starts to oink, and grunt. 'Peegh! Ees the best een Espain.'

Chrissie is devastated. 'Rosa! You know I am vegetarian. Steak or beef, and pork, as we call pig, are both meat. What is there in these places for me to eat?'

'Nothing!'

So here we are, this fine Friday morning, en-route to this famous buy a dolly, with one notable addition to our navigation aids. A sat-nav. Chrissie came back with it from her last trip to the UK, which I regarded as a snub to my cartographic skills. We drove from Washington DC to New Orleans, and back again via the east coast, with my pen and ink maps, and only went wrong, ooh, just about every day actually. A present from her brother, who'd updated his car to a model with a built-in system, so gift horses and all that, Plus, amusingly, it comes complete with a chirpy Australian 'Crocodile Dundee' character, who refers to me as his 'mate', which might become decidedly un-amusing after a few miles, we shall have to see. *Still, beat them at cricket last summer, didn't I? But what if he knows that, and sends me the wrong way? Poor losers, aren't they, Australians?* Still, for now, he implores me to 'take the motorway, it's time to cruise', and so we do.

I reckon buy a dolly is all of four-hundred miles from our place, and there are actually a few numbers in the bottom corner of the screen, which might or might not refer to the exact distance, the trouble being I need my glasses to see the road ahead, but have to remove them to read small print, so what with Mister Dundee and his 'keep straight on, too easy mate', and being keen to avoid crashing, I ignore them. Must be getting close now, however, and what a weird place this is, like how I imagine the other side of Pluto to be, only with roads. The countryside is dominated by flat-topped mountains, as if a giant hand has come down and planed them off. They seem man-made, like gigantic slag-heaps, but cannot be, as they go on for miles, like a huge, drab, layer cake, with each step progressively smaller than the one below, seemingly devoid of vegetation, stark, haunting, frightening even, I certainly wouldn't want to be out here at night knowing these brooding hills are looming in the darkness. The sun has disappeared too, rendering the whole scene like some twilight world devoid of colour, or life. 'Jeez mate, stick yer boot down, get outta this hell-hole' cries Dundee, in my imagination.

We reach the outskirts of the city, population over three-hundred thousand, famous for its university, according to something I read on the internet, but it didn't mention the large prison blocks though, did it? Hang on a minute, it is not a jail, they are apartments, block after block of featureless, never-ending flats, without balconies. Is that even legal? Don't people need somewhere to breathe? Communist-era, Iron Curtain architecture, in a flat monochrome, surely even students, if that what this is, need a railing they can vomit over, after a hard night's partying? Still, Rosa will have secured something a little more upmarket, I am sure. Or not. After a couple of quick turns, Dundee announces that 'you have reached your destination. Windows up, grab those sunnies, and don't let the seagulls steal your chips!' Blimey. 'Best of luck here, ya Pommie bastard!' he is thinking, recalling the last Ashes series, and stifling a wry chuckle.

We are in a side street, surrounded by dark, forbidding apartment blocks, four of five stories high, although I cannot be certain as the whole place is making me shudder, contrasting this with Andalucia, the warmth, the colour, the sunshine. Chrissie whips out her Spanish phone and texts Rosa, then we exit the car and stretch our aching limbs. It is precisely seven o-clock. 'This is strange' she ponders, 'what is different from home?' There are families out and about, on their evening *paseo*, but something is missing… 'It's the silence!' she chuckles.

'The noise, or lack of. Nobody is shouting, bellowing across the street, hollering from their balconies, calling out to their friends three streets away, singing, clapping, nothing. Are we actually still in Spain?' *How the hell do I know, it is depressing the life out of me, and we've only been here less than five minutes. And how could anyone holler from a balcony? There aren't any.*

Our friend appears, smiling, pleased to see us, and all is forgotten amid the kissing and flopping, proving that some things never change, however mournful the scenery. 'Plees, follow me, I show you my floor. Sorree, flat!' she grins. 'Did you have good journeee?' Through the communal front door and into a phone-box, masquerading as a lift, don't ask me which floor as all I can think of is *how would they get a coffin out of this building? Standing up, certainly not horizontal, that's for sure. Must be a stair-well, somewhere?* The problem for me is that I suffer from claustrophobia, and always have, ever since I was a kid. I am a fresh-air fiend, and cannot stand being cooped up, in enclosed spaces, or even wearing heavy clothes, hats, scarves, woolly jumpers, round necks, thick jackets. I would rather my hair got wet than put up a hood, and in hotel or guest-house rooms I always rush to the window and let some outside in. Even walking in the street, I hate people behind me, invading my space, and have to stop to let them past, which causes endless problems for Chrissie when we are out shopping, looking around to find I am not there. *Quite convenient at times, this claustrophobia…*

Still, her flat is pleasant enough, bright and modern, and at least the view is of the other apartment blocks, and not those creepy mountains, but this lack of outside space is giving me the willies. 'Would you like tea, or beer?' *Well a beer is known to cure the willies, they say….* Up go the corners of her mouth. 'Ees possibly too late for you Eengliss people to go to cit-ee now, because you like to eat at eight, eight and half, not like us Espanee people, at eleven! So maybe we eat in bar here, and I show you cit-ee to-morrow? There ees good restaurant here, called *La*

Teta y La Luna.' The corners stay up. 'I think you enjoy thees, Juanee!'

I will indeed. Always liked pubs with the moon in the name, which is what la luna means of course, although no idea about the teta bit. The Full Moon, the Half Moon, had many a pint in those establishments, and we always called into the Moon and Sixpence, on visits to the Wye Valley, although sadly that has closed recently, according to a bloke I sat next to on a plane not so long ago. And what about George Orwell's favourite pub, the Moon Under Water? Or even, have Wetherspoon's recently opened a venue in buy a dolly? Surely not?

So a quick shower, and change of clothes, then into the phone box again and out across the grassy area between the blocks, proving it must rain here on occasion for there to be grass, and we approach a bar with outside seating declaring itself to be *La Teta y La Luna*, according to the sign affixed to the window. A delightful caricature of a white crescent moon on a black background, and the legend *Cafe Cantante & Lounge Club.* 'Doesn't *cantante* mean singer?' Chrissie enquires.

Our friend is struggling to keep a straight face. 'Yes it does, and do you know the meaning of *la teta*, Juanee?'

Suddenly a waitress with tattooed forearms, but thankfully all her own hair on both sides, approaches and hands us a menu each. 'Will you join us in a bottle of wine, Rosa? Red or white, or would you prefer something else?'

Thankfully our friend indicates a preference for red, and so I order not our usual *vino tinto de casa*, house red, which in Spain is usually superb, unlike the UK where house wine gets you some unspeakable, vinegary dregs for fifteen quid, but a *Ribero del Duero*, which I am told originates not a million miles from here, and will hopefully mark me down as a bit of an aficionado. Or a bit of a prat, who knows? Especially if it turns out to be twenty euros a bottle, given that I didn't bother to study the wine list. *Well us experts don't need to, do we?*

I then turn my attention to the bar's logo on the front of the menu, in greater detail, for any clues about this *teta*. The moon even has a notch out of his or her face, to signify a mouth.... but hang on.... is this one of those optical illusions, where the brain recognises one image, but if you concentrate, another suddenly appears? So the white part of the picture depicts a crescent moon, with a mouth, but the black part... is a breast, with a nipple? No, surely not? This cannot be. This is a family place, there are kids on the next table for pity's sake. I raise both hands to my chest, in a squeezing, cupping action, and gaze, open-mouthed at our friend, who is nodding, and grinning widely. As is the waitress, who, seemingly with some sixth sense, has hung around for the fun. Chrissie meanwhile looks horrified, as realisation dawns. The tit and the moon. You wonder there haven't been complaints. I shake my head in disbelief, in case the whole thing is a mirage, but no, there it is, unmistakably a boob. 'The teet and the moon' giggles Rosa. 'A surprise for you, no?' It certainly is, and to prove it I dig my phone out of my pocket and take a snap of the window. They will never believe this, next time we are in the Rose & Crown.

As the initial shock wears off Chrissie and I start to see the funny side, and by the time the wine arrives we are laughing along with Rosa. 'We talk about the man in the moon in Britain' she giggles, 'but I've always thought he was a bit of a teta!'

'Didn't he come down too soon once and go to Norwich?' I splutter, feeling somewhat lightheaded after the day we've had. 'Or was that Delia Smith? I know porridge was involved somewhere. Can't remember now!'

The waitress returns with her notepad to take the food order, but in all the hullabaloo I haven't even as much as glanced at the menu yet, apart from study the celestial body parts on the cover, so decide to go with whatever Rosa is having, her being a local and all that. My wife on the other hand, being female and therefore more than capable of multi-tasking, is going for the veggie burger, always a safe option, even if they do taste like cardboard. 'So what are we having, Rosa?' I enquire, as I don't really trust the woman not to be pulling another prank.

'Boor-gerr especial, con costillo, ees delicioso' she confirms. 'How you say costillo in Eengliss? Pantha?'

Not a clue, obviously, although I am certain it is nothing to do with the singer Elvis Costillo, of *Oliver's Army* fame, or a big black cat. 'We will have to wait and see, Rosa!' I smile.

Meanwhile my choice of wine is going down a storm, clearly more than a notch or two above the house stuff we usually imbibe, so, taking a deep breath I turn to the back page of the *carta.* Oh my God, I've just died and gone to heaven. Seven euros-something. Rejoice.

The food arrives, towering burgers filled with slices of belly pork, four of them, with crackling of course, and a mound of spiral-cut chips. The veggie option is no slouch in the wow stakes either, stuffed with, well you'd have to ask Chrissie, but stuffed it certainly is. Mine is so big there is no way even a gob the size of mine will go round it, so I have to divide it into the component halves, as do the ladies, of course.

And thus the evening proceeds, with hilarity. And the bill, when it came, must have been entirely moderate, as I've forgotten. So there you go. I don't usually like to recommend places, as everyone has different tastes, but for a fun evening if you are ever in the vicinity of buy a dolly, check out the tit, the moon and the panther. Just don't ask me where exactly it is, although I know an Australian bloke who could probably give you directions…

The following morning at eight sharp comes a knock on our bedroom door. 'Plees to wake up! Brax-fass! Coffee! Reechard Bowgan!'

Reechard Bowgan? Is that a bloke, or something to eat? I passed a somewhat disturbed night, although whether that was to do with feelings of confinement or the pork belly, is impossible to say. Still, upwards and onwards. I stumble into the sitting room to find Rosa settling down to watch television, which strikes me as odd to say the least, especially when there are guests present. 'Coffee, jam and cheese in kitchen, take plees. Reechard Bowgan begin now.'

You know what? I've managed to get through sixty-three years of my life without ever having heard of this person, so presented with the choice of sitting down to watch him, whoever and whatever he is, or breakfast.... I mean, it's not as if she is catching up with re-runs of *Only Fools and Horses*, that one with Batman and Robin for example, is it? In the kitchen there are indeed slices of cheese and Spanish ham laid out, plus coffee in a pot, but no sign of the jam, which I knew there wouldn't be, as every single Spaniard always refers to ham as 'jam'. I pour a coffee and select a few items just as Chrissie appears. 'Quickly!' I giggle, 'grab your breakfast, Reechard Bowgan is on now', and from the lounge comes the sound of cheesy music, the like of which I haven't heard since the days of *Jackanory*. The TV screen is filled with cartoon balloons floating past, each one displaying the flags of different nations, they then disappear to be replaced by a huge one bearing the legend *Ingles en TVE*, and flanked by the Stars and Stripes, and the Union Jack. This miracle of nineteen-seventies animation then vanishes, to be replaced by a grey-haired old bloke, with an open-neck shirt, sinister, hooded eyes, and a comb-over, sitting at a desk on which a miniature electric guitar in a perspex case, a mug containing coloured pencils, and a microphone from the days of Technicolor and CinemaScope, have been artfully placed. This is more than my brain can cope with at this time in the morning. TVE is the main Spanish channel, similar to the BBC in Britain. Are they really showing English classes on national TV? On a Saturday morning, prime-time kids hour? What is wrong with *Multicoloured Swap-Shop* starring Noel Edmonds? *All right, all right, don't answer that.*

Mr Bowgan, as I assume this is he, begins to speak. 'Hullo and welcome' he drawls, in a mid-western American accent. A banner then appears at the foot of the screen, announcing RICHARD VAUGHAN. Chrissie is giggling, but I have had enough of this already. 'Rosa' I interrupt, 'this man is called Vaughan, not Bowgan. His diction is terrible, he is mumbling, even I am struggling to follow what he is saying. And this is certainly not the *Queen's English*, as we say.'

She smiles. 'Well ees impossible for Espanee people to say Bowgan.'

'Vaughan.'

'Bowgan!. Fffown. Fffawn. Sorree, ees not possible for we. In Espain he is always Bowgan.'

I am not having it. 'Look, this is supposed to be an English lesson, so you must try to pronounce the name of the teacher correctly! That is basic! The first step. *Good morning Mister Vaughan, good morning everybody!* Vaughan. V.v.v.v. Please try!'

'Fffawn.' *Ah well, has to be better than Bowgan, doesn't it?*

Chrissie and I watch, fascinated, as old Bowgan bumbles his way through the programme, following the script of a textbook in his flat, unemotional delivery. A completely different scenario from what we do of course, with no audience participation, but the whole lesson reminds me of a particularly long, boring, wet afternoon in school about fifty years ago, my mind racing over subjects entirely unrelated to the subject in hand, girls, the rugby next weekend, girls, accompanying Killer King to the pub tomorrow lunchtime, girls, a bag of chips on the way home, and finally, girls. *Even Noel Edmonds would be preferable to this.* There is just no animation in his voice, Bowgan I mean not Noel Edmonds, so it is with huge relief that Rosa reaches for the remote, and puts us out of our misery. 'He is rubbish!' our friend declares, dismissively. 'Not so good as you two.' *Yeah but he has his own TV programme, and, presumably, a healthier bank balance than ours. Plus I don't even have a comb-over. Such is life.* Suddenly she leaps out of the chair, dispelling my fond recollection of the girl Killer and I persuaded to visit the Cross Hands that day. She even paid for the chips I believe. 'OK, we go to my car, and I take you to cit-ee. We can get lunch maybe, Eengliss lunch, at one of clock, not Espanee lunch, at three! What time you must to leave, travel to Abbey-la?'

I drag my thoughts away from that girl, and her chips. *Who was she again? Actually, I do remember it well....* 'Well, my Australian friend tells me Abbey-la is eighty miles, so if we are away by three, that will be fine.'

She frowns. 'Australian free-end? Who you Australian free-end? And what is eighty miles plees?'

Increasing her vocabulary, aren't I? 'The voice on our sat-nav is Australian. He is very funny. And in the UK we use miles, not kilometres. Eighty miles is about one hundred and forty kilo-metres, more or less.'

She is still frowning. Storing away the new words no doubt. Learning more from us than the old bumbler, for certain. 'What is sat-nab plees?'

'Sat-nav. Short for satellite-navigation, a small electronic de-vice for your car, showing directions to different places.'

She grins suddenly. 'Ahh, ay-pay-essy. Een Espanee we say ay-pay-essy.'

My turn to smile. 'Gee-pee-ess. In English, gee-pee-ess.'

So we pile into the phone box and down to the car garage under the block, the parking bays in which seem even smaller than those in Malaga airport, squeeze into her beaten-up Renault and along endless streets of endless apartments, before alighting in a free car park opposite what appears to be the older part of town. We stroll across an ornate bridge over a deep, wide river. 'Thees ree-verr Piss-you-gra', confirms our guide, and indeed it does look decidedly murky, although I decide against the rather obvious schoolboy joke. Breaks my heart to leave it go, because, come on, when will the river Piss-you-gra ever come up in conversation again? A once-in-a-lifetime chance has passed me by.

Then suddenly, the panorama is transformed. Ornate gardens, narrow streets, exquisitely decorated churches, public buildings, facades, shops. Delightful. This is what we came to see. I have just one question, however. 'Rosa, could you explain where the old houses are, in this city? Across the river, there are new apartments. Then this side, is the city centre, shops, churches, old buildings. So where did people used to live, before the apartments were built, maybe twenty years ago?'

She exhales, grinning. 'I will try! When Espain change to euro, was much money, a lot of, a lot of money, from banks, many people, how you say, especulate, building flats, apartments, here in thees cit-ee were built flats, people buying two, three flats, for especulate. Een many cit-ees in Espain happen thees. I think in buy a dolly no body want old houses, people want new apartments, I think demolish old houses. Then come creesis, many years, disappear money, jovs, big problems, no jovs, no money, banks take flats, too many flats, big problems.'

Chrissie smiles sympathetically. 'So did you get your flat cheap, if there are too many for rent?'

Our friend roars with laughter. 'Of course! Was cheaper to rent now than when builded!'

Across an ancient plaza, she indicates a stone building, with a massive iron chain embedded into the stone lintel above a window. 'Thees Palace of Pimentel, one of most important in the city. Around five-hundred years ago here was born King Felipe second. Ees legend that through thees window, where hangs chain, King Felipe was taken out when born to be baptized in the chur of San Pablo, because if he left through door of palace he should to be baptized in the chur of San Martin. However, ees legend only, for the baptism of he a passage elevado was built between the chur of San Pablo and the palace so that the royal family could pass through without stepping on the street. As passageway was elevado, one of the windows was used as exit from the palace, without us knowing with certainty which one could to be.'

'What a delightful story' Chrissie smiles. 'Is it true?'

Our friend's mouth turns up. 'What do you think!?'

'So what did the Royal family have against the church of St Martin?' I enquire. 'Was the church of San Pablo prettier, you know, for the photographs?'

She still has that twinkle in her eye. 'I think next to San Pablo chur was pub! Now come on, I show you bar of Donkey Hottie.'

My wife's ears prick up at this news. 'Is this a man, Donkey Hottie?' she hopes, panting slightly. 'And will he actually be there?'

'Oh yes!' our student titters. 'He very famooos Espanee man. He be on display in bar thees day.' *Oh please no. She cannot surely mean… not after all that belly pork?* She leads us through more narrow, winding streets, until we find ourselves outside a sunny cafe/bar with two huge barrels either side of the front door, menus in the windows, and a swinging sign bearing the legend *Fierabras. Auto Pull.* Now I have to say I was expecting a sleazy dive with blacked-out glass and a seventeen stone meathead in a badly fitting suit and a curly wire in his cauliflower ear guarding the door, so this comes as a total shock. I burst out laughing. It is the *Auto Pull* bit of course. Who, or what, is being automatically pulled? My leg, probably, knowing Rosa, although I have to confess my mind first leaped to other, ruder, conclusions. *'Fierabras'*, she confirms, as if that explains every-thing perfectly. 'Ees medicine of Donkey Hottie. It make he big and strong.' And she squeezes Chrissie's arm in a 'two girls together' kind of a way. I meanwhile glare back at the pair of them in a 'well I don't need any medicine to make me big and strong' fashion, holding in my gut and puffing up my chest, proving once and for all I can actually multitask.

My wife is keen to get inside, clearly, as she tugs her student's arm. 'Come on, are we going in?' I am tempted to wait outside in the sunshine while the pair of them grab their share of leer-ing, automatic pulling or whatever is about to happen, but hey, I'm a modern man, I have nothing to be ashamed of, although if you believe that you'll believe anything. Before I get a chance to decide either way however I feel a nudge in my back and we are heading for the door. To be confronted by the life-size figure of a man dressed in a suit of armour, a white pointed beard and a black floppy hat, perched on a throne on top of the bar. And standing next to a pillar is what appears to be the same bloke, this time clutching a shield. Who is this sup-posed to depict? Sir Lancelot? Surely not, he was one of ours, wasn't he? Some famous Spanish knight? Hmmmm, let me think. Nope, not a one. There were clearly conquistadors and fidgety little fellows stomping about in chainmail, hundreds of years ago, but none of them are famous on the global stage, are they? Probably, when it came to the actual fighting, they were sat under parasols well away from the battle, having a tapas. Chrissie meanwhile is clearly hoping the figure will burst into life, rip off his breast plate, whip out a little white towel and a bottle of baby oil, and start gyrating, before her very eyes.

'Who is this, Rosa?' I enquire, bemusedly.

Up curls the mouth for the umpteenth time this weekend. 'Donkey Hottie, of course! You not know he? You not read the book? Cervantes? Donkey Hottie? Sancho Pantha?' What? This is a literary figure? I delve into the crevices of my mind. Cervantes? Didn't he write *Don Quixote*, about some windmills, and a little fat bloke on a donkey. Used to think it was pronounced Don Quick Oats, like the Scottish breakfast cereal, when I was a little boy. Never read the book, of course, as what was it in comparison to *Charles Buchan's Football Monthly*, or the *Beano?*

I bet I know someone who has read it, however, as she is ashen-faced with shame, and serve her jolly well right, if you ask me. It's the Spanish pronunciation of the letter 'O' of course. Us Brits say *Fernand-O, Albert-O, Romer-O,* whereas the locals are more like 'aww.' Fernand-aww. Oh, I am going to love this. My wife slumps onto a stool, just as the fat Spanish waiter arrives. 'Rosa, we pronounce it Key-Hoatie, in English' she groans, covering her face with her hands. 'Don Key-Hoatie. I thought you were saying Donkey, you know, a burro, and Hottie, a sexy person who is hot, it's what us ladies say about such a man, a hottie!'

I, meanwhile, have my hands two feet apart, like an exasperated fisherman, nodding my head. 'Donkey. We both thought this was a strip-club!"

Our friend squeals with laughter, and has to grip the table for support. 'Oh my GAAD! Donkey Hottie!' The startled, portly *camerero* is grinning, amid all the hilarity, although clearly without a clue why, until a rapid-fire burst of Spanish puts him right, whereupon he starts to gyrate, like a walrus on an ice-floe, and mimics unbuttoning his shirt. Rosa then staggers over to the bearded figure standing unemotionally by the pillar, and indicates the groin area, under the breast-plate. 'I don't think so!' *Ingles en TVE* with Reechard Bowgan was never like this, that's for sure.

I really need a beer, but daren't risk one, in my weakened state, plus the fact that I'm driving, later, so make do with a lemonade, or a lee-mon as it's known in these parts. 'I have order you a ration' our pupil smiles, which I know to be a plate of something, although she doesn't specify what.

'Which ration?' I giggle, casting around for the non-existent menu which the Spanish stripper has completely overlooked, in his haste to get his kit off, an image which will surely disturb my sleep, this night, and many others to come.

'Pantha!'

'Is that Sancho Pantha, or belly pork pantha?' I giggle.

The corners of her mouth have been more or less permanently up, since we arrived. 'Ees the same thing!' And she taps her stomach. 'Pantha. Sancho Pantha mean Sancho beeg belly! You eating belly of peegh.' It's all coming back to me now, Don Quixote and Sancho Panza, although I always pronounced the 'Z' in Panza. Not very nice, is it, naming someone Sancho big belly? Imagine that nowadays? There'd be uproar. Different times of course. And wasn't Cervantes a contemporary of Shakespeare? He could be a bit rude, too. The Elizabethan era, wasn't it?. And suddenly, for no particular reason, the image of Blackadder, Baldrick and The Queen of Spain's beard flashes before my eyes. 'Why you laughing, Juanee?'

I possibly don't have sufficient of my allotted three-score-years-and-ten left to explain about the Queen of Spain's beard, but luckily, or unluckily actually, at that moment a large bowl piled high with crunchy pork belly, this time cut into inch-long strips, is placed in front of me by the wobbly waiter. I attempt to avert my gaze from his hairy, deliberately exposed chest, but fail. Blimey, don't they eat anything else in buy a dolly? The girls meanwhile get a mixed salad each. 'Rosa, what are you doing to me?' I cry. 'We are going to Se-go-bia tomorrow, you tell me I have to eat that coachy-something there, I had pantha last night, I will start to look like a pig, soon!'

Predictably, and entirely unamusingly, my wife mutters 'too

late, you already do', which I resolve to store away in the corner of my brain, and dredge up on another occasion, like she does. I cannot help laughing of course, and so the lunch continues, hilariously, although I cast envious eyes on the salads, from time to time. Order a bottle of water to go with your pantha, should you decide to visit, as it's as salty as hell, and trust me on this; don't under any circumstances ask the waiter to dance.

Rosa drops us back at her flat where our little white SEAT is waiting, suitably rested, raring for the off, and Dundee similarly appears to have spent a peaceful night. We kiss, flop and hug, even though we will be speaking to her on Skype later in the week, and we turn south, away from the flat-top mountains, towards Abbey-la, through rolling vineyards, past enticing wineries. We've only gone about ten miles however before I start to curse. 'What on earth is the matter now?' my wife enquires.

I sigh, dramatically. 'I have a head like a sieve. I forgot all about it. I meant to ask Rosa what that 'auto-pull' was all about.'

CHAPTER 14. ABBEY-LA.

Eighty miles later, just as Dundee seems to be gearing up for another big finish, we round a bend and bump straight into a huge stone wall. I don't mean literally, of course, but it is gigantic, like about ten castles all rolled into one, one minute nothing, just a normal town, then suddenly, whoa, what is this? Comes as a hell of a shock, actually, even though we were expecting a *wall of stones*, as described by Rosa, and I bet this stretch of road is an accident blackspot, for first-time visitors. I am attempting to gape, and steer, all at the same time, then suddenly spot a road on the left which leads across a grassy bank, up a slope, below the wall, so I swerve alarmingly across the oncoming traffic and park up. 'Mate, turn around when you can' cries Dundee, 'and if those back-seat drivers don't keep it down, well ditch 'em at the next servo!'

'I thought you said you came here before, on your bike?' Chrissie mutters.

'Why don't you all stop going on at me?' I wail. 'Unplug him, he's done for the day. And what's this about my bike? Yes I came here before. So what?'

'Well how come you failed to notice this wall?' she giggles. 'I know you are the most spectacularly unobservant man in the entire universe, but even you must have spotted this. Both ends are out of sight, it's that long, for pity's sake. It must be a hundred feet above us, perched on that hillside, the turrets bulge out like Sancho Panza's gut. Or about fifty Sancho Panza's guts. The battlements, that massive gateway, I bet you can see this from the moon!'

It is rather large, I have to admit, and she does have a point. I rub my hands across my eyes, then take a gigantic swig from my bottle of water. God that pantha was salty. 'Look, I told you. It started teeming down, I had to shelter in a garage, get my waterproofs on. Maybe I came through a different way, perhaps there is a bypass, who knows? But I didn't see it, all right? Besides,' and I step out of the car and ease my aching back, 'I don't think it was here, three years ago. Look at those stones, they are brand new. I bet the cement is still wet! And that grassy bank has just been turfed, look, there is not a single weed sprouting through the cracks in the wall. And I don't think it is even proper stone, it's that reconstructed stuff, probably assembled in panels, like the scenery on a model railway, stuck with Airfix cement. Give it a tap, it will sound hollow.'

My wife has her head in her hands, and mimics banging her head against the car roof. 'You're hallucinating, right? Not even you could be so monumentally stupid. You are thicker than those walls. Must be all the crackling you've eaten these past two days. Wet cement.... Most of this dates from the twelfth century, some even earlier, little Anna was telling me, she studied it for a college project. The wall is two and a half kilometres in circumference, apparently, no doubt you can tell me what that is in miles, or all you all porked out?'

'About a mile and a half' I confirm, automatically, in a split second, proving my brain is still functioning. Just about. 'But the twelfth century? More like the twelfth of October. This year. It just looks too perfect to me. Where is the pollution stuck to it? Where are the signs of conflict, of invaders?'

She closes her eyes, as if addressing an idiot. 'Pollution? Have you seen any factories, these past two days, these hundreds of miles we've travelled? Some old farmer burning a few vine clippings maybe, but heavy industry? And invaders? Would you even bother? These walls must be, what, seven men high, forty feet? Close the gates and the city is impenetrable. Obviously, there has been restoration over the years, and I know what you mean about the stones looking suspiciously clean, but look at the angle of the late afternoon sunshine, slanting in, bathing everything in a warm glow. Come here in the morning with the sun on the opposite side, it will look entirely different.'

She is correct of course, as she usually is, about the sunlight, me being a monumental idiot, and the crackling. This place is spectacular, breathtaking even. We've been to walled cities before, York and Chester spring to mind, St Malo in northern France where we went on the ferry to celebrate our engagement, all of them magnificent, but I cannot recall anything quite like this, perched on the hillside, gently sloping from left to right, the towers of several churches peering enticingly over the battlements at the highest point. Suddenly the porky fog clears and I cannot wait to explore, gripped by that special fever which takes hold whenever a new location presents itself. 'Come on then, back in the car, and let Mister Crocodile guide us to the hotel!'

She giggles. 'Ahh, who needs him? Leave the car here, it's perfectly safe, just grab the bag from the boot, and follow me!'

I am puzzled, quite naturally. 'What, did little Anna know where we were staying? Did she draw you a pen and ink map? One woman giving directions to another wom...'

'SHUT UP! That sexist remark will cost you, sunshine. I will get us to the hotel, directly to the hotel, without passing 'GO' and you will owe me the two hundred pounds. A big present. A very big present. Zip the lip, and get thee behind me!' And she stalks off up the track. *Well I was only joking, wasn't I. She knows that, surely?*

We approach the gateway, two huge half-round towers, or Sancho Panza's guts, to give them their alternative name, which I do craftily tap as I pass, just in case, checking all the while for traces of Airfix model cement, of which there is none. They must be all of sixty feet high, with a smaller archway between them, where a massive iron-studded wooden gate might have hung, in days of yore, or last Tuesday, I am still not convinced, and suddenly I am glad we left the car behind, as the streets within are a maze. Well worth the two hundred not to have to drive this. 'Round to the left' she smiles, although I cannot fathom how she can be so confident without a plan or electronic assistance of any sort. I even check her ears, surreptitiously, for evidence of cables, or Bluetooth devices, and fail. Narrow cobbled streets, a tiny flower-bedecked square, everything carved from this suspiciously clean-looking stone, and suddenly she is delving into her bag. 'Now then, I'll just get myself checked in, what did I do with my passport? Ah here it is of course.'

I almost run into the back of her, not looking where I am going, or paying attention, as usual. 'Why did you stop here, and why are you looking for your passport now? Why don't you leave it until we get to the hotel, if we ever get there that is, at this rate.

Told you I should have… where are you going?' She disappears into a doorway, annoyingly marked *Hotel,* and so, grinding my teeth, I follow, into a tiny reception, staffed by an unsmiling, middle-aged woman behind the counter, who is proffering a registration card. 'How did you find this?' I whisper, although predictably she ignores me. Suddenly, through the door barges a breathless, younger woman, who, ignoring the fact that we are clearly in the process of checking-in, proceeds to bark about a hundred different questions at the receptionist, including the phrase 'I have my car outside', and to her eternal shame the employee breaks off from serving us and starts to answer. Not *'I am serving these people a moment, but I'll be right with you'*, but she actually hands her a registration slip. Taps away on the computer, and begins the process. This is not untypical, I have to say, such displays of ignorance, and blatant pushing-in, but I am scandalised nevertheless. I hold out my hands, palms upwards. 'Er, ola?'. Nothing, and old misery actually holds up her hand, as if I am a naughty schoolboy needing to be taught a lesson. I stroll across the room to the window, where a TripAdvisor sticker has been affixed, tap it casually, then make a writing gesture, as I cannot recall the Spanish for 'this is going down in my review, don't you worry.' Water off a duck's back of course. For two pins I would walk out and find somewhere else, but Chrissie arranged this one on her own Booking account, and has already paid, I imagine. *But it did go down in my review, don't you worry.*

Eventually we get our key, which my wife snatches up with a venomous glare, and she can do venomous glares far better than me, let me tell you. We find our room, on the top floor as previously requested, to avoid the sound of insomniacs trip-trapping about above, hopefully, and I fling open the French doors to let some outside in, revealing a delightful courtyard below, complete with tinkling fountain. Bang goes a restful night's sleep, as tinkling fountains and my bladder are incompatible, a fact I decide to keep to myself, as I don't want her to feel she has made an unwise choice of venue.

She joins me at the balcony, and peers out. 'Oh terrific' she giggles. 'I suppose I'm going to have you weeing about fifty times during the night, with that damn fountain. Remember that guest house in Beer, in Devon, with the babbling brook outside the window?' As if you'd ever let me forget, *mon petit chou*, although the beer in Beer had a lot to do with it, as I recall.

After a quick freshen-up, we head out to explore, retracing our steps through the archway, and head uphill, keeping the wall to our right. 'So come on, out with it' I grin. 'How did you find the hotel so easily? Did you memorise the directions?'

She sighs, stops dead, and turns around. 'See those yellow things fixed to that post? They're called signs. They have writing on them. Hotel names. You should try it some time, you know, concentrating, instead of wandering along with your head in the clouds. I simply followed the signposts. It's easy, when you get used to it.' *Signposts for hotels. Who knew?*

At the top of the slope the land levels out and the wall bears to the right, clearly the upper limit of the old city. A sign proclaims that wall-walking is available for a small charge, which is certainly something we can do in the morning, but for now across a delightful tree-lined *plaza* is an exquisitely ornate church, the Basilica of San Vicente, built in the twelfth century, according to our audio-guide, to house the remains of St Vincent and two other martyrs, Sabina and Cristeta, killed during the Roman period, their bodies interred elsewhere for the intervening millennium. Massive stone pillars support a magnificent cross-arched ceiling, but the undoubted masterpiece is a huge rectangular tomb, described as a cenotaph, ten feet by six maybe, covered by a steeply shingled roof embellished with gold leaf, supported by four carved marble pillars, and below, a stunning three-storey stone model of a basilica, embellished with delightfully sculpted, painted religious figures, depicting the torture and subsequent crucifixion of the trio, some on horseback, each around twelve inches tall, in different poses and clothing, their features alternately exultant or supplicant, some bent in prayer, others gazing in adoration. At the foot of the structure, exquisitely carved arches afford a glimpse into the crypt below. We stand in awe, transfixed, and for a moment I wish I could somehow be whisked back in time to the Middle Ages, to witness in person the skill and dedication of the original masons who carved this monument, seemingly from a single block of stone.

Suddenly, our reverie is shattered by a chattering, selfie-stick wielding group of tourists, and the peace evaporates, although I shall treasure those brief moments of silence and wonder, and vow to return again. Meanwhile, time to leave. We emerge into the gathering dusk, street lights twinkling, bars and restaurants preparing for the free nightly show, enacted all over Spain, of the evening *paseo*, young and old waking from their siesta to gather, and gossip, in groups large and small. We follow the wall past it's highest point, the top end of the rectangle, assuming of course that the far side, which we haven't yet seen, is a mirror image. We will find out tomorrow, hopefully, and my heart beats a little faster at the prospect. I place my arm around Chrissie's shoulder and give her a little squeeze, as I sense she feels the same. 'Can you remember what Rosa said about the pork and beef, the coachy and the chooly, which one was which, and what town was famous for what, excuse my mangled English?' I giggle.

She smiles, in sympathy, or perhaps in pity. 'Chooly was here, for sure, but I cannot remember if it was pork, beef, or witch. As basically I don't care. But I think you are about to find out, because this restaurant ahead has a sign board with photographs, for dim people like you who cannot tell the difference!' *It was pity..*

'I think I would recognise the witch, because neither pork

nor beef is served with a broomstick' I sniff, 'but the pork....
BLOODY HELL!' I recoil, in horror, and stumble across the
street, plonking myself down at a table outside a tiny bar, to the
surprise of the waiter who is leaning against the door-frame,
and order two beers, whether she wants one or not, and if not,
I will drink them both. *As basically I don't care.*

'What was that all about?' she grins, joining me. 'Blimey, you
have gone white! What on earth has happened?'

My beer arrives, and I take a gulp. 'See that signboard? No, actually do not look at that signboard. You're a fishetarian, right?
Well, it will give you nightmares. *Chuleton* is indeed the beef,
and I'm a flexitarian, but it will give *me* nightmares. I cannot
eat it. I don't want any. Let's go for tapas.'

She doesn't understand. She hasn't seen the photo. 'But you know
I don't mind you eating meat, when we're out like this. You
know you love beef, or steak. Just go ahead and order it, I don't
mind. This is a special occasion, we're on holiday.'

I drain my glass and nod at the waiter for another. 'Well you
will certainly mind if I order that. *I* will mind, trust me. I can't
order it, for three reasons.'

'What reasons?' *She hasn't seen the photo.*

I can see the signboard out of the corner of my eye, so turn my
seat slightly, so that I cannot. 'Well firstly, it is huge, gigantic,
like half a cow sat there, on the plate. The platter is one of those
great oval things people hang on their walls, actually *we* have
one in *our* dining room on the wall, it belonged to your granny,
I think, one of your grannies?'

She nods. 'Nanny Cole, yes.'

'Right, well this *Chuleton* is hanging off the edge. It's like a
doormat. It looks disgusting, far, far too big. The sign says
approx one kilo. A KILO! That is what, two-point-two pounds,

about thirty-five ounces? Jeez. That is four regular portions, for Pete's sake. It is for sharing, obviously, like the Spanish do, but who am I gonna share it with? The Five-Thousand? And secondly, it is thirty-two euros. THIRTY-TWO! Hell, I wouldn't pay that for a suit, let alone a steak! And thirdly, worst of all, it reminds me of Constance.'

'Who the devil is Constance?'

I'd forgotten she was into reggae, when she was a girl. 'Remember the Pink Floyd album *Atom Heart Mother,* the one with the cow on the front cover? The brown and white cow? Well, she didn't have a name, apparently. Storm Thorgerson, who designed many of the early Floyd album covers, said he simply drove out of London and photographed the first cow he came across, 'your regular cow, your standard cow, a cow qua cow' was what he said. And we Floydonians, as our select group of layabouts who were into the band called ourselves, felt that was unjust, that she didn't have a name. Now, at that time, the Floyd didn't have a title for the new album, when suddenly a story appeared in the press about this woman who was the first British heart patient to receive an atomic-powered pacemaker, and the headline ran 'The Atom Heart Mother is named.' And this woman was called Constance. The band thought this was such an off the wall article, they used it as the title of the album. But we didn't. We referred to the album as Constance, sprawled round Willerby's front room guzzling Taunton Natural Dry, someone would say 'hey man, put Constance the cow qua cow on' and so the name stuck. And it remains one of my favourite albums to this day. So I am not eating her. And that is final.'

She regards me with a dispassionate air, stands, delves into her bag, and signals to the waiter for the bill. 'What a delightful story, albeit factually incorrect.' The waiter arrives, she hands him a five euro note, and tells him to keep the change. Yes, you truly can get three beers for under a fiver in this country.

It appears we are leaving so I rise from my seat, angling my body away from the signboard, although the damage has already been done. 'What was incorrect?'

She strolls off down the street, then half-turns and calls out over her shoulder 'Because everyone knows that cow was called Muriel.'

Keeping the floodlit wall to our right, we approach a Chinese restaurant on the left. 'What about this?' I enquire, 'you like Chinese, and I can have beef chow mien, pretend it's chuleton! Chuleton chow mien, what about that?'

She turns up her nose. 'I don't really fancy Chinese, we can get that at home, can't we? I was hoping for something a bit more special, as we're away. In fact, I was planning on buying you a chuleton, seeing as how you're such a devoted husband and all that. Mind you, I wasn't planning on spending thirty euros!'

No call for sarcasm, is there? After a few more steps we reach what appears to be the main gateway into the old city, and on the left is a large square, lined with bars and shops, all doing brisk business. She grabs my arm, excitedly. 'Right, remember that uncalled-for sexist remark you made earlier, about the map? Well I've just seen what I want. Follow me, please!' *Oh no. Handbags. A handbag shop, has to be. This is going to cost, big time.* She leads me to a bakers shop, where in the window is a huge display of gingerbread men, all carefully laid out on a platter. Or actually gingerbread women. Gingerbread nuns, to be precise. Four inches tall, flared habit, white wimple surrounding a marzipan face on which eyes, nose and mouth have been drawn, together with a large cross on her breast, and rosary beads in her hand, in black food colouring, I imagine. 'There you are' she giggles. 'One each, please!'

I burst out laughing, and not simply because I have just saved a shed-load of money, although I cannot help but wonder if this is not slightly disrespectful, poking fun at religious figures? Still, they are for sale after all, and this is a right-on bakers, with crusty bread, cakes and pastries, not some cheap joke shop, nevertheless I hesitate. 'What is the Spanish for 'nun', can you remember?'

Dictionary-woman delves into her memory. 'Mon-hha. Mon-hhay is monk, mon-hha is nun. Off you go!'

The shop assistant has clearly witnessed us dithering outside. 'Do you like nooons?' she smiles, in broken English.

'Si, dos nooons, please!' I splutter, unable to keep a straight face.

She places them carefully in a bag, I pay her, then carry the confectionery outside, delving into the wrapping with my mouth open, ready to decapitate the poor smiling nooon. My wife beats me to it however, snatching the figure from my very jaws. 'Not now, you great pig, you'll spoil your dinner! Speaking of which, I am just about dying of hunger. Are we ever going to eat today?'

All along the edge of the square are tables and chairs, occupied by excitable Spaniards, indicating there might indeed be purveyors of nourishment. Suddenly, comes a familiar refrain. 'JOSE POR FAVOR! MARIA POR FAVOR! ANTONIO POR FAVOR!' A Hundred Montaditos! That'll do, as they say!

'Don't even think about it!' she objects. 'I'm not coming all the way to this so-called gastronomic paradise to visit Hundred Montaditos! Very nice, in it's own way, but I don't fancy eating in Woolworth's tonight, thank you very much. What about that one next to it, looks a bit quieter, a proper Spanish place. There's a menu outside, let's have a look.' Through the window we can see low ceilings, exposed beams, swords and shields and other antique paraphernalia, dark wooden furniture, plush chairs. Seems ideal. I can eat anything, off any menu, any where, apart from a four-foot steak, so I am OK, always, but Chrissie needs to satisfy herself there is sufficient veggie, fishy stuff to satisfy her tastes, before entering. 'Looks good' she smiles, 'garlic mushrooms to start, and I fancy that broccoli with sauteed vegetables. Come on, I'm starving!'

'Well if you're having garlic mushrooms, I'd better have them too!' I chuckle. 'Maybe we can get a big one, between us. And that hake *a la plancha* sounds good. In we go!' *Plancha.* A hot-plate. Many Spanish dishes come *a la plancha*, and are yummy, let me tell you!

We snag a quiet table for two, and, caught up in the moment, I order a *Ribero del Duero* from the elderly, diminutive waiter, for the second evening running. *Well, I saved on the nooon, didn't I?* After a respectable delay, the mushrooms arrive, served in a *cazuela*, a glazed earthenware dish both oven and flame-proof, another extremely popular method of preparing food in this country. And not a breadcrumb in sight either, bought-in frozen from a catering supplier. Indeed no, these fungi have simply been cooked whole in olive oil, with chopped garlic, and little... pink... squares... of... what?...

'Oh take it away, please!' she recoils. 'They've put diced ham in it. Why the hell would they put ham in a vegetarian dish? That is completely ridiculous.' The waiter has disappeared, mean-while, so we cannot ask him, but surely it must have been shown on the menu, *including diced ham*, whatever that is in Spanish. *Jamon*-something I imagine? 'No of course it wasn't' she sighs, more exasperated than angry. 'Do you think I would have ordered it if there had been? Look, there's a pile of menus on the bar, grab one will you please?' She turns to the first page, under the heading *primera plata*. First plate. 'There you go look, *champinones con ajo*. No mention of ham.' And she pushes the *cazuela* towards me. 'You'll have to eat it. I'll be OK with just the main course.'

Not right though, is it? Now I have to admit to being, not annoyed exactly, frustrated sometimes perhaps, at the limited choice available to her, and veggies generally, particularly in inland Spain. But this town is hardly the backwoods. There is a world heritage site outside the restaurant door, for pity's sake. Surely they should have got to grips with this, in the twenty-first century? 'No, I'm not accepting this' I tell her. 'You ordered a starter, and you're going to get…. ah, there he is look, I can just see the top of his head!' And I gesture him across. *'Hay jamon'* I frown, politely but firmly.

Now then. The Spanish word 'hay.' One of my favourite words. An extremely versatile word, although it has nothing whatsoever to do with dried grass. Actually pronounced 'eye', it means 'there is'. *Hay jamon.* There is ham. A statement of fact. *Hay jamon con mi champinones.* There's ham in my mushrooms. But the word can also be used as a question. *Hay jamon?* Is there ham? *Or, no hay jamon?* Isn't there any ham? Eye? No eye. Brilliant! And it applies to singular or plural, too. Or it does in rural Andalucia.

Old shorty studies the fast-congealing dish of fungi. 'Si' he agrees.

Deep breath. 'But my *moo-herr* is vegetarian' I wince, hating the fact that I have to refer to Chrissie as 'my woman', on account of there being no Spanish word for 'wife.' There is 'husband', *merido*, indicating our level of importance in society, but a wife, or partner, is just 'a woman.' The Dark Ages, or what? 'And' I continue, opening the menu, 'there is nothing in the *carta* about ham. *Champinones con ajo.* No eye the word ham.' And I push the dish towards him.

He regards me as if he is unable to grasp the concept of vegetarianism. 'But in Spain we always put ham in mushrooms.' he confirms, unhelpfully.

Another deep breath. Don't argue with me, sunshine. I'm the customer here. I explained it once, I'm not saying it again. I flap my hand over the dish, dismissively, and turn my head away. He picks it up, reluctantly, then suddenly, a smartly-dressed, educated-looking woman on the neighbouring table barks a fusillade of irritated Spanish at him, then turns to us. 'I sorree, een Espain we are so, how you say, old fashion-ed? We no understand customs of north of Europe. Are no many vegitarianos in thees countree. Es meat, always meat. We so embarrass-ed.'

Chrissie smiles warmly. 'Thank you, but please don't apologise. The restaurant should know this! We understand how Spain is so traditional. Don't worry, really.'

All right for her to say don't worry, but my belly is rumbling. 'I wonder what they are doing with those mushrooms now?' I giggle. 'Hosing them down, or picking the bits of ham out one by one with a cocktail stick!'

'Or not bothering at all,' she frowns. 'Look, our mains are arriving.' And sure enough, a slightly younger version of the original waiter approaches, bearing my fish and her sauteed vegetables, which he places before us, with a flourish. '*Approveche*' he smiles. Bon appetit. We certainly hope so, my friend.

My eagle-eyed wife has spotted something, however. *Oh what the hell is wrong now? She can be so finicky sometimes.* She slumps back in her chair, and covers her face with her hands. 'I just don't believe it. Look at this. They've only gone and put the diced ham in the broccoli. Have you ever seen anything so completely and utterly stupid? Putting meat into the vegetables. What is wrong with these people?'

I stare in disbelief, dumbstruck. Ham in broccoli? Just as well we aren't staying the night, as I really don't fancy pork in with my Cornflakes. Or a pile of it on my pillow, in lieu of a chocolate. I frantically scan my fish for signs of pig infestation, and find none. 'Well look' I frown, 'we have two choices. Send yours back, which means you'll be eating long after I've finished. Or, raise a fuss, and send both back, stick a cork in the bottle, pay for that and walk out, then go to Hundred Montaditos. Or, and this is three choices actually, you have my fish, and I'll have the broccoli. The ultimate sacrifice. An hour ago I was looking forward to a nice juicy steak, and now I'm volunteering to eat the guinea-pig food, in recognition of the love and affection I feel….'

'Oh crap! Will you pack it in!' She smiles nevertheless, as is only right and proper, when I've offered to save the day. 'Would you really do that? You are so sweet.' And she reaches across and squeezes my arm. 'Now give me your plate, before it goes cold! And give that idiot waiter a bollocking, next time he returns.'

'What, the check-back?' I giggle, handing over my plate. 'Is everything OK with your meal, sir? That concept hasn't reached these shores yet!'

So we proceed with our meal, and I have to say the broccoli with sauteed vegetables was absolutely delicious, lacking the flavour and texture of a nice juicy steak perhaps, and the diced ham didn't bring anything to the party, either, and the constant envious glances at my wife's plate was probably a mistake, although she did place a sliver of her fish onto mine, which only made matters worse, actually, and dreaming of Hundred Montaditos next door, through that wall there, just a few short steps away, did me no good either. So frankly it was a relief when it was all over. Foregoing desert, in the sure and certain knowledge there would be diced ham in it, I call for the bill, *la cuenta*, which duly arrives courtesy of the younger waiter, and quite honestly I have had enough conflict for one day, and come to the conclusion that explaining to these savages that putting meat in with the veggies is a bad idea would be like beating my head against a brick wall, so decide to leave it there. And I rarely check bills, either, feeling it to be bad form, somehow, to scrutinise, like some old miser, as if I am suspecting the premises of cheating. My wife however is less generous of spirit. And just as well. 'Look at this! Look what they've done! They've only gone and charged us for the mushrooms!'

My turn to stare angrily at the ceiling. More conflict, and sadly the witnesses, the couple on the next table, have long gone, as has the original waiter, seemingly. I call the younger one back, and indicate the entry for garlic mushrooms. 'We didn't eat this' I tell him, and he is welcome to smell my breath, if he doesn't believe me. *'Era jamon con los champinones.'* There you go, another simple word worth it's weight in gold. *Era.* Pronounced *erra.* Was. There was ham in the mushrooms. Also works as *no era.* There wasn't. It wasn't. 'We are vegetarians' I continue, losing the will to live. *'No comido los champinones.'* I think that is correct, but if it isn't, I don't know what we will do. Fight a duel, with that pair of antique flintlocks, screwed to the wall in the corner, possibly. Just get me out of here.

He digests the information, slowly. 'Si. Eye jamon in the mushrooms.'

Progress I suppose. He's admitted it. Sort of.

'No nos gustas jamon in the mushrooms' I tell him. We don't like ham in them. I think. 'Ask your *companero.'* If he can actually find his elderly colleague, that is, as he seems to have disappeared off the face of the earth. And I hand back the bill, with a slashing gesture across the erroneous entry. *'Quitar.'* Which is not a middle-eastern emirate, but indicates I need it knocking off. Probably.

He scuttles off, out of the back door and homewards, it seems, as five minutes pass, companionably, as I am still basking in the righteous glow of donating my meal to my wife, and we still have a third of the wine to polish off, having paced ourselves in anticipation of multiple courses, instead of just the one. Because no way are we having a pudding here, for obvious reasons, which is a shame as I am ravenous, broccoli not being all that filling. Still, Chrissie has two nooons in her bag... I am just about to stand and start tapping my imaginary watch, angrily, although at whom is difficult to say, and if someone doesn't return and sort this out very shortly we are off, when a head appears in the far corner and the original shorty *camerero* is weaving his way around the tables, with our bill in his hands. A revised bill, hopefully. He will smile, apologetically, hope we enjoyed our *segundo plato*, the main course, hand over the amended account, sorry about that ham business, and wish us a *buenas noches*. Er... Nope. He appears to be arguing about it, although it is difficult to make out what he is saying as his false teeth seem to be loose. I grab the incorrect bill, gesture for him to give me his pen, scratch out the *champinones* and scrawl in capital letters, *ERA JAMON. NO COMEMOS*. Was ham, no eaty. I then perform a quick mental tally of the two main courses and the wine, which scandalously comes to nineteen euros-something, fish a twenty from my wallet and slap the bill, the pen and the money onto the table. Chrissie stands, we turn away, grabbing the wine bottle, and stroll casually out into the street. 'If you hear running footsteps behind us,' I whisper, theatrically, 'ignore it and keep going. If we are apprehended we can split up! See you back at the car, get the engine running. I was a marathon runner, they'll never catch me!'

'Yeah, twenty years ago' she giggles, unkindly, but truthfully. 'But what is the legal position over here, do you think? In the UK you're supposed to leave your name and address, with a disputed bill, I believe.'

'Who cares?' I sniff. 'We paid for what we ate, not our fault if they put meat in the veg, is it? I'm just so damned annoyed.'

She squeezes my arm, 'what, you didn't get your *chuleton*, you mean? I told you to get one, and that I would pay.'

I smile, ruefully. 'No, not that at all. Having seen that picture, I've gone off steak for life! No, I'm just angry that I effectively gave that little waiter a fifty-pence tip. Now hand over that nooon, I'm RAVENOUS!'

The following morning we head out for breakfast, generally a pleasurable task in this country of pavement cafes, and sure enough, around the corner from the hotel, is a tiny square with tables and chairs arranged enticingly outside a small bar. I passed a fitful night to be honest, what with gnawing hunger and Niagara Falls cascading away outside the window, so I'm glad of a sit down. We order *tostada con tomate*, half a crusty loaf slathered with chopped tomato, drizzled with olive oil, and Chrissie makes a point of specifying hers *'sin carn-ey'*, without meat, a serious point for all you veggies out there, as if they can slap ham in the broccoli, you never know where it will turn up next. *Cafe solo*, heart-stoppingly strong espresso, and *zumo naranhha*, fresh orange juice produced from the type of machine you might have found in the amusement arcade at the end of the pier, where the waiter places about a pound of whole oranges in a tube at the top, and after a brief flurry of mechanical squeezing and squelching, the juice duly arrives from a tap at the bottom, completes our order. We gaze admiringly at the various stone buildings surrounding the plaza, and I cannot wait to climb the battlements later, for a bird's-eye view, providing I can summon the strength, but something is puzzling me. 'What is different here, from the UK? I cannot put my finger on it, but there's something missing somehow.'

She grins. 'The rain? Chain-store-lookalike cafes? McMuffins? All of the above? I don't know, you tell me!'

'I can't think. I've been on prison rations since yesterday! If I'm not fed soon, I will collapse... ah here he comes now. Stand back, this will be like a pack of ravening hyenas!' I fall upon my breakfast, and it disappears in record time. I slump back in my chair. 'By Gaw, as they say, I could eat another one of those! Anyway, I've just remembered what it is, what is different from Britain.'

She rolls her eyes. 'Well brush the toast crumbs off the side of your face, and put me out of my misery, please!'

'The morning papers. Have you noticed? Nobody is going for the morning paper. Strolling along with the dog, calling in the newsagent. Pulling up in their cars. You just imagine a place like this, a crossroads, in the UK, how much busier it would be. It's really noticeable, isn't it, and its all because there is no big tradition of the daily paper in this country. Down on the Costa of course they have traditional newsagents, selling the British and German papers, plus those English language freebies, but away from the coast they just don't do that.' And I smile to myself, fondly recalling how my faithful retriever Nelson loved to accompany me after breakfast each morning, sitting patiently outside the shop while I nattered briefly with 'Pete the Paper.' Nowadays our news comes electronically, which is progress I suppose, but sometimes it's just not the same, is it? Sitting here has brought it all home, and I feel a small pang of nostalgia.

'Yes, fascinating' my wife groans. 'Now, if you've finished wallowing, would you care to outline what we are up to, this morning, and what time we need to leave for Se-go-bia?'

I snap back to the present. 'Right, well Se-go-bia is only about forty or so miles, so as long as we're on the road by three, that should be fine. I think we should certainly walk the walls this morning, get the perspective of the old city, then see what happens. Check out of the hotel now, leave the bag there, pick it up when we leave town? Sound good to you?'

'Sounds good to me' she grins, 'but I have to get some *Yemas de Abbey-la*. They are sweets, local sweets. Anna told me we cannot come here without buying a bag of *yemas*. It's the law, apparently!'

So we check out, I grab my camera, and we head towards the top of the old town along the main thoroughfare, lined with shops, churches and other important buildings, all delightfully constructed from the local honey-coloured, suspiciously recent-looking stone, keeping an eye peeled for these *yemas*. Ahead we spot a black labrador pulling a middle-aged fellow enthusiastically up the slope, as nutty labradors do, tail swishing with pure joy, panting, tongue lolling, sniffing, straining. The labrador, obviously, not the bloke. Suddenly, the dog crouches, and deposits a steaming pile in the middle of the street, right bang smack in the middle, the most prominent part, as they always do. *And the guy just walks away.* The dirty, filthy swine. I am outraged. This is not some skanky piece of wasteland, it is the main street through a world heritage city, not that that should matter of course. Pick it up, you heathen. And he is a respectable-looking chap too, not some scruffy oik. I am speechless, but only for a split second. I am not having it. 'HEY!' I bellow. He turns, innocent look on his face. 'TOMAS!' I holler, aggressively, gesturing furiously at the offensive mound. Now I realise that shouting 'take' is not the correct expression, but in my moment of anger I have forgotten the words for 'pick it up', but he understands, right enough. Without any embarrassment whatsoever, without acknowledging me in any way, he pulls a plastic bag from his pocket, bends, scrapes up the offending faeces, and strolls casually away.

Chrissie meanwhile is shaking her head in disbelief. 'The savage. I was going to say something, if you hadn't. But what is it with you and this town, all this conflict? Up there through that arch is the restaurant, from last night. Can I suggest you keep your head down, for the remainder of our visit? Just look at the scenery? Before you get yourself arrested?'

I cannot help laughing. 'I don't think Abbey-la likes me very much! That deluge when I was here before, and now this visit. But none of this is my fault, is it, putting meat where it's not needed, leaving piles of crap in the road? And as the great Kenny Rogers sang, 'someone should do something about it, how hard can it be, and maybe that someone is me.' And whatever Kenny says is just fine as far as I'm concerned!'

We pass through the main gateway again, into the street of our escapades last night, and I do indeed avert my gaze, in case that photo of the chuleton is still there, or there are police cars lined up outside the restaurant. Suddenly Chrissie spots a sign board, not far from the bakers selling the nooons. 'Look, *Yemas de Abbey-la!*' she cries, delightedly. 'Let's get a bag and we can eat them walking along the wall.' In front of us is an old woman, bent and stooped with age, being guided slowly across the cobbles by her daughter, or a carer possibly. She raises a bony hand, and points shakily at the sign. *'Benga!'* Come on! *Yemas de Avila*. Let us get some *yemas de Avila*.' We smile warmly at this delightful tableau, and I am intrigued the old woman uses their full title, *'de Avila'*, as she is clearly a local out for her morning stroll. In Cornwall for example you would never hear a resident referring to a *Cornish* pasty, merely a pasty. Curious, and another little nugget to add to my already overcrowded brain. Which, as my wife would undoubtedly tell you, is full of such trivia, yet when it comes to important stuff...

We step back to allow the pair some space inside the tiny shop, and a great deal of excitable conversation ensues between them and the female assistant. I imagine this could well be a weekly treat for the old lady, a little ritual enacted every Sunday morning, and not for the first time I am gladdened by the ability of the Spanish to turn a mundane transaction into an event filled with joy and laughter. Even the days of my youth, when sweets were sold loose, making a selection from the ha'penny and penny trays in *The Chocolate Box* was something of an ordeal, what with Mr James glowering over us kids, miserable old sod as he was. Little fun in purchasing tuppence-worth of *Fruit Salads*, I can tell you.

The old lady must have a sweet tooth as she emerges from the shop with about a pound of the things in a paper bag, or whatever that is in kilograms, then spots us studying the display in the window. Hand trembling, she unwraps the bag and holds it out to us graciously. *'Degustacion!'* she smiles. A tasting. Chrissie daintily selects a yema, smiling, me likewise, as daintily as possible given that I am not particularly dainty, and I study the famous confectionery, which I had never even heard of half an hour ago. About half the size of my little finger, a lurid yellow in colour, slightly coarse in texture, I decide to do the dainty thing and bite the top off... and my eyes cross, and my tongue explodes. Sweet? Hell's teeth. This is off-the-scale sweet, like marzipan with added sweetness, with extra sweetness thrown in for good measure. Were I in a field, or out to sea, I could spit the vile concoction out, but clearly that is not an option in front of the smiling old girl, so I decide to swallow, and pray that no internal organs are irreparably damaged on the way down. Chrissie meanwhile is nodding her head, although whether in delight or whether her tonsils are about to detach themselves, is impossible to say. Consummate actress as she is, she gives a virtuoso performance out of thanking the pair very much, whereas I merely roll my eyes, convincingly as it turns out, although only I know that I am about to choke, and we move away.

I still have the other half of the thing in my palm, but dropping it down a drain is not an option in case the pair are watching, and I have no wish to be responsible for an ecological disaster, and I don't particularly want to shove it in my pocket, in case it burns a hole in my trousers, or worse, my thigh. What I really need is for one of those pesky pasty-stealing seagulls from St Ives to swoop down and pluck the thing from my fingers, whereupon I could wave my fist, dramatically, feigning anger, all the while giggling hysterically, privately. Revenge. 'Quick, have you got a bottle of water in your bag?' I gasp.

'MMM, MMM, UGGGG, AHHHH' she replies, puffing out her cheeks like a demented hamster, all the while rooting around desperately in the depths. Triumphantly, she snatches up the bottle, and takes a massive swig, rinsing her palate like a Frenchman in a wine cellar, selfishly leaving about an inch in the bottom for me, most of which I manage to dribble down my chin.

'So are you getting any *yemas de Avila,* after all that?' I wonder. 'Maybe take a bag home for Anna? It is the law, you know! Go on, I dare you!'

She glares at me for a few seconds, considering the challenge, then grins. 'That is a good idea, actually. Well done! Anna really loves them, for some inexplicable reason. We'll be back here again later I assume, when we've circumnavigated the walls? Don't let me forget.' *As if I could. I'll be tasting the thing until Christmas.* 'And what did you do with the other half of your *yema?*' she continues. 'You only bit the top off. Do you have it secreted about your person, somewhere?'

I cannot help a conspiratorial giggle. 'I flicked it into the open doorway of our favourite restaurant, as we were passing just a few seconds ago. I have a different shirt on this morning. They can't possibly recognise me!'

The first point to consider about the *Walking the Walls* experience is that only around two-thirds is actually open to the public, according to the sign in the ticket office, reinforcing my original opinion, perhaps, that the other side isn't actually finished, yet. Probably get round there to find the scaffolding still up. Spanish builders eh, what are they like? They promise to get it completed by the thirteenth century, yet here they are in the twenty-first, still standing around, shouting. Or sat under a parasol, more likely. Secondly, and more seriously, will we be able to get off, if we spot something we would like to visit? Like that open-top bus that goes round many tourist destinations? *Hop on, hop off, Wall Experience?* The problem with a 'flying' visit like this is that we cannot possibly see everything in one go, so we are regarding this weekend as a taster, as I am sure we will be visiting Rosa again next year, and can therefore identify the buildings we would like to explore in greater detail on a subsequent trip. Like that exquisite octagonal roof and round, leaded windows for instance. Will we ever be able to find it again, however, from ground level?

The walk begins at the highest point of the old city, laid out like a carpet before us, following the contours of the land in spectacular fashion. The only slight annoyance is that we are directed to the right, anti-clockwise, and we've already seen that bit from down below, but an entirely different perspective from up here, of course. The first thing we recognise is St Vincent's, outside the walls, somewhere we will most definitely visit again, then what appears to be a cathedral, or a large church, on the inside. This really is frustrating, actually, they did provide us with a plan showing the names of the different gates, for example the gate of *peso de la harina*, which I think translates as 'weight of the flour', where foodstuffs came through originally, I imagine, but inside the walls is a complete blank apart from the outline of the streets. Maybe there is a smart-phone app, for those with that sort of technology, and I'm sure we could have found one of those excellent *Eyewitness* guides, on eBay, if we'd thought about it. Or a newsagent-cum-bookshop here, had one existed.

Every twenty yards or so is a turret, and we have great fun poking our heads through the battlements like a pair of juveniles playing *wall whack-a-mole*, admiring the surrounding countryside, marveling at the buildings below, small squares, parks, gardens, and in one location, directly below us, a tuk-tuk parked next to a signboard. For me however the most enjoyable sections are the occasional glimpses of the wall as it curves gently around to the left, at the lowest part of the town. Away to the right, across some fields and trees, half a mile distant, possibly, we spot a group of coaches parked up, and small groups of tourists gathered around four stone columns supporting a roof, providing a shelter of some sort. 'Is that a Roman remain, do you think?' I puzzle. 'Looks a bit strange, stuck there, and very small to warrant tour groups? Must be something fairly important? Reminds me of a massive four-poster bed! Did giants walk this land, at the dawn of time?'

She narrows her eyes, studying the artefact. 'I think it's a view-point, look, all the people are facing this way, staring in this direction, taking pictures. Nobody is taking the slightest bit of notice of the four-poster. When this walk comes to an end, and we have to get off the wall, I think we should head over there, check it out.'

'Don't be daft' I scoff. 'The land over there is lower than here, surely? There cannot possibly be much of a view of the old city. Besides, I am still suffering from the after-effects of that damned *yema*, which was all your fault, by the way. I don't think my poor legs could make it that far!' And I grip the stone-work for dramatic effect. 'And look! There is the car, parked below by that grassy bank. Can't we drive over there, if we must? I think it's a waste of time, personally. You go, and tell me what it was like.' *If looks could kill…*

The lower portion of the walled city consists mainly of houses, which look suspiciously modern I have to say. Not *Barratt Homes* modern I don't mean, but less than a century, for sure. There must have been original housing down this far, presumably, otherwise why go to the trouble of extending the fortifi-cations, but what happened to the original dwellings? *And why didn't we have the sense to get a guide book?*

At the bottom of the slope, as the battlements continue to

the left, the walk comes to an end, sadly, and we have to get off. Exiting through a gateway which the map describes as the *puerta del puente*, the door of the bridge, we emerge into traffic, roundabouts and pedestrian crossings. I am rather hoping my wife has forgotten about visiting the four-poster, and that we can continue following the wall, at ground level, around the far side, which may or may not exist, but sadly no. 'Come on, this way!' Down through some trees, across a bridge, avoiding tour buses and bewildered-looking visitors, we emerge breathlessly on a grassy bank, topped by what the signpost describes as *los cuatro postes*. 'You were right!' Chrissie giggles, 'it is the four-poster, but someone has nicked the roof!'

'Well big deal' I puff. 'Who cares, I can't see damn-all... Oh my giddy aunt! Will you look at that?' And there it is, the whole city, laid out before us, encircled spectacularly by the fortifications, an irregular U-shape, the horizon dotted with church towers, the jumble of streets and houses below, the battlements and turrets, fluffy white clouds against an azure-blue sky, the honey-stone bathed in the late autumn sunshine. My heart sings, and my soul rejoices. I slump down on the grass, and drink in the whole magnificent, uplifting scene.

Chrissie joins me on the ground. 'Wouldn't this make a wonderful jigsaw puzzle?' she breathes, softly.

'Well it would, but I'd probably have to let you complete it!' I whisper, smiling. 'That is a great idea, actually. We could stick it to a board, get it framed, hang it above the patio window, maybe. The perfect momento to the perfect day. A real talking-point. Wouldn't it be great if we came across one in a shop, here?' Suddenly, some hairy-legged hiker in beige multipocketed cargo shorts, immaculate walking boots with brown woolly socks tucked in, and a ski-pole, stands directly in front of me. The moment is gone. Stifling the urge to grab his stick and shove it somewhere unpleasant, and painful, we rise to our feet, shaking our heads, then retrace our steps back through the *puerta del puente*, and continue our anti-clockwise circuit through the maze of streets, keeping the wall to our right.

Attempting to traverse the hotch-potch of narrow lanes without a guide-book is an object in monumental stupidity, and I cannot believe we have been so foolish. Or that I have been so foolish, as it is yours-truly who usually supplies the maps and guides, being a Capricorn and therefore organised to the nth degree. I blame old Crocodile Dundee actually. He brought us here, so the least he could have done would be to guide us around, explain what everything is, don't you think? *Not forgiven me for scoring over two-thousand runs against them, last summer, clearly.* What we are therefore doing, and this is no hardship actually in these delightful old streets, to hopefully ensure we see everything there is to see, regardless of whether or not it needs seeing, is more of a zig-zag, a left-then-right-then-straight-on-for-a-bit, and it is in this manner that we arrive at an old church, an entirely symmetrical four-storey grey stone facade flanked by two bell towers, a delightful *plaza* and about a hundred milling, chattering Spaniards. Thirty or so chairs have been thoughtfully laid out, so gratefully I plonk myself down, while Chrissie wanders off to see what is what. She likes doing that sort of thing. Gives her a little break from me.

'You cannot sit there!' I glance up to see an earnest-looking young man with a short-back-and-sides, brandishing a clipboard, bearing down.

I smile warmly. 'Two minutes only' I lie, as I'm going to need five, at least, and there is absolutely nowhere else to sit.

'You cannot sit there' he repeats. 'You need a ticket for the *obra*.'

A performance of some sort. 'How much is the ticket?'

'Two euros.'

'One ticket, please!' Has to be worth it, as suddenly I am overcome by fatigue. Chrissie can always stand at the back.

He seems somewhat flustered suddenly. 'You cannot buy ticket here, for this you must go to the tourist office.'

'And where is the tourist office, please?'

He frowns in concentration. 'Top of the town, through the gate of *peso de la harina*, turn left, it is there. Where you get all tickets. Tourist office, sell maps and guides.' *If he mentions jigsaw puzzles I will scream. The tourist office. Where we bought the wall tickets. They sell maps and guides apparently. Is there something hard I can beat my head against?* 'But you cannot sit there.'

Suddenly, salvation appears, in the form of twenty or so Spanish teenagers, most of whom are carrying identical backpacks. A church group, possibly. They fling down their bags and sprawl across the chairs, as only teenagers can. And the noise! A Rangers v Celtic Scottish Old-Firm derby crowd makes less racket than twenty Spanish kids. Mister Earnest was struggling with me, now he simply gives up, and scuttles away. Through the melee weaves my giggling wife. 'BLIMEY, WHO ARE YOUR FRIENDS? CAN WE GO SOMEWHERE QUIETER?' And she flaps a leaflet at me. *Good job I didn't buy that ticket…*

She leads me towards the church doorway, where we can at least hear ourselves think. 'This is the convent of St Teresa of Jesus' she confirms. 'I am translating this, so bear with me, but it seems quite straightforward. She was a Carmelite nun born in fifteen-fifteen as a noblewoman, her house was actually under this building, and those are the coats of arms of her parents' families, carved on the front of the church, up there. And we can visit the place where she was born, in what is now the crypt. She is one of the patron saints of Spain. She was a writer, religious reformer and theologian. She performed a miracle by saving her injured nephew when a building fell on him, and it is only one-fifty for us pensioners to visit. Are you coming?'

Cheaper than a seat? Why not. Inside the convent a service appears to be in progress so we tiptoe around so as not to disturb the congregation, a ludicrous notion given the noise filtering through from the outside. Rangers have just nicked the winning goal, it would seem. We are however able to admire the richly engraved altar-piece, and religious artwork adorning the walls, but it is the family home we are better able to esteem, in relative tranquility, the centrepiece of which is a single, wooden four-poster bed with rich crimson hangings. A delightful stained glass window depicts a young Theresa in a white flowing robe, hand in hand with her nephew, accompanied by a horseman astride a magnificent white steed, although for me the *piece de resistance* is the view through an opened window of a small walled garden, featuring stone sculptures of the girl, aged twelve or thereabouts, clutching a prayer book, with the boy, surrounded by fallen stones, a number of which he has arranged into the shape of a church building, seated on the ground around her feet. An interpretation of the miracle, I imagine, with perhaps the little church representing the nephew's grateful thanks at his salvation?

Weaving our way back through the crowds, past the sprawling kids, none of whom have given up two euros for the privilege, we decide to exit the old city through the gate of *La Santa*, the saint, and complete the circuit from the outside, following the wall to the top of town, then through the gate of *peso de la harina* one final time to the hotel to retrieve our bag, having first purchased a bag of *yemas* for Anna. They can then go in the boot of the car for the remainder of the holiday, under the spare tyre, to avoid possible contamination. This final section of wall, the secret side, the one I doubted actually existed, is a delight, with a broad, paved boulevard running alongside, occasional glimpses of the countryside to the south of the town through the trees... deciduous trees... with piles of fallen leaves on the ground... Yippee! Like a couple of kids, *'through autumn's golden gown we kick our way'*. Justin Hayward of course, *Forever Autumn*, and something we truly miss, living in Andalucia, the home of scrubby pines and evergreen olives. So here we make up for it, to the bemusement of a group of Japanese tourists, but hell, we've not done this for years. 'Hang on a minute' my wife laughs, 'these are horse chestnut, aren't they? And where there be horse chestnut, there be conkers! Quick, look, over there, grab them, before someone else does! Yay! Conkers! We can take a bagful back for Louise!'

Indeed. Conker trees they are. Not the solid, sturdy, venerable variety you see adorning British village greens, these are young, lithe, whippy Spanish trees, but conkers nevertheless, the tell-tale spiky outer cases littering the grass, some already open, yellowing, the very colour of autumn, the rich, luxurious, deep-brown nut peeking out seductively, just waiting to be prized open, taken home, carefully drilled, knotted string threaded, soaked in vinegar or baked in the oven if you were a cheat, which I never was, I promise, then taken to the playground to hopefully smash Dave Tout's champion *sixer* to oblivion. And Dave Tout along with it, if my aim was off, which it invariably was. The hours I must have spent, in the days of my youth, and not just my youth either as I taught our girls this, lobbing bits of fallen branches into conker trees, to encourage the bounty to fall. And our elder daughter Louise was, and still is, terrified of spiders, and used to adorn her bedroom, and outside her door, with a protective shield of conkers, in the belief they acted as a repellent, whereupon our faithful retriever Nelson felt it his duty to retrieve and redistribute the nuts around the house so that we never knew where they'd turn up next, the cause of much pain, and a great deal of swearing, to tread on one, barefoot, particularly the instep, in the middle of the night, en-route to the bathroom.

Soon, my pockets are bulging with the nuts, proving, perhaps, that within every man lurks the schoolboy he once was. I glance at Chrissie and cannot help giggling to witness her gently placing her collection into a plastic carrier bag. 'Where did you find that?' I demand, wincing, reminded as I am that conkers are notorious for finding every painful crevice within a pocket, and groin, as every schoolboy knows.

'In my handbag, of course' she smiles, 'you know me, prepared for every eventuality!'

'Well grab hold of this lot then!' I grimace, rooting furiously in my pockets, and dropping several large handfuls in with hers. 'And don't worry, I'll carry them' I add, forestalling the inevitable protest, wondering, maybe, why I had not thought of transporting a plastic bag halfway across Spain. *Obvious really. I don't have a handbag...*

She glances at the sizeable pile within. 'I think we have enough now, don't you? Just remember, we have to get this lot past Malaga airport security!'

'No!' I frown, gazing anxiously at the fallers still strewn across the grass, because, once again as every schoolboy knows, you have to gather every single conker, before the big kids come for them. 'I want to keep a few for myself, thread them up, and teach my students how to play. It's obvious Spanish kids know nothing of this tradition, judging by what is left here. What sort of a country is this, not playing conkers? You know, you could even teach Victor!'

'Oh really?' she sniggers. 'Can you see Victor doing that? He would probably be sat on the sidelines with a glass of milk, *Ship or Sheep* open on his lap 'thees ees too danger-oos!'

Tearing myself reluctantly away, against all my youthful instincts, we complete our circumnavigation of this delightful old town, rounding the final corner, to be confronted by a curious, larger-than-life-size sculpture of a nun, St Theresa presumably, in later life, adopting the strangest posture, sprawling against a wall, right hand resting on an opened book, head and upper torso canted back, as if tossed and blown by a sudden gust of wind, or drenched by muddy, oily puddle-water by a passing juggernaut. Eyes firmly closed, lips pursed, her whole demeanour displays, for me, intense irritation, as opposed to the angelic smile of her youthful self back in the convent. The sculptor has done her no favours, certainly. 'Looks like someone just gave her a *yema*' Chrissie laughs. 'And speaking of which, there is the shop, still open. You wait here, we don't want any more theatrics, do we? I won't be long.'

'Get her to wrap them in a layer of insulation!' I cry, to her retreating back.

A few minutes later she returns, carrying, at arms length, like one of the Three Kings approaching downtown Bethlehem, a brightly coloured package. 'Here you go, a kilo, in a sealed polythene bag, and I told her they were a present so she kindly wrapped them. Stick them in with the conkers, will you?'

I recoil. 'No fear! I'm not having my precious conkers polluted! I came halfway across Spain to get them. It was your idea, Anna is your student, you carry them! And how much were they?'

She grabs the carrier, and a brief tussle ensues, which she wins, of course. 'Not telling you. And it was your idea, don't forget!'

I narrow my eyes. 'I said, how much were they?'

She sighs. 'Don't worry, I paid. Your precious credit-card remains unscathed.'

I decide to leave it there. Besides, I can maybe trick her into a confession, during an unguarded moment. 'Well, if they were more than five-bob, you was robbed!'

Through the *peso de la harina* for one final time, we wind our way back towards the hotel. Which cannot come quickly enough, with the weight of my precious conkers, and these cursed *yemas*. Have you ever heard anything like it? A KILO? Hell, I only meant two ounces. Suddenly she stops abruptly, narrowly avoiding a pile-up involving danger-oos confectionery. 'Oh look' she hisses. 'A bookshop. A closed bookshop. A closed-because-it's-Sunday-and-they-only-work-Spanish-hours bookshop. Which we passed yesterday evening when I'm willing to bet they were open because-they-work-Spanish-hours bookshop. And what is that in the window? An Avila guide. And what do I spy on the shelves towards the back? Jigsaw puzzles by any chance?'

I take a deep breath and gaze, in exasperation, at the heavens. 'Oh well, don't worry about it, don't blame yourself, it was an easy mistake to make, it wasn't your fault. We've had a great couple of days here, haven't we, even though we didn't really know what we were looking at? And we'll be back, for sure. Next time, you will be better organised!' And I step back, and hold up the carrier as a shield, from the inevitable wallop.

We eventually reach the car, stow the bag, and the *yemas*, and fire up Mister Dundee. 'Hey mate, what's that terrible honk?' he complains, 'open the window, will yer?' As we drive slowly away, I gaze in the mirror for one last, fleeting glimpse of the battlements. I loved it here. We loved it here. But I tell you what, those walls really do look suspiciously new...

CHAPTER 15. SE-GO-BIA

With only forty or so miles to our next destination, we can afford to take our time, and puzzle over my latest quandary. Namely, how can two different towns, so close together, be famous for two entirely different dishes? Every single Spaniard we spoke to about visiting Avila and Segovia said the same thing; chooly-ton and coachy-knee-o. Not what there was to see, simply what there was to eat. And most hadn't even visited. I reckon it's a fairy-tale, or a marketing wheeze. Chrissie however is far more charitable. 'It's exactly the same in

Britain' she argues. 'Bakewell tart. Wensleydale cheese. Melton Mowbray pork pies. Stilton. Have you ever been to any of those towns? No. But I bet if a Spaniard, or anyone else, told you they were visiting those locations, you would tell them they simply had to try those delicacies.'

I remain unconvinced. 'What I am saying is that we didn't see a single cow, on the way to Abbey-la, no lush meadows, green pastures full of herds of cattle. And have you spotted a single pig yet, on this journey? Not a one. I think they buy them in, both places. It's just not feasible, to me, for one to be famous for this, the other for that, when they are virtually next door to each other. The hand of cynical big business, for sure.'

Mind you, the countryside is changing, becoming wilder, rockier, with each passing mile. The light, too, has a strange, slightly eerie quality, diffused somehow, despite the bright sunshine, reminiscent of Dartmoor, or possibly the Peak District or the Yorkshire Dales, although I've never been to either, as my wife was keen to point out. Maybe the altitude, although this is hardly the foothills of the Himalayas, but it does make a welcome, pleasant change from the harsh glare of the south. Suddenly, she sits bolt upright. 'Blimey, look at that woman, lying down.'

Instinctively, I hammer on the brakes, juddering to an inelegant, spluttering halt. 'Where? Is she injured? Is she OK?'

She has her hand over her mouth, tittering helplessly. 'Sorry, she's not a real woman, it is that mountain, over there! On the horizon. The shape of a woman, look, she is on her side, her head is on the left, her hip on the right, then her leg outstretched. Can you see that?'

I am struggling to hide my fury. 'I've just burned an inch off the tyres and the brakes all because of some woman who's been dead about a million years… oh yes, I see what you mean. Like a giant sculpture. Uncanny, the likeness, but don't do that again to me, please, my nerves cannot stand it! And if the bag of *yemas* has burst in the boot, you are clearing them up!'

Soon, a little town appears, sitting snugly into a valley, and Dundee confirms we have indeed arrived. Remarkably, I spot both the hotel on the right, and a free station car-park opposite, so I glide effortlessly into a vacant space, switch off the engine, then jump out and theatrically examine each of the tyres for signs of excess wear. Which earns me a gentle kick on the back-side. One of the things I love about this country is the apparent unwillingness, or reluctance, of local authorities to monetize car parking, unless your name is Malaga airport, as we have seen, and to me it is indicative of how councils here encourage the public to shop locally, which in turn aids local business. The Town Hall is out to help, rather than screw the local taxpayer for every last penny. Might be worth trying in the UK? Just saying.

Our 'hotel' turns out to be a large bar with a small guest house attached, and we enter to find the proverbial old man with a dog watching TV, the dog I mean as the old man is watching us, and a woman of indeterminate age beside the bar, who might or might not happen to be the proprietor. Three pairs of eyes are following us as we enter, the dog no doubt bored with the action on the telly, and I feel like a gunslinger entering a Western saloon, albeit without the benefit of a Colt forty-five should it turn ugly. Not that I am expecting trouble, but I always feel that frisson of apprehension right about now, in case the place denies all knowledge of our booking. 'Good afternoon, we have a reservation for tonight' I smile, in my best text-book Spanish, having been warned by our local friends not to use the sloppy Andalucian dialect in this part of the country, where they apparently speak correct. Sorry, correctly. We have to pronounce every letter 'S' for example, *'buenas dias'* and not *'bwenna dia'*, *'adios'* and not *'dee-aww'*, if we don't want to come across as uneducated peasants. Heaven forbid. Not that this place resembles the Court of King Felipe, mind you.

She grins, gappily, and beckons us through to a lobby, where
she disappears into a cupboard, slides back a pane of diffused
glass, revealing a reception the size of a ticket booth in a small-
town, pre-war cinema. She is a strange one, and no doubt,
clearly having had a psychotic 'oh sod it' episode when getting
dressed and applying her make-up this morning, deciding, on
the spur of the moment, to utilise everything in her cosmetics
box, to avoid complicated choices. Orange hair scraped back severely across her scalp, eyebrows highlighted and lengthened
by black felt-tip pen, sparkly green eye-shadow, eye-liner from
a tin of Hammerite, leaving her lashes in clumps, every finger
adorned with chunky silver rings, or possibly knuckle-dusters,
and red lipstick with the merest hint of Coco the Clown. Her
ensemble is complimented by a frilly white blouse, a volumin-
ous, batik-print skirt, depicting a herd of elephants all moving
in different directions, and flip-flops. Is she channeling her pirate, pantomime dame or circus look, or a combination of all
three? But hey, whatever gets you through the night, as they
say, and I can hardly shout, dressed as I am in a short-sleeve
shirt, when every single Spaniard is trussed up in a winter
coat. She probably thinks I am bonkers.

Anyway, her people-skills are far superior to the miserable
woman of yesterday, and this is all decidedly, refreshingly non-
corporate. Check-in takes but a few, brief, pleasant moments,
she hopes we will join her for breakfast in the morning, and
hands us a plank of wood, engraved with the number eleven,
with a small key attached. Why do they do that in country hotels? This hunk of timber certainly won't go into my pocket,
without causing catastrophic damage all round, I doubt it will
even fit in Chrissie's bag, and everyone takes the key off anyway, don't they? One of life's little mysteries. Up the stairs to
the first floor, then, oh no, no, no, please no. A fountain. An
indoor fountain, slap bang in the middle of the landing, and

not a million miles from room elev.... oh God, not again, my waterworks will not stand this torture two nights running. Standing over six feet high, ceramic, glazed in multiple colours like Joseph's coat, shaped as a giant triffid, roots, branches, a mouth, and teeth, all combined in some nightmare-inducing, post apocalyptic vision, and an unwelcome reminder of my schoolboy English Literature classes. *The poems of Robert Frost, The History of Mr Polly,* and of course, *The Day of the Triffids.* And there was me, a simple *Beano* reader.

My wife however is fascinated. 'Ooh, it reminds me of one of my carnivorous plants, at home. Do you like it?'

'Certainly not.'

'Hmmmm. Do you think it is a suitable ornament for a hotel lobby?'

'Absolutely not.'

'Do you think it is plumbed in?'

'Christ, I hope not!' I splutter. 'This object wouldn't emit a gentle tinkle like the one last night, more like a powerful jet from a water-cannon at a Parisian riot!'

She ponders a moment. 'Is this the weirdest hotel we've stayed in?'

'A candidate, for sure.'

'So do you want to see if we can find a Travelodge somewhere?'

'Not in the slightest!' I grin. 'You know me, I like weird, weird suits me.'

She giggles. 'So is that someone I can hear having sex in room twelve?'

My senses snap to attention, having hitherto been turned down to about two on the dial, where they usually reside, and to my ears comes the unmistakable, rhythmic sound of creaking bed-springs, accompanied by soft, feminine whimpering, and heavy male grunting. A leisurely spot of late-afternoon coitus is indeed taking place, unless she is administering CPR. One never knows how to proceed in these situations, does one? Do I cough, theatrically, break into a round of applause, or tap on the door and enquire if she needs me to summon an ambulance? None of the above. We proceed in a British manner, keeping calm and carrying on, tiptoe to our door and stumble into the pitch darkness, whilst I grapple with three pairs of blackout curtains, which I am about to rip unceremoniously from their rails, before Chrissie comes to my rescue and gently untangles the mess, revealing an unspectacular view of the station car park, and platform two. 'Do you want to check if our bed-springs squeak, also?' I purr, romantically.

'No need' she snorts, derisively, 'they will, under the weight of your fat arse.'

See what I mean? Anyway, we have this bridge of stones, and castle of Disney to find, and like any intrepid explorer I know the way into town, having previously expanded the map on the Booking site, *as we have no guidebook, you see.* Out of the hotel and turn left, basically, which is more or less what David Livingstone did, up the Zambezi. After a quick freshen up, all is quiet next door, indicating they are either basking in the afterglow, or in the back of an ambulance, and we follow the nondescript main road in a generally downhill direction, to where the good bit starts, hopefully. And it takes a while to start, I have to say, even though I knew it was a mile or so from the centre, when I made the booking, for reasons of economy, failing to take into account the fact that we would have already been on our feet for over four hours, this morning. I've cocked-up, again. Chrissie is complaining, as are my legs. 'See what happens when a man, a tight-wad man, is allowed to book the accommodation?' she groans. 'Remember the hotel last night?

The one I booked? Right bang slap in the middle of town? But oh no, you couldn't do that, you had to book something right out in the sticks, run by a woman from the end of the pier show, with a John Wyndhamesque figure stuck outside our room, and a copulating couple banging away next door, just so you could save a few quid?' *What can I say. Guilty as charged.*

Suddenly, thankfully, we have arrived. The road levels out, we pass a colonnaded church on our right, turn a corner, entering what appears to be a pedestrianised street, and there it is, towering over the surrounding buildings, dominating the landscape. A viaduct. An ancient, browny-grey stone, multi-arched viaduct. Or is it an aqueduct? Cannot tell yet. What is the difference? One is a pathway, one a waterway? A canal? A railway? Could be, there's a station up the road. We need to get closer. The avenue is, I don't know, thirty feet wide, flanked on either side by attractive four-storey buildings, in tasteful pastel shades, complete with wrought-iron balustrades, cafes and bars crowded together, jostling for business, at street level, and crossing at right-angles is the duct, the whatever-duct, the we'll-find-out-shortly-duct. From back here we can only see three arches, double arches, one on top the other, the bigger at the bottom, entirely symmetrical, and it is difficult to tell just how wide the structure is, or how tall. Transfixed, dodging the milling tourists, we edge slowly towards it, savouring this once-in-a-lifetime moment of discovery, as the panorama opens up, and the true scale of the monument is revealed.

Breathtaking, awe-inspiring, we are now in a massive plaza, and there it is, our something-duct, claiming the space, standing tall, and proud, as it has for the best part of two millennia, for surely this dates from the Roman period. It must be approaching a hundred feet high, constructed from rough-cut stone, each one precisely the same height, two feet or thereabouts, and varying in width from a foot to maybe three, placed, seemingly without benefit of mortar, so that it would be possible to count them. At the base, each pillar is maybe six feet square, narrowing imperceptibly as they rise, so this is clearly an aqueduct, for drinking water I imagine, as the top can only be four feet across. To the right, it climbs gradually up a hillside, lined with cafes, each arch progressively shorter in height, to maintain the horizontal aspect, although there must be a 'run' of a couple of degrees to maintain the flow, but which way, right to left or vise-versa, is impossible to tell with the naked eye. How did they do that? To the left meanwhile, it reaches a rocky cliff, topped by a castellated wall, then disappears into what appears to be a fortress, complete with a spire.

At the foot of what I presume to be the 'central' pillar is a stone cross, fifteen feet high, and directly above that, in the middle of the second, smaller row of arches, is a small shrine, dedicated to what appears to be a religious figure, a later addition I would imagine. Chrissie grips my arm and I fully expect her to gush admiringly at the magnificence of the whole scene. Not a bit of it. She starts to sing, softly.

'Honey! Na na na na, na na,

Ah, sugar sugar, na na na na, na na,

You are my candy girl,

And you got me wanting you!

What the...? 'Why are you singing that American, comic-book crap by some non-existent group of...'

'The Archies!' she giggles. 'Get it? The Archies, the arches, all these arches, reminded me of the song. *I'm gonna make your life so sweet, hey hey hey, pour a little sugar on it baby...'*

I remove my arm in disgust. 'Here we are, confronted by two thousand years of history, here I am, trying to fathom out how the whole thing worked, and you have a head-full of some frivolous, throw-away ditty, which I despised by the way, and will now be humming for the rest of the day. AND it knocked Bobbie Gentry off the number-one spot, for God's sake, that soppy, cartoon shi...'

She retrieves my arm, and squeezes it tighter. 'Don't worry your tiny man-brain about it, I've figured it out already! The spring, or stream, rises on the high ground to the right, not a million miles from our hotel, I imagine, and was diverted by a series of channels, or leats, into the aqueduct, from where it ran, right to left, into that castle. What I find curious...'

'You cheeky swine!' I splutter. 'That was my idea! I thought of it first! You read my mind!' And I attempt to release her grip, but she is not letting go, and a small tussle ensues.

'As I was saying, before I was rudely interrupted' she continues, tightening her hold, 'what is strange is that we were taught in history classes at school, that in Britain, settlements originated next to a regular, reliable water supply, namely a river, and fortifications grew up there. In Spain however, they tended to build their castles on high ground, and were forced to rely on rainwater, which they stored in those huge stone reservoirs within the foundations, you remember we've seen those strange features in several of the forts we have visited in Andalucia, what do they call them, *al-he-bays*? And as we know, zero rain falls for seven months of the year, and the remainder is fitful, to say the least. So maybe that was what happened here, there simply wasn't enough rain water to sustain the growing city, up there behind those walls on the left. Mind you, *we don't have a guide-book, do we?* But that is what I think happened.'

Possible, isn't it? She might be correct. 'What I was wondering' I smile, 'is what the people who lived down here thought about them sticking a dirty great aqueduct outside their windows, blocking the light. Just imagine it, waking up one morning, open your windows, out on your balcony for a stretch, inhale the fresh morning air, WHAT THE HELL IS THAT? What did the Romans do for us? Nicked our sunshine, that's what, just so those rich bastards up on the hill could have a bath. That is what I think happened. Always the little man who gets trodden on, isn't it? Especially when there are Romans involved!' And I suppress a giggle.

She drops my arm in mock disgust. 'Even you aren't that dim! This street is less than a hundred years old, I imagine, it only exists to keep the tourists fed and watered. Speaking of which, is there any chance of us getting a morsel to eat, this night? Are you planning on sniffing out some *coachy-knee-o*, any time soon?'

There is indeed, hopefully, although firstly I suggest we climb the steps to the left, below the castle, to maybe gain sufficient elevation to look down on the actual watercourse, atop the structure, to satisfy my curiosity as to what the flow might have been. Sadly not. After puffing our way breathlessly as high as we can go, we are still a good few feet shy, although a wonderful aspect opens up of the aqueduct, straight as a die for, ooh, four hundred yards, before it curves sharply to the left, the land gaining altitude all the while, the arches be-coming progressively shorter until the lower row disappears altogether on the bend, the top of the structure meanwhile perfectly horizontal. *How did they do that?*

Disappointingly however, to our left, on the opposite side of the structure from where we were first standing, all pretence of antiquity disappears amid a whole swathe of land un-necessarily cleared for what appears to be a dual carriageway, complete with a roundabout, a coach park, zebra crossings, road signs and about an acre of tarmac, all going absolutely nowhere as there is a dirty great *bridge of stones* in the way. Town planning at its most hideous. Like the council held a 'how can we comprehensively bugger-up the surroundings of an ancient monument' competition. Mind you, the best candidate certainly won, so that is all right then.

Averting our gaze from this prime example of twentieth-century cultural vandalism, concentrating instead on this marvel of first or second century engineering, and in my case, at least, ensuring I don't trip headlong and break my neck whilst admiring said engineering, we descend the stone steps back to street level in search of nourishment. 'So are you intending to pay for my coachy-knee-o?' I enquire pleasantly.

'What?'

'Well, you remember you said last night you were going to buy me the chooly-ton, on account of me being such a wonderful husband, and an all-round ruddy nice bloke, but all I ended up with was hammy broccoli, having donated my fish to your cause? Well I just wondered if you intended making-good on your promise, that was all?'

She smiles warmly, and grips my arm. 'Of course! Providing it's not thirty euros!'

An image of the doormat-sized steak flashes through my mind. 'Hell, I hope not, I don't need any more surprises like that. What can this stuff be, a pork chop, or a cutlet, something similar? Much less than a tenner, for sure. So shall we check out these restaurants up the hill, then the ones in the main street if the veggie options don't look good? And for heaven's sake remind me to specify *sin carney*, when we order yours, we don't want a repeat of last night's chaos, do we?'

Enticingly, although somewhat precariously, tables and chairs have been set out on the cobbled street, and I chuckle to myself at the thought of spending the entire meal gripping the table, to prevent myself either tipping backwards, or sliding forwards, depending which way I was facing. 'We cannot eat there!' my wife giggles, as if reading my mind. 'You would have your food in your lap, or in mine, for sure! We need to find OH

THE POOR THING, GOD THAT IS DISGUSTING, GET ME AWAY FROM HERE.'

I have not been paying attention. I am thinking of something else. I am facing the other way. Always I am facing the other way. I turn, to see her with her head in her hands, retching, and there, on the wall behind her is a sign, that sign, the sign I will forever associate with Segovia, in my mind. Eighteen inches square, maybe, a sign, a hateful sign, bolted to the wall, bearing the legend *Cochinillo Asado para llevar*. Below that, the English translation. *Roasted suckling pigs made to order.* And below that, to my horror, is an illustration, a photograph, or a painting, I know not which, and care even less, of a baby piglet, lying on his or her stomach, legs spread out front and back, eyes open, lips parted in a grotesque grin, in a roasting dish, skin basted, seasoned, browned, cooked. Sickening.

Shocked to the core by this graphic, hideous notice, in the *street* no less, the restaurant clearly oblivious to the sensibilities of passers-by, I step quickly between my wife and the image, slip my arm around her shoulder and lead her gently away. 'I am sorry' she sniffs, composing herself, 'but I cannot possibly sit there and watch you eat one of those.'

'I cannot possibly sit there and eat one of those' I reassure her. 'It is vile. How could anyone...' And I shake my head, in a futile attempt to dispel the trauma from my mind. Distressingly, this area appears to be *Cochinillo Central*, as out of the corner of my eye it appears that every different location has cartoon illustrations, or in one place, a life-size, authentically-coloured model, in the windows. Gratefully, we make it around the corner, into the pedestrianised street, without further mishap, or images of you-know-what. It is our fault of course, my fault, for failing to carry out any research whatsoever, which would have at least prepared us for what to expect. The problem now of course is to find somewhere safe to eat, somewhere devoid of dreadful pictorial matter. A vegetarian restaurant perhaps?

Well fat chance of that, in this country, away from the coast, or outside of the big cities, particularly in this citadel of meat. *What to do?*

Glancing around, it becomes apparent that dusk has caught up with us, lights twinkling in the street and in the bars, reflecting majestically on the stones of the monument, bathed in warm, golden tones against the deep blue of the evening sky. Spectacular. The soft murmur of conversation drifts lazily into the air, indicating that the customers are tourists, at this relatively early hour, the Spanish all being at home, still, gossiping, getting ready. The place will liven up no doubt, when they arrive, later, by which time we will be safely tucked up in bed, hopefully, as I am flagging, and I imagine Chrissie is too. *What to do?* Suddenly, from behind me, comes a familiar refrain. 'JOSE, POR FAVOR! MARIA, POR FAVOR! ANTONIO, POR FAVOR!' A Hundred Montaditos! To the rescue! Our saviour! Where is it? Get in there! Grab a table! I cast around, frantically, to see that my wife has already beaten me to it, having claimed the perfect table for a spot of people-watching, at the edge of the melee, where she is already perusing the menu. She giggles, as I approach. 'Where have you been? Right, number eleven please, cream cheese, tomato and guacamole, number eighteen, goats cheese and pesto, number fifty-six, brie, caramelised onions and honey mustard, and a *campechana* salad, lettuce, tuna, hard boiled eggs, olives and onion. Oh yes, a glass of *tinto de verano*. Go on, hurry up!'

I decide to string it out, however, while I am making my selections. 'So you don't mind eating in, what was it you said, Woolworth's?'

'Yeah, well, I learned my lesson, all right?' she huffs.

I narrow my eyes, theatrically. 'Well, I cannot wait to tell our Spanish friends about how we came all the way up here to this capital city of *Cochinillo*, and you dived into Hundred Montaditos! Mind you, so did I! Oh by the way, did you slip my Swiss Army knife into your bag, like you usually do, for cutting up the oranges on the journey?'

She rolls her eyes. 'So how else did I manage to hand you segments of orange, and apple, on Friday, yesterday and today? And why are you asking me this now, when I am about to flake-out with hunger?'

I put on my serious face. 'Well I might need it later, with that triffid, outside our room.'

'What?' she splutters, 'are you planning on fighting it, with that thing for getting the stones out of a horse's hoof?'

I break out into a huge grin. 'No, but if it is fountaining away when we get back, I'm gonna take the damn plug off!'

So anyway, her choices eventually arrived, as did mine, were devoured with apparent relish, and let me tell you, not a trace of chopped ham was to be found anywhere. Which has to be a result, right? Particularly in Woolworth's.

During the night, as always, I wake to attend to a call of nature, to feel her shaking in the darkness, apparently in tears. I instantly sit bolt upright and scramble blindly for the bedside light switch, knocking the TV remote, and Gideon's Bible, off the table. 'What is wrong? Are you OK?' I whisper, not wishing to add to her distress, or disturb our fellow guests. She has her hand across her mouth, but is laughing, not crying, and puts her finger to her lips, in a 'shush' gesture. And through the wall comes the unmistakable sound of rhythmic mattress abuse and protesting bed springs, this time to the accompaniment of male whimpering, and heavy female grunting. 'Bloody hell!' I splutter, all pretence of neighbourly goodwill evaporating. 'She is giving him one now! What is it next door, the honeymoon suite?'

Chrissie is dabbing her eyes. 'I think I would want somewhere better than this for a honeymoon, don't you? The Seychelles, rather than platform one?'

'Well I feel like holding up a scorecard, like that Craig Revel Horwood bloke on Strictly Come Dancing.' I snigger. 'That rumba was grounds for divorce. FOUR!'

'I think they deserve a little song, don't you?' she grins. 'Come on, after me, one, two, three, four *'Honey! Na na na na, na na, Ah, sugar sugar, na na na na, na na.....'*

Next morning, bleary-eyed, we stumble down to breakfast, to find another couple already seated, oblivious to their surroundings, looking mightily chipper for this time in the morning, tucking in to what appears to be breakfast for five. Double rations of *tostada*, plus a large plate of *churros*, the deep-fried lengths of fatty donut beloved by Spaniards, with a pint of dipping chocolate, to ensure the arteries get a good coating. She is about eighteen stone, with dark Charles the Second ringlets down to her shoulders, like someone has inflated a spaniel with a bicycle pump. He meanwhile resembles a coal-miner who hasn't surfaced for over a week, or bothered to wash or change his clothes, before he came out. He needs sandblasting, followed by a good hose down. And there, on the table, is what looks suspiciously like a plank of wood engraved with the number twelve. *Oh my God.*

Chrissie meanwhile has already found a table, on the opposite side of the room, and has been collared by the proprietress, who is enquiring whether we passed a good night. *Yeah, apart from my sweat-drenched nightmare featuring some invasive killer weed rampaging outside our door, roots heaving and pulsating, tentacle-like branches writhing and contorting, the two of us fighting it off with a pair of tweezers and a flat-head screwdriver from a Swiss Army knife, all the while attempting in vain to rip out the plug, interspersed by recorded highlights of the Segovia sex olympics in the next room, with commentary by David Coleman, we slept like babies. At least there were no trains.* Our host has changed her attire, all of it, to a fetching shade of navy blue, yet to my untutored eyes at least, she is wearing the same make-up. Now look, I'm a bloke, I don't understand these things, I've never worn lipstick, unless you count that night at the rugby club, where it was forcibly applied, by several burly prop-forwards, but not to my lips. Chrissie rarely wears cosmetics, as I tell her she doesn't need it, which must earn me a few brownie-points, surely? She is more of a perfume girl, not, sadly, the feminine equivalent of 'Old Spice', but the eyewateringly expensive variety they sell in airports. 'I only need the merest little puff' she always claims, a sentiment with which I wholeheartedly agree. But I do know this. My Mother used to perform her nightly ritual of make-up removal, with her jar of *Oil of Ulay*, as it was known in those days, chattering away whilst Dad and I attempted to watch *Sportsnight, Match of the Day*, or other far more important pursuits. Maybe it is different nowadays.

The lady takes our order, which contains no *churros*, or pints of chocolate, and flip-flops away. My wife holds up her hands. 'Don't say it, DO NOT SAY ANYTHING. I saw the key on their table, OK? Let's just leave it there, shall we? Breakfast will be here in a few minutes, and I would like to enjoy it without further input from you.'

'I am merely disappointed' I grimace, standing, having spotted a pile of A4-sized tourist maps on a side-table next to the bar, 'I am disappointed she didn't give us one of these yesterday, I wasn't planning on mentioning the Danish porn-stars next door whatsoever.'

'SHUT UP!'

I wander across the room, grinning, and gently extract a map from the heap, then spread it out on our table. 'Now look at this. That brown line must be the aqueduct, and it begins not far from here, in *Avenida del Padre Claret*. What is that, Father Red-Wine Avenue? So after breakfast, I think we should head over there, and follow the thing from its source, down the hill where we were last night, then up the steps, into the old city, which must be that oval area with a wall around it. It looks like there are dozens of monuments, but that big one on the far left, protruding out over the river below, number 21, yes the *Alcazar*, the palace, or citadel, which might just be this castle of Disney? Let me translate, centuries eleven to fourteen, constructed *sobre*... over a Roman fort... residence of the Kings of Castille in the Middle Ages... it was a state prison... converted to the Royal College of Artillery in 1764... suffered a big fire in 1862... took until 1896 to rebuild, thirty-four years, typical Spanish!... it doesn't actually say that of course, but reading between the lines... and we can visit most of the monument. So how's that for a plan?'

Breakfast arrives, and is consumed leisurely, yet even after we have finished, and paid the extremely modest bill, the porn stars are still ploughing away at theirs, Charles the Second having upended the jug to her lips in order to ensure the last remaining droplets of chocolate aren't wasted. This is a good thing clearly, as it means we can pack our bag and vacate the room before they return and continue where they left off last night. It's not the sound of the mattress I mind particularly, but Coleman's voice can get a bit irritating, I find.

Father Red-Wine avenue is easily found, after one or two wrong-turnings, and the odd blind-alley, but as we approach I cannot help a modest chuckle... no scratch that, I feel as boastful as hell, for there it is, in front of us, the new-born aqueduct, the infant aqueduct. And not another tourist in sight. Down in the town, I bet there are hundreds milling around, yet here we are, at the source, alone, and I cannot help but bask in the glo....

'IS THAT IT?' complains my unappreciative wife. 'A wall? You brought us all the way over here to look at a WALL?'

'Nay, nay and thrice nay!' I splutter, offended. 'Not merely a wall, but a baby aqueduct. Look.' And we approach the admittedly ordinary-looking four-foot high structure, which features a channel down the middle, big enough for my arm, maybe, but hardly the Zambezi, it is true.

'So if this is the end,' she sniffs, 'how did the water get in there? The channel is four feet off the ground. I know the Romans were clever, but even they couldn't make water run uphill. Could they?'

I am still doing my best to look displeased. 'But this is not the end, is it? Don't you see? This is the beginning, the start, the commencement. This is a metaphor for life itself....'

'Oh will you ever cut the bullshit and just take a damn picture!'

'Well, stand next to it, then, as I need some perspective, and wipe that scowl off your face at the same time!' She pokes out her tongue, indicating I have won this stage of the argument. Possibly. I think this is delightful actually, not her rude gesture I don't mean, but this little beginning, or what is left of it, as clearly there must have been some method of feeding the aqua into the duct, back in the day. 'What was the name of that fellow on Bodmin Moor, in the time of King Arthur, condemned forever to scoop the waters from Dozmary Pool with a limpet shell?'

'John Tregeagle?'

'Well perhaps they had someone like him here, or a slave, or maybe the lie of the land was different before they built that church...' and I unfurl my map and consult the key... 'the Convent of San Antonio the Royal?'

'Yes I am sure. Just take the picture will you, I am getting stiff here.'

'Would that be old-age stiff, or porn-st...'

'JUST TAKE THE DAMN PICTURE!'

Sounds like I have just gone two-nil up. But this really is lovely. The commencement of the monument is marked by two courses of thick, un-faced stone, on top of which are balanced two clearly much older fragments of column, the lower engraved with a stylised elephant, with a figure on his back, the upper depicting the arches of the aqueduct. Picture secured, we follow the wall, keeping to the left, the top being dead level of course, down a slight incline, and after around a couple of hundred yards, it is taller than us, and we can no longer see into the channel. A little further on is a single-storey, one-roomed stone building straddling the structure, a pump house is my first thought, but they didn't have steam in those days, although perhaps a much later addition? Or to somehow regulate the flow, possibly. There are no clues, and far too high to peer through the barred windows. A mystery. This building heralds the first deviation in the course of the wall, as it bears slightly to the left, but very much in the Roman style, straight line-bend-straight line, and still a solid construction, fifteen feet high now, with no sign of the arches which did so much to decorate the structure, and cause people to break into song, lower down in the town.

Then suddenly, there they are, baby arches, a couple of feet high, no more, a little wonky I have to say, as if the builders kept the better, more regular blocks for lower down, and used these 'seconds' for further up, out of the way, where only intrepid British tourists would see them, and for the apprentices to practice on. There must be a dozen or more of these 'see how you get on, but if you make too many mistakes you get thrown to the lions' arches, and another bend to the left, before the pattern regularises itself into the flawless construction we so admired yesterday. Concentrated minds, no doubt, the threat of becoming lunch for Leo. Ahead, we spot a sharp right-hand turn, not a right angle, but not far off, and the beginning of the second, lower row of arches, as the street descends more steeply. 'Loved their straight lines, didn't they, the Romans?' I smile, 'think of the roads they laid, in Britain. The Fosse Way, Ermine Street, straight as a ruler, in many places. But I wonder why they didn't put a curve in here?' My wife is rolling her eyes, a gesture I choose to ignore, as I'm on a mission. 'Just imagine, in the winter here, the water cascading down the channel, up there, in a gale, hitting that sharp corner, it would come splashing out, don't you think, on the people below, and over that building there'.... and I unravel my map again... 'AN AR-TILLERY ACADEMY! Can you believe that? Trying to keep their ammunition dry, a bit of a wind gets up, and they're cursing again, our gunpowder's soaking wet all because of those posh bastards up there in the castle? It was not all sweetness and light, let me tell you, in Roman times!'

She regards me with pity. 'Are you taking a photo? Can we please move on from the wild fantasies circulating around in that tiny object you call a brain? Soaking wet gunpowder, oh please.'

I take my shot, but I haven't finished spouting, just yet. 'Well, I think we'd better cross over, through the arches, to the other side, because if we stay over here, we will be passing those *Cochinillo* restaurants, around that bend, down the hill, with the pictures of you-know-what on the walls, and we don't want that again, do we? You see, my tiny brain does have its uses, doesn't it?'

So we pass through, to the 'other side', and the whole panorama opens up of the aqueduct sweeping majestically across the valley to the castle. There can be little doubt the prospect is far more extensive from this side, it is just a crying pity the surroundings resemble the end of the runway at Gatwick airport. It was bad enough last night, bathed in the golden rays of the setting sun, but in the harsh light of day the brutality of the scene is criminal, in my view. Surely some gardens, trees, shrubs, flower beds would have perfectly complimented the magnificence of the structure? Hang your heads in shame, you town planners responsible for this.

Climbing the steps to the old city once again, it soon becomes vividly apparent there is way more to see here than Avila, and that I have boobed, massively, in planning just the one night in this city. Antiquities are on virtually every corner, churches, bell towers, convents, arches, columns, pillars, turrets, plazas, public buildings, private houses, mostly carved from this gorgeous, honey-coloured stone, mouldings, gargoyles, grotesques, all thrown together in a kaleidoscope of styles from centuries past, a breathtaking jumble of architecture, and not a single runway in sight, praise be. And this tourist map is causing me grief, too, depicting as it does our hotel, on the extreme bottom right, and this castle of Disney, this *Alcazar*, about as far to the top left as it is possible to go, without ending up back in Avila. We're simply going to run out of time.

My wife however is still finding something funny. 'Sorry to have to tell you, but our neighbour, Juan-the-soon-to-be-retired-dustman, has beaten us to it! He's been up here building walls. Look at that, have you ever seen anything like it, on a major public building? A Spanish wall, for sure, built on a Friday afternoon, from whatever was left lying around. Quarry tiles, all stacked on top of each other, like a plate of sandwiches, then crumbly cement, held up by planks of wood, horizontally, and left to dry, like lath-and-plaster, with insufficient lath. Then a patch of rubble-stone, which looks like it came out of the bottom of a fish-tank, one section of decent stone, some more sandwiches, and finally a spot of rendering any self-respecting chimpanzee would be ashamed of. Then the electricians came along and literally nailed that cable from one side to the other, but didn't bother to pull it tight, so that it droops like a one-string fiddle. All topped off by a nineteen-sixties summer-house from a suburban garden in the Home Counties. Now look behind you at something the Romans built!

Giggling, as she is absolutely correct, the thought processes behind whoever built, or possibly repaired this wall unfathomable, I consult my map again. 'I'll have you know this is the convent of Santo Domingo de Guzman and the tower of Hercules. A Medieval strong house, apparently, although clearly not that strong as most of it has clearly fallen down, at some stage!'

I tell you what though. For a Monday morning, in the depths of Autumn, there aren't half some people about, tour groups, many of them from locations as diverse as the Far East, and the United States, reflecting the year-round nature of heritage tourism in this country. It is the same where we live, in that 'Golden Triangle' of Malaga-Seville-Cordoba-Granada, which are a joy to visit, and hugely popular, outside the traditional summer season, and clearly similar here, side-trips based around Madrid, I imagine. All of which means I do not really need to bother following the map, we are just going with the flow, literally, past pavement cafes, trinket shops, and in one particularly delightful row of ornate facades, purveyors of local ceramics. Now Chrissie is potty about pottery, boasting an extensive collection in the distinctive 'Granada' design based around stylised pomegranates and palm leaves, in deep blue and wishy-washy green, much of it sourced from the allegedly 'original' seventeenth-century factory in that city, situated on the fringe of the *Albaicin*, that maze-cum-rabbit-warren of whitewashed stone cottages and flamenco caves straddling the hillside below the *Alhambra* Palace. But this Segovia motif is delightful, a parallel design centred around a blue-grey floral swirl, bordered by a deeper blue, fringed in pale orange and lemon, finished with a wavy, fine-brush pattern in the blue. Recalling suddenly my ham-fisted attempts at slip-glazing in my schoolboy ceramics-class years, I can appreciate the skill involved in creating this art. Providing I am not called upon to dust the pieces, of course.

The window of one particular shop is chock-full of plates, urns, vases and bowls, but a distinctive water-jug catches our eye. 'Look at that!' Chrissie giggles, 'it reminds me of that old cow of a ward-sister at the hospital. A wide bottom and a narrow neck!' Indeed. I cannot claim to have known the woman, but this vessel is of striking and unusual design, probably nine inches in diameter at the base, no more than three at the top, like a circular chunk of china Toblerone, with a pouring lip and a braided handle. From a practical point of view I imagine it would be an absolute swine, splashing the liquid everywhere, like those stainless-steel teapots they used to provide in olde-worlde teashoppes, but I can picture it in pride of place on our marble-topped coffee-table.

Just the one slight reservation however. Apart from the price. 'Are you sure you want a momento of this town? Won't it, you know, remind you of a certain you-know-what? Last night? The unmentionable?'

She is grinning. 'What, the porn-stars, you mean?'

I roll my eyes. 'You know very well I don't mean them. I am referring, as you know full well, to that vile image fixed to the restaurant wall. And if you buy this jug, I don't want you thinking of that, every time you do the dusting.'

She is really laughing now, as she skilfully applies the finishing touch. 'Well I was rather hoping *you* might buy it, and *you* flick the duster around, once in a while, so I don't have to!' *Stiffed again.* 'Actually' she continues, 'I love it here. It's incredible, the architecture, that cathedral with the massive tower and cupola, that Italianate church tower, everything. I've forgotten about the you-know-what, and I think you buying me, sorry, us, that jug would be the perfect souvenir.'

Get yer wallet out, Jonno.... Which I do, of course, and the nice lady in the shop agrees to hold the jug for us while we visit this Alcazar. 'Castle of Disney' she smiles, enigmatically.

'With Mickey Mouse?' I grin, unsure now what to believe, as they are all saying the same thing, 'castle of Disney'. Rosa of course, but also most of the library group back home, the majority of whom admitted they had never even been here, apart from Marie when she was at school, which is a sobering prospect if ever I heard one... Spanish school kids? Oh please no, for the sake of my eardrums, and sanity. And now this woman in the shop, who must live at the end of the street, or thereabouts.

'Possibly Donald Duck!'

Let us hope not. I always preferred Goofy. Anyway, we're not going to have to wait long as the old city appears to be nar-rowing appreciably, we cross a small park, and there it is, this castle of Disn..... A French Chateau! Stout, stone, four-storey walls, narrow windows, steeply-sloping grey-slate roofs, round towers on each corner topped by tall, conical 'witches hats', and a rectangular tower topped by circular battlements, it could have been lifted straight out of the Loire Valley. Califor-nia or Florida this is not. Uncle Walt never came here, for sure. And besides, it is stone-coloured, not various shades of candy-striped pink. No cheesy music is playing. And there is no Main Street USA. Disney my eye.

Chrissie, however, disturbingly, can read my mind. 'Don't for-get that we were in Walt Disney World Florida with the girls for the twenty-fifth anniversary of the park, when they decor-ated the castle in various pastel shades, like a giant birthday cake covered in sweets. If you ignore all that, picture that cas-tle in its natural state, then try to imagine this one without those side walls, just the towers with conical roofs all bunched together, I think this looks absolutely like Cinderella's castle! I know you have zero imagination, but please try!'

Remove the colours, and the walls? Blimey, I struggle to remember what day it is. I narrow my eyes, cast my mind back over twenty years, and concentrate... oh my word, do you know what? It is! I can see it now, this has to be the inspiration for the Disney people, or one of the inspirations, certainly. They copied this, for sure. I mean, visiting with the kids, all those years ago, the Magic Kingdom truly was magic, I loved it there, and even to this day it remains one of my favourite places we have ever visited. I know, I know, entirely manufactured, commercialised to hell and back, but it brought out the big kid in me, the whole experience, and that's just the way it is. Having my photo taken with Minnie Mouse was one of the highlights of my life, and now, all these years later, here we are at the source. Two sources in one day, the aqueduct, and Cinderella's castle. I think I am going slightly mad, but in a good way you understand, and a shiver runs down my spine.

My wife however continues to demonstrate her telepathy skills. 'You didn't seriously think... no, surely not... even you aren't that dim... you did, didn't you? You did! You thought this was going to be some sort of a theme park here.'

'I don't know what I was supposed to think' I cry, indignantly. ''Castle of Disney, castle of Disney', that is what just about every Spaniard has been saying since we announced we were coming here.They didn't say 'Walt Disney drew inspiration for Cinderella's castle from the one at Segovia!' Did they? Couldn't articulate that I suppose, so how was I supposed to know what to expect? No, I wasn't anticipating a theme park, of course, I just thought there might be one or two of the figures dressed up, you know, Mickey, Donald, Snow White, that kind of thing, maybe a Disney shop. Anyway, were here now, so are we going in, or are we staying out here debating my mental deficiencies all day?'

She has her head buried in her hands. 'Snow White. Oh please....'

We enter the ticket foyer, a large space indicating this might be a popular attraction, although sadly, or fortunately depending on your point of view, no trace of cartoon mice, ducks or heroines. There is however, regrettably in my case, a large group of schoolkids. French schoolkids, no less. Teenagers, mid-teens by the seem of it, behaving as teenagers do, the girls swiping their mobiles, crowding around, giggling, pouting, the boys jostling, pushing, shoving, play-fighting, maybe fifteen in total, making enough noise to wake the dead, and, distressingly, no sign of any teachers. Sat in the cafe no doubt, having abandoned their charges for the afternoon, or simply handed in their resignations. Deep joy. We have history, French schoolkids and me. Dating from the mid-seventies no less, when a new cross-channel ferry service was launched from Plymouth to Brittany, overnight sailings to St Malo, initially, then Roscoff, latterly. As part of the publicity for the new service, they even arranged a stage of the Tour de France on the new Plympton by-pass, when the whole entourage came across on the ferry for a quick scoot up and down the most boring road in Christendom. Of course, for romantically-inclined young men, as I was in those days, and still am, when allowed, the opportunity arose to whisk one's fiancee abroad for the weekend, a beguiling prospect for any young lady, surely? I recall to this day a line from the poem I composed, in French, inviting her on this luxury cruise. *Dans tes bras je trouve heureusement tout complet.* In your arms I find complete happiness. Or something like that. Unfortunately, my tickets arrived in the name of Mr & Mrs Elliot, and my mother, who had taken delivery from the postman, furiously accused me of engineering a clandestine weekend of pre-marital hanky-panky with 'that girl', as my betrothed was known in those days, a ludicrous notion in the middle of the storm-tossed English Channel with my intended bringing up her boots in the bathroom, *and hoards of adrenaline-charged French schoolkids screaming and shouting in the corridors the entire night.*

'Let them go first' my now-wife giggles. 'Some boring old castle, they'll be in and out in five minutes. We can follow behind. A long way behind!'

The madness is still upon me, however, and I feel a pang of nostalgia for the antics of the Gallic hordes of forty-five years ago. 'Remember that night on the St Malo ferry? And can you recall the words of that poem I wrote you?'

'Huh' she scoffs. 'I don't think I've ever been so ill. And that poem? All about finding happiness inside my bra, wasn't it? Some rugby-club ditty, no doubt.'

'Arm!' I cry. '*Bra* is French for arm, as you know very well. In your arms I find complete happiness. I meant every word then, and it remains so today.'

She squeezes my *bra* and pecks me on the cheek. 'Well that is lovely of you to say so. Now please get the tickets, and don't forget to tell them you're a pensioner!'

A pensioner. Where did all that time go? My thoughts echo down the years. Must be the madness still. It's enough to make you well-up.

All is quiet on the western front as our visit begins, armed with a complimentary coloured pamphlet outlining in brief detail the various rooms we will be passing through, beginning with the Throne Room, consisting of a richly carved and molded ceiling in the *Mudejar* style, which my guide informs me is the type of ornamentation used in Catholic Spain following the reconquest, but based on original Islamic art, and we are advised to gaze upwards periodically, throughout our tour. The walls are hung with rich deep red velvet drapes, and on a raised dias are a pair of sumptuously carved wooden thrones. Next comes the Galley Room which features not the kitchen, as I had first thought, but a crimson and gold-leaf ceiling in the shape of an inverted hull of a ship, albeit a flat-bottomed one, and certainly not something I would care to sail across a boating-lake, let alone an ocean. On the wall at the far end is a painting depicting the coronation of Queen Isabella, emerging through an archway, golden crown placed regally on her head, veil pulled back, long ivory-white gown sweeping majestically to the floor, her adoring public congregating on the steps below.

My favourite room however is the Hall of the Kings, and immediately the exquisite, haunting flute of Thijs van-Leer, from the early-seventies Dutch rock band Focus, starts up in my head. Always, there is music playing there, from the moment I wake, until I drop off last thing at night, which undoubtedly goes a long way in explaining my apparent absentmindedness, because, as surely we all know, recalling the third verse of *Stairway to Heaven* is of far greater importance than whether, say, we need any cheese this week? Now, van-Leer aficionados will have already twigged that the song to which I am referring is actually *House of the King*, not Hall of the Kings, but hey, who is splitting hairs, especially when Focus tracks are on my internal juke-box? *Hocus Pocus, Janis* and *Sylvia* will be on any minute now. Anyway, the kings in question here are those from the ancient realms of Asturias, Leon and Castille, dating from the eighth century, depicted as Toby jug-like figures, fifty-six in total, each maybe eighteen inches high, delightfully carved from wood I imagine, arranged in an exquisite, continuous frieze of gold leaf around the tops of each wall, the ceiling above adorned with 'Tudor-rose' style heraldic, floral motifs, presumably representing each king, set in an hexagonal pattern, again decorated in gold leaf with a royal blue background. The major disappointment is that the statues are simply too high off the ground to study in detail, which they certainly deserve to be, the individual facial features, postures, colours and modes of dress meriting far more than a cursory glance.

And a number appear to be women, Queens, not Kings, so perhaps this room requires renaming, in these more enlightened times?

Time is pressing. Reluctantly, we tear ourselves away, for the final room, the Armoury, where, unfortunately, the day heads rapidly downhill. As can be gathered from the title, this *salon* is home to all manner of arms from the Medieval period onwards, swords, shields, cannon, six-foot pikes featuring steel, crescent-shaped axes and vicious spikes, a crossbow, and a knight in shining armour sat astride a fibreglass horse wearing, and I swear I'm not making this up, a crimson velvet miniskirt with golden tassels. The bloke I mean, not the horse, although come to think of it, the nag is similarly clad, albeit slightly more modestly, his or her cape reaching the knees. All part of the regalia I imagine although maybe this is a secret weapon? A guy in a short skirt turns up on the battlefield, and the opposition all die laughing.

And the afternoon deteriorating? *The French kids are all crammed in here.* Misbehaving mightily, seemingly re-enacting a famous French victory from the Middle Ages. *Nope. Me neither.* Astonishingly there is no sign of any guardians, custodians or security staff whatsoever, which leads me to wonder if the weaponry on display are reproductions, shipped in from China twice a year to replace any damage inflicted by rampaging school parties. Probably explains why the suits of armour on display look suspiciously thin, barely more substantial than a tin of baked beans. Delve inside you'd likely find a label bearing the legend *Made in PRC*. Thankfully however, the implements of war are screwed down, the pikes secured by a substantial iron rod, the crossbow in a glass case, and there is no gunpowder in evidence, thus ruling out any low-flying cannonballs. Astoundingly bad behaviour however, Chrissie has already been side-swiped by a girl who simply barged in front of her, without a by-your-leave, or an apology, but it is this pair of lads who are enjoying an imaginary sword-fight who are causing the most concern, oblivious as they are to the other guests, women, children and pensioners among them. *And me, two yards away.* Still, the Three Musketeers were French, weren't they? *En Garde, Pussycat!* Or was that Tom & Jerry? Forget now.

The pair are thrusting and parrying like d'Artagnan and that other bloke, or maybe they are both pretending to be d'Artagnan, a bit like us kids all wanting to be Bobby Charlton when we played football, who knows? Suddenly, the first d'Artagnan takes a mighty, decapitating swipe at the second one, who ducks, half-turns, stumbles, swerves and, unseeingly, lunges in my direction. And I have less than a split-second to avoid what could be a nasty clash of heads. D'Artagnan-Deux is going full pelt, or at *grand vitesse* as they say in France, he's a big lad, too, easily my height, albeit lacking a few stone, and there will be carnage. Now, fifty years ago, on the rugby field, I would have gone low, tackled him around the waist, ripped away the ball and channeled it back to Killer King, my old partner in crime, who would have been following up, a foot behind my right ear, then like the raging, snorting bull he was, gone rampaging up the field. Cannot do that here of course, in a heritage attraction with a hint of Disney, and besides, these days whole seconds pass while my creaking corpse responds to signals from my equally dilapidated brain. Nor can I step smartly out of the way as Chrissie is directly behind me, still nursing her sore shoulder, and there are the women, children and pensioners to consider. Too late, the split-second is up, I am going to have to take the hi....

BOOF!

'*MERDE!*'

Gallic gazelle meets English elephant, and down he goes, all arms and legs in an ungainly heap, and his compatriots all roar with laughter, although none of them enquire as to the state of my manly chest, albeit insulated by several layers of protective blubber, which took the brunt of the impact. Now then, I speak better French than Spanish, or I did fifty years ago, having studied it in school for five years, with a certificate to prove it, as opposed to my Spanish which I mainly pick up in bars, but do you think I can remember the French for 'look where you are going you idiot?' Or did I ever know it? I'll let you into a little secret; for my French composition exams I memorised a series of about fifty stock phrases, all grammatically correct, which I could link randomly together to answer more or less any questions on the paper. But I don't think 'it was a fine day, the sun was shining and the sky was blue' is going to be a lot of use here. So I give him one of my stares, and tap the corner of my eye with my finger. He is still rolling around theatrically, groaning, when in a flash some expression on his face reminds me of my own self, all those years ago, when I was sixteen, and some of the horseplay which took place, on school trips, which I am not going to tell you about, in the cold light of day, other than that much of it involved the rapid consumption of scrumpy, on the back seat of the coach. No, it is the teachers I blame, or the lack of them, abdicating their responsibilities, allowing their charges to rampage through a castle, whilst they sip *cafe au lait* and puff away on a pack of *Gauloises* on some terrace. So I extend the hand of *Entente Coardiale* to d'Artagnan-the-Second by grabbing his arm and hauling him to his feet. *'Je suis désolé'* he whispers, suitably chastened. I smile, warmly, *'moi aussi'*, and Anglo-French relations are restored. *Mind you, I still haven't forgiven them for that night on the ferry...*

Two flights of stone steps take us up to our final destination, the roof of the tower of John of Castille, and let me tell you it is a fine day, the sun is shining and the sky is blue as we emerge, breathlessly, and take in the stunning panorama. And realise what idiots we've been. Or rather, I realise what an idiot I have been, not allowing sufficient time, but we really do have to leave now if we are to reach our next destination before night-fall. OK, so Rosa has been going on at us to visit her for months, but what with one thing and another, we were in the UK for most of August, and so on, and so forth, so this trip was hastily arranged, the Spanish were all telling us about the cursed meat dishes, but I could have looked at the internet, or bought a guidebook, or simply asked around. Excuses, excuses. And I failed. As if reading my thoughts, Chrissie squeezes my arm. 'We have to return, don't we, next year? Look at all that, the old city laid out before us. Turrets, battlements, towers, spires, the walls, the wooded slopes below, the mountains beyond. And look behind you, at the back of the castle, standing proudly above the countryside below. That is what the Cinderella castle was modeled on, the central tower with 'witches hat' roof, and the four, smaller, round towers on each corner, each with the same style roofs. That is the part Disney copied, almost exactly, and I bet if we went down to that road below and drove along, there would be the most stunning view of all this, perched on the cliff, dominating the skyline. We simply have to return next year.'

Of course we can, easily, in twenty-twenty. 'Well, we have Sri Lanka in February,' I smile, pleased that my gaffe has been apparently forgiven, 'so what about coming here again in say March? See it in the early Spring.'

She winces. 'Well, something else is happening in March, a sur-prise, so not March, and then we have Easter, all the parades, and I know they want me to carry Mary Magdelaine again, so later in April, or early May, for my birthday. There you go, we can come up here for my birthday, but do me a favour will you?' I am all ears, especially at the thought of a surprise in March. She looks me in the eye. 'Let me choose the hotel, PLEASE!'

CHAPTER 16. TOLEDO

'There's that knocking-shop I went in by accident, when I was here on the bike last year. I told you about it, remember?'

We are in another Roman city, this one built inside a horseshoe bend on a river, protected on three sides by a steeply-sided gorge, and on the fourth by a substantial stone wall. This time, however, I have the slight advantage of a previous visit, so I know more or less what to expect, not that I imagine my wife will be all that keen on exploring the aforementioned 'attraction'.

She stops dead on the pavement, and narrows her eyes. 'I beg your pardon?'

'That place there, I went in thinking it was an hotel, but it turned out to be a house of ill-repute. I told you about it when I got home, remember?'

Her eyes are blazing, she folds her arms, decisively, and takes a couple of steps back. 'You most certainly did not. Do you think I would have let you into my bed if I'd known you'd been cavorting with whores?'

'I wasn't cavorting with anybody' I wail, plaintively, 'least of all whores. I told you, I'd been riding all day, I was all stiff...'

'I bet you were.'

I take a deep breath. *Why did I mention it?* 'I was all stiff as I'd been caught in a Biblical deluge in Avila, remember? I decided to press on, soaked to the skin, try to outrun the storm, this was the next big town on the road, I saw the sign 'Hostal Marie-Carmen, that sign there, look, so I decided to stop for the night. A hostal. You know what a Spanish hostal is. Not a grotty bunkhouse full of sweaty Australian backpackers, but a small hotel. A completely respectable small hotel. Hostal Marie-Carmen, there is the sign, look.'

Her eyes are still burning, with cold fire. 'So you conveniently ignored the other sign, that silhouette of the woman in a catsuit and thigh boots, brandishing her tail like a whip? A likely story.'

'WHAT? What silhouet.... oh my God, that wasn't there last year. That is new, look, you can see that is new. The Marie-Carmen sign is older, anyone can see that.'

'A likely story.'

'Look, I told you about this. I went inside, thinking it was rather dark, then I realised I still had my Aviators on, when suddenly a middle-aged woman came forward, and again I thought it was odd she was only wearing a negligee, I had this funny feeling, anyway I said I was looking for a room for the night, she smiled and said 'this is a club, not a hostal. The hostal is around the corner.' And suddenly, as my eyes became accustomed to the gloom, I spotted three younger women lounging on a sofa, with next to nothing on. I must have blushed to the roots of my hair, luckily it was dark, then I stammered 'gracias' and beat a hasty retreat.'

'A pack of lies' she hisses. 'As soon as we get home, I will be re-examining the credit-card statements, see if I can spot the odd hundred euros disappearing.'

'It wasn't a hundred, it was only fifty' I blurt out, realising, too late, what I have just admitted. Well not admitted, as such, merely reported, but now I am up to my neck. *Why did I mention it?*

The reply is predictable. 'And. How. Do. You. Know. It. Was. Fifty?'

'Because, and I told you all of this at the time, as I was going out the door she called over my shoulder 'it's only fifty if you want to come back later!' And I know you remember this because when I got home, Maggie and Colin were there, staying in their holiday cottage, and we went out for a drink with them that night, and they both know Toledo, and Colin said something like 'Hmm, Hostal Marie-Carmen you say? Only fifty euros? Hmm.' in that deadpan way of his, and we all roared. You remember.'

'I remember no such thing. And if you think for one minute that Maggie and I take one iota of notice of what you two boring, disgusting old farts are rambling on about, you are very much mistaken. We were chatting happily about colleagues past and present at the hospital, who is doing what to whom, not listening to you pair of perverts.'

She remembers, I know she remembers, with her elephant-like memory, and I brighten, visibly. 'Anyway, never mind all that, there's our hotel, look, just along the main street, with the tables and chairs outside the cafe under the awning, and the small parking area, so if we check-in now, I will get the fellow to open the barrier, and I can nip back and get the car. OK?'

She surveys the scene, but refuses to budge. 'The hotel is in the same block as your knocking shop. Two sides of a rectangle. The hotel in the front, the whorehouse up the side street. The two are connected. I'm not staying there. It was bad enough last night, do you think I want to be kept awake by banging headboards and cries of fake passion, all night long? And besides, you will be prowling round like a randy tomcat, trying to locate some subterranean back-passage, sniffing-out some clandestine entrance. Not a chance. You can stay here if you want, I will be in that place across the road.'

Now it is my turn to be offended. 'Tomcat indeed. What rubbish. The two are not connected, the hotel backs onto an inner courtyard. I had a wonderful night's sleep there. And besides, I've already paid, via the booking site. So please come on. *Please?*'

She is unable to hold back any longer, and bursts into uncontrollable laughter, holding on to the wall. 'Oh my God, I love it when you beg. You should have seen your face. Of course I remember this tale. Only you could stumble into a brothel and ask for a room for the night. Maggie was in fits that evening!'

PHEW!

So we check-in, I park the car, we freshen up, then head out for the evening. And I have a surprise up my sleeve. Hopefully. 'Right, I am taking you to a lovely little bar I discovered last time, providing I can find it again, of course!'

She frowns. 'Will there be strippers, pole dancers? Do you want to go on your own?'

I roll my eyes. 'Oh will you pack it in. Of course there will not be strippers. It is a pincho bar, actually.'

'A pincho bar?' she echos. 'What is that, where some semi-naked woman shimmies past, you pinch her arse, and stuff a tenner into her thong?'

'Just give it a rest, will you? A pincho is food, a small plate, like a tapas, from the Basque country. Actually the Basques claim it pre-dates tapas in the rest of Spain by hundreds of years. What they do is slice up a thick crusty baguette, but diagonally, so that each slice resembles the hull of a ship, then they place the food on the top. It could be a slice of meat, or fish, or vegetables, salad, anything really. And you just help yourself, the pinchos are in glass cases on the bar, you take whatever you want, and then you pay at the end. Each one has a cocktail stick in it, holding down the food, different lengths of stick, with three different prices, depending on the size of the stick. *Palillos* they call the sticks I think, each pincho is between one and two euros, and they count the sticks at the end and total up the bill. It's really good, and something completely different, and of course, there will be no nasty surprises on the menu! I only found it by chance last year of course, and I hope I can find it again. It is quite small and intimate inside... oh yes and the waitresses wear tee-shirts and jeans. No flesh on display whatsoever, I promise! So, are you coming?'

Despite being the main route into town from the north, this street is delightful, parks, gardens and old stone buildings either side, shaded by trees and shrubs, with plants and flowers set out behind wrought iron railings in formal gardens, a bandstand, and every fifty yards or so, wooden kiosks selling sweets, ice creams, hot dogs and cheap kiddies toys. 'This is really special here after the sun goes down' I smile. 'On the way back later you will find tables and chairs under the trees, and these kiosks turn into bars, all generations sat around gossiping, enjoying a drink, the low murmur of conversation, because this is not Andalucia so no-one is shouting, they put lights in the trees and it is a magical atmosphere. We can stop and have a beer here after the pinchos, if you like.'

Ahead now is the old city wall, built from honey-coloured stone, with a gateway, two massive, stout towers, flanking an archway topped with a fresco depicting a mythical, feathered, two-headed eagle with a breastplate featuring a coat of arms, and clawed talons, from which hangs a slaughtered lamb. I take a photo, then attempt to dismiss the gruesome image from my mind, as I've had sufficient nightmares on this trip, thank you very much. Through the arch we are confronted by a secondary wall and gatehouse, forming in effect an enclosed pen, double security so that any invaders breaching the first entrance would be trapped, able to be cut down at leisure. And guess which grotesque emblem adorns the space between the two rectangular towers? Correct, my double-headed gryphon, my phoenix, picked out in gold this time, on a fiery red background, a virtual guarantee of a disturbed night.

We pass gratefully into the old city, stepping back in time to a Dickensian world of cobbled streets, higgledy-piggledy buildings, shops and restaurants with bow-fronted, mullioned, leaded windows, all build from this rich, golden stone, glowing now in the rays of the setting sun. Chrissie, unsurprisingly, finds something to buy. 'My mother would love it here! Look, a marzipan shop!'

I can feel the accumulation of Brownie points coming on. 'Well, this is the principal route through the old town, I actually rode my bike up this way, the morning after my distressing hostal experience. We will be coming back this direction tomorrow, so you can buy her some marzipan from me, and we can take it over on our pre-Christmas visit. A token of my esteem for my wonderful mother-in-law. And you never know, she might then feel inclined to pop down Kelvin's butchers, and get me some of his wonderful Cumberland sausages, and fry them up each morning! In fact, get her two sticks, or packs, or whatever it comes in. Hell, get her three lots!'

'Get stuffed!' comes the not-unexpected reply. 'I will say the marzipan is from both of us. Why should I pander to your fat guts? No, it will be from both of us. And besides, that way she might make me some of her creamy, dreamy porridge!' *Well who cares, as long as I get my breakfasts?*

We pass through yet another ancient stone arch, thankfully devoid of winged creatures, and the road widens as it climbs, above the city wall, and to our left a panorama opens up across the pan-flat water meadows adjoining the river, to the east of the town if my sense of direction serves me well, presumably the same river which plunges spectacularly into the U-shaped gorge which serves as the main defence of the original settlement. The gradient steepens, curves to the right past shops dispensing reproduction Medieval weapons which appear suspiciously similar to those on display in the *Alcazar* de Segovia, and we arrive breathlessly in the main square of the town, *Plaza de Zocodover*, according to the sign. Two hundred yards across maybe, flanked gracefully by colourful four and five-storey buildings, not particularly old seemingly, although adorned by decorative wrought iron balconies, with shops and cafes on the ground floors, tables, chairs and parasols laid out in the Spanish fashion, although disappointingly, the central area presenting a complete absence of anywhere for the public to sit. Because I need a rest. 'Continue…. around… to the… right' I wheeze, understandably, as it's been a long day, and I am in severe need of a cold beer and a pincho.

My wife seems unimpressed about something however. 'You swine! You cheeky swine! Pinchy bar my eye. Burger-flipping-King, you're taking me to Burger…. AND MACDONALD'S! You utter bugger, I cannot believe this, after all…

'Shut up!' I pant. 'Just ignore the emporia of all things burger, we are not going to either of them, of course. The pincho bar is around to the right, up that little street there. And it's pincho, not pinchy. No pinching takes place. Just give me a hand up and I'll show you!'

Another fifty yards, past hamburger heaven, or hell depending on your point of view, on the right as predicted, and there it is, small and intimate, split level due to the slope, and hey-presto, through the window, are the pinchos, in their little glass cases, on the bar, *palillos* standing tall, beckoning, *eat me, eat me*, a sight for sore eyes. And there is our table, vacant, waiting for us, drawing us in, as if we needed any encouragement. We are greeted by a friendly young lady, dressed with decorum in company tee-shirt, and jeans, with no sign of any tenners about her person, who shows us to our table, and proceeds to explain the concept, *'help yourself and save the sticks,'* and the pricing *'small sticks one euro-twenty, medium one-fifty, large one-eighty'*, then takes our drinks order. *'Large beer sir?'* She can tell I'm British, clearly.

The bar counter is L-shaped, six or seven feet long maybe on each side, and the little glass cases are two-storey, one on top the other, so thirty in total, I would guess, each containing a mouth-watering offering. I want them all, of course, and I've played rugby with blokes who could most certainly eat thirty pinchos at a single sitting, although this is neither the time or the place for gluttony, or a rousing chorus of *Oh Mister Fisherman,* so I reckon a round half-dozen should suffice. Probably.

Chrissie meanwhile is champing at the bit, although her choices are somewhat more limited. 'I think you will find the veggie and fishy ones are placed randomly, so you will need to seek them out' I giggle. 'Do you want me to lift you up so you can see them all?'

She regards me with scorn. 'Just you watch me! Stand back, I'm going in!' And she strides purposefully across, and grabs a plate. Now, from my elevated vantage point I can envisage two minor problems with her selection process. Firstly, the bartop is somewhat higher than you would encounter in a pub, so she might struggle to see into the containers on the higher level, I'm not sure, we shall find out, in the next few seconds. Secondly, the bar is not designed for leaning on, drinking, gossiping, as it is strictly a buffet counter, and customers should really sit at a table, in the Continental fashion. But guess what? Yep, there are two young blokes, tall ones, leaning on the bar, drinking, gossiping, and obstructing her view of the food. No problem, they will realise she cannot see, surely, and move politely away. Nope. They remain resolutely in place. I imagine she can see possibly four of the cases, the rest are blocked by these sprawling fellows, so she smiles and asks them politely to move. Which they do. About two feet. And they carry on chatting away, completely oblivious. *Or are they?* So now she can examine around eight. Again she gestures for them to shift, which they do, but once again a couple of feet only. Either these guys are infernally stupid, or being deliberately obstructive, I cannot decide which. Big blokes, a little woman, man-spreading, no need of it, is there? And I am just about to stride across and shoo them away when she settles the matter decisively, in her own way, by barging between them forcefully, actually nudging one of them aside, so that he slops a small amount of his beer on the floor. Which has the desired effect, as they move away, sheepishly, and sit down. Five-foot of woman routs twelve-foot of man.

Now she has a clear run of the selections and chooses three, then returns to our table, grinning widely. 'Blimey!' I exclaim, 'I thought I was watching the *Pontypool Front Row* in action, then! The way you cleared that pair away. Excellent!'

She places her plate down, and sits. 'Pontypool Front Row?' she echos, dismissively. 'There were three of them, from Pontypool, weighing-in at fifty stone in total, I imagine. There is only one of me, coming in at less than, ooh, eight stone.' And she grins, wryly. 'Stupid great lumps, I asked them to move, nicely, twice, I wasn't asking a third time. Anyway, I've cleared the way for you, so off you go. Do you want to climb on my back, so you can reach?!' *Touché.*

At that moment the waitress appears from behind the bar with a mop, rolling her eyes. 'Estupid people! There is a sign on the wall, *do not obstruct the cabinets.* Are you OK?' Chrissie assures her that she is indeed unscathed, as I rise to make my selections, three only, for now, including the smoked salmon one, which I've been anticipating, drooling over in fact, ever since we arrived in this town. Ever since I came here last, actually. Suddenly, there is a clanging sound behind me, and I very nearly have a lap full of fish, before I've even had a chance to take a bite. Someone is ringing a hand-bell, and shouting *'caliente!'* A gentle tinkle, you understand, not something from a school playground, but a shock nevertheless, especially with seafood finely balanced. Ignoring the interruption, in the interests of avoiding greasy stains, a tray is suddenly thrust under my nose, causing much merriment from across the table, and a male voice enquires 'hot pinchos sir? Feeesh, cheeps and peeeees? Shosh-shage? Eengliss pinchos!'

Oh my God. Little plates of fish, done in a tempura batter, a handful of chips, and *mushy* peas, no less, although I'd love to hear a Spaniard enunciating *mushy*, and separate platters featuring fat, porky bangers, all mounted skilfully on the crusty bread, speared by the *palillos*, the long, expensive ones it would appear, but who among us really cares? Have I actually died? Have I arrived in Heaven? I tell you what, it cannot get much better. And it would be rude not to, wouldn't it? The least I can do, relieve him of one of each, and my wife, who has a soppy grin on her face, likewise, although she naturally avoids the shosh-shage. 'Cooo!' she leers, as the waiter makes his way towards the other diners, 'I wouldn't mind slipping a tenner into his briefs!'

'Well go right ahead' I splutter, disinterestedly, concentrating instead on spearing a couple of chips, having deferred the pleasure of the smoked salmon until later, 'as long as you take the money from your purse, and not my wallet! And will you please stop gawping?' She has her head swiveled around, checking-out the retreating figure, in a manner unbecoming a woman of her age. *Honestly.* 'And eat up your fish 'n' chips, before they get cold.'

She turns to face me, the waiter having vanished somewhere. 'Sorry? Did you say something?'

'I said, eat your fish and damned chips.'

She gazes round, theatrically. 'Fish and chips? What fish and chips?' I point furiously at the plate on her side of the table. 'Oh that fish and chips. I didn't know they were there. I must have been mesmerised by something, hypnotised in fact. I don't want them, I have three pinchos already, you will have to eat them. I am sure you will find room, in that cavernous belly of yours!'

Oh well. Be rude not to. The least I can do.

The following morning, after the best sleep of the trip, thankfully devoid of images of winged beasts, or invasive plants, we enjoy a leisurely breakfast in the pavement cafe outside the hotel, then set off to explore. We retrace our steps towards the city gate, past the park, where we did enjoy a magical couple of beers last night. Magical? Is that an exaggeration for what must surely have been the fairly mundane consumption of a glass of amber nectar? Well now, one of our favourite pastimes in this country, possibly *the* favourite, is the ability to sit out, and the willingness of the locals to shove a few tables, chairs and parasols into just about any vacant space is a joy to behold. Grotty industrial estates, even filling station forecourts, are brightened considerably by the image of people lounging, gossiping with their friends, over a coffee, or a beer, the passage of time of secondary importance. And so it was last night, under the trees, under the stars, the townsfolk promenading unhurriedly through the park, with all the time in the world, family groups, three generations, meeting acquaintances, catching-up, a free nightly show, unscripted, un-choreographed. Yeah, magical.

Instead of passing through the gateway, we instead turn to the right, following the city wall from the outside. 'This leads down to the river, I think.'

Chrissie frowns. 'I thought you said you'd explored on your bike, last year? Perhaps you had *other things* on your mind, after all?'

I shoot her a mild *I refuse to rise to the bait* stare. 'Well clearly I didn't have time to look at everything, as I was, after all, anxious to get home to you, my sweetness. I simply went through the gate, up to Zocodover, then took a left at the burger joints, and around the town on that side. I've never been down this way. But if you imagine the river gorge as a U-shape, with the city on the inside, we are around the eleven o-clock position here. So if we follow the wall down to around eight, all will be revealed. I think!'

So down the hill, the wall towering above us, to the left, a magnificent mansion perched on the hillside high above..... and a massive, ugly zig-zag scar cut into the cliff face..... and a hideous, concrete, pedestrian subway dug *under* the wall. What the hell? For a few seconds we are dumbstruck at this vandalism, this desecration, and stand, in abject horror. The city engineers who created the runway next to the aqueduct in Segovia have been here also. How was this ever allowed? And where does the underpass actually go, as the other side of the wall is a huge, towering escarpment? I turn away in utter, complete disgust. OK, this is not my city, my country, but heritage belongs to all of us, surely? Us citizens of the world? Chrissie meanwhile has approached the mouth of the tunnel, and beckons me to join her. 'It's an escalator' she confirms, unenthusiastically. 'It goes all the way to the top, look. And they've covered it with a roof, but left the side open, for the view, presumably. Must be something worthwhile at the top, a castle, a spectacular panorama maybe, to justify this desecration? Come on!'

Disbelievingly, we pass through the tunnel and step aboard, rising slowly up not one but around six separate escalators, each with an inter-connecting walkway. My wife giggles, like a schoolgirl. 'Ground floor, perfumery, stationery and leather goods, wigs and haberdashery, kitchenware and food, going up!'

'Yeah well' I scoff, 'at least at Grace Brothers you could get off at each floor. This is more like a multi-storey car park stuck on the side of a world heritage site. And who do you think you are? Mrs Slocombe?'

'Cheek' she scoffs. 'Miss Brahms, I thought! You, of course, are more like Young Mr Grace!' *Well at least she didn't call me Mr Humphries.*

At the top is a viewing platform, covered by a concrete canopy, although the vista is decidedly average, and that is talking it up. The best bit is directly below, down a scruffy, weed-strewn earth bank to the top of the wall, a wall dating from the Middle Ages in case anyone had forgotten, then out across some non-descript suburbs featuring Lego houses, what looks like a hospital dating from the eighties, and a bypass. Lovely. Well worth it, you city authorities. Congratulations.

We are now inside the city walls of course, after this unfortunate diversion, so continue in a generally downhill direction along twisting cobbled streets lined by gorgeous honey-stone buildings, and soon we reach the gatehouse of a Medieval stone bridge, turreted battlements on one side, a conventional pitched roof the other, with a window into what appears to be a small room below. 'Wouldn't that make a wonderful holiday let?' I smile, 'forget a shepherd's hut in some boring old field, or a yurt, what about this? I'd close the bridge, stop the tourists coming across, I could fish for our supper, grill it on an open fire, suspend a white *Rioja* over the parapet to chill, enjoy a romantic supper on the roof of the tower....'

'Aren't you forgetting something important?' my wife queries, unimpressed seemingly.

'Matches to light the fire? A corkscrew? A hook for the fishing line? I was a Boy Scout, you know!'

She shakes her head. 'Nope. Your bladder. And that river. With a weir. Hell, it was bad enough in Avila, with that tiny fountain, you wouldn't get a wink here, would you? What is it, two hundred yards wide?'

Ah yes, the river. For the first time we are able to appreciate the natural defence of the old city, and the monumental barrier confronting any would-be invaders. A rocky chasm, a sheer drop in places, dense vegetation lining the bank on the southern side, meaning any attacking force would be unable to gather in sufficient numbers to mount a serious challenge. And then the river itself, benign at first glance, and I quite fancy a dip, actually, in this warm sunshine, but closer inspection of the murky waters reveals dangerous currents, shoals, and the depth is unimaginable. The weir is a more modern addition of course, to stem the flow I imagine, but it is not difficult to picture the unwary being swept to a watery grave, in days of yore. Plus, of course, any assailants making it across would then have the city wall to conquer. *Unless they took the escalator.*

From here we have several options. 'We can either descend to the river bank, or follow the streets. We are at eight on the clock face, and we need to get to around six, or five, then head inland, up the hill, towards the centre of the city, meandering our way through the streets, past the cathedral, eventually back to Zocodover square, where awaits you the highlight of the entire trip. The number-one of the past five days. In fact, I would not be exaggerating if I said this was the most incredible thing we have witnessed in this entire country, in the time we've lived here. In my opinion, anyway. I know I severely ballsed-up with the other places, not having a guide-book or doing any research, but I've been thinking of this since I came here on the bike, itching to show you one day, and that day has arrived. Prepare to have your little socks knocked off!'

She ponders a moment. 'Hang on. Zocodover square? With the beefburgers? Am I getting a Whopper? That will make a nice cha.....'

'SHUT UP! Do not mention burgers again, or you're going straight home! You know very well that is not what I mean. So what is it to be, streets or path?'

She giggles, and squeezes my arm. 'Oh, you've got me all excited now! A Big Mac!' I wrestle my arm free, and fish around for the car key in my pocket. 'No! No! Only joking! I think that the path would be delightful, the rocky gorge towering above on the opposite bank, but maybe we'd see more of the actual city, the architecture, from the streets?'

And she was correct. Narrow cobbled lanes, churches, squares, statues, history on every corner, all lovingly carved from this sumptuous, creamy stone. An Elizabethan-style, half-timbered, balustraded building in a pretty square laid out with box-hedging... and a monstrous, concrete toilet block, slap bang in the middle... No. Not again, please. It's a good job Prince Charles isn't here. Why, oh why do they keep doing this? These people must be *insane.*

'Calm down.' Chrissie smiles, 'it's a museum of something. *Museo del Greco*, it says. Is that El Greco, the painter? Was he associated with Toledo?'

'Well who the bloody hell cares?' I rage, ' surely... hang on, El Greco? The Adoration of the Magi? That is one of my favourite paintings, with the Virgin sitting on the steps of a colonnaded building holding the Infant Jesus in her arms, the Wise men kneeling, bowed, around her. We studied it in art-history classes in school, but only in a book of course. Is the place open?'

It is indeed, and not only that, admission is free. Sadly this means the leaflets are in Spanish only, although with my own translator in tow, this is no biggie, as they say. 'This is the only museum in Spain dedicated to El Greco.' she begins. 'He was born in 1541 in Greece, obviously, his name was.... blimey!... Domenikos Theotocopoulos.... he came to Spain in 1577 and through an intermediary.... secured commissions from the King of Spain, Phillip the Second.... the King didn't like the works.... this place was actually his house.... no it wasn't....'

'Well make up your mind!'

She flashes one of her stares. 'Oh, hark at Mister O-Level French. Would you like to do the translating? This is not actually his house, but a reconstruction of what it might have been like. Happy now? Anyway, to continue.... he died in 1614.... some of the paintings here are originals, but the earlier ones, including, you were right, the Adoration, are reproductions.... that is what it says, more or less. So, was this the big surprise you promised?'

Well, I'd love to say it was, but honesty prevails. I had no idea this place was tucked away, these little streets never echoed to the throaty rumble of my bike, but what a joy, what a discovery, to stumble upon this place. We are enchanted, mesmerised, as we proceed slowly through the original house, or not as the case may be, and the modern wing, the concrete outhouse. And of course, I still have this big surprise up my sleeve. The original part of the museum features ceramics, portraits, furniture and various artifacts, all displayed in a church-like space with an ornate, geometrically patterned ceiling, but the highlight for me, in the new extension, is a collection of thirteen portraits, each around three feet by two, of Christ and the Twelve Apostles. Depicted on plain backgrounds, head, shoulders and upper-bodies, Jesus is gazing directly at the viewer, whereas the disciples are glancing six to the left, six to the right, each performing some task, St Andrew bearing the Cross, St Peter clutching a pair of silver keys, St Matthew with quill and manuscript, St John the Evangelist holding a golden goblet from which an exultant dragon is rising, St Bartholomew gripping a chained demon. The attention to detail is exquisite, the facial features, the eyes, hair and expressions, simply stunning. 'You notice there is no place for Judas Iscariot?' Chrissie whispers. 'He was replaced by St Paul. I remember this from our Confirmation classes, some said Matthew was the substitute, but he was a disciple, not an Apostle. Paul was appointed by God.'

Moving along, sadly, as time is pressing, we reach a selection of the artist's later works, which appear more intense, more stylised, flights of fancy as opposed to true likenesses, two of which cause me to bite my tongue in annoyance, as they could well ruin my surprise, if Chrissie notices, realises, as she is certain to do. *View of Toledo* from 1596, and *View and Plan of Toledo* from 1608, both created from elevated positions, *and I know the whereabouts of these locations. Curses.* My wife is studying the former intently. A dark, angry, almost violent sky, the old city cascading down the hillside, the vivid green of the vegetation, the turbulent waters coursing through the impenetrable gorge. *And my big surprise about to be rumbled.* 'Look at this,' she frowns, 'that is where we were earlier, isn't it? The city wall, the gatehouse on the bridge, your bed and breakfast accommodation? He is looking down on it all. Is this real? We have to go there!' *Damn.*

'I think this is a figment of his imagination' I lie. 'You can see how his style has become vivid, fanciful. He clearly visited the bridge, which is only just along the street from this house which wasn't actually his house, then imagined how it might appear from above, peering down from the sky. In the days before aeroplanes, or drones.' *Say anything, any old rubbish, to put her off the scent.*

Annoyingly, she then spots the other work. 'And look at this one, that is the same view, on a sunny day, from a different location, further along presumably. If you ignore the heavenly host of angels, the fellow sprawled across the Horn of Plenty, and the chap holding up a giant parchment, there is the old town, stretched out across the hillside. Where is that viewpoint?' *Oh Hell.*

'But look at the date' I protest. '1608, just a few years before he died. He's clearly gone off into the realms of fantasy. I mean, when was the last time you saw angels cavorting in the sky? And the Horn of Plenty is a pub on the road from Cornwall to Dartmoor. We went there one evening, years ago, before the kids were born, remember? Anyway, where is my favourite, the Adoration of the Magi? Is it here, can you see?' *Keep bluffing, keep talking. Might just have got away with it.*

Helpfully, she scans the gallery, seemingly forgetting about the viewpoint. 'Here it is, look. Unfortunately, according to the label, it is a reproduction, not the original. But tell me please, Mister O-Level Art, why are the Holy Family and the Three Kings gathered around a Roman temple? Where is Away in a Manger? A Stable All Forlorn?'

I stand in awe, transfixed, as my mind is cast back fifty years. Could I ever have dreamed, all that time ago, studying the masterpiece from the pages of a school-book, that one day I would behold the original, or if not the original, then one produced in the school of El Greco by a contemporary, a student of his. Or maybe it's a Chinese knock-off, produced by the thousand in some greasy sweat-shop, who knows, but I recall vividly the brush strokes of Mary's cloak, in particular, how it flowed to the ground around her feet, the hand of the Infant Jesus gently caressing the gift offered by the supplicant king, and this version is identical, to my untutored eye. 'The scene represents both provocation and reconciliation, I think. Yes, traditional images of The Nativity show the stable, and the manger, the cattle, but El Greco chose to place the scene at the heart of the enemy, the Roman Forum, with Mary actually sitting on the steps. As a boy, I always felt this was an act of revenge by the artist, aggressive, almost. Yet looking at it today, maybe he was reminding us that irrespective of our religious or other beliefs, the birth of the Son of God is something in which the whole world can rejoice. Our world, one world. It is a simple, yet powerful message. My youthful self relished the thought of him thumbing his nose at the Romans, nowadays perhaps I feel the opposite.' I smile, ruefully. 'Art is in the eye of the beholder of course, people will form their own interpretations, but this is actually the second work of El Greco with the same title, Adoration of the Magi, the earlier one he painted on the side of a box or a chest, I forget now, but it was set in a similar location, a Roman villa or temple. He is definitely sending us a message, down the centuries, it is up to us all whether or not we choose to listen.'

Time to move on. We wend our way through the delightful maze of streets, in a generally uphill direction, catching occasional, provocative glimpses of an ornate grey-stone bell-tower, topped by a spire, which I am assuming is a large church, a cathedral even. What is around this corner? Where does that little lane lead? I could spend all day doing this, wandering aimlessly around this warren, unsullied by commercialism, not a shop or bar all morning so far, no enticements to spend my hard-earned. My type of town. If only there was somewhere to sit. So it is with some relief that we emerge into an irregular-shaped square, flanked on one side with what appears to be the town hall, provincial, national and European flags fluttering daintily in the breeze, an ornately carved three-storey frontage book-ended by solid, square towers.... and benches! I almost sprint, as fast as my aching limbs will carry me, and bag the last one, ahead of a small, bored-looking tour group who clearly regret signing-up to follow the strident woman with the loud voice and the umbrella, reciting parrot-fashion into their ear buds. 'The Gothic cathedral was begun in the early thirteenth century' she is informing the disinterested party, most of whom are taking selfies,'and completed in 1493'.... and I cannot help giggling. What, two-hundred and seventy-five years or thereabouts? Must have been Spanish builders, clearly. 'The main portal is the Door of Forgiveness, and next to it the Door of Hell.' *Well you can see how that would come in handy, can't you? Try Hell first maybe, see what it was like, and if not....*

Up the slope to the left is a 'Bridge of Sighs'-type structure, joining the two buildings either side of the street, but up high, a Bridge of High Sighs if you like, perhaps for those on their way back from Hell, who knows.... wait a minute, did she say cathedral? Now, no sniggering at the back, thank you very much. Such was my haste to rest my aching pins, I didn't notice it, all right? They sneak up on you, do Spanish cathedrals, hiding in plain sight. For the past half-hour or thereabouts, one minute it is there, the next it has vanished, and this one sits right on the street, hemmed-in by the surrounding buildings, no manicured lawns sweeping majestically around the structure. And such is the tightness of the space, it will not fit entirely into the viewfinder of my camera. Umbrella-woman is still going strong, although clearly wishing she'd paid more attention in school, and that she was elsewhere, the Caribbean possibly, sipping cocktails on some tropical beach, instead of guiding these smartphone-swiping heathens. 'The city of Toledo was re-conquered peacefully by Alphonso, King of Leon in the eleventh century, and part of the agreement for the transfer of power was that the original mosque on the site could remain, and its traditions co-exist. While he was away from the city however an armed force stormed the mosque and installed Christian emblems and artifacts....' then suddenly the whole group is moving off, across the plaza, and her words are carried away by the general hubbub.

'Quick, follow her and find out what happened next, then come back and tell me!' I chuckle. 'I'll wait here and save your seat.'

'I won't dignify that remark with a reply' she sniffs. 'But what a shame we cannot see the whole building, everything around here is so closed in. It would be wonderful to be able to just step back and admire it in its entirety. There is no such place, I suppose?' *There is actually, but I'm not telling you. Yet.* 'Anyway, are we sitting here all day, or are we going inside?'

I puff out my cheeks in frustration. 'Well, it will take us four hours or thereabouts to drive home, and we need to grab a bite to eat before we leave. We cannot do it all. The time we spent in the gallery we could have used here, although I wouldn't have missed El Greco for the world. And we still have my special surprise don't forget. So I guess we will have to leave the cathedral until next time.'

She eyes me suspiciously. 'Are you still serious about this so-called surprise? I don't trust you. It's probably some lap-dancing club. Come on then, let's get it over with.'

Oh, is she going to be eating her words.... Pressed back against the far corner of the town hall, I take a couple of truncated shots of the cathedral facade, then we continue up the hill, past gift shops now, cafes, bars, boutiques, the whole tourist scene, emerging into the main square, where suddenly I am grinning like the Cheshire cat. It is here! The highlight of the whole trip! I will be basking in the glory, any moment now! 'There you are madam' I gloat, in triumph, with an expansive sweep of the arm, 'Ta-da! Your carriage awaits!'

Her little face falls, and she visibly deflates. 'You. Cannot. Be. Serious. All morning you've been banging on about this. A Noddy train? You utter, steaming idiot. A ridiculous little Noddy train? Do you know, I will swing for you, I really will. The most incredible thing we've witnessed in this country, you said. You promised. If you expect me to get in that, you have another think coming. You go, if you like, it will suit your tiny mind, parading round the streets, everyone laughing at you, but I'm off back down the cathedral.'

I grab her in a massive bear-hug, and steer her, laughing, towards the opened door of the little carriage. 'You'll just have to trust me, OK? Come on, in you get. You need to be on the right-hand side. Chop-chop!'

'Chop-chop? I'd like to chop you into little pieces. I will get you for this, I really will.' Reluctantly, she climbs aboard, still grumbling mightily, while I dash to the kiosk to get the tickets, then after a short wait we are off, rattling across the cobbles, heading out of the old city. 'Oh this is nice' she whines, sarcastically, 'the by-pass. A filling station. A splendid view of the motorway. How delightful, you certainly know how to treat a girl.'

I smile, enigmatically, but remain silent, for now. *About another five minutes, by my reckoning.* She is correct, of course. The scenery is mundane, and that is being kind. We are traversing what I imagine was the northern relief road before the motorway was built, and I can feel my fellow travellers becoming restless, wondering quite why they have shelled-out for a tour of the 'burbs, with the glorious historical centre, where they thought they were heading, disappearing rapidly behind us. We could do with umbrella-woman, to enliven the journey, and explain that we are travelling clockwise around the old town, and are currently at around twelve noon. *Four minutes.*

We cross the river, so are now on the outside of the fortified city, then suddenly swing to the right, signposted *Camino Valle*, leaving behind the depressing outskirts, and heading into wilder territory. Chrissie is on the right, as instructed, next to the window, with a good view of the surroundings, whereas I, from my somewhat loftier plane, have the perfect vista of the carriage ceiling and therefore have to crane my neck, like some fat greedy swan chasing a slice of stale bread, across her lap to check our progress. *About two minutes now.* 'Get your great head out of it' she giggles, sensing perhaps that something exciting is about to happen, as we are passing an ancient stone bridge, guarded by formidable towers on each bank. The gradient steepens and we are climbing the hillside all of a sudden, cliff-face to the left, river to the right, and slowly but surely the southern, natural defences of the original settlement are becoming apparent. Or they are to those of us not playing with electrical devices.

The little choo-choo plods valiantly upwards, engine straining, when abruptly Chrissie almost leaps from her seat. 'Oh my God, oh my God, get me out of here! There is nothing below us!' She is gripping my arm, painfully, head turned away from the window. 'Quick, swap seats! NO, don't move! We will tip over, we are on a suspended roadway, bolted to the cliffs, you swine, sitting me next to the window! Is this your idea of a surprise?'

'Don't worry' I smile, reassuringly, clutching her hands, peering through my window. 'We are turning inland, around that hairpin bend.'

'Hairpin bend, hairpin bend? Get me off this damn train!'

One minute. She has her face buried in my shoulder. 'It is safe now' I whisper, 'we are back on terra firma. Don't you want to take a look at the view?'

'Oh sod the view. I won't forget this, you bugg.... Ooh, will you look at that! Incredible. What a stunning panorama. Are we stopping? Can we get out?'

We can indeed. The rickety conveyance shudders to a halt, the doors are flung open, and the passengers, animated suddenly, make a dash for the little wall above the sheer drop, phones raised, chattering, posing, pouting, peace signs even. *Oh pleeese.* 'Come down this way a few yards' I grin. 'We have plenty of time!' And there it is. As painted by El Greco, and photographed by millions. The view of Toledo. One of *the* views, in my opinion. Spread out below us, enclosed by the horseshoe bend in the river, climbing the hillside, the skyline dominated by a massive square palace with towers at each corner, and the cathedral of course, or certainly the tower and the top half of the nave, as I knew it would be. Turrets, battlements, towers, arches, roofs and houses, a chaotic eruption of terracotta and stone, rolling and tumbling down the hillside to the river below. Breathtaking. But climbing *and* tumbling? How is that even possible? Well, as I see it, some of the buildings appear to be balanced, one on top the other, barely a space between them, like kiddies' building blocks, yet in other places they have seemingly fallen, brushed by some giant hand, gravity having taken over, a glorious jumble of history.

'So' I whisper, 'was I right, or was I right? Is that one of the stunningest sights you have ever seen?' *Stunningest? Is that even a word? Well it is now.* 'One of the best in the world?'

She is shaking her head, in wonder, not disagreement. 'In the top ten, certainly. But what about the top of the Empire State building, or the Eiffel Tower? Venice? The Grand Canyon?'

'Absolutely' I concur, 'I've told you before I would be happy to die in Venice, for you to tip my corpse into the Grand Canal and watch me float away. Or sink to the bottom more like! But those views are linear, horizontal. What I think is so special about this is the circular nature of the scene, as if we're viewing it through a fish-eye lens, with the river cradling and protecting the city in the palms of its hands, inside the horseshoe bend of the gorge at the bottom, and the roofs of the buildings completing the circle at the top.'

I am unable to read her expression. She either agrees, or thinks I have finally lost my tiny mind. 'So you knew this was here, didn't you? All that rubbish about El Greco flying a drone? The Horn of Plenty serving beer? Did you come here on the bike?'

I am chuckling at the memory. 'Well I almost didn't make it, actually. I was trying to get on the motorway, heading home along that road with the filling station, I knew nothing about this of course, and I came up behind the choo-choo, plodding along, and I just couldn't get past, traffic, speed humps, all the rest of it. Then the train seemed to veer to the left, so I saw the opportunity to nip up the inside, to the right, when suddenly the damned thing swung across my path, up that valley road back there, so I had to turn with it to avoid getting splatted. It was like a Mr Bean sketch actually, with all these tourists open-mouthed at the sight of a biker careering crazily alongside, teeth and buttocks clenched. Well, they couldn't see my buttocks, hopefully! Anyway I just managed to squeeze past, then saw the city open up to my right and almost fell off as I wasn't looking where I was going. So that suspended roadway you were shrieking about was almost my watery grave! Then I got here and parked up, I was just taking off my helmet when the train pulled in behind me, I thought for a second the driver was going to give me a bollocking, then suddenly I was swamped by tourists. Anyway, I didn't want to spoil the surprise for you, actually I cursed when I saw the painting, I thought you would figure it out, which you did, so I was just spouting any old rubbish to put you off. Which is par for the course....'

She squeezes my arm. 'Bless you for that! So, *View and Plan of Toledo* must have been painted from this very spot, although there are no Heavenly Hosts today, and I assume his earlier work *View of Toledo,* with the bridge and the gatehouse, and your bed and breakfast, from further along, the way we are heading?'

'Correct. I don't think the train stops there actually, but don't worry, we can come this way in the car on the way home, stop wherever we like. Without the crowds too!'

She ponders for a moment. 'So why didn't we simply drive up here, and save the ten euros or whatever on the train ticket?'

'Fourteen actually. Seven euros each.'

'Fourteen euros? For this? You must be mad. That would have paid for lunch.'

I flash her my full 'I know best' smile, guaranteed to annoy the hell out of her. 'Well, I wanted a fun, romantic conveyance, to maximise your experience. I couldn't get hold of a 1965 E-Type Jag at short notice, so this was the next best thing.' And I pull an imaginary chain, imitating a train whistle. 'Wooo wooo!'

She almost chokes. 'Romantic? Sat behind that annoying woman bursting out of that canary yellow sundress in all the wrong places, tapping away on her phone with those tarty stick-on fingernails the entire trip? Call that romantic?'

I am still in annoying mode. 'I do actually. Years from now, when we're old and grey, you will look at the photos and recall this moment. 'Blimey' you will say. 'Remember that woman in the yellow dress? How she almost slipped out of it every time the train went around a bend?' And I give my chain another tug. Wooo wooo!'

'Old and grey?' she echos. 'Years from now? One of us in this marriage is old and grey at this moment. AREN'T YOU?'

'So what was your favourite place on the trip?' We are on the motorway, heading home after five fantastic days in the middle of Spain. The A4, *The Motorway of the South* as the sign enthusiastically proclaims, no doubt attempting to alleviate the boredom of the flat, monotonous scenery of Castilla la Mancha, but failing. Confusingly, the road is also designated as the E5, the reason for which I have been unable to obtain a logical answer, the best suggestion from our Spanish friends being that it is also a 'European route.' Possibly.

I allow my mind to drift momentarily from the bone-rattling concrete surface. 'Everywhere!' I smile. 'It was a fantastic break, we saw so much, and there is still a lot to visit, next time Rosa invites us. What I would really like is to design my own coffee-table style book, with glossy photographs, firstly of the tomb in St Vincent's, those individual figures, then the Walls of Avila, from the four-poster bed. Then, the Roman Aqueduct taken from the end of the runway, and inside the House of the King, all those individual little thrones around the walls. Next, the shot of the Disney castle, from the tower of John of Castille, and that will take care of Segovia. Then in Toledo, the three El Greco paintings, obviously, then finally *that* view. Never going to happen of course, as indoor photography was prohibited at all those venues, so I have no pictures to create an album you can order online. So I will need to rely on my memory, which as we all know, is not what it was!'

My wife squeezes my knee, sympathetically. 'So, no pictures from Buy-a dolly?'

'Oh yes!' I chuckle. 'I thought I'd have a photo from Buy-a dolly on the front cover.'

Oh, which one? That massive chain hanging from the window? Or even better, the figure of Donkey Hottie?

I pause a few seconds, for dramatic effect. 'The tit and the moon, of course!'

CHAPTER 17.
THE (SPANISH)
SANTA SPECIAL

'No, you are not getting a train-set.' It is the best time of day, for me. A Rick Stein special has been lovingly prepared, and enthusiastically consumed, a couple of beers are lining the walls of my stomach, and now I am slumped in my armchair, feet up, nursing a glass of red, Classic FM on the speaker, catching up with the day's news on the internet. The only way this could be improved upon is if we were outside, on the terrace, but it's the middle of winter, and although the days are pleasantly warm, it can go off a bit parky, halfway up a mountain, after sunset. Still, spring is just around the corner.

I actually want to burst out laughing at my wife's comment, but with surprising self-control, after the beer and wine especially, I shoot her a *I have no idea what you are talking about* look. 'Sorry?'

She knows me, of course. 'You heard what I said, you are not to buy another train-set. You know what it will be like, oh just an oval of track, with a little tank engine, a couple of wagons, and a guards van. Then we all know what will happen next, don't we? Another oval of track, slightly bigger. Then there will be points, and sidings. Next will come stations, with the little people waiting for the trains. Then a village, with a pub, a church, a post office, a chip-shop. Then there will be a Flying Scotsman, because there simply has to be a Flying Scotsman, with those expensive LNER teak coaches. And of course you will have to make a base-board, and commandeer the old bodega and tool room for the layout, and before we know it you will have spent hundreds of pounds we don't have, just to recreate your boyhood, which didn't actually exist as your mother wouldn't let you have a train-set, and I can't say I blame her.'

I am struggling to keep a straight face. 'I have no idea what you mean. I am browsing pornography websites, actually.'

Nope. Didn't work. 'Indeed you are browsing porn. eBay porn. I'm gonna set some parental controls on that bloody website, stop you going on it. It's an addiction, every damned night you are on there, looking at rubbish. If you want something useful to do of an evening, write another book.'

One last try. 'What nonsense. Parental controls. Addiction. I might admit to a fleeting glance at eBay, occasionally, but I really...'

'I CAN SEE THE REFLECTION, OF THE LAPTOP SCREEN, BEHIND YOU, IN THE PATIO WINDOW! What is it, Hornby, mixed freight? Actually, sit forward in the chair, just a minute.' Puzzled, I shift forward a couple of inches. 'No, more that that, edge of the chair, that's it, perfect.' And she shoots out her hand, like a cobra striking, and grabs me comprehensively by the Crown Jewels. 'Now, turn it off' she hisses. 'You don't need a train-set.'

Incredible, the grip. Painful, too. 'Look' I splutter, 'if you're trying to initiate sex, just give me five minutes, will you? There is a bid ending shortly for some curved platform sections....'

She pulls her hand away in disgust. 'I knew it. You've bought it, haven't you? Go on, admit it.'

I still have one last trick up my sleeve, however. There is a chance, a slim one admittedly, but the possibility exists that I might just get away with this. 'Do we still have those Christmas cake decorations? You know, the Father Christmas, the snowman, the tree?'

She narrows her eyes. 'Yes, of course, they are upstairs with the rest of the decorations. But stop trying to change the subject, and admit you are a conniving....'

I smile, warmly. 'Yes, I admit I have bought us a very inexpensive train-set. It's an 0-4-0 tank engine, actually the original was built in the Swindon works, designed by the engineer Mr Holden, around a hundred years ago, it was originally intended for the Wrington Vale railway in Somerset....'

'US?' she wails. 'US? What is all this 'us' business? Do you think I want to be playing the Fat Controller with a train-set? Us? You do talk some utter crap sometimes. Sorry, no, you talk utter crap the whole time!'

'Au contraire, my sweetness' I grin. *Told you I might have got away with it.* 'The Thin Controller. The Extremely Trim Controller. The Glamorous Waif-Like....'

'CRAP!'

I am undeterred. 'You know how many of the heritage railways in Britain organise 'Santa Special' trains around the Christmas period? Where the kids get to meet him, have a ride on the train, get a present after? Well I thought I could rig up our train to run around our Nativity village, here.' And I wave my hand at the corner of the room, where our *Belen* will go, very soon hopefully. 'And we could use the Father Christmas cake decoration, sit him in one of the wagons, maybe cut up some Christmas paper to look like presents, stuff it in the truck behind him, and have our very own Santa Special. And,' I eye her solemnly, 'we could enter the town competition for the best Nativity village, the only Santa Special in Spain. Guaranteed to win hands down! So what do you think of that, my Almost-Invisible Controller?'

She exhales, dramatically. 'A Nativity Santa Special? What a wonderful idea. I am sure Mary and Joseph won't mind the Chattanooga Choo-choo rattling past the stable, when they are trying to get the baby off to sleep. And the shepherds will be delighted about Casey Jones blowing his whistle all hours of the day and night, scaring away the sheep. The Three Kings meanwhile will absolutely love having to dodge the Cannon-ball Express, to avoid being mown down, whilst following the star. You have had some ridiculous ideas in your time but....'

'Whoa! Just hold on there one minute, please, while I make something abundantly clear.' It is my time to look stern. 'Those trains you just mentioned were *American*. We are having no foreign rail-*roads* around our Nativity. Ours will be the Great Western Rail-*way*. The GWR. God's Wonderful Rail-*way*. The baby will be lulled to sleep by the gentle chuffing of the locomotive, and the clip-clop of the wheels on the tracks as they pass sedately by. And I thought I might base the eventual layout on the West Somerset line, between Blue Anchor and Dunster. Difficult to represent what is effectively a straight line on an oval, I am sure you will agree, but I reckon I can get the stations bang-on. And thank you for the advice about the sidings and the village, plus the baseboard in the tool room of course. Great idea! I don't know what I'd do without you!'

She shakes her head, then grins. She has no doubt remembered that the visiting Spaniards will need to be provided with a res-torative glass of *Anise*, and a biscuit. The possibility exists that she might take a sneaky sip herself, whilst dispensing.... *Told you, didn't I?* 'So when is this train-set arriving? Don't forget we are in the UK next week for our pre-Christmas visit.'

I shoot her an *oh you just remembered the Anise* look. 'Well, it's not coming here of course, postage would be too expensive, and it wouldn't arrive until Nativity is over! No, I am having it sent to Charlie. We can collect it from her next week.'

'What?' she objects, 'how can we bring that damned great box back? We only have cabin bags, and don't forget I need to get two tubs of *Celebrations* into the luggage. And the Christmas cake.'

Now it is my turn to protest. 'Why are you buying *Celebrations?* You know I hate those miserable little Mars Bars. How many times do I have to tell you I prefer Cadbury's Roses? For pity's sake. And, let me tell you, I won't need the train-set box. The control-unit is the size of twenty fags. The loco is about four inches long, the trucks even smaller. The biggest thing is the track, and that will be in bits, in a bundle, so I thought I could put everything in my socks, in the case, no weight, easy.'

She sighs. 'The *Celebrations* are not for your fat guts, you know very well they are for our Spanish friends at the library group, and the neighbours. And don't tell me they sell sweets in Spain, which I know you were about to say. I make up sparkly little bags, remember, half a dozen choccies in each, hand them out with their Christmas cards. *Un regalo desde Inglaterra.* Present from England, they love it. So while you're demonstrating God's Wonderful Railway, I can be dispensing *Celebrations.* And the Anise!'

Ah yes, I recall this rigmarole, from last year. 'Don't know why you're wasting your money on sweets for the neighbours, most of them have very few teeth! Can you imagine Juan the Dustman with a miserable little Mars Bar in his gap? And Loli with a Milky Way stuck in hers?' Then I turn serious, dispelling all thoughts of Loli's Milky Way from my mind.. 'And talking of Christmas cards, I just wanted to remind you it is the last posting day in the UK next week too. I mean, I will get a pack of charity cards for my students, hand them out when we get back, but if you are making ours for the family, as I know you like to do, hadn't you better make a start? I know you can knock them up fairly quickly, but you've got your cousins in Yeovil and Paignton, and the Truro crowd, the Penzance lot. Your brother's gang in Nailsea, my cousins in Northampton. Your mum, and her neighbours. I don't want to put you under any pressure, I know you've got a lot on and all that, but...'

She is glaring now. 'Put that laptop down.'

'Look, I told you' I grin, 'if it is nooky you are after, I just have this bid on the platform....'

'If I wanted nooky, as you so quaintly put it,' she hisses, 'I am sure there are any number of much younger men around here, most of them with their own teeth, who would oblige. Now. Put. That. Laptop. Down.' I hastily comply. 'Now turn your head to the right. And tell me what that is, hanging from the ribbon, on the wall?'

I grip my knees together, just in case, then do as commanded. 'Er, Christmas cards?'

'Correct. Now turn to the left, and what do you see on that wall?'

Cocked-up again, haven't I? 'Looks like Christmas cards to me.'

'Right. And where did I go, in October?'

I wrack my brains for a second or two. Got it! 'Well who could forget that nightmare trip to the airport, in that bloody Fiat! You went to visit your mum for a few days.'

'So what was I doing, ensconced in my craft-room the whole of the previous week?'

Getting fed up with this now. 'Oh how the hell should I know? I was down Miguel's, plastering that cursed ceiling, earning some money. Who cares what you were doing, swanning around in your craft room?'

I relax the grip on my knees, because us guys find it painful, keeping them together like that. Too late. The cobra has struck again. 'Well I'll tell you what I was doing. I was making Christmas cards, for YOUR friends, for YOUR relatives. And that is the result you see there, on the walls, cards from the UK.'

'Ah, don't be ridiculous' I frown, 'no way did you post a load of

Christmas cards off in October. People would think you were completely potty, sending out cards in October.'

She buries her head in her hands. 'Oh please save me from this imbecile. I made the cards. I wrote the cards. I wrote the envelopes. I put the cards in the envelopes. I stuck the envelopes down. I took them to England. I went to the post office. I bought the stamps. I stuck the stamps on the envelopes, and left them with my mother. Then, the first week of December, she walked to the post box, and posted them. I remember telling you, it was about fifty cards, she had to make two separate trips to the box. And DON'T say you were working in Miguel's.'

Well I was though, wasn't I? But yet another argument I have lost, through not paying attention. Christmas cards in October. Huh. Who knew that was a thing?

Anyway, we get our trip to Britain, my railway pieces get stuffed inside my socks, including a second oval of track and some points, so that after Christmas I can get on with laying out the scenery on the base board, and the contents of two tubs of miserable little Mars Bars get tipped into the cases and smoothed into the gaps, together with a Christmas cake, and by some miracle we avoid a bag search at the airport, so now here we are back in Spain, the Nativity village is set up, and God's Wonderful Railway all ready for the big switch on, hopefully gliding peacefully past the stable, avoiding disturbing any lambs, and well out of the path of visiting Wise Men. Mind you, if any Roman centurions stray onto the track, tough titty to them.

Our biggest problem now is one of logistics, and bearing in mind my track record in cocking things massively and spectacularly up, I consult my wife on the subject. 'Have you given any particular thought to Loli? Bearing in mind she has fallen out with virtually the whole street, at one time or another, and with us over the cats, before too long, do you think it would be wise to get her, Isabel and Fernando in first, give them their sweets, then usher them out, before the other neighbours arrive?'

Chrissie regards me unfavourably. 'Not at all, I know how much you love hearing foreigners swearing at each other. I thought how maybe we could light a small bonfire and arrange to the smoke to waft across Loli's patio, then hear her and Mercedes hollering YOU DAUGHTER OF A BITCH! at each other. Possibly leave a small item of broken, worthless furniture in the street and take up ringside seats as her and Leopard-skin Woman play expletive-laden tug of war with it. Or what about sprinkling a few drops of urine on her doorstep and sit back as Cruzojo and her employ every variation of the Spanish C-word at each other. What a morning that was. YOUR DOG IS A C-WORD. NO YOU ARE A C-WORD. WHO ARE YOU CALLING A C-WORD, YOU C-WORD? YOU DAUGHTER OF A BITCH! And all the while the eight-fifteen from Blue Anchor to Bethlehem would be chugging round the village, dispensing peace and goodwill to all men. DON'T GIVE THAT C-WORD ANY ENGLISH SWEETS, NEIGHBOUR. Wouldn't that get Christmas off to a wonderful start in these parts?' I am laughing so much at the memories I have to sit down. 'And another thing' she continues, 'Loli only gets one bag of sweets, not three bags because there are three of them, as she asked for last year. Every other couple only get one bag, between them, twelve sweets in the bag, six each. Loli's bag has eighteen, so it's the same for everyone, OK? There is her bag, with her card, and all the other cards are with the bags. Right? I've been doing all this while you've been buggering around with your train set, and don't for one moment think I have forgotten about how we were much too late to enter the Nativity competition, which you clearly knew about, this pretence about a Spanish Santa Special, when you really just wanted a train-set all along.'

I am still roaring with laughter. 'Yes, we might have been too late to enter, but you still have the anise to dispense, don't you? And here is the locomotive, ready for the off, with Father Christmas in the truck behind, surrounded by all his 'presents', so get the glasses ready, I am about to knock on her door, light the blue touch-paper, and stand well back. Let Christmas in Santa Marta commence, and may the best rottweiler win!'

I step into the street, then am suddenly riven by doubt. This is a religious country after all, what if the locals don't appreciate a train running around a Nativity village? Father Christmas only became popular here fifteen to twenty years ago, presents are usually brought by the Three Wise Men. There is no tradition of heritage railways in Spain, they won't therefore have a clue what a Santa Special is, and model railways are not even popular, or common. According to my students, it was all Scalextric when they were kids, those rubbishy racing cars which came off on the first bend, and then disappeared under the sofa, or got carried off by the dog. What if I am inadvertently about to cause offence?

Too late. Loli is already in the street, hovering outside our door, no doubt alerted by some sixth sense, or the bugging device we are convinced she has planted. 'GOT OUR ENGLISH SWEETS, AND OUR CHRISTMAS CARD, NEIGHBOUR?'

I smile sweetly, through gritted teeth. *And a Merry Christmas to you, too.* 'Yes, and a special surprise! Come in please.' Oops, I will need to unbolt the double front doors, to enable Fernando to pass through. Whatever weight he lost during his hospital stay, he has put back on, and then some. One consolation however, he no longer resembles Jonathan Ross, which can only be a good thing, in my book. I squeeze past, operate the controller, and the eight-fifteen pulls majestically out of Blue Anchor, bang on time.

For a second or two there is a stunned silence as the trio take in what for them must be a huge shock, and I nervously tweak the controls to speed the train up, down the back straight, then slow it down as it passes the stable. No baby inside yet of course so Mary and Joseph gaze impassively as Father Christmas glides serenely by. The sheep appear unconcerned, the Three Kings maintain their regal expressions, although sadly the Centurions are keeping well back. *Come on, say something. Anything. Must be ten seconds, already. No Spaniards have, in the whole of history, ever kept quiet for this long.*

Suddenly Fernando's bulbous countenance creases into a wide grin. 'FERRO CARREEEE, NEIGHBOUR!' Yep, a railway.

'QUE PRECIOSO!' hollers Loli, inflicting, possibly, irreparable damage to my eardrums.

'Did you buy this in England, neighbour?' Isabel whispers. Well it sounds like she is whispering, although hopefully my hearing will return, some time during the next few days.

'Yes' I croak. 'This obby is very popular in Britain.' *There you go, who knew the Spanish for hobby was obby?*

I am expecting maybe a short discourse from Fernando about how he had a Scalectrix when he was a nipper, but no. Maybe Santa, or whichever King deigned to squeeze down his chimney, only dispensed an orange, or a few nuts. Chrissie hands over the Christmas card, plus one bag of sweets for each of them, and we stand back, expecting not gushing gratitude, but a short *gracias* at the very least. Not a bit of it. 'Got any more, neighbour?' Incredible, isn't it? The hide of a rhino, this woman. Personally I would give her another bag, just to get rid of her, but am under strict instructions, although ever the coward, I leave the blunt refusal to my wife.

'No.' There. That was fairly emphatic, I would have thought. Our grasping neighbour would have heard the steel in Chrissie's voice, and left it at that, realising maybe the baggage restrictions on Ryanair were such that we could only squeeze one tub into our cabin bags, and that she was being a trifle ungrateful in requesting second helpings.

Not a bit of it. 'You have more here, neighbour' she protests, having noticed the cards and bags for the other neighbours, and thinking perhaps that being first in the queue entitles her to swipe the lot, and stuff everyone else.

'No. One bag each' comes the unsmiling reply, and I have to say I am starting to resent even bothering to impart a small gift to these heathens. I could, after all, have squeezed another small station into my luggage, had it not been for these miserable little Mars Bars. The other neighbours are not like this, of course, behaving with grace and dignity. It is only Loli. Always Loli. *Just as well the Anise is in the kitchen.* I glance at Isabel, and shake my head, imperceptibly, in a kind of *you've got all you're getting so kindly get this woman out of my sight* kind of way, and she takes the hint, steering her sister by the arm towards the front door.

Suddenly, from the street comes the sound of raucous Spanish shouting. Oh please, please please please, let this not be Mercedes. Anyone but Mercedes. Not with Loli on the prowl. Tis the season to be jolly, of goodwill to all men, and women, although asking for love and sisterly understanding between our neighbours is expecting a bit much, to be honest. *Come on Richards, get a grip.* I will not tolerate someone getting called the son of a whore, in our house. If that is what happens, they are being ejected, and that is that, Mars Bars or no Mars Bars. I know someone who will eat them, and imbibe the allotted Anise, *don't I darling?*

Mercifully however, the gappy grin of Juan-the-soon-to-be-retired dustman appears around the door, followed by his buxom, orange wife, who, shorn of her fluffy white dog, seems diminished somehow. 'Come in neighbour' cries Fernando, as if it is he dispensing the Yuletide jollity. 'The train is waiting for you!' And squeezing his gut through the door, the three of them depart, Loli casting an envious eye on the remaining parcels of sweets, with me taking up the role of Primark store detective, to ensure she doesn't swipe something, on the way out. She resists the temptation, although I bolt the door, just in case she is trying to lull me into a false sense of security, then pop back when I am distracted, driving the train.

Strangely, the reaction of Juan and Susanna is broadly similar to that of our first visitors. Initial shock, then laughter. They are not sure what to make of it. And I still have a slight feeling of trepidation, that we are being disrespectful, despite the shitting gypsy figure taking a poo behind the stable, which is a Spanish tradition, after all. I pour myself a glass of Anise, and decide I am being overly sensitive. They all think we are bonkers, anyway, lying in the garden, having a sandwich at one o-clock, splashing around in the pool in the middle of winter, not bothering to take an umbrella if there is even the merest hint of rain, on the horizon. Driving a train around a Nativity village? Just one more morsel of gossip, for down the town in the morning.

And so the evening passes. A spectacular success, I decide, as we bolt the door for the final time. Whether everyone made it I have no idea, and my wife has no clue either, the state she was in. Will need to check which cards are left, in the morning, and deliver them by hand. I can leave the railway where it is for now, in case any judges in the *Best Blue Anchor to Dunster* section of the Nativity village competition actually show up. Besides, I need to wait until we get to the caravan over the New Year, when I can pop into the DIY warehouse at the end of the Malaga airport runway for the materials for the base-board. In the meantime, I can spend my evenings building and painting the model stations, platforms, with the little people waiting for the trains. Then a village, with a pub, a church, a post office, a chip-shop....

The following evening we head out for our regular *paseo* around the town, and notice that Betty Boob opposite has her blind up, proudly displaying a floodlit Nativity on a table inside the window. And not some crappy figures about three inches tall from the Chinese Bazaar, and Multibuys, such as we have. No. These are at least twice that and more, beautifully finished, incredibly detailed, and must have cost an absolute fortune. The Holy Family, of course, three wise men in all their glory, a collection of shepherds, an angel and various animals, none of whom appear to be squinting horribly. A wonderful display. Chrissie seems agitated, however. 'Shit', she whispers. 'Quick, back home, right now.'

I open the front door I last closed but two minutes ago, and we step inside. 'Was that *shit, how come the local rag-and-bone man has a wonderful Belen which makes ours look as if it came from a Lucky Bag?*' I enquire.

She is distracted by something, clearly, but still manages to regard me pitifully. 'No, it was shit we didn't give them a card, or any sweets, last night. I totally, sorry, *we* totally forgot them. I haven't made them a card. Because they are new here, since last Christmas, so when I was making the cards, and packaging up the sweets, they completely slipped my mind. And imagine what they must have thought last night, with all the hullaballoo going on over here? Anyway, like the good little woman I am, I have some cards in reserve, for just such an emergency, so while I run upstairs and get one, grab twelve *Celebrations* out of the tub, please.'

I decide against telling her I have no idea where the chocolates actually are, so rummage vaguely in the sideboard, *with one eye and one hand*, as mother used to describe dad's half-hearted efforts at looking for stuff, until I locate the disputed confectionery, then laugh like crazy as I prise off the lid to discover there are but eight left. 'I told you two tubs wouldn't be enough, didn't I?' as she returns clutching a card and a homemade, sparkly grab-bag.

'And whose fault was that, filling the suitcase with railway rubbish? she fires back. 'But not to worry, we can chuck in a handful of Jelly Babies, can't we? They are English sweets, just the same.'

Now, I have to tell you the Jelly Babies, MY Jelly Babies, are a major source of domestic disharmony, in this house. She likes Liquorice Allsorts, which I cannot stand, so she effectively gets to nibble on both, whereas I only get the Jellies. We have two large novelty plastic containers, about ten inches high, one shaped like Bertie Bassett, with his liquorice nose, cheeky grin and pictures of the various Allsorts across his belly, the other shaped like a smiling Jelly Baby, and every time we go to the UK we stock up on a couple of bags of each, then decant them into the respective containers when we get home. And guess which container becomes depleted the quickest? Correct. Occasionally, I catch her sneaking a crafty Jelly Baby from my stash, to which I always react in mock anger, but I cannot retaliate and nick one of hers, as I really cannot tolerate the taste.

Years ago, I ran the Bodmin Moor marathon, in November, in the driving sleet, and recall a guy in our running club, parked in a layby just down the road from Jamaica Inn, around the half-way point, handing out Jelly Babies to exhausted runners. Nothing, before or since, has quite hit the spot in the way that small handful did. Kept me going all the way to the finish. Bless you, Neil.

'Can't we give them half and half, a few Allsorts as well?' I growl, to no avail as quick as a flash, she whips MY container from the sideboard, snaffles a handful of MY sweeties, stuffs them and the remaining Celebrations into the sparkly bag and pulls the drawstring tight.

She opens the card, then giggles. 'What are their actual names, can you remember? I cannot put *to Betty-Boob and Limpy,* can I?'

I fold my arms in a huff. ' How should I know? None of this is anything to do with me. You made the cards, and the bags. This is all your idea. I could have got some more platforms into the case if it hadn't been for those cursed sweets. You drank all the bloody Anise last night. You are giving away my Jelly Babies. You sort it.' She fires me a glare, and my face creases into a huge grin. 'Er, Bettina and Javier, I think.'

She addresses the card, slides it into its envelope, and picks up the bag of disputed loot. 'Right' come on. Your turn to be Father Christmas!' We step across the street, I tap on the door, and Betty pokes her head out as if maybe she thinks we are double-glazing salesmen, or religious do-gooders.

'*Feliz Navidad!*' I cry, proffering our gifts. 'We love your Belen!'

She appears decidedly unimpressed, seemingly more interested in something around her feet. She bellows a command, then after a short period of agitated shuffling, opens the door fully, and beckons us inside. 'Come in' she smiles. '*Pasa, pasa*, but mind the kittens, *los gatitos*, don't let them escape!' I grit my teeth, and silently curse. Of course there had to be kittens, as her un-neutered tabby *Me-me* parades herself seductively up and down the street most evenings, attracting the attention of the local Toms, a surly, ragged bunch, who then gather in large numbers under our bedroom window in the middle of the night to engage in furious bouts of shrieking, wailing intercourse, during the mating season. Which seems to be just about always. I glance down and spy a diminutive ginger-and-white scurrying beneath the sofa, but of the remainder of these alleged *gatitos*, there is no sign.

'A present from England' Chrissie grins, as Betty expresses her thanks, launching into a monologue, an unstoppable outpouring of words, of which we are able to just about follow, but it is a struggle, let me tell you. At least I am spared the bear-hug Amador received. Against the wall, the seven-foot telly is playing, mercifully with the sound muted, and in the gloom I suddenly spot Limpy, sitting impassively at the kitchen table, rolling an Impressive mound of cigarettes, surrounded by piles of copper coins, reminiscent of a scene from a Dickensian work-house. Betty is still droning on in her child-like voice, and we, having lost the thread completely, or I have certainly, are nodding and smiling sympathetically. We could be agreeing to anything quite honestly, and I am longing to escape, if I could ever get a word in edgeways, although now we are getting a tour of the garden, it appears. Quite why I have no idea, as it is pitch black outside, but she flings open the back door and beckons us to follow. What could actually be out there? Her view of a dark mountain in the darkness? A life-size Nativity, perhaps? This is what I call an 'uphill house' of course, on the wrong side of the street to get the view of the town below, stretching out across the olive fields, accompanied by spectacular sunsets. *Reminds me of a book I read once....* No, at best she will have a view of the mountain, or possibly not, depends on how close the street above actually is. The hairpin bends weave their way up the side of the steep, rocky hillside, and what you get is a matter of geography, and pot luck. Dutch Dick's old house just along the street had no view, just a concrete terrace and a thirty-foot stone wall, supporting the terrace of the house above. Janie and Nigel's further down is likewise, yet Miguel's, their ruin next door which I am currently renovating, has a spectacular uphill garden, on three different levels. Pure chance, dependent on the configuration of the roads and houses above.

Chrissie trails Betty through the doorway, and exclaims, loudly. *Must be a life-size Nativity.* I follow, and receive a huge shock to the system. *Oh my God.* The thirty foot wall is there, right enough, but rather than in a perpendicular style, as walls invariably tend to be, this one lies in a grotesque heap on her patio, an ungainly accumulation of rocks, stones and soil, with the occasional tree root and weed sprouting through the devastation. I am struck dumb, momentarily, unable to think of a single appropriate comment to convey my shock, and sympathy at their misfortune. *Madre Mia* is a phrase the Spanish use, although often at some mild aggravation, as in *Madre Mia, Jose the Pan had no muffins this morning*, or as a form of rebuke, *Madre Mia, look at all that dust on her front door*. Wildly inappropriate in these circumstances. This is a *Madre-W-T-*

F-Mia situation. A *Madre-how-the-bloody-hell-did-that-happen-Mia* state of affairs. Our Spanish classes at the library have left us totally unprepared for such a situation, which will be the basis of a complaint to our dear friends down there next week, but for the moment, in total shock, I glance upwards at the now entirely unsupported earth bank, and the unguarded patio of the house above, teetering over the abyss.

I turn to Betty, who has herself fallen silent. *'Madre Mia'* I whisper, pathetically. *'Eye seguros?'* Is there insurance? Not *do you have insurance*, or *do the people above have any insurance*, simply *is there any?* My vocabulary is totally inadequate.

She shakes her head, sadly. 'No eye.'

A million thoughts go racing through my mind, in English, but in the language of our adopted country, not a single one. I feel totally inadequate. Chrissie however is on the ball. *'Hablado con Ayuntamiento?'* she enquires. Have you spoken to the Town Hall? Good one. That was to have been my next question, if only I could have articulated the phrase. Surely the Council has contingency funds for uninsured losses such as this, which could, quite seriously, result in catastrophic damage during the next deluge of rain to the actual foundations of the house above? The neighbouring cottages too. And this is not going to be a cheap job, believe me. Dutch Dick had a large hole open up in the wall above his patio during heavy rain, but that was only, I cannot remember exactly, but no more than three feet square. It required a week's work by a skilled team of specialist craftsmen to repair the damage, support the stonework, dig out the earth behind, rebuild the masonry to include adequate drainage, and back-fill the soil. Well, that is what it required, but what he actually got was a ragged group of Moroccans to brick it up one afternoon and poke a length of secondhand plastic drainpipe through. Still cost him six hundred euros mind you. And they stole all the grapes from his vine. I suspect the fact he was back in Holland at the time might have had something to do with both the extortion, and the theft.

'*Puta Ayuntamiento*' she replies. *So that is a no, then.* She launches into another monologue, the gist of which being that when it rains, the earth washes through the back of the house, clogging the drains, causing all sorts of problems, not only for them but the Kissy-Kissies next door, who are constantly complaining. When they are not kissing, presumably. A forlorn attempt has been made to cover the rubble with a tarpaulin sheet, a hopeless task as the pile stretches the full width if the house. Like sticking a Band Aid over the hole in the Titanic. Surely they could have afforded another few sheets, to cover the worst of it? They are only a couple of quid, in the Chinese bazaar. Hasn't Limpy been able to find anything, on his thrice-daily trawl around the streets? Actually, I have an old one in the shed which used to cover the pool. They can have that, tomorrow. And I think there is one in Miguel's, too.

I have to get out of here. I feel unbelievably sorry for the pair of them, but other than more questions which we are unable to ask, and some lengths of secondhand tarpaulin, there is nothing we can do. 'We are very sorry' I frown, as we edge towards the door. Limpy looks up from his coins and his fags, and grins. The giant TV is still playing. A fugitive kitten darts across the tiles. And our present, and card, are lying pathetically on the table. Some Christmas it will be, in this house.

CHAPTER 18. A CRAPPY CHRISTMAS

'Twas Christmas Eve, Babe,

In our bathroom,

And Chrissie said to me,

My feet are getting wet!

Apologies to The Pogues and Kirsty McColl for mangling the lyrics of what many regard as the greatest Christmas song ever recorded, and I would include myself among that number, but that is actually what happened. More or less.

Enjoying my third mug of coffee, with my feet up and the newspaper on my Kindle, I suddenly hear my wife calling out in distress. 'Help! The bathroom is flooded!'

I leap to my feet, and rush through to the back of the house. 'Are you, er, decent?' I enquire, tapping on the door.

'Of course I am!' comes the anguished response. 'Quick, get the mop and bucket. There's water all over the floor.'

Rapidly, I retrieve said items from the kitchen patio, thankfully remembering where they actually are, and with a calming air I enter the bathroom, to find a film of water trickling in my direction. Not a tidal wave it has to be said, but clearly it shouldn't be there.

'I pulled the flush' she wails, 'the bowl filled up then overflowed. What are we going to do?'

I glance at the toilet bowl. 'Were you, er, doing a number one, or a number two?' *Get the preliminaries sorted first, is my motto.*

She shoots me one of her *oh you blathering idiot* glares. 'A number one. For pity's sake, just get on with it.'

I pass her the mop and bucket. 'Well, this happened to me, yesterday, the bowl filled about three-quarters, but it didn't overflow. There must be a blockage down there. You mop, while I carry out some tests.' I turn on the taps of the bath, the sink, and the bidet. 'There you are, look' I continue. Everything is backing up. An obstruction in the main sewer pipe, under the floor. Hang on a minute, while I perform a final test.' And strolling sedately through to the kitchen, I flash her one of my *trust me, I am a professional* smiles. I turn on the kitchen tap. 'Right, the kitchen sink is draining perfectly, look. This means the blockage is down there, between the bog and the kitchen.' And I point to the affected area, under the floor. I think.

'So what does that mean?'

I suppress a chuckle. 'It means we will be washing in the kitchen, for the foreseeable. Showers are out, until I can get it sorted. The bathroom is out of bounds, from right now. Where is the Spanish phone?'

'What?' she splutters, 'who you gonna call? Poo-busters?'

I have never heard Del-Boy described as a 'poo-buster' before, but smile to myself at the apt description, as I dial his number. ''Ello mate!' cries the diminutive Cockney. 'Ow ya doin'?'

I assure him we are fine and dandy, all things considered. 'You remember when you had blocked drains, back last year, and told me about this machine you had? Can you tell me how it works?'

'Yeah, mate. It's a pressure washer, actually, the main unit is about the size of a small vacuum cleaner, you plugs in into the mains. Then the water has an input hose, which clips to an outside tap, with a snap fitting, about twenty foot of pipe, and the outlet is a smaller bore pipe, about thirty foot, really thick, sturdy, with a steel wand on the end a few inches long, which goes down the sewer. You switches it on, and feeds it in until you reaches the blockage, then wiggles it about, like. Christ, mate, get in the way of the jet and it'll take the top of yer 'ead off, it will. Like I say, it is a pressure washer really, for cleaning mould off yet walls and tiles, but you daren't use it on a Spanish wall, as you'd have no wall left! Serious!'

We giggle together, at the thought, but I have just the one question, to which I probably know the answer, but I have to ask, for the sake of my sanity. 'So this metal wand, will it go round the U-bend of a toilet bowl?'

'No mate' he confirms. 'You gotta take the bog up, then you can shove the wand and the pipe down the elbow-bend of the sewer.'

Deepest joy. That is my Christmas gone down the pan. Or not, as the case may be. 'So could I possibly borrow it from you, please?'

'Course you can, mate! Gimme a shout in the New Year, I'll dig it out for yer.'

THE NEW YEAR? 'Christ, Del, I need it today, we have a bit of an emergency here, the sewer is blocked, between the bathroom and the kitchen. We are, as they say, up shit creek.'

He laughs, heartily, at our predicament. 'Sorry mate, no can do. I'm off to England, right now, to stay wiv Jade, meeting her family an' all that, back the second of January. I'm actually walking down the bus station as we speak, with me suitcase. Getting the coach to Malaga, in 'alf an hour. Anyway, wass the problem? You got that bog on the downstairs landing, overlooking the street, doncha?'

In frustration, I gaze at the heavens for inspiration. We do indeed have a second toilet, the original in the house, clearly, before the kitchen and bathroom extension was built onto the back of the house in the nineteen-seventies. And this facility does actually reside at the top of the stairs down to the basement, next to the window onto the street, where we like to imagine Jose Ocana Pastor sitting, killing two birds with one stone, performing his daily 'duty' whilst chatting to the neighbours. *Having a poo-poo, Jose?* We've never used this artefact, as you'd struggle to cram a six-foot Englishman into the space, but it does cause much merriment when new friends come to call. We could I suppose use it for the next ten days, at a push, literally, and I could always soap myself off under the garden hose on the downstairs patio, even though it is the dead of winter. But Chrissie? Washing in stone-cold water on the patio? Forget it. Suddenly, inspiration arrives. 'What time is your flight, Del?'

'Well, the coach gets to Malaga bus station around half-two, then I gotta wait around for the airport bus, get there say half-three, the last check-in is four, I think. Flight leaves around six. Manchester. Christ, the frozen norf. That's nearly bloody Scotland, innit? Why couldn't she come from somewhere civilised?'

'Oh yeah' I snigger. 'Civilised, like you, a man who puts Daddies sauce on a roast dinner? Anyway, listen to this. What if I take you to the airport? You go back home now, dig out the pressure thingy, I'll collect you about one, stick it in the boot, that will give us plenty of time, I can drop you at departures, save you all that mucking about. What do you reckon?' Out of the corner of my eye I can see my wife waving her arms around like a madwoman, but ignore her. I am playing an absolute blinder here, and don't need the distraction.

Del jumps at the chance, of course, to save himself the bus fares, and have someone civilised to chat to, on the journey. We make final arrangements, and he rings off. Before I've even had time to put the phone down, Chrissie steams in. 'You idiot. I cannot believe this. Have you forgotten what day it is?'

I rub my hands across my face. Been a hell of a morning, so far. 'Er, Monday? No, hang on, Tuesday. I gaze out the window, vacantly. Yes Tuesday. Definitely Tuesday. So what?'

She turns away, shaking with laughter. Or anger. 'This is like talking to the living dead.' *It was anger.* 'It's Christmas Eve. Remember that? We get one every year. And who is coming here tonight, for the traditional Spanish Christmas Eve meal? *Not a clue, and who cares, quite honestly? Father Christmas? I've secured the pressure thingy. Nothing else matters, right now.* 'Nigel and Janie. Remember them? They're flying in today, we have the turkey ordered from the mother-in-law of Jesus, which needs to be collected, right now, so YOU can get it in the oven, so YOU can start the Christmas meal, which YOU have insisted on preparing. Half-six for seven, YOU said, and now you're swanning off to the airport giving a free lift to that stinky old reprobate.'

'That is a bit unfair, actually' I protest. 'Del has cleaned himself up, since he met Jade. Blimey, he even uses a razor, nowadays. I got him that after-shave, in Poundland, remember? And don't forget' I add, as she seems about to completely blow her top, 'it was you who got them together, wasn't it? I told you it would all end in tears, didn't I? So now it's come back to bite you on the ass, hasn't it? Anyway, I cannot worry about bloody Christmas. I have this mega job to plan, these drains to unblock. The toilet pan is cemented to the floor, isn't it, so I have to get the angle grinder out, and try to cut the cement seal, and get the pan up without breaking it, and without ruining the tiles. That means removing the guard on the grinder so I can get it as flat to the floor as I can, which is bloody dangerous, then wedge myself into the gap between the bog and the corner of the bathroom wall. Then, assuming that works, I have to get the pan up without breaking the sewer pipe. Then, I have to try to unblock the bloody thing. I've never done anything like this, I have no idea what to expect. I'll need the patio door and the bathroom window open to let the choking dust escape. It's gonna be hell in there. So sod Christmas. It's just been cancelled.'

She seems about to burst into tears. She's worked so hard, behind the scenes, making the cards, decorating the tree, assembling the Nativity village, the sweets for the neighbours, everything. Maybe I've been a trifle harsh. I place a comforting arm around her shoulder, which she brushes away, irritably. 'I'm so worried' she wails. 'I've been having nightmares, all week.'

'All week?' I echo. 'But this flood only happened half an hour ago. Why have you been having nightmares all week? Come on, sit down here and tell me all about it.' And I steer her to the sofa.

'It's that house opposite' she sniffs. 'Bettina. I keep dreaming we have a deluge of rain, the foundations of the houses above wash away and crash onto her patio, then the torrent continues, through her house, and the Ox one side, the Kissies the other, across the street and into ours. I dreamed last night Fernando was swept away, floating down the street like Moby Dick.'

'Well if that happens' I snigger, 'all you have to do is cling onto him, like a life raft! White-water Fernando-rafting in fact! But seriously, if Bettina's did flood, her front door is slightly down the hill, isn't it? So I think the water would simply run away down the street. Leopard-skin woman might get a little muddy, however! That collapse is a problem, a huge problem, and I have no idea what her and Limpy are going to do, but I really don't think we have anything to worry about.' *All very well me acting brave, but I had the same nightmare, more or less. Not the bit about Fernando of course, in mine it was Jonathan Ross floating away. Which made it a dream, not a nightmare....* 'Anyway, sorry about the Christmas dinner, but I simply cannot be in two places at the same time. I have to get that pressure thingy, we cannot be washing in the kitchen for the next ten days. Can't you message Janie and suggest we have it in their house? Seems the logical solution, to me.'

She fails to be reassured by my suggestion. 'Don't be ridiculous.

They are still in the air. They don't land until mid-day, then they have the hire-car to collect. They're not getting here until about four. We cannot possibly expect them to put on a Christmas dinner, they'll barely have time to have a shower and get changed.'

'Well lucky them!' I sneer, 'a shower, imagine that? So you'll have to take over then, won't you? You know what to do, you did the Christmas lunch for about thirty-five years, before we came here. Besides, you are better at it than me. Remember I dropped the pan of roasters, last year? And there are no Christmas dinners in the Rick Stein Spanish cook-book, are there, so you are better off taking over. Anyway, sorry, but I have a lot of planning to do. I have to get all my tools organised, laid out in the bathroom so I can start straight after breakfast tomorrow. I need to check I have some of the Super Blanco waterproof tile adhesive left, get my trowels, buckets up from the woodshed. Extension lead, spirit levels. I need to go through every stage of the job in my mind, rehearse grinding away the toilet pan cement. The bathroom needs to be stripped of everything that isn't nailed down. Shower curtain, bog seat, everything has to come out.'

She looks me in the eye. 'So what about the turkey? You arranged it, with Jesus. I don't even know his mum-in-law. How heavy is it going to be? It really has to go in the oven, soon. Who is going to carry it up the hill?'

Well me, clearly. Cursed turkey. They are not that common, here, actually. The Spanish usually have seafood with their family dinner, on *Noche Buena*, Christmas Eve. Bernard Matthews would not have made his fortune in this country, let me tell you. Chrissie and I usually have a chicken, given that it's only me who eats it. This year we need something bigger, of course, with our friends coming, so weeks ago I mentioned it to my student Jesus, he of Baena fame, which we still haven't managed to visit, by the way, and he suggested his mum-in-law, who runs the butchery shop in the square, to see what she could suggest. And the following week, hey presto, all arranged, collect it from the shop on *Noche Buena, por la manyanna*, which is right about now, as I've just been reminded. Cursed turkey. I don't even like it that much, actually prefer chicken. One year, I remember, not long after we were married, we decided to ditch tradition and have something else, beef possibly, Chrissie will remember, but it just wasn't the same, so the following year it was back to a turkey again. When the kids were younger, Louise would have a few slices of breast, me likewise, Chrissie and Charlie wouldn't touch it of course, so most of it ended up inside the dog. Loved Christmas, did Nelson. Partial to sprouts too, which did nothing to improve his flatulence.

My wife coughs, exaggeratedly. 'Er, hello? The turkey? Are you expecting it to stroll up the cobbles on its own? Does it know where we live? We don't want Fernando making off with it, do we? Are you sitting there all morning, gazing into space? Or are you going to GET YOUR FINGER OUT ANYTIME SOON?'

Cursed turkey. 'Right, so I've told you what I need to do, before I leave here around twelve-thirty, to collect my fragrant buddy. How about you run through what you will be doing, so we can agree a division of the labour?'

'What, apart from preparing and cooking a Christmas dinner from scratch, which I only found out about five minutes ago, and for which WE DON'T EVEN HAVE THE MAIN INGREDIENT YET? Getting the Christmas tablecloth and napkins out, the best crockery, our Engagement-present cutlery set, the festive candles, decorate the cake, and the other one-hundred-and-one things a woman needs to sort out to ensure everything is looking Christmassy, which blokes assume just happens automatically, and don't even notice? Those things do you mean? Then going down Janie's this morning, as I do every time they come, switching on the electric and water, and giving the place a thorough dust, sweep and mop?' She pauses her litany of Christmassy tasks,then suddenly wails. 'My shower. Oh Hell, what am I going to do about my shower?'

'Wait until Boxing Day?' I snigger, unhelpfully. 'I told you, the bathroom is out of bounds. The best we can do is use the kitchen sink, there is hot and cold water, we'll just have to make the best of it. Listen, if, if, if, and they are big ifs, *if* I can get everything done tomorrow, including unblocking the drains, then wiping down every surface in the bathroom, including the light fittings, to clear away the dust, then we can probably have showers Christmas night. The toilet will have to wait until Boxing Day, to give the cement time to dry. We have the second toilet, don't we? Don't worry, everything will be fine. IF.'

She remains unconvinced. 'But my hair, I need to wash my hair. Even you, with your minuscule barnet, will need a wash and brush-up before dinner, after two hours with that greasy urchin who, sorry to disappoint you, still reeks of damp dog, even with a hint of Poundland's finest dabbed on.'

'Ah don't worry about me' I giggle. 'I can have a sluice off on the Sombrero, when I get back. You will have to use saucepans, to swill your hair. Or what about this' I hastily add, as she seems about to lodge a formal protest about rinsing her hair with kitchen utensils. 'Have a shower down Janie's. Clean the rest of the house first, leave their bathroom to last. Have your shower, then mop out the cubicle, wipe down the glass sides, bingo, job done! See, takes a bloke to organise this stuff. I bet I could have the dining room looking Christmassy in half the time you take!' And I duck, to avoid the incoming slap.

She ponders this a moment, which I take as a sign that my excellent idea about the shower has taken root, not that she will ever admit it of course, and she will pay me back for the Christmassy jibe, sure as eggs is eggs, when I am least expecting it. 'So what about Janie and Nigel? They are sure to need a wee, some time during the evening, aren't they? And where will they wash their hands. What about towels?'

I rub my hand across my face, and sigh exaggeratedly. 'They will have to use the bog at the front, overlooking the street, same as us, won't they? Christ, Nigel is a fireman, they will pee anywhere, that lot. Make a chalk mark six foot up the wall and he will....'

'Shut up! I wasn't thinking of him, you blokes are all like dirty dogs. It was Janie I was talking about, I cannot see her wanting to go in full view of the street, even if there is a blind in the window. You know how particular she is.'

'Well who cares?' I shout, starting to get irritated by this turn in the conversation. 'Who do we think is coming? Royalty? The Queen of bloody Sheba? We are in the middle of a crisis. They will have to use our facilities, or go back to their place for a slash. Her family are all West Ham fans, aren't they? What does she have to get all particular about? Probably use tin baths, on a Friday night, in front of the fire, I bet! She can wash her hands in the kitchen. Just put a few hand towels out, Jeez.'

She remains unconvinced. 'So what if they need a wee when I am getting dinner ready? And really, I will need a quick shower after I've finished cooking, while you serve it up, give me chance to change. I wanted to wear that new dress you bought me. I don't want to be smelling of Christmas dinners now, do I?'

Did I buy her a dress? Slept since then. And I forgot about the Christmassy thing, didn't I? It doesn't just involve making the dining room look festive, it also includes the hostess. Me? I might change my chinos. I am getting sick of this piffle, I have important things to be getting on with, so I stand, signaling an end to the conversation. 'Well, the whole house will have a Yule-tide aroma of roasting fowl, won't it, so nobody will notice, will they? Or perhaps you could pretend you are wearing the latest perfume. You know, Chanel Number Six Pigs In Blankets, or Brut Thirty-Three Roasters, Yves Saint Laurent Stuffing Balls? Send them a Facebook message, which they will pick up when they land, outlining our predicament, telling them to have a tinkle before they come here. Now, I am off to collect the confounded turkey as nobody else is volunteering. Where's my wallet?'

Christmas Day dawns, well I'm not really sure how it dawns to be honest. I spent a restless night, images of whirling, screaming angle grinders inches from my ears disturbing my sleep, visions of sewers blocked by fat-bergs the size of footballs, which is why, for the first time since the Christmas morning when I was sixteen and so horribly hungover I failed to emerge from my pit until Boxing Day, my Festive Fry-Up has been cancelled. For some strange reason, considering the Christmas lunch she was in the course of preparing, Mother used to insist on serving a good old British blow-out for breakfast, lest we became peckish during the morning. Dad and I used to wolf it back of course, a tradition I have continued throughout our married life. Today, however, a couple of slices of toast, and I am struggling to get those down, to be honest. My stomach is in knots, and we still have the charade of the present-opening to get out of the way, before I can get down to work. Deep joy.

Del-Boy was conveyed to Malaga airport safely, benefiting from civilised conversation en-route, although he spent much of the journey with his head out of the car window, puffing on a never-ending supply of kerbside roll-ups which any self-respecting hobo would surely have discarded, all the while urging me to smash our ancient crapper to smithereens and get a modern, close-coupled version, dismissing my protestations that we quite liked our traditional cistern at the top of the wall as befitting an ancient cottage and not wishing to turn our bathroom into something which might be encountered in a Travelodge. Fell on deaf ears, of course. Carried away on the fag smoke, more like.

And the party went well, plumbing arrangements not withstanding. The turkey turned out to be a monster, easily capable of carrying Fernando away, let alone vice-versa, although I will still be eating it come Easter Monday, being without benefit of Golden Retriever. It's times like this I miss the old boy. Nigel meanwhile caused uproar by rolling up the window blind next to our reserve toilet and mooning across the street, in the general direction of Betty Boob, which caused me, shrieking with laughter, to crash through the front door and capture the image on my phone for posterity. He resembled one of those women you see in Amsterdam, I felt, so I've been told, although I am unable to check this morning as my phone has been confiscated, it appears.

I mentioned the charade of the present opening? I should have said the embarrassment, as Chrissie has divided the hoard into *his and hers*, the latter pile dwarfing mine spectacularly. In fact, mine is not even a pile, consisting of but one rectangular shape, around eight inches long, three wide and the same high, maybe. Still, it is pleasantly wrapped, which is some consolation, but considering I have one wife and two daughters, a meagre return I feel. Chrissie's stash is boosted by her students of course, all of them female, and barely an evening has passed these last few weeks when she has failed to return home bearing gifts, and grinning boastfully. My pupils on the other hand, all blokes, have donated precisely diddly. Not even a single Christmas card. I gave them each one of course, in aid of the RNLI this year, a wintry scene depicting a dusting of snow across the deck of an old fishing boat, bobbing serenely in a Cornish harbour, a happy bunch of ruddy-cheeked kids building a snowman on the quayside. Miserable Spanish. They have no tradition of sending Christmas cards it appears, although they all love gazing at ours. *Eengliss traditional, yees.* If the popularity of a man is reflected in the gifts he receives… 'Hang on a minute, what about Lydia? Hasn't she got me anything?'

My wife titters helplessly. 'Yes she has, but I put it in my pile. She has addressed it to *Cristina and John*. My name first. Besides, it's something soft, unlikely to be for you, a scarf or something, and you know how much you hate being bundled up, round the neck. Anyway, are you going to open your present?' *Note the accent on the singular.*

'No' I wince, through gritted teeth, 'I'm going to savour the anticipation. You go ahead, I want to enjoy feminine re-gifting, in all its glory.' And I narrow my eyes, and nod knowingly. I was wrong. Present after present was clearly bought with Chrissie in mind, a series of highly individual items of great charm. *Curses.* Even Lydia's, a scarf as predicted, in girly colours. You wait until I see her, in the New Year. She is C-Level English, she will understand a dose of good old British sarcasm.

Soon, it is time for mine. She hands it to me, barely able to keep a straight face. 'This is from the three of us.' I heft the thing in my hand. A box, most definitely, and were I a betting man, a railway locomotive I would say. I tear off the wrapping, never being one for saving the stuff, bearing in mind a forty-foot roll is about a quid, to reveal an illustration of a mobile phone on the top, the Apple logo on one end, the legend *iCloud* the other, the words *iPhone 8* on the side, and *64GB* on the bottom. Yeah, right. These things are about a thousand quid, aren't they? This has to be a wind-up, right? They've got hold of an Apple box from somewhere, Charlie, I am guessing, who always seems to have a succession of cracked and dilapidated iPhones in her possession every time we see her, and they've stuck a loco inside. Which is great, actually. Just what I wanted. I've been dropping hints about a GWR 64xx-class tank-engine on eBay recently. Maybe this is it?

My wife is watching my eyes intently, an enigmatic smile on her face, as I separate the two halves of the box, the bottom sliding cleverly from inside the top, to reveal an actual mobile phone. A Chinese copy, has to be, and actually I will be annoyed if it turns out to be genuine, as I regard extravagance, particularly at Christmas, as faintly vulgar, and they know that. I lift it from the plastic tray, and turn it over, revealing the word *iPhone*, and another Apple logo. The front and back appear to be made from glass, but the frame is metal and the whole thing has a quality feel. *Surely not?...* Chrissie, sensing perhaps my hesitation, is unable to contain herself any longer. 'It is not the latest version, obviously, we are not made of money, but it is new, never been used, an ex-display model. You must blame Charlie, it was her idea, she was sick and tired of you calling her up, constantly, after you dropped your iPod last summer and broke it, then tried to transfer your entire music library to a memory card to stick in your ancient clam-shell. She was calling me, *for God's sake tell Dad to get an iPhone,* then we were all stuck for something to get you, this was before you bought the train set of course,when she saw this somewhere and that was that. Problem sorted! Don't you like it?'

She can detect the slight hesitation on my face, no doubt. 'Of course I like it' I smile, 'I am stunned, quite honestly. Thank you all so much, I will call Louise later, as soon as I get this flaming bathroom sorted. Problem is, I will need to ask Charlie how it works, won't I? I have no idea, quite honestly, and I'm a little scared, not scared but apprehensive, and she will need to guide me through it, step by step, which is gonna take hours!'

She grins, widely. 'No need, it is all set up, ready to go. You need to put it on charge, then you are all set. All your music is on there, you just press a couple of buttons and off you go!'

'How can that possibly be?' I frown. 'I need to connect it to the laptop, where my iTunes library is stored, so it can transfer across, 'sync' they call it. I will need to find out how to do that first. She will need to explain that.'

'Not so!' she laughs. 'Everything is up in the clouds, these days. Remember when we were on the turkey and tinsel weekend at the end of October in Weston? When Charlie and Andrew came down on the train? You and Andrew snuck off to the bar to sample the single malts? Well us technically-minded girls went up to our room, Charlie connected the phone to the hotel Wi-Fi, entered your iTunes account details on the phone and it all started downloading, automatically. It was really strange to see, actually, the list of albums getting longer and longer, the whole thing took about half an hour I suppose, but by the time we dug the pair of you out of the bar, it was all done.'

I am puzzled, quite frankly. 'How did she know my iTunes log-in details? I don't understand.'

'The little black address book, with our passport numbers and all that, which you always insist on taking every time we go abroad? It was all in there! Anyway, the home screen has a few icons, a calendar, a calculator, alarm clock, maps, camera, photos, messages, the music, and of course the phone has its own Wi-Fi. We converted your old Tesco pay as you go to what they call a Rocket Pack, which includes data, so you can use the internet out in the street, or down the garden, or wherever you like. It is connected to the house internet in here of course, but outside it switches to your own data. Fifteen gigs a month or something, Charlie said that should be plenty and you can always change it, it is still pay as you go, no contract, but renews every month.'

'So how did you know my Tesco Mobile log-in details?'

'Er, the little black book? Oh, I forgot, your email account is on there too, you just press the Yahoo button and your messages appear. And I swapped your SIM card over last night too, while you were snoring away. That disgusting photo of Paul's backside turned up as well, but I managed to delete it.'

'Ah you spoil-sport!' I huff. But how did you get my Yahoo log-in details?'

She rolls her eyes. 'Er, the little black book? Blimey, you have everything in there. Do you know you even have the password for the Isle of Wight ferry?'

I smile warmly at the mention of a life-long friend, from early family holidays, when I was about five, that time my mother was horribly sea-sick when the boat was still tied up in Lymington harbour, until a couple of years ago and a short hiking trip around West Wight. And I feel a tingle of excitement about my latest Christmas present. An iPhone. Just imagine. Didn't see that one coming, did I? I reach behind my chair and bring forth Chrissie's present from me, expertly wrapped I'll have you know. 'There you go, not really much of a surprise, but I saw this, and thought of you! Grabbed from under the noses of those Japanese women in that department store in Cardiff!'

She giggles at the memory. 'Not anything of a surprise, really, seeing as how **I** chose it. **I** saw it and thought of me! **I** brought it home in **my** suitcase! But thank you so much, I love it!'

'You haven't even opened it yet!' A Radley bag, of course, what else is a man to do? A large white one depicting a wintry scene on one side, two scarf-clad Scottie dogs frolicking in the snow, one of whom is poking his head out of a kennel, a robin perched on the end of his nose, Christmas trees zigzagging up the mountainside, and a blue and white spotted leather dog pendant dangling from the strap.

'Anyway' I continue, 'enough of this jollity. Wish me luck! Are you meeting Janie and Nigel for their walk around the mountain this morning, while I get on with this?'

'Not blooming likely!' she frowns. 'I'm staying here. Bandages and sticking plaster to the fore. A mop handy, for the blood. Not wishing to tempt fate of course, but severed digits are on the cards, this morning. Do you think I could walk round some mountain with you in mortal danger? I will be right here, listening out for cries of pain.'

Well thanks for the vote of confidence. I already have my work head on however, concentrating too hard to be offended. I performed a dry-run yesterday, before leaving for the airport, and came to the conclusion that the job would be a piece of cake, were it not for the bath, the sink, and the bidet. Imagining the bowl as an oval shape, the front and the left-hand end should be a doddle, the right end a slight problem, although doable, but the far side next to the wall, damn near impossible. I even tried lying in the bath, gut resting agonisingly on the rim, but had to give up on that position, after about five seconds. There is simply no space in which to stretch my ample frame. Now I know what you're thinking, because I wondered the same thing myself. *Why doesn't he simply cut the steel wand off the end of the pipe, so he can shove the bare tube around the U-bend, switch on the pressure-washer, save himself the bother of demolishing half the bathroom, and have an end to this drama?* Well, all yesterday morning I was hoping, nay praying, there would be a little jubilee clip I could undo, to simply detach the wand. All the way up the zig-zag road, hands gripping the steering wheel, right up to the moment Del carried the equipment to the boot of the car. Blast, blast and thrice blast. The pipe was molded, factory-fitted to the wand, to cut it off an act of wilful destruction of a piece of kit that is not mine. 'That is brilliant, mate, thank you so much for letting me borrow it' I smiled, through gritted teeth, as he got into the car, and rummaged for his first roll-up.

So. Angle grinder ready, mask and goggles in place, switch on, here we goooo.... within seconds the air is filled with choking dust, visibility down to just about zero, and I have to switch off to allow the room to clear. Wafting away the smoke, wiping my goggles with a thick leather-gloved finger, I note I have cut through less than an inch. What the hell is this stuff they used? Throughout our time in this country, I have joked about the porous, crumbly nature of Spanish cement. Not laughing now, am I? And so the morning progresses. Lying on my back, knees up round my neck, head bent at an impossible angle, slowly, but surely, muscles screaming, I make it around the clock-face, and feel the bowl start to move a fraction. Blessed relief. I lie there, savouring the moment, stretching my legs up the wall to allow the blood to flow. Resisting the impulse to grip the bowl to haul myself into a standing position, I struggle to my feet and lurch through to the kitchen, where my waiting wife bursts into uncontrolled laughter. 'You look like a ghostly Christmas snowman! Come out to the patio and dust yourself off. Well done! Is that it? Here, drink this.'

Never before has a plain glass of water tasted as sweet, and I drink deeply. 'That's the first part done, yes, but now comes the critical moment. Grab that length of plank if you can, position yourself next to the pan, and when I lift it, drop the wood over the hole, to prevent Uncle Bob making a bid for freedom.'

'Ah you great baby! With all the noise you've been making, Uncle Bob and his whole family will have decamped to the coast, for a Christmas break! Even the cats have run for cover! Loli was in the garden, shouting, earlier, but I ignored her. Do you fancy a turkey sandwich by the way? Keep your strength up? We've plenty left!'

I stretch my back, to ease the knots from my spine. 'Not at the moment, thanks. I still have the sewers to attend to. Now, take hold of the wood, and after three. One, two, three, GO!' And I gently lift the bowl, screwing my eyes tight shut and crossing my legs, in case any resident vermin should go galloping across the bathroom floor, until I hear the reassuring sound of the plank dropping firmly into place. I carry the bowl out to the patio, turn it upside down, and stand it in its rim. And bask in the glory. Take a bow, Sir Jonno. You are indeed a star. Undamaged. A result of the first order. Under every toilet bowl there will be a pudding basin-shaped protrusion, which forms a seal with the sewer pipe. On modern ones there will be a rubber grommet, to make the whole thing watertight, but on these examples from an earlier century, not. Which is why the floor flooded yesterday of course. But hey-ho, if it was good enough for ole Joe Shepherd, it is good enough for us, and I can always dab a bead of mastic around the joint when I refit it later.

I stand on the patio, and breathe luxuriously. 'Got time for a cuppa?' Chrissie enquires, placing one on the table. 'So what now, the machine? Is the danger over? Can I stop worrying?'

'You can indeed' I laugh, lightheadedly, still feeling the warm glow of success. You can put away the plasters, and the bandages. The threat of blood is over. Just let me tidy the angle grinder away, If you could plug the machine in, while I connect it to the tap, then if you stand by the wood, and lift it so I can shove the wand down the hole. But first, I have to whack the plank, a couple of times, with this hammer.'

What is that, Morse code?'she giggles.

'It is indeed!' I reply, deadly serious. 'Morse code, in rat-speak. 'It means 'don't' whack, 'pop' whack, 'your' whack, 'head' whack, 'out!' whack.

She rolls her eyes. 'Actually I'm closer to this damn sewer than you are, holding this flipping wood. Can you get a move on, please?'

I flash her a watery smile. 'Just one moment, please, I have a final addition to my ensemble,' and I nip out to the patio, and return clad in a pair of rubber gloves, in a fetching shade of pink.

She was crouching against the bathroom wall, now she is laughing so much she slumps to a sitting position. 'Oh wow, you really know how to turn a woman on! A cement-covered, stinky old builder in a pair of Marigolds! That is really doing it for me, let me tell you! Sex bomb, sex bomb, you're my sex bomb! Can I shove a couple of dollars into your jeans?'

'Ah shut up' I growl. 'If you think I'm putting my bare hands down a sewer, think again.' I waggle my fingers seductively, and grin. 'Yeah well, they were all I had in my tool box, OK? Must have got two pairs for some job I was doing in Miguel's. Anyway, when I shout go, I need you to lift the plank, stand it against the wall, then run like hell, as I'll be shoving the wand down the hole with one hand, and switching on the machine with the other. I have no idea what will happen next, it might all come fountaining out, and you will be in the direct line of fire. All right? Ready? GO!' In the enclosed space, the noise of the thing is deafening, and the force of the jet so powerful that for a split second my aim goes awry and I send a fugitive burst across the bidet, but I manage to bring it under control and ram the wand down the hole, causing it to froth and bubble like a witch's cauldron. Mercifully, the jet appears to be getting through whatever vile concoction is causing the obstruction as there is minimal backflow, so gritting my teeth I reach into the pipe and attempt to wiggle the wand around the elbow bend, where it can perform as advertised, and blast whatever blockage is down there away to the main sewer under the street.

Suddenly, horrifically, I feel a pair of teeth sink into the back of my hand, and screaming wildly, I stagger to my feet, glove shredded and blood welling from the wound, and with just about the presence of mind to kick the plank across the hole, I lurch into the kitchen, almost knocking my startled wife clean off her feet. 'I BEEN BIT, I BEEN BIT, RABIES, LOCKJAW, BERRY-BERRY, DYSENTRY, CHRIST ALMIGHTY'. And ripping the tattered Marigold from my throbbing wrist, I dive wildly under the kitchen sink, emerging with a small bottle of bleach, and fighting blindly to unscrew the top, I pour around half the contents over the affected area. Which sends the pain level sky-high of course, but at least the poison should be contained. I am hopping around like a scalded cat, heart pounding in my chest. My worst nightmare has come true. 'TETANUS. WHEN WAS MY LAST TETANUS SHOT?'

Chrissie springs into action, of course. 'All right, calm down, sit there, let me see?' She produces a small pile of serviettes, and proceeds to dab the area gently. 'Blimey, you were lucky, the scratch has missed all those veins. In a minute when the bleeding stops you can run it under the tap, then I can dress it properly.'

I am outraged. 'Scratch? Scratch? It was a bite I'm telling you. I felt the teeth sink in. Jesus. And turn that bloody pressure washer off, will you? The noise is driving me insane. That is it.

I am finished with it. Tomorrow we call a plumber, or if I die of raging gangrene in the night, you will have to call one.' She heads into the bathroom, and switches off the infernal noise, then I hear her moving the plank. 'DON'T TOUCH THAT! THE BLOODY THING IS STILL IN THERE! DON'T LET IT ESCAPE OR I WILL ACTUALLY DIE!' And my whole body is shuddering.

She ignores me, and instead strolls through to the hallway, then returns clutching a little silver LED torch. What is this, to check if my pupils are dilated, or whatever it is they do on *Casualty*? Instead she returns to the bathroom, and I hear the wood being shifted again. Several minutes pass, and I lift the tissue to check if the infection is spreading up my arm yet. Thankfully, for the moment at least, the bleach has done its job. Eventually she returns, and sits calmly next to me in her patio chair. 'Let me see the cut? Mmmmm. Much better. I'll put a dab of Germolene on it in a moment.' I am about to protest mightily about describing my villainous gash as a mere 'cut', but she over-rides me. 'Tell me, are the drainpipes in the bathroom all made from lead?' I am about to kick off again but she raises a hand. 'Humour me a moment. Are they?'

'Who the bloody hell cares...' then I catch sight of the fire in her eyes. 'Er yes, the sink is, and the bidet certainly, remember that fuss we had with the copper washer reacting with the *agua fuerte* a couple of years ago? The bath I have no idea as it is under the floor, but I imagine so. Why?'

'And is the sewer pipe asbestos, or fibre of some kind?' She still has the look on her face.

'Not sure, but almost certainly yes. Jade's runs through her basement and hers is, so I imagine ours will be the same.'

'So the lead pipes of the bath, the sink and the bidet all join the main sewer, under the bathroom floor, right?'

I know what this is. She is taking over the whole job. Picking my brains, before stepping in, and saving the day. ' I imagine so', I confirm, cheering up considerably. 'Just the other side of the elbow bend, I think. I've not actually plucked up the courage to look down there, yet.'

'So, with your extensive knowledge of Spanish plumbing, do you reckon the place where they join is a pre-formed section with neat little junctions, where the pipes can snugly fit? Or do you think the original bodgers who installed this just banged holes into the sewer pipe and rammed the lead pipes through, sealing the joints with any old plop they had to hand?'

I am really grinning now, at the mention of Spanish plumbers. 'They bodged it. One hundred per-cent!'

She smiles sweetly, as she administers the *coup de grace.* 'In which case, do you possibly think that this alleged attack by a disease-ridden rodent was actually you catching the back of your hand on a rough, unfinished, badly sawn, protruding length of lead pipe? The bit of lead pipe you can actually see sticking out, if you peer down the hole, and snap on the torch?' She sits back in her chair, and nods her head, implying there is more to come. She has not finished with me yet. 'Do you remember, back when we first moved in here, that evening when all those Brits turned up, most of them uninvited? And one of them, I forget who in all the hubbub, but somebody told us not to put toilet paper down the pan, in this country? You poo-pooed the idea of course, excuse the pun, load of crap you said, excuse the pun again, this is not a Third World country you said, of course you can put paper down there, you said. And so we have been, ever since. Despite just about every cafe or bar in town, the new part of town, having a notice up asking patrons not to throw paper *hygenico* down the pan? And them putting a little flip-top bin there, for that purpose? Disgusting, you said. What sort of country is this, you said. So you were wrong, weren't you? And that Brit, whoever it was, who had lived here longer than us, and therefore knew best, was right, weren't they? So you have cocked up again, haven't you? You didn't listen, did you? This is all your fault, this completely ruined Christmas Day, isn't it?'

Before I have time to comment on that distinct possibility, however, there comes a disgusting sucking noise, and then a whoosh, like a small underground explosion, or rockets going off. My grinning wife places her hand to her ear, theatrically. 'Oh hark. Could that be the blockage, wending its way to the sewage plant, or the sea, or wherever it goes? I think so. In which case, let me put a tiny plaster across your minuscule scratch, so that you can get on AND FINISH THIS BLOODY JOB?'

CHAPTER 19. AND THE WORLD TURNED

'Was that Peter Stringfellow-lookalike character here last year?' We are relaxing peacefully on our sunbeds under our favourite palm tree, sheltering from the hot tropical sunshine, at our Sri Lankan beach-resort hotel. The one I was forced to book, after losing that bet about the car repairs, a few months ago. The Indian Ocean is lapping peacefully on the white powdery shore behind us, the infinity pool is calling, from just across the lawn, a spicy omelette and several cups of strong black coffee are nestling comfortably in the pit of my stomach, and all is well with the world. But one of our fellow guests is puzzling me. I recognise him, surely. Not from the TV of course, he is not the real Stringfellow, in those scruffy yellow board-shorts with the faded bit around the groin, although these days, you just never know, do you? Stranger things have happened.

'What, that little poser, with the scrawny blonde wife, her with the mouth like a cat's arse, you mean?' giggles Chrissie. 'No, I don't think so, but you're right, he does look familiar.'

The situation resolves itself that evening, over pre-dinner drinks on the terrace, when Stringfellow and cat's-arse stop for a quick chat. 'Where do you live in England?' he enquires.

'Spain!' I chuckle, 'but we lived in Cornwall for many years, before we emigrated a few years ago.'

'Ooh, my God, we live in Cornwall too!' cries the blonde.

'Whereabouts were you?'

I can feel the warning pressure of Chrissie's foot under the table, but I wade straight in, as I always do. 'Newquay' I smile. 'Still got a bungalow there actually, which we let.'

He runs his fingers through his thinning locks, frowning. 'Oh my God, so do we! Just up towards Fistral, by the golf course. So where is your place?'

'Down towards Porth' I grin, still without the faintest clue who this pair are.

He laughs. 'So you know Graham Law, Paul Linden, Pete Miles, all that crowd!' he laughs. 'The Bunt brothers, Jack Trelaske, all my good mates?'

We do indeed. Poseurs the lot of them. They used to ride their motorbikes to the local pub and line them up outside, despite it being quicker to walk, then stand around, gurning for the tourists.

'So what are you called?' I enquire, the penny still not having dropped.

'Phil Davies, and this is Hannah, but everyone calls me P-D' he confirms.

'Chrissie and John' I nod, rising to shake his hand, still slightly embarrassed that I cannot fathom who on earth they actually are.

Luckily my wife steps into the lull in the conversation. 'So did you know Jill Turner?' she wonders. 'Lived along Tower Road. Jill and her husband Harry were good friends of ours, from years ago, but Jill sadly died just a few days before we came away. Her funeral is the twenty-first of this month, sadly we're unable to go, as we will still be here then.'

He looks vaguely at his wife. 'Yes, we did, you remember, Phil?' she pipes up. 'We knew their daughter better, the eldest one, they had one of those long dogs, you know, the labrador-basset crosses, they were all black apart from the brown one.'

'Well, everyone is really worried about Harry' Chrissie continues. 'They were such a devoted couple, childhood sweethearts, known each other for ever, did everything together. Nobody knows how Harry is going to cope. And he is such a private man, won't talk about his feelings, he's not on Facebook or anything, and their three daughters are spread around the country, they all have their own families, it's going to be so difficult to keep an eye on him. Ellen, the youngest, is staying at the moment, she is passing on messages from us, he is a Tottenham Hotspur supporter so John is gently ribbing him about how rubbish they are, you know, but we cannot help worrying about him.'

'Anyway, I can feel the gin calling' smiles Stringfellow, ignoring everything Chrissie has just said, 'so we must dash! Lovely to see you, and we'll have another chat tomorrow.' And the pair of them wend their way unsteadily towards the bar, for what will clearly not be their first beverage of the evening.

'Blimey!' I splutter. 'What a strange pair. Are they addicted to gin, or what?'

My wife shoots me one of her superior looks. 'So have you worked it out yet? Has it penetrated that thick skull of yours?'

You cannot help laughing, can you? Mind you, she has known me for forty-five years. She is correct. I can be rather slow on the uptake, especially after a couple of Sundowners. 'Um, well, phew, er, no, not really' is the best I can manage.

'Your old mate in the town' she persists, like she is addressing a baby. 'Clive. Remember him, do you?'

'Of course!'

'And his wife, or should I say EX-WIFE?'

'Madge!' I cry, triumphantly. 'Whoever could forget Mad..... Oh bloody hell!'

She leans back in her chair, nodding, while my grey-matter gets itself into gear. 'And, what do remember about Madge?'

'Shit, oh my God! She was having an affair with that P-D, wasn't she? They got caught having it away in the pub car-park, didn't they? And then, a few days later, she came into the pub and announced to everyone that P-D was the love of her life, and that she was moving in with him, didn't she? Christ, that must have been twenty years ago, easy. And poor Clive never got over it. I saw him a few years ago when I was back there decorating the bungalow. They are still separated, or divorced. And we have to spend the next couple of weeks here with that weaselly bastard, who was shagging my best mate's wife.' And I feel myself tensing-up.

'But it is worse than that, isn't it?' she smiles. 'Don't you remember what happened, that night in the Institute, when we were in there with Jill and Harry?'

'OH! HOLY! CRAP!' The fog of all those years, and more importantly, all those pints of Abbot Ale in the Institute, clears, and I am transported back in time to that night, standing, with him backed against the wall. I bury my head in my hands. 'Oh God. Yes of course. He came in there that night, didn't he, mouthing off about Clive, saying horrible things about him, what a total loser he was, and I snapped, told him to get his sorry ass out of my pub and never come back. And I don't suppose I've had anything to do with him since. And now, in the middle of Asia of all places, we have to spend the next two-odd weeks with the bloke. And right now, the pair of them are in the bar, piecing together the story, recalling what happened that night, and who we are, and the whole holiday is turning into a sodding nightmare.'

Chrissie meanwhile is rocking with laughter. 'I wouldn't worry. The pair of them were pissed right up that night, they're pissed now, so I doubt they remember anything about it. And besides, talking about his affair is probably verboten in their house. He is still with that Hannah, clearly. Just forget about it.'

Now it is my turn to giggle.'I suppose you are right, P-D probably was rat-arsed that night, I know I was. But it's still going to be awkward, at the very least, next time we see them.'

The rest of our evening, dinner then a few more cocktails on the terrace, passes without incident, and the Stringfellows appear to have taken an early night. The calm before the storm.

Next morning, Chrissie is checking her Facebook messages before breakfast, when suddenly she starts to wail, uncontrollably. 'Oh, no, Harry is dead.' And she convulses into tears. I rush across to hold her, and my first thought is *suicide?* She struggles to control herself. 'It's a message from Ellen,' she explains, brushing away the tears. Harry was admitted to hospital a couple of days ago with cardiac problems, after Jill died, but he just slipped away peacefully last night. He died of a broken heart. The girls are trying to arrange a joint funeral for the same day as Jill's. Can you imagine anything sadder than that?'

I cannot, and feel as if I've been hit for six. The poor girls, having to bury both parents, at the same time. To me, that is unimaginable. Chrissie dries her eyes. 'Tell you what, would you mind giving me ten minutes? Would you take the towels down to the sunbeds, and I'll catch up with you at breakfast?' We hold each other tightly, which is all there is to do in the circumstances.

In a complete daze, I wander across the hotel gardens, and the first person I see is Hannah, setting up her own sunbed. I sit down heavily on the end, and take a deep breath. 'I'm afraid we've just had some terrible news....'

We talk it through, and actually I find it helps to get it into the open, to try to get some perspective on the whole sad situation. I then stumble to our beds, slump down, then whip out my phone, scroll down to the music section, and select *With or*

Without You by U2, the song I most associate with our friends, dancing together to a live band at the Institute, all those years ago. And it is here that Chrissie eventually finds me, tears streaming down my face.

After breakfast P-D approaches our table. 'Such sad news about Jim' he confirms.

'Er, Harry?'

'Oh yes, sorry, Harry. Like we said, we didn't know him that well, we knew their eldest daughter much better, forget her name now, but a horrible situation for her and her sisters.' *It certainly is, pal, even if you can't remember our friend's name.* 'Anyway, I wanted to say goodbye, we are leaving this morning, we can't stand it here any longer, some of the guests are so working class, not our sort of people at all. This hotel claims to be four-star, but it's more like two, actually, like Asian Butlin's. Two new English couples have moved in near us and the blokes have shaven heads, for God's sake. Another couple are leaving their wet swimwear hanging on the balcony railings instead of the clothes horse, I spoke to them about it but it was like conversing with pork. I actually had a forty-five-minute meeting with the manager yesterday, told him what he is doing wrong, how he could improve the place, but he just didn't get it, so we've found another hotel near Colombo, five-star. It will suit us better.'

I actually want to punch the air and perform back-flips, then apologise for the fact that my father was a mere pleasure-steamer operator, but supreme self-control enables me to mumble something about how sorry we are they are leaving, and how we hope to look them up next time we are back. And with a wave, he is away to reception, to order his taxi. *Oh bugger, I meant to suggest we have a pint in the Institute.*

Later that afternoon, at High Tea, a decidedly working-class event at 4pm for anyone who might be feeling faint between lunch and dinner, we bump into Lynn and Alan, a couple from the New Forest we have become friendly with over the past week. Slightly younger than us, they both have a wicked sense of humour, and we have spent a few hilarious evenings with them in the bar. 'You know that bald bloke with the long blond side-pieces?' Al giggles. 'You call him Stringfellow or something, but we don't know who that is, do we Lynn, cos we're too young? Anyway, he came up to me yesterday and told me to take our towels off the balcony, and put them on a clothes horse, but we're too young to know what a clothes horse is!'

'It's because you are low-class, Al' I giggle. 'Leaving your skid-marked budgie-smugglers lying around. Just as well you don't have a shaven head. So what did you say?'

His wife is laughing fit to burst. 'He told him to eff-off, of course! What a tosser! Just as well they have cleared off as we'd have had a row, for sure. D'you know where they've gone?'

'Some five-star place near Colombo, he told me this morning, will suit them much better than being near you riff-raff!'

Our friends are doubled over. 'Oh my God!' Al splutters. 'He'll love it there! Full of Russians! We had a night there last year, absolutely hated it, grey-faced, porky, fag-breath Ruskies, looked like they'd spent ten years in the gulag. Pushing, shoving, ignorant savages! Anyway, he said they used to know you, years ago, didn't you live in the same village, or something?'

'We did' I titter. And if you have five minutes, I'll tell you a funny little story about them...'

'Ooh, I love your stories!' Lynn smiles. 'I downloaded your book today, it's hilarious. So come on, we're all ears. Let's hear it!'

I pause for dramatic effect. 'Well now, about twenty years ago, the Stringfellow character was having an affair.....

Time passes quickly, and all too soon it is the day of the funeral, nine o-clock in the morning in the UK, half-three in the afternoon here, and to mark the occasion as our friends would have appreciated, I order a G&T for me, a V&T for Chrissie, their favourite drinks. We touch glasses, fondly recalling all the good times. 'God bless you, Jill and Harry' Chrissie whispers.

I meanwhile have a song running through my head, a Tottenham Hotspur song which Harry and I used to sing occasionally, towards the end of the evening. I can hear him now, belting out the lines, glass in hand, but never spilling a drop.

'Nice one Cyril,

Nice one son,

Nice one Cyril,

Let's have another one!'

Unsurprisingly, dinner that evening is a subdued affair, although I have something to impart. Something important. 'I've been thinking, lately, this past week or so.' I announce.

Chrissie smiles, then rolls her eyes. 'This spells bad news. Always does, when you start thinking. Come on then, let's hear it.'

I giggle, softly. 'Well you don't have to worry, but I want to make a few changes in my life. After what has happened these past few weeks, it makes you think, doesn't it, reassess priorities? After what happened to Jill, and Harry particularly. Firstly, I have to start taking more exercise, running, cycling, I have those two bikes, stuck in the woodshed, doing nothing, which is ridiculous. I have to find the time to have a little ride, a couple of times a week, just a few miles, nothing drastic, and I thought before breakfast, before it gets too hot? And other mornings, a little jog, just around the streets, and I thought maybe you might like to come, you know how you used to enjoy it?'

She reaches across and squeezes my hand. 'I've been thinking the same thing, actually. We've become too lazy. I think that is a great idea. So what was the other idea?'

I take a deep breath. 'Well, I want to give up the building work, for other people. It's getting too hard, clambering up and down ladders, I keep getting injured, I didn't enjoy it down Jade's place, and Miguel's is almost finished, I know Nigel will have some more jobs for me down there, but I have to think of what is best for me. When that fireplace fell on me was the final straw really, I could have been seriously hurt. So that is what I've decided. And I thought I could concentrate on the students, Lydia is keeping on at me for extra sessions, she wants to take her C-level next, of course I've had to turn her down, as I have no time in the mornings. And then I thought I could concentrate on getting the next book finished. I've made good progress this holiday, an hour or so a day, up on the terrace, but I have no time. Time, time, it's all about time, and we are supposed to be retired, after all. I feel I'm just chasing my tail, and it has to stop. Then I thought how we could go out together somewhere, midweek, say Wednesday mornings, we'll still have the afternoons in the garden of course, but we have to prioritise ourselves from now on.' She has her mouth open, about to object. 'Oh and I thought I could help you, putting the mop around, now and again!'

She chuckles, softly. 'Yeah, I've seen your mopping. I thought Noah had paid us a visit! That is all well and good, but I don't want you getting stuck in the house, you need to get out now and again, and working down Miguel's does that. So think carefully before you give it up, OK? Of course, I don't want you having any more accidents, and I do worry about you especially up on roofs, and you know I never wanted you to get involved at Del's place, when we first came here. But promise me you'll think about it.'

'I have thought about it, trust me' I smile. 'Since Harry died

I've thought about little else. So I'm decided, as soon as we get home, it's all change. Jogging and cycling before breakfast, and more time for us.'

Be careful what you wish for, Jonno....

All good things come to an end, and we are on the final day of the holiday. The twenty-fifth of February, two-thousand and twenty. The taxi to the airport is coming at three, after lunch, and at two-forty-five I am still bobbing around in the pool, chatting to a lady from Bodmin, about the people we know, and those we know of, which in Cornwall is just about everybody. Climbing out of the water for the final time, quick change, lob my wet shorts in the bin, a final glance around, committing the whole scene to memory, then off we go. Into a different world, utterly unaware. Colombo airport is a complete nightmare, three security checks, all the guards wearing face-masks, looking sinister, only their eyes visible. And I have to be honest, I hate this image. The most expressive part of the face, the smile, completely obscured. Do security guards actually smile? Well, you know what I mean. Far more prevalent in the East, of course, and we even see a few people with face coverings in Spain, during the olive-flowering period. Over the past few weeks we have been reading in our online newspaper of this new virus which has been spreading from China, and appears to have arrived in many other countries of Asia, and one or two in Europe, too. Sounds quite nasty, although hopefully it can be contained, as the SARS virus was a few years ago. I said reading about, although merely scanning the news would be more accurate, as we're on holiday of course, plus the fact that the paper arrives on our devices at around half-three in the afternoon Sri Lankan time, so by the time Chrissie has had a quick glance, I only get around fifteen minutes before high tea is served. And I cannot miss that, can I, low-class oik that I am?

Anyway, thankfully the check-in desk of our Middle Eastern

airline is completely mask-free, as is the upper shopping area, where we bag a couple of seats, then take it in turns to go browsing. 'Ooh look, there's that jewellery shop where you got me that elephant pendant, last year' giggles my wife, expectantly. I pretend not to hear. Must be all that sea-water in my ears, these past three weeks.

The departure gate is a total bun-fight, pushing and shoving, and that's just the staff. The plane is no better, like Ryanair, only with seats which partially recline, but not enough to make a ha'pence worth of difference to anyone over five feet two, and no sign of screens or any entertainment systems whatsoever. Are we seriously expected to travel half-way across a continent to Abu-Dhabi in this? For a national flag-carrier this is an absolute disgrace. I would ask a steward about an upgrade, if only I could locate one amongst the horde of humanity stampeding down the aisle, so after my groin has been assaulted by the third piece of carry-on I take the only available option and subside into my seat, bolt upright, plug in my earphones to muffle the sounds of wheezing chests, switch on some music at maximum volume, and pray the next seven hours pass quickly. Which they didn't, of course. I hope whichever Premier League football club this airline sponsors get relegated, come May.

If Colombo airport was a bun-fight, Abu-Dhabi is a cattle market. We are discharged from the plane in some far-flung corner of the airport on this Arabian Night, herded into buses, packed cheek-by-armpit, and after a seemingly never ending, bone-rattling tour, hanging grimly onto a ceiling strap with one hand, a metal pole with the other to avoid being flung against our fellow sufferers, the doors hiss open allowing a cloud of diesel fumes to permeate our lungs, and we scramble gratefully into the terminal. 'I am never doing this again' I growl at Chrissie, as we join the disorganised scrum for security. 'Next year, we are flying direct to wherever we go. Prisoners get treated better than this.' She rolls her eyes unsympathetically.

'I mean it' I continue. 'Shoe-horned into that manky plane, and now treated worse than a herd of buffalo? We paid for this, don't forget. Never again will I transit through this hell-hole.'

The security line is a haphazard affair, and that is talking it up, snaking as it does across the concourse, round a length of metal barrier and back again, allowing those who perhaps missed the bursts of throaty exhalation on the first pass to savour the delights on the second. The black-masked guards resemble Mafia hit-men, and in my sleep-deprived state I am having difficulty interpreting their barked orders, which might or might not be something to do with sea water, although I suppose 'tablets and lap-tops in a separate tray' is the same in any language.

Having noted the price of a bottle of Italian Blue Ribbon cooking-lager is the equivalent of eleven-quid, we forgo the delights of the Five-Star Shopping Experience and head directly to the gate, as displayed on the departure board, taking up a pair of seats as far as possible from large families picnicking on the pungent contents of home-made, foil-wrapped packages, involving, surely, bribery and corruption on an industrial scale, to get these concoctions through customs. My single, unopened packet of Mints With The Hole almost didn't make it, let me tell you. 'Aren't we getting anything to eat, on this flight?' Chrissie giggles, sniffing the air, like an inquisitive bloodhound, then recoiling. 'Maybe we should have stolen something from the hotel lunch buffet!' *Now why did she have to go saying that? My black dal lentils with garlic naan and poppadoms was exquisite, on a different planet from the unidentifiable slop we were served on the first leg of the journey. Animal, vegetable or mineral? Who knows?*

Suddenly down the corridor flounces a gate-dispatcher, who exhibits signs of total meltdown when he discovers three-hundred-odd passengers crowded into his personal fiefdom, without permission. He hastily grabs a mike. 'Plees, you must all exit the gate now. We need to check your boarding passes. Plees exit immediately. You should not be here.' *Don't get shirty with us, pal. Only one of us was late to this party. You.*

Amid groaning, wheezing, coughing and the sound of rustling tinfoil, we rise as one, and attempt to steamroller our way through the exit, all except us and a few other sharp-eyed customers who have spotted a second door at the far end. Flouncy spots us. 'You cannot exit ther….' *Too late sunshine. I'm already out. My extreme dislike, bordering on obsession, of large crowds and the associated pushing and shoving is genuine, we have tickets, with numbered seats, and some of our fellow passengers seem, ahem, somewhat unhealthy, and that is being kind. Let them all go first. We can wait.*

Readmission to the gate takes up a good forty-five minutes of everyone's life, by which time boarding seems overdue, unless this plane has about ten separate entrances. Our friend's moment in the spotlight has arrived, however. 'Good evening ladies and gentlemen, welcome to your flight to London Heathrow. We would now like to invite those seated in rows one to six to commence boarding.' *Hmm. Six rows, eight or nine seats to a row, unless we are on another Ryanair lookalike. What is that, fifty-four passengers, maximum? So why have over two hundred people just stood up and made a bolt for the airbridge?*

We are among the last to board, and I have to say are duly impressed. A wide-bodied plane, seat-back screens, USB ports, plenty of legroom. The middle aisle, so two seats out of four, and by tradition I take the one on the aisle, Chrissie the inside one, as my bladder is the weaker. One slight problem however. The couple next to her are furiously spooning something horrid from tinfoil packages… She glares, whereas I cannot help a quick snigger… until I glance across the aisle next to me and spot… you've guessed it. 'Chicken chow-mien, do you think?' I groan. She has her hand across her mouth, however, as if she is about to burst out laughing, or gag.

All things considered, the next seven hours pass reasonably well, I manage to doze off between films, no checked bags to collect, Heathrow customs is rapid with our e-passports, and before we know it we are in the exit to the terminal, contemplating the next stage of the journey, in the cold, grey light of an English winter morning. And here we face a choice, a decision to be made. I don't know about you, but when I book a holiday I seldom worry about the return leg of the journey, caught up as I am in the excitement and euphoria of travelling somewhere new. Which is why we now face a ten-hour layover before our flight to Malaga this evening. And as many of you might already know, there are no flights to that destination from Heathrow. We have to get to Gatwick. And the only way to do that on public transport, without heading into Central London and back out again, is on the coach. And the coach company know this, and price the journey accordingly. Pounds for miles covered, it would be cheaper to charter a rocket from NASA.

So my original plan was to spin out the day in the terminal at Heathrow, looking round the shops, something to eat, before the coach to Gatwick around two PM. But you know what? Two hours in the taxi to Colombo, three hours at the airport, seven hours on the first flight, another three hours at Abu-Dhabi and seven hours on the second flight. We haven't encountered fresh air for twenty-two hours. I've been poked, prodded, shoved, coughed at, sneezed on and and subjected to other people's recycled air for almost a complete day. If I don't get out into the open soon, my head will explode. I wonder what Chrissie thinks? 'Instead of staying here in this madhouse, why don't we head down to the coach stand and see if we can change the booking, head to Gatwick now, and go to that hotel where we stayed on the way out, you know, the one on the A23 just outside the terminal, with that lovely quiet lobby, and maybe we can get a little nap there, tucked away in the corner, before the Malaga flight?'

She narrows her eyes. 'Oh, that wouldn't possibly be the hotel with the massive, free-for-all breakfast buffet, would it? That place where you ate so much, you could barely get your seat-belt done up, for take-off? Where you weighed so much the pilot could hardly get the plane to leave the runway? Would it? Don't you think you've had enough breakfasts, these past three weeks? You and that omelette-boy were on first-name terms come the end. I'm surprised you didn't get his address, add him to your Christmas card list.'

'Would that be a yes?' I giggle. 'Anyway, when are we back in the UK next? May? You surely don't begrudge me one proper fry-up to last me the next three months? And don't forget, they have that porridge you like, and those Danish pastries!'

The National Express bus stand resides in the bowels of the terminal, where there is indeed free air, albeit with a hint of damp concrete and a smidgen of internal combustion engines, although it hasn't passed through anyone else's lungs, which can only be a good thing. I breathe deeply, and rejoice. Thirty minutes pass, during which time coaches headed to every corner of the UK, apart from Gatwick, add to the nauseous cocktail, but eventually ours arrives, the Eastern European driver lumbers down the steps and confirms that, as she only has one other passenger, we are able to swap our tickets. We climb gratefully aboard, to be assaulted by the sound of nasal Aussie shouting from a middle-aged bloke, with a ridiculously large pair of headphones clamped to his head, seated halfway back, bellowing into his mobile. 'YEAH MATE, JUST TOUCHED DOWN IN, LIKE, LONDON?' *Well you presumably bought the ticket, to, like, London? Mate?*

We grab the front seats, on the left, to enhance the vista of whichever motorway we will be travelling down, I plug in my, like, tiny ear-buds, call up something by Led Zeppelin, slouch down.... and breathe. But not for long. Before I've even had time to press play, a kerfuffle on the pavement reveals a shouty young woman, Eastern European again, but a different accent from the driver, enquiring if she has time for a last smoke before the bus leaves? 'I leave in four minutes' barks the driver. 'If you not here, I go.'

Shouty fumbles into her bag like a woman possessed, lighting up before she has the ciggy between her lips, almost, gulping greedily at the smoke as if her life depends on it, which quite possibly it does. Seeing the driver taking her position behind the wheel, she takes a final lung-busting drag, hurls the butt into the gutter, climbs aboard.... *and throws herself into the seat behind us.* I hang my head in sheer, utter, dejected disbelief. She has the whole bus to choose from. Why, oh why would she pick that particular one? She reeks of fags, yet has the cough from hell, a deep, throaty, liquid growl, which makes Keith Richards sound like a ten-year-old kid with his first pack of Woodbines. Then, as if the morning couldn't get any worse, it suddenly does. She whips out her phone. Whatever did we do in the days before mobiles? Read books? Play a few Led Zeppelin tracks? Enjoy a brief respite from the hurly-burly of the day? Nope, she calls what I assume to be her boss, in heavily-accented but admirably fluent English, to discuss some changes, cough cough cough, she would like to make within her team, which is not reaching its full, cough cough, potential, sadly. It appears that Kirsty is unsuited to a customer-facing cough cough cough role, and therefore needs to be moved cough to a more admin-based position cough. In her place cough cough cough she feels that Ryan choke is showing enormous potential cough choke hawk and could easily step into the recently vacated cough space.

I suddenly feel overwhelmingly sorry for poor Kirsty, and would like to sit her down, face to face, to explore whether she feels she has not been receiving the full support of her line manager, and maybe a one-to-one air-clearing session would be beneficial? Or perhaps she would simply prefer to stab her in the eye with a pencil? Ryan meanwhile, whom I had initially envisaged as a spotty school-leaver, could in fact be a hunky, toned gym-bunny, who perhaps has been developing his enormous potential in ways un-imagined by the boss? Let us hope he has a poor sense of smell, in that case. I turn to Chrissie, and grin. 'Is Ryan giving her one, do you think?'

In our sleep-deprived state, we dissolve into hysterical laughter. Which seems to be our only option, apart from moving seats of course, and why should we? Deprive ourselves of this delightful panorama of the M-whatever-it-is, in the process of being widened into what seems to me a death-trap, devoid of a hard shoulder? Sadly, my phone is getting low on battery, and this old bus has no USB charging points, so Led Zep is off the menu. As is phoning someone, and bellowing. *So it's the Kindle, then.*

Mercifully, shouty seems to be winding-up her call, and we relax, slightly, at the prospect of little peace, apart from the coughing, and the Aussie, who is still banging away, like? Sadly not. She calls her mother. I know this, despite not speaking a word of her language, as *Mama* cough cough is universal, right? I close my eyes, and count to ten. Not only has the speed doubled, but the volume also. There is an article in the online newspaper about Coronavirus deaths in Italy, but quite honestly I am unable to concentrate in this bedlam.... suddenly there is a fusillade of coughing from behind, and something hits me on the back of my head. Instinctively, I put up my hand to brush whatever it is away, and my palm and fingers come back wet, and slimy. Outraged, I leap to my feet, turn and thrust my mucous-covered limb in her direction, in a *didn't they teach you to put your hand in front of your mouth* gesture. Water off a duck's back. She glances up, disinterestedly, and resumes her conversation. Furiously, and I might have used unprofessional language, although I was so angry I cannot now remember, but I am guessing I did, I stamp furiously down the aisle and into the toilet. Where there is no water in the tap, nor paper towels, or even a toilet roll. National Express, you are an utter disgrace. I cast around to find somewhere to wipe my hand, I actually consider removing a sock and wiping it with that, or even in desperation on a coach seat, but in the nick of time remember that Chrissie usually carries a pack of wet-wipes in her bag, so banging my way to the front of the bus again and making a huge scene, so it proves, and I am finally able to remove that evil woman's filth from my person.

'I've had enough of her' I rage. 'I'm going to the back, are you coming?'

She regards me unsympathetically, from her refuge, curled up in the corner of the seat, against the window. 'No, I am fine here. Besides, we are almost there, surely? You go, if you want to.'

I cannot believe she is not supporting me in this. I've just been hit by flying phlegm, for pity's sake. I glare at her for several seconds, then snatch up my Kindle and hurtle to the back of the bus yet again, throw myself into a seat, and fume.

I must have nodded off, actually, as I open my eyes to find we are pulling into the South terminal. We want the North however so no need to move yet, but suddenly I am aware of a kerfuffle down the front. Shouty is off again, but at Chrissie this time. 'Your cough husband is mental. I feel sorry for cough cough you. You are racist. He is cough racist. I will report you. I cough pay for my ticket.'

I cannot help a frisson of satisfaction. Maybe if she'd followed me to the back, she might have been spared this barrage of abuse, although my wife is more than able to handle herself, against the tirade. I cannot hear her reply, as she is speaking at a normal volume, but whatever she is saying, our accuser is getting more and more agitated, shouting, coughing and hawking, particularly so when I poke my face round the seat, grin widely, and wave her a fond farewell. The driver has heard enough, as have we all, although the Aussie seems totally un-aware, like. 'Get off the bus, now' she commands, and stands, in all her yellow-jacketed glory.

Is there to be a stand-off? It certainly seems like it, as Shouty has paid for her ticket, demands every last second of her purchase, and is not going quietly. Our saviour raises herself to her full height, which is impressive, unfolds her arms as if she is about to draw a weapon, and steps forward a pace. 'Get. Off. The. Bus. Now!'

For a couple of seconds the ladies eye each other, malevolently, as if national pride is at stake, the Battle of the South Terminal. Sadly however, as I love a good ruck, particularly if other people are doing the rucking, Shouty decides to leave it there, and edges down the steps. 'You are racist. Cough cough reach for her fags. They are racist. I will report you all.'

The door clatters shut, and the driver resumes her seat. 'Fockeen foreigners.' she hisses, as we glide gently away. 'Always they trouble. I hate thees dogs!'

The short hop to the North terminal is an anti-climax after all that, although I remain in my seat at the back, to convey my lingering annoyance. Besides, you never know what other bodily fluids might be clinging to my original seat, do you? Better be safe, than sorry. Or wet. As we depart the bus, we compliment our driver, as we always do, *cheers drive*, although I do gently point out the complete lack of facilities in the toilet, in case she might want, I dunno, to run the vehicle through the service station, before resuming the next journey. I actually want to inform her I will be emailing National Express about the matter, when we get home, but lack the courage.

Into the terminal and the first job is to give my hands, arms, face and the back of my head a jolly good swill, with soap and water. I emerge, several minutes later, wetter than I was before. Chrissie is aghast. 'What the hell? What is that in your hair? Tissue paper. NO! Toilet paper.'

I grimace. 'Well, I washed the back of my head, before I realised they only have those bladed hand driers, which almost rip your skin off, but are very little use as a hair-drier. No paper towels of course. But at least they had bog-roll, unlike National Express. Never mind, it will drip-dry, en-route to breakfast. Come on, after all that, I am starving!'

She stares, in exasperation. 'You cannot possibly go to that hotel with toilet paper in your hair. They will think you have escaped from an institution. Come here, bend your head...' She starts rubbing, and for a second I am a six-year-old boy again with Mother doing the same, to rid my person of various noxious substances... and after brushing the little white flakes from my jacket, I am passed fit to resume the journey.

We exit the back of the terminal and along a roadside footpath, towards the off-airport, smaller and more intimate offering from a budget chain, where we stayed, dined and breakfasted on the outbound leg. Thoroughly enjoyed it, actually, which is why we are now returning, for the breakfast bit, and hopefully some peace and quiet, and a lack of crowds, and conflict. Stringfellow and Cat's Arse wouldn't have liked it mind you, as there is a smattering of the lower orders on display, as we enter the lobby and place our cabin bags in the quiet corner, having first checked with reception they have no objections, returning customers as we are. And breakfast we do, twice in my case, thoroughly justified I feel, as May is a long way off, right?

Fully sated, we head back to the lounge, sit back, eyes closed, and drift away. Premier Inn, you are absolute stars. Particularly Elena and Marianne. Give those ladies a pay rise. They say, don't they, that travelling east to west you get back the eight hours, or however long the time difference is. Well if that is true, I don't know where those hours have gone. Still, maybe catch up on a few of them righ....

Whenever I wake from a cat-nap, which is every day, without fail, I have no idea how long I have out, could be a minute, could be an hour. I therefore glance at Chrissie, for a time-check. 'Forty-five minutes!' she grins. 'You look better. HEY! Where are you going?' Ignoring her, I leap to my feet and, grabbing my phone, head rapidly across the lobby, and out through the front doors.

Five minutes later I return, grinning like the Cheshire Cat, with important news to impart. 'Remember our fortieth wedding anniversary, that day in Bristol, when we met up with the kids for the first time in ages, Louise came down from North Wales, Charlotte was there of course, plus the boyfriends? In the shopping area that afternoon, bottom of Union Street, you went off to look in a craft shop, and I sheltered from the rain outside that department store? And you came back and I was listening to some music playing in the shop, sounded like one of those girl-groups, not the Spice Girls or anyone like that, but I had no idea who they were? And that night, out for the meal, I asked the youngsters about the song, couldn't remember many of the words, but I did have some of the tune, *na na never gonna live without you, without you,* but they didn't have a clue. Remember? Louise even had an app on her phone, and I sang into that, but it drew a blank of course. Remember?'

She rolls her eyes. 'How could I possibly have forgotten? But does this story have a purpose?'

Indeed it does. 'Well, just now I heard the same track playing softly on the loop here in reception, so I memorised some of the words, typed that into Google, and it turns out it is by someone called Alicia Keys, not a girl-band at all, and called *Try Sleeping With A Broken Heart.* And then, I went into my iTunes account and downloaded it onto my phone. How about that, then? I am a techno wizard. I is dahn wiv da kids, nah wot I mean?'

She buries her head her hands. 'Should you really be playing about with this right now? Shouldn't you be relaxing? We are not due to be back home until just before midnight, don't forget.'

I grin widely. 'I am relaxing. This is relaxing. And to prove it, I'm just gonna get my earphones out, play the song through properly, then be away to the land of nod, I promise!' And so I do. A powerful number, R&B I suppose they would call it nowadays, but in my day maybe soul? Her vocals are confident, and she seems a strong lady, not some little girl lost. She clearly regrets losing her lover, but is telling him so, on her own terms. But to me, as a former drummer in our senior-school rock band, it is the beat, a powerful rhythm, which dominates the record. Not a rock beat at all, of course, and not even an actual drummer, simply a machine, but the outstanding feature of the music. I attempt to follow the drum pattern, in my head, as I always do. Wow, takes me a few bars, but finally I get it. Boom, boom-boom, boom-boom, boom. Then I try to work out how I would play it, on my beat-up Premier kit, as if it were still 1971, and get hopelessly lost. Bass and tom-tom, or simply bass? Or are beats two, three and six a snare-drum? Suddenly I am all imaginary arms and legs, as I was in 1971, if you'd ever been unfortunate enough to hear us, but by the time the second verse comes along, I have it, and can even start to overlay some vocals. *And all the time you were telling me lies. So tonight, I'm gonna find a way to make it, without you. Boom, boom-boom, boom-boom, boom.* What a great piece. And it will be in my head for the rest of the day, I promise you that. *Boom, boom-boom, boom-boom, boom.*

Suddenly I feel pressure on my shoulder, and wake to find Chrissie standing over me. 'Come on, time to get moving. Stroll back to the terminal, through security for the final time, one last bout of pushing and shoving, but no conflict, hopefully. Please?'

Suddenly, I don't want to leave. This has been far and away the best part of the trip, so far, and with the orange airline to look forward to, most definitely the best part of the trip. Gathering up our belongings, we offer again our grateful thanks to Elena and Marianne, and head out into the grey February afternoon.

Still, sunshine tomorrow, all being well. A lie-in, then an afternoon in the garden. Probably uncover the pool, give the pump a blast, a quick trip to the supermarket, then one of my Rick Stein specials. Prawns and potato in that picante sauce, possibly? What is tomorrow? Thursday? Probably start the first jog of my new regime on Friday, in that case. Get the tyres pumped up on one of the bikes too. Janie and Nigel are coming sometime, so a quick word with them about quitting, in a nice way, of course. Maybe wander down the town for a tapas with them, and they usually want to visit the pizza place during their stay. Lovely. Ease back into our Spanish life. It was a great holiday, despite what happened to our dear friends, plus the past thirty hours or whatever it was. Learned my lesson there. My soul fills with joy at the prospect of our return to Spain. Life is good.

Or it was until we reach the terminal, and encounter the departures board. EasyJet to Malaga. Flight delayed. By at least ninety minutes. The pent-up rage returns, in an instant, and I cast around for something to kick, but find only my wife, who herself is fuming. 'Even if we leave at seven-thirty, that will gone ten before we get to Malaga, add the Continental hour, means we're not getting home until two in the morning. Why did you book EasyJet? Always it's EasyJet who are late. Why didn't you book Norwegian, who we came over with?'

I glare at the board again, willing it to change it's mind, claim it was all a big mistake, that the flight will be on time after all, and that we will have the plane to ourselves, with champagne all the way. Nope. 'You know very well why I didn't book Norwegian. Their flight was leaving an hour later than SleasyJet. I know, I know, now they will be getting to Malaga before us. With the benefit of hindsight of course… next time you can organise the bloody bookings.'

She shoots me a *well I could hardly have made a worse cock-up, could I?* look, but instead takes me by the arm. 'Well there is nothing we can do about it, is there? Come on, get your belt off!'

I grin, lasciviously. 'What here, in the middle of the terminal? Oh, go on then, if you insist!' Which earns me a whack, but at least it breaks the tension. I do of course get my belt off, plus the laptop and tablets in separate trays, then we settle down to wait, one last time. Actually, I don't mind Gatwick, plenty of shops to troll around, nothing I would remotely want to buy mind you, particularly that place selling laptops and tablets, plus phones, and cameras, all at prices which, I swear, are higher than the High Street. Still, gives me something else to moan about. On my way back to our seats however I spot a passenger information desk, so approaching the middle-aged lady sweetly, with a smile on my face, I have a question. 'I know this is nothing to do with you, but there are six delayed flights on the board, and five of them are EasyJet. Do you have any explanation for that?'

She gives me a knowing look, then comes out with the typical corporate spiel. 'Well, it is late in the afternoon, the planes are not actually here of course, all coming in from different locations, so naturally any problems during the day has a knock-on effect.'

Not having that. 'Yes, but they have five separate flights, to different locations, all due to leave within a half-hour period. So that is not one single hold-up, is it? It must be five different hold-ups, surely? We are reasonably frequent fliers, mainly from Malaga to Bristol or Manchester, and in our experience it is usually them who are delayed.'

She reaches under the desk, to either press an alarm to have me escorted from the premises, or to present me with a silver hammer, for hitting the nail on the head. Or perhaps she is scratching her knee. She glances suspiciously from side to side, then lowers her voice. 'You didn't hear this from me, but yes, you are correct. More often than not, it is them who are late.' And she folds her arms, emphatically. Conversation over. *So*

Norwegian next time, then.

The time passes agonisingly, but eventually the terminal thins out, leaving only Malaga, and I think Faro, left. We have been eyeing our fellow travellers suspiciously, for some time. Who is going where? Please let that couple with the screaming baby be going to Faro. They will like it there, much better than Malaga, for kiddies. Faro Beach. Been there many times, although we always drive from our place of course. Great traditional hotel across the causeway, Super Bock lager, crusty bread with sardine pate, in their bar, overlooking the lagoon. God loves it there, let me tell you.

Suddenly, the board springs into life, and both flights are called. Different gates of course, but four hundred frustrated passengers start scrabbling for their carry-ons. Too late people, we are ahead of you. We have perfected the drill, on these budget flights. Get to the gate, pronto, to have any chance of finding an overhead locker anywhere neat your seat, by the time the speedy boarders have had first dibs. So I have had our cases lined up for the last half-hour, and the moment the gate flashes up, I am away like a greyhound chasing the hare out of the traps, with Chrissie trailing in my wake. And then, racing up towards the line, she passes me on the outside, and wins it by a short nose. We take a seat as close to the actual gate as possible, no sign of any babies yet, but the speedy boarders are causing me concern. There are quite a few of them. In fact, there are a lot of them, on the privileged side of the barrier. More, actually, than on our poor side. Curses. Still, for what we paid for this flight, fifteen quid each or thereabouts, who can grumble if our bags are not quite where we'd like them?

Boarding is finally called, almost two hours late, and I try to ignore the fact that the Norwegian passengers will be touching down very soon. And fail. Curses. A seemingly never-ending line of smug speedies pass us, although I try to ignore them. And fail. Curses. Finally it is our turn, although most of the speedies have not even made it to the air bridge, yet. 'Not very speedy, are they? Chrissie giggles, although I refuse to feel amused. We are all boarding through the front door, although you would have thought, wouldn't you, that someone at Gatwick might have cottoned on to the fact that planes have two entrances nowadays, arranged a set of steps at the back, and then, here's a thought, announced rows one to fifteen to the front, the remainder to the rear?

Just then I glance out of the airbridge window, and note with dismay a crowd of passengers hurrying across the tarmac, the first of whom are already mounting a hastily arranged set of back steps. 'Look at those bastards!' fumes the bloke in front, turning his head and generously allowing me the full force of his doggy breath. 'I paid for speedy boarding, and those cheap bastards are getting on before us. I'll be contacting Easy-Effing-Jet, you see if I don't. And why ain't we effing moving?' A wave of outraged discontent crackles down the bridge like summer lightning, although so concerned are they to be losing their paid-for advantage, and who can blame them, that they have possibly not realised that those of us boarding at the front yet seated towards the back, will soon be confronted by those squeezing past in the opposite direction? And have they seen the size of some of those bums in the queue ahead? I predict a riot.

Now. I have never dispatched an aircraft, and probably never will, as once this book is published I expect to find myself blacklisted, especially by this lot. Which can only be a good thing, quite honestly. Do I sound bothered? But surely anyone with a modicum of common sense could surely have foreseen carnage in the aisle? Couldn't care less, clearly, get the gate cleared of troublesome passengers, and knock-off early. *That* is what you should be complaining about, Mister Doggy.

Carnage is an understatement of the scene which confronts us, once we cross into the fuselage and survey the gangway. The stewardesses are dead on their feet, bless them, with painted-on smiles of greeting, and amusingly, the pilot is on the PA urging us to take our seats as quickly as possible to avoid us losing our take-off slot, a laughable notion given that every other plane in the western hemisphere departed hours ago. Apart from Faro, presumably. An old woman with an unfeasibly large posterior is battling her way up the aisle, dragging a Peppa Pig suitcase, deranged look on her face, as I breathe deeply and contort myself into a position from the Kama Sutra, possibly, to allow her to pass. Someone ahead in the scrum reeks of garlic, so much so that it would be a blessing almost if another passenger were to break wind, right now. Ahead, a sweaty student is attempting, and failing, to force a backpack the size of Cambridge into the locker, and his choice of language, when the stewardess orders him to place it under his seat, would surely disgrace a freshers-week all-night rave, with extra drugs. I meanwhile have passed into a trance-like state of fatigued indifference, caring only to avoid having my testicles caressed yet again by this enraged woman's elbow, as she attempts to uncoil her seat-belt from her neighbour's armrest. And the chap forcing his way behind me is extremely excited at the prospect, let me tell you. I glance behind me, in case he wishes to swap phone numbers, although I would then need to inform him I never go all the way on a first date, when suddenly I catch the merest glimpse of Chrissie. It must be hellish in these circumstances, poor love, at five-feet-nothing. I am struggling to breathe at my loftier elevation, and what air there is seems to be tainted by egg sandwiches. Or maybe armpits. Is there actually a difference?

She catches my eye, and glowers, as if this were all my fault. Oh hang on, she actually thinks it is. I smile, sympathetically, as I attempt to think of a quip, to lighten the mood. 'Next time, remind me to book with a proper airline, like Norwegian.' Which earns a rumble of approval from the scrum, but also a glare from what I assume to be the chief steward, who is kneeling in the seat opposite, like a traffic cop in a jam sandwich perched on one of those 'police only' humps on the M5, pretending to look busy.

Mercifully, I reach our seats, which appear to be just up from the emergency exit. Not, sadly, the ones to the rear of that door, with ten feet of legroom, but a pair, instead of the usual three, with a gap between the inside one and the window, perfect for one of us to slide into, painfully, should we nod off during the flight. *Chrissie can have that seat, then. She never nods off.*

With a final heave, she emerges from the ruck, brushing someone else's dandruff from her shoulder, volcanic look on her face, although whether directed at the fugitive scalp scrapings, or me, is difficult to determine. 'So are you going to stow those bloody cases, or do I have to do it myself?' *It was me.* I glance around woodenly, as if the thought hadn't entered my head. Which it hasn't. I truly have passed into another universe. Still, only another three hours or so and we will be driving through a balmy Spanish night. I am having the windows down the whole way home, not only to vent my lungs, but to dispel any lingering little white flakes. And the egg sandwiches. What else can possibly go wrong now?

Indeed. Screwing up my eyes, all the better to focus, I glance across the aisle, and notice, for the first time, the couple with the baby, who, thankfully, seems to be asleep. *So no Super Bock for them.* Then, yes you guessed it, there are no spaces in the overhead lockers, not ahead, or behind. 'There is no room anywhere' I whisper, so as not to wake the snoozing infant.

She elbows me aside, grabs the first case and rams it into the gap, then, with a venomous glance, repeats the gesture with the second. 'Don't you worry, I can manage' she hisses, then tearing off her coat, with unnecessary force I feel, subsides into her seat. I do likewise. 'Got any room over there for my jacket?' I venture, smiling my best *you know you love me really* smile. Well, it was an old jacket, all said and done.

Two minutes. Two blissful, relaxing minutes. I use the time wisely, uncoiling my earphones, and dialing up Alicia Keys for another run-through, before down the aisle stomps chief head-honcho steward. 'You cannot leave those there' he bellows, waking the slumbering nipper in the process. 'That is the emergency exit.'

I have my mouth open to reply, but Chrissie beats me to it. 'No, that is the emergency exit' she growls, pointing through the gap and tapping the door. Great response, that. Wish I'd thought of it.

He takes a deep breath, and a step back. Not what he was expecting, clearly. Not his fault the flight was late, is it, without having to deal with these wise-ass customers? And I bet his lot aren't paying overtime, either. And tomorrow morning he has it all do do again, while we are enjoying a leisurely breakfast on the terrace. And, as I said, this flight is costing less than what National-robbing-Express charged for forty miserable miles, devoid of bog-roll. Now. If he'd only smiled, just a little one, then said something like *well that is where the door opens, so we need to keep the area clear,* or something like that, that would have done. We'd have grinned, sheepishly, oh silly us, and found somewhere else for the cases. No idea where mind you. Out on the wings, perhaps? But all would have been well. No. Not him. He had to go and spoil it, by raising his voice at my wife, and making a fraught situation worse. 'That is the emergency exit. Move the bags, now.'

I rise calmly to my feet, reach across and pull both cases out, and place them in the aisle. I fix him with a look. 'If that area has to be kept clear, don't you think a sign saying so would be a good idea? How were we to know that?There are no more spaces, so I suggest you radio the pilot and get him to open the hold.' I grin, picturing the Captain, hand on the joystick, revving the engines, gagging to be off, pull a massive wheelie, then a call comes through...

He stalks off towards the back, then returns. 'There are a couple of spaces, row twenty-nine, on the left, and row thirty, on the right.' He nods at the cases. 'You have to do it, I'm not allowed to touch them.'

Pushing one bag ahead of me, towing the other behind, I suddenly become aware of the change which has occurred these past few minutes. I am the only person standing. Everyone else is comfortably seated, belts on, tray tables upright. And fifty pairs of eyes are glaring, in my direction. How did that happen? How could that possibly have happened? We were first in line of the non-speedies, for pity's sake. And a voice echoes from somewhere near the back. 'Bloody well hurry up, will you. We are waiting to leave!' Mortified, I hurry back to my seat, and fasten my belt. We are never late. We hate those who are constantly late. A special circle of Hell should be reserved especially for them. Me, in fact. Us. I want the floor to open and swallow me up. And then, judgement from above, perhaps. The baby starts to wail. Piercingly. Our very own circle of Hell. I flash a watery grin at my wife, switch on Alicia, and close my eyes. *Boom, WAAAAAAAAA. boom-boom, boom-boom, WAAAAAAAAA boom.* One of the major problems with babies I always find. They are rubbish at rhythm. Cannot keep time for toffee.

The rest of the flight passes uneventfully. The little 'un nodded off eventually, as did I. Chrissie managed to find six Euros for two black coffees, she even dug out two battered Kit-Kats from her bag. No idea how long they'd been there, but by Gaw, they went down a treat. I did however take my bathroom break at the front of the plane, where I am less well-known.

Soon, the lights of Malaga are visible below, the pilot executes a perfect landing, we taxi to a halt, and in unison, amid a waft of stale breath and body odour, the whole plane rises to its feel. Except me. Chrissie gives me a nudge. 'Are you awake? We've arrived. Not getting, er, up?'

I place my hand on hers. 'I'll have a little wager with you. I bet we depart from the front of the plane.'

'Well so what?' she replies, sarcastically, whipping her hand away. 'We usually do, at this airport. What is your point?'

I sigh, exaggeratedly. 'My point, dearest, is that our cases are at the back. No way can I collect them, until that lot have departed. We're gonna be last off the plane.'

She buries her head in her hands, and starts to wail. Not as loud as the baby, thankfully, and I do manage to catch snatches of her strangled oaths, including 'Norwegian', 'next time' and 'cock-up'. Next time? There's never gonna be another next time, like this time, trust me on that.

A few stragglers are all that are left as we make our way to the front of the plane, past the relieved hostesses and the shell-shocked head-honcho. Time to bury the hatchet. 'I bet you're glad all that's over!' I smile.

He rubs his hands across his eyes, and face, then breathes deeply. 'The same every night, mate!' he mumbles. 'You were right, earlier. Nor-bloody-wegian are far better than this shit-shower. I'm joining them, next month!'

Through customs, then deep, blessed relief. A warm, balmy, velvety Spanish night. At last, at last. We climb the stairs to the arrivals level, where Chrissie can sit, under the stars, while I collect the car, providing I can remember where it is, under the motorway bridge, in the free unofficial parking spaces, and assuming it starts. Then a gentle cruise, along the motorway past Malaga, front windows down, giggling like a couple of teenagers on our first date, until we face a choice. Turn inland, signposted Seville Cordoba and Granada, and home, or straight on a few more miles, where lies the caravan. My choice, always my choice, as in, can I stay awake another couple of hours, do I feel safe, and alert? Or do I need to get my head down? Or does Chrissie actually feel like driving, which is her choice, of course, but one she rarely exercises. 'Well, I feel bright, and awake, so I think we can press on for home, if that's OK with you? There is no food in the caravan of course and I think we both need to get back to our own bed, don't you?'

She smiles in the darkness. 'Bright and awake? You weren't even born bright and awake! But are you sure you're OK? We can always buy some bread and milk at the campsite in the morning. I don't want you nodding off, halfway.'

I assure her I am fine, and so we turn left, up into the mountains, and the prospect of a good night's sleep ahead. We natter companionably about the holiday, ignoring the blip that was the journey home, and the very special country that is Sri Lanka. Twenty miles from home however I am beginning to wish I had taken her advice. I am completely overtaken by fatigue. Not just tiredness, which would be understandable, but a numbing pain throughout my body, feeling both hot and cold, all at the same time, disoriented, dizzy, and a pounding headache. I grip the wheel in an attempt to dispel the sensation, which helps, but I'm only just going to make this. Chrissie, of course, keeping a watchful eye, cannot help notice. 'Are you OK? Do you want to pull over? Shall I drive the rest of the way?'

'No, I'm fine' I lie, 'we'll be home in less than ten minutes, but I tell you what, I've really had enough, now. I'm at the end of my endurance. I'm gonna flop straight into the sack and not move for a month.'

'Oh no you're not!' she chuckles. 'You reek of taxis, boarding gates and other people's spit. Straight into the shower for you, Sonny Jim, *then* you can flop all you like!'

I steer erratically through the town, and by a miracle end up, more or less, outside the abode of Percy Anna, in our usual spot. Did we drag the cases across the cobbles to home? Must have done, as I vaguely recall telling Chrissie to forget about them, until morning. Did I get my shower? No idea, as I fell into the worst nightmare of my entire life…

I am spinning, in the pitch dark, perfectly upright, hands at my sides, feet together, in some kind of cylinder, with only a bright, blinding, flashing light, on and off, on and off, and a pulsating rhythm, a drum beat, the Alicia Keys beat, louder and louder, as I turn, faster and faster, falling, falling, into the abyss. **Boom, boom-boom, boom-boom, boom.** My whole body throbbing, pounding to the noise, and the excruciating light, over and over, relentlessly. Then, the walls of the tube are closing in, slowly, inexorably, squeezing, compressing, preventing me from breathing, gasping for air, my chest, my head, my life…. then oblivion.

EPILOGUE. By Christine Richards.

John was always the most stubborn of men, on those rare occasions he had something wrong with him. Typical bloke. *Oh I'm fine, waste of time going to the doctor, nothing they can do, I will get better on my own. My immune system will protect me.* Always his immune system. But not this time.

That first night, I woke to the sound of stifled groaning. Not shouting, not crying out, but a muffled keening, as if someone had him wrapped in the quilt, squeezing. Or like he was inside a strait-jacket, struggling to move. I sat up, switched on the bedside light, and the sight which greeted me will be with me until my dying day. Lying on his back, his face was crimson, bloated, engorged, his eyes bulging. And seemingly not breathing. Quickly, I shook him by the shoulder, gently at first, then when he failed to respond, urgently. Nothing. Was he having some kind of seizure, or heaven forbid, a heart attack? I knew I needed to get him into the recovery position, so climbing out of the bed and running round to his side, I started to roll him over, pushing under his shoulder, then his back, until I had him halfway, when mercifully he gave an almighty shudder, and a deep, choking breath. He rolled back, panting for air, twice, three times, his chest heaving, then finally, just as I was considering some form of mouth-to-mouth, or chest compressions, he came to, opening his eyes. Before I could stop him, he stumbled out of bed, crashing into the wardrobe and falling against the window wall, where he ripped back the shutters, flung open both panes, and hung there, gasping. 'I..... can't.....breathe....' he wheezed, 'can you....open the other windows....at the back. Air....I need air....' And he tumbled on the bed, overcome by a fit of coughing. A deep, chesty, rasping bark, over and over, fully thirty seconds, greedily sucking in the chilly night air starting to flow through the room, until gradually the bout subsided and he lay there, panting, a look of sheer terror on his face.

I placed my hand on his shoulder, in an attempt to reassure him. His skin felt so cold. 'Don't worry, you were having a nightmare, that is all. Look, cover yourself up, you'll catch a chill in this air.'

The fit of coughing returned. 'Burning....I am burning....so hot, so hot....water....please....no, don't worry....I need to splash....my face.' And he was struggling to get to his feet again, when another spasm hit him, and he subsided on to the quilt. '....Jeez....what is....this...?'

'Stay there' I told him, pointlessly, 'I will get you a drink, and a flannel.' I started to hurry downstairs, when suddenly l heard groaning behind me, and there was John, stumbling on the landing, hanging onto the banister with one hand, swinging alarmingly, and instinctively I flattened myself to the wall, in case he let go or slipped, and sent the pair of us crashing to the floor. 'Stay there.' I shouted. 'I said, I will do it. Get back into bed before you hurt yourself.'

'....need a pee....' he grinned, painfully, and by some miracle he made it to the foot of the stairs without injuring either of us. Annoyingly, our bathroom is located on the ground floor, involving a nocturnal flight of stairs, both during the colder months when we inhabit the top floor, and the basement summer kitchen apartment during that season. Straining my ears in case of further mishap, I heard him flush, then splashing from the sink, before he reappeared, face and hair still damp, not having bothered to towel himself off. He staggered into the lounge, his whole body wracked by a fit of coughing, and collapsed on the sofa, a three-seater, luckily, and therefore able to accommodate his ample frame, more or less. I dashed to the bathroom, fetched him a towel, then ran downstairs for the spare quilt, and his pillow, to make him comfortable on the settee.

'....You go back to bed....' he wheezed, '....I'll be.... fine here.... don't worry....' As if. Actually, his coughing seemed to have eased slightly, although it was excruciating to watch him gasping for breath, twice, three times, before it finally came, all the while a look of terror on his face, as if that breath might not come.

Did I sleep that night? I was hours, seemingly, getting off, although I must have done, eventually. It was well gone nine when I woke, instinctively listening out for sounds from below, of which there were none. Poor chap must still be asleep, I thought. Silently, I got dressed, then tiptoed downstairs, to find him gone, the quilt all in an ungainly heap on the floor, the pillow thrown across the room. The bathroom and kitchen were empty, he was not out on the terrace, and the back door still bolted, ruling out a visit to the garden or the covered Sombrero patio. Suddenly, from the street came the sound of horrid, throaty coughing, which is par for the course in this country, and nothing particularly unusual. Then the front door crashed open, and an old man staggered into the hallway. So appalled was I at this appearance of my husband that my hands instinctively flew to my face, as we stood there in mutual horror for a brief second. '....Needed air....house closing in....I feel so....claustrophobic indoors....cannot stand it....' he raged, bouncing off the wall, wrenching back the patio door and crashing into one of the plastic chairs, chest heaving.

Instinctively, I flapped around for a few seconds, attempting to hide my embarrassment at his appearance. 'Right, stay there, I'll get the coffee on, do you want any breakfast?'

'....no, nothing.... we have nothing....here....need to go shopping....'

I smiled, and sat down next to him. 'Sorry, I forgot to tell you, last night when I was trying to drop off to sleep, I picked up a Facebook message from Lydia. The cats are fine, by the way, although I haven't had chance to se them yet this morning. Anyway, she has actually been staying here off and on during our holiday, you remember we said that was OK, things have been really bad between her parents again, over her father's affair, and she just had to get away. So she went out to get us some basic supplies, we have milk, bread, tea, coffee, cheese, ham, cereal and all that, which means we have enough for breakfast, and lunch. Wasn't that good of her? So what do you want, toast, cereal? You have to eat something, keep your strength up.'

He stared at me blankly. '....Uh, don't think....I want anything....'

'Come on' I persisted, 'what about a small bowl of Cornflakes? Here's your coffee, look.' I shook out a small quantity of cereal, about a quarter of what he would normally polish off, added the milk, and placed it in his hands. For a moment I thought he would drop the whole thing, then gradually, hand shaking, he picked up the spoon, and placed a small amount between his lips. And I am ashamed to admit I had to look away in disgust. He was eating, or trying to eat, with his mouth open, sucking in air at the same time, and bits of half-chewed Cornflake and dribbles of milk were running down his chin, and onto his shirt. He thumped the dish onto the table, struggled to his feet, cried out '…I'm off to bed….' and, one stair at a time, disappeared from view. I broke down then, feeling utterly lost and isolated, without support, in this foreign country, so completely alone. And this usually strong man, reduced to this state, in just a few short hours.

He slept until around midday, I remember, by which time I'd regained my composure, having been to the fruit shop for, among other things, a two-kilo sack of tangerines, then busying myself in the kitchen. The thump thump on the stairs heralded his arrival. 'Look!' I grinned, giving him a big hug, 'I've made you your favourite, mushroom soup! I thought it would be easy for you to swallow. Doesn't is smell wonderful?'

He sniffed the air around the bubbling pot, then subsided into his patio chair. '….Cannot smell anything….' he wailed, burying his head in his hands.

'Oh well don't worry' I blustered, crushed. 'Here, try some, just be careful, it's still boiling hot!' I ladled a small amount into a bowl, he waited a couple of minutes, then took a tentative sip. 'Is that good?' I smiled.

He grimaced, eyes seemingly centered on something in the distance, staring right through me. '….Can't taste anything….can't smell….don't bother making this again….lost my balance….my vision is like….looking through binoculars….all black round the edges….'

How I held it together then I'll never know. 'Well, I imagine it's your blocked head, with this man-flu, don't you?' I couldn't resist that little jibe, with him dissing my soup.

He still had problems focusing. '….No….not a blocked head….no cold….no runny nose….no sore throat….just my breathing….and this evil cough….where's the Flockodene?….'

Oh no, not the bloody Flockodene again. Many years ago, after we were married, John discovered this cheap, over-the-counter cough mixture called, if I remember correctly, Pholcodene.

He jokingly mispronounced the stuff Flockodene, and so it has remained, even though you don't seem to be able to get it these days. Any cheap old crap will do, always referred to as Flockodene. Actually cough linctus is expensive in Spain, so every time we go to the UK, especially in the autumn, he keeps on about it.'*Don't forget to go in Poundland for the Flockodene.* And John being John, he refuses to follow the recommended dosage, choosing instead to swig the stuff from the bottle, as and when. Which is why I always get two bottles, one for me, one for him. I took a deep breath. 'I think this has gone way beyond Flockodene, don't you? We need to get you an appointment with the doctor.'

I knew what was coming next, of course. '....Oh I'm fine.... waste of time going to the doctor....nothing they can do....I will get better on my own....my immune system will protect me....what day is it?....'

Infuriating man. Wish I'd added chilli flakes to the soup. Might still do that actually, tomorrow, when I warm it up again. He is eating it, even if I have to force-feed it to him. 'Uh, Thursday. Janie and Nigel are coming on Saturday, for a week, so I've messaged Janie warning her not to come here. I said we will contact them first, when you are better.'

He took another couple of sips, sensing, perhaps, my acute disappointment. '....I'll be fine by Saturday....just a twenty-four hour thing....tell Lydia I'll see her on Monday as usual....'

He still couldn't see it. Waste of breath trying to argue with him. Actually I'd already cancelled his students for the whole of next week, mine too as I was bound to get infected with this, whatever it was. 'Anyway, the sun is out, why don't you see if you can make it to the garden, *after you've eaten your lunch.*' I emphasised that last bit, just to show him who was in charge. 'Lie in the sun, *make you feel a little better, hopefully.*'

Of course, he didn't get any better by Saturday, or the one after that, either. A couple of times, we struggled down to our friends' house, spoke to them from across the street, listening to Nigel banging on about the work he had to do finishing off in Miguel's, Janie all the while rolling her eyes and lamenting, while the blokes were droning on about drains and sewers, her wasted holiday. We were unable to join them in the evenings, of course.

The days, those endless days, settled into a pattern. John would stagger along the street as soon as he got up, in a vain attempt to rid himself of his feelings of claustrophobia, then after a small bowl of porridge with honey, which he found easier to digest, he would sit on the terrace, tapping away on his laptop for an hour or so, updating his manuscript for this book, then after lunch, always home-made soup, French onion, spicy tomato, *with added chilli flakes*, which he never twigged, we would repair to the garden. I moved to the downstairs bedroom, as I generally do when one of us is sick, and John described how he would fall asleep, then wake around two in the morning with the light still on and his Kindle propped against his pillow, and spend the rest of the night gasping for breath, tossing and turning. He even tried plugging in his ear-buds and playing gentle folk music on his phone, in a futile attempt to drift off to sleep. Ralph McTell, James Taylor, Don McLean, all his old favourites. His main concern that week, his only concern in fact, was that he would forever associate that music with memories of the evil virus, and acute breathlessness. Don McLean reminded him of sitting his college finals, apparently, James Taylor of cycling to Minehead Youth Hostel in about 1971, Ralph McTell of some tiny folk club in Cornwall around the same time. Yawn. On and on about it, becoming tearful, that *Fire & Rain* would never be the same again. And still stubbornly refusing to see the doctor.

I meanwhile was nearing the end of my tether, and on the Wednesday, I think it was, I let it all out. 'Listen to me, I am getting grief from the girls, every day, that you have to get tested for that Coronavirus. You cannot go on like this, there is something seriously wrong with you, they are worried sick, I am worried sick, and you are being bloody selfish, quite honestly. Think what this is doing to us. Louise reckons there is an NHS website you can look at, you answer some questions about your symptoms, and it tells you if you have it or not. So I will keep on and on at you until you do. I know you think I am nagging, but just do it, for God's sake.'

He buried his face in his hands, a common feature of that week. '....Will you ever stop keeping on....so what if I....have Corona-bloody-virus?....there is no cure for it...same as flu....nothing the doctor can do....anyway....we've been nowhere near bloody China....have we?....'

I completely lost it. 'You stupid man. You stupid, stupid man. Where were we, last week? Asia. And that other hotel, just along the beach, where we went for a drink, that evening. Where did most of the guests come from? Who was laughing about them with their washing out to dry, on the clothes horses, on the lawn? Like a laundry, you said. And what about the airports, crammed into that little plane, the security queues, the departure gates, that gate in Abu-Dhabi, everyone coughing and spluttering?'

At least he had the grace to look sheepish, as he switched on the laptop. '....Right....here it is....NHS....listen to this....no....no....no....no....none of it....satisfied now? ....only the cough....and it says dry cough....I don't have a dry cough....I have the wettest cough known to man....I have so much phlegm....mucous....I cannot clear it....that is my problem....the Flockodene is working, gradually....so tell the kids....thanks for their concern....but I officially don't have it....right?....'

I was so relieved, actually, although I still had my doubts. 'You sure you didn't cheat? You answered the questions truthfully? You promise?'

I thought he was about to explode. Instead I got the hollow-eyed glare. '....I will not....dignify that....with a response....I don't have Corona-effing....virus....official....it was that train....back from Colombo....dose of flu....the flights and airports....were too soon....couldn't have come on....overnight....'

We had gone to Colombo, on the train, for our wedding anniversary, a few days before we came home. Stayed in a lovely little hotel, not the posh one with the Russians I hasten to add, but the return journey to our beach resort was a total nightmare, standing the entire journey, the carriages so crowded that people were literally hanging out of the doors, face to face with our fellow travellers in the sweltering heat. John actually managed to snag a seat in a doorway for the final half-hour of the trip, legs swinging in the breeze, but that was his theory. He got his 'flu' on the train. The flights to Abu-Dhabi, Heathrow and Malaga, and the phlegmy coach, were too soon for a virus to have incubated. Of course, the gaping hole in that theory was that he could equally have contracted Corona on the train, but he couldn't see that. Wouldn't see that.

He managed to struggle down the street on the final Saturday to wish Janie and Nigel a safe trip, and to apologise for not being able to get together. Next time, we promised. May. Babs and Andy are coming over then, too, so we can have a lovely get-together. Janie actually beckoned me to one side, while Nigel was summarising the state of his pipes. 'Do you think John is getting any better? He looks worse to me, to be perfectly honest.'

I shook my head in despair. 'I agree, but you know what these bloody men are like. It's like banging my head against a brick wall. He just won't see it. Actually I'm getting it from both sides, the kids are keeping on at me, he says the NHS website confirms he doesn't have it, so what can I do? He refuses to bother the doctor, but all this will end in tears, I just know it will. A crisis is just around the corner.'

It arrived the following morning, the Sunday. The eighth of

March. He went for his pre-breakfast air, as usual, before I got up, so I hadn't seen him that morning. While he was gone I decided to do him a couple of boiled eggs, as a little surprise, and a slice of toast, cut into soldiers. The problem is I am rubbish at boiling eggs, always have been, and can never seem to get it right. Time and time again he has told me how he likes them done, soft. *When the egg water is boiling, bubbling, put the toast down, and when it pops up the eggs are ready. Easy.* Yeah, easy to say. He came barging in through the front door, and immediately I could see all was far from well. He lurched into the bathroom, where I could hear him coughing, and retching, before throwing himself into his patio chair. 'Look, I've done you a couple of boiled eggs. Stay there, I will pull the table up to you.' He stared at me, as if I were a total stranger, then grabbed his spoon and began attacking the first egg like a madman. Usually, he is so precise, tapping gently and removing an almost-perfect circle of shell, but this time he had lost all co-ordination, ripping the shell with his fingers, sending fragments across the table. I was praying the egg was correct, runny, but had to look away as he thrust his spoon in, open mouthed, and took the first tentative bite. He gagged, gasping for breath, then let the virtually hard-boiled mouthful drop onto his plate. Throwing down the spoon, he slumped back in the chair. His eyes were red and puffy, and he seemed barely coherent.

'....So sorry....cannot go on like this....you were right....need to....see the doctor....antibiotics....Flock-odene....not working....antibiotics....kill this infernal cough....cannot see straight....head banging....almost fell in the street....'

I stood, and put my arm around him, overcome with relief that at last, at long last, he had seen sense. 'All right, we'll get you to the doctor, the problem is it is Sunday morning, I doubt they are there at the surgery, and I have no idea if there are emergency GP's in this country. We could try at the cottage hospital, there is bound to be someone there. Do you think you can walk, or shall I get Marie or someone to give us a lift?'

With a supreme effort he focused his eyes. '....Walk....can walk....quick....have to get out....can't breathe....air....'

Scrabbling for my jacket, and his medical card, and leaving everything else, my bag, purse, the Spanish mobile, our UK mobiles, his wallet, I dashed outside to find him slumped against the wall of the house, clinging to the wrought iron around the windows. Remembering, just in time, to lock the door, I caught up with him as he lurched down the street, weaving from side to side, taking his arm, firmly, and guiding him, like a pair of drunks, towards the clinic. Was I angry with him, for delaying seeking medical help for so long? Probably, although I cannot now remember, with everything that has happened since. My abiding memory of that morning, that whole day, is fear.

What should have been an easy ten-minute stroll took three times that, with frequent pauses for breath, but we got there eventually to find the place seemingly closed. Lights off, nobody home. 'Hang on here a sec' I told him, leaving him clinging to the railings by the front entrance, 'I'll just pop round the back, where the ambulances go. Someone must be there surely?' I hurried around the back to find two ambulances parked up, and what I assumed was the emergency entrance, mercifully, open. Sticking my head around the door, I spotted a man in a florescent yellow jacket, a paramedic I assumed, middle aged, short, stocky, dark, typical Spanish build, horned-rim glasses with thick lenses, although quite honestly I wouldn't have cared if he'd been fifteen feet tall with three heads. Next to him on the bench seat was a much younger woman, blonde, elegant, dressed in nursing scrubs. 'Emmer-hen-thia! Mi merido. No respiro!' I cried, remembering, possibly, the Spanish for *emergency, my husband can't breathe*. Actually I'd been rehearsing it, all week, knowing this moment would come, eventually. The message got through. They leaped to their feet and followed me through the door, to find John, arms outstretched like a circus tightrope walker, staggering towards us. From there they took over completely, consummate professionals as they were. One on each arm, they guided him inside, and sat him gently on a chair.

The paramedic then reached for a cellophane packet and produced a short, grey plastic tube, which he placed on the middle finger of John's right hand. An oximeter, I assume. He waited a few moments while it booted up, then bent to study the reading on the LCD display. 'Whoooo!' he murmured, eventually. Was that good, was that bad? It was bad, I assumed, as the nurse suddenly sprinted off down the corridor, returning moments later with a saline bag and assorted tubes, which she hung from a stand in the corner. The paramedic meanwhile was concentrating on his English. 'Ingles, yes?' I nodded. 'Plees, not to worry. Take off your jacket, and shirt.' Struggling, John did so, and I stood there, transfixed, as he unbuttoned his shirt to reveal, on his abdomen, the largest bruise I had ever seen in my life. An almost perfect rectangle, fully a foot wide, six inches deep, as if someone had dipped a paint roller in a tray of mahogany varnish and inscribed a stripe across his stomach.

John must have seen me staring, as he glanced down at his discoloured torso, presumably for the first time in many days. '....bloody hell....coughing?...'

The medico seemed decidedly unimpressed, as he gathered up his stethoscope. 'Haematoma. Now, plees to breathe, normal.' Easier said than done, as John attempted three consecutive breaths, before being overcome by a fit of violent coughing. Eventually however this subsided, and our saviour was able to complete his readings. He replaced his instrument on the desk and grabbed a walkie-talkie, into which he barked a few brief instructions, sending the nurse galloping away for a second time. He turned to John. 'You have arrhythmia, of you hare. You must to go to hospital, now.'

John looked totally stunned, me less so as I had suspected

where all this was leading. Still a hell of a shock, of course. From Flockodene to an emergency ward, in less than an hour. 'Which hospital, and how do we get there?' I enquired, nervously.

'Granada' he replied, smiling reassuringly. 'Ees good hospital, of university. We take he now, in ambulancia.' I had temporarily lost the power of speech, and pointed to myself. *What about me?* He reached forward, and patted me on the arm. 'Of course, you also.' He then reached into a drawer and produced a blood pressure cuff which he wrapped around John's upper left arm, as the nurse returned with a sealed packet containing cannula equipment.

John now had a look of sheer panic on his face. He knew what was coming. Terrified of needles. Seventeen-stone rugby forwards he could take in his stride, but a tiny injection? Forget it. This all stemmed from his first blood donor session, with a group from his office, when he watched the needle being removed from his arm, then slumped across the bed as a tiny bubble of blood seeped through the resulting hole. His giggling colleagues felt obliged to take him for a restorative pint of Guinness, on the way back to the office, thereby setting a precedent for all future donations. But he never again looked at the needle.

On this occasion, he was asked to position himself on a tubular-framed, wheeled bed, as the medico inflated the cuff and proceeded to insert the cannula, then connected the assorted pipework, I assume, as I too was staring intently at the ceiling. By the time I turned around, the paramedic was placing self-adhesive pads across John's chest, the nurse pulling a clear plastic oxygen mask around his nose, and wrapping a blanket around his shoulders, with his jacket and shirt across his feet. With the medico pushing, the nurse guiding the frame supporting the drip and cylinder, and me following behind, we made our way down the corridor and through the double doors to the waiting ambulance. An everyday occurrence for them of course, a terrifying one for us. A driver stepped out of the vehicle, indicating the passenger seat, then the three of them shunted the bed, and my bewildered husband, into the back, the medico climbed in with him, and we were off, the nurse remaining outside with the walkie-talkie in her hand, advising the hospital we were on the way.

At least there was no siren, although I did catch a brief glimpse of our reflection in a shop window, with the blue lights flashing. I half turned in my seat, and through the glazed partition could see the medico attaching wires from the ambulance's ECG monitor to the pads on John's chest. That did it. Up until that moment I'd held it together, but the with combined effect of the flashing lights, the mask, the drip and now the wires, tears flooded my eyes. The driver, sensing my distress, reached behind him and tapped on the glass, and the reassuring voice of the paramedic came to me through the gap in the partition. 'Not to worry plees. Now you are safety.' He turned to John. 'You worry, to have Coronaviroos?' Now what did he mean by that? Was he saying John had the virus? Surely not, they took no swabs, or bloods. Or was he speaking generally? John murmured something in reply, and I was relieved that his breathing seemed easier, already, with the oxygen.

Granada hospital? No idea there was one, although a place that size there had to be, of course. Several, I imagine. My MRI scan and polyps operation were in Jaen, and we regularly pass that hospital, next to the park-and-ride tramway with no trams, every time we visit that city. But Granada? We always approach along the southern ring-road, then up the hill to the Alhambra Palace, and park near there, following a delightful wooded path down to the cathedral, and shopping streets. Where is the hospital, and how will we get home, when this is all over? And when will it be all over? Heart arrhythmia? Irregular heartbeats, I know that much, but too slow, too fast, or a mixture of both? Will it all go away, when John recovers from his virus, or will he need tablets, medicine, or heaven forbid, an operation? How long has he had this? When did it start? Did the virus cause it? What will I tell the kids? When should I tell them? Now, when we get to the hospital? No, best leave it until tonight, when we get home. If we get home tonight. Can I sit with him, next to the bed? Will he have to stay in? Will there be a put-you-up bed, for me? Or will I have to go? Will need to get a taxi, in that case. Someone in the hospital will arrange it. A doctor will come to see us, explain everything, what is happening next, the treatment, when he can go home. Tell the girls then.

If you gave me all the tea in China I could never find that hospital again, especially after all this time. I recognised the villages on the way into the city of course, but when we eventually turned off the motorway I was totally lost, the outer suburbs a blur of endless, featureless apartment blocks, as I gazed blindly out of the window, glancing back, occasionally, to ensure all was well with the patient. Eventually, we reached our destination and the unloading began, the exact opposite as the start of the journey. I followed the procession into the building, where the medico turned to me. 'Thank you all very, very much for all your professional help' I told him, in my broken Spanish. Must remember to get them a tin of biscuits, next week, for them to enjoy with their elevenses.

In my distressed state I'd forgotten he had a little English. 'Not to worry, plees, ees nothing. Now, you must to wait in room of relations. Thees way plees, follow to me.' And he led the way along a corridor. I just had time, and the presence of mind, to turn as John was wheeled away in the opposite direction, on his bed, half sitting, half lying, surrounded by the clutter of equipment. He gave me a frightened smile, and a little wave, as he disappeared from view. Choking back the tears, I bade a final fond farewell to the last friendly face I was to see for many a long hour, then slumped into an uncomfortable armchair in the corner. It was ten past ten, according to the clock on the wall.

I glanced around at my fellow relations. There must have been well over twenty people in that room, adults of all ages, with a smattering of kids, all chattering away at the same time, more like a social club than a cardiac department. Out the corner of my eye I could see a young fellow staring at me, although when I glanced in his direction he immediately looked away. On the wall opposite a TV was playing, with the sound turned down, some low-budget Western judging by the costumes, the star of the show a woman with unfeasably large breasts bursting from a low-cut, frilly blouse, who should have known better at her age, in apparent argument with a much younger girl over some trifling incident. Hang on a moment. Was this *Bandaleros*? John told me about it once, when he and Del were working at Tony and Jo's place. Every afternoon Tony would toddle off to the bar to watch his favourite series, set on the border between Spain and Mexico, he claimed. So what was this, on a Sunday morning? The omnibus edition? Poor Tony. Died of a heart attack over a year ago, and Jo returned to England. Oh my God. And there I was, in a cardiac... tears welled in my eyes again and I buried my head in my hands. Didn't want to make a scene, in front of all these people. What was happening, next door, or wherever they took him? He cannot be far away. When will I get an update? When will somebody tell me something? Anything. My head was swimming, I needed to get out, get some air, a tea or a coffee, something to do, to stop me thinking, thinking the worst...

Into the room strode an orderly, a porter, wearing a face-mask, the first one I'd seen that morning, who spoke briefly to a large family group opposite me. 'Excuse me' I said, in my best schoolgirl Spanish, as he turned to leave. 'Is there somewhere I can get a drink please, coffee, water?'

He glanced at me briefly. 'Only a machine, in the corridor, turn left' he grunted, dismissively, then walked away, having a bad day, clearly. Charming. Not that I was expecting a branch of M&S Simply Food, or WH Smith, of course, but a little sympathy and understanding wouldn't have gone amiss, surely?

'He was telling you there is a machine in the corridor to the left' came a voice, in perfect English, from opposite. The young chap, from earlier.

I smiled, gratefully, even though I'd understood the porter's words. 'Thank you.' I studied him in more detail. 'Are you from Santa Marta?' I asked. 'I am sure I recognise you. Aren't you Amador's friend?'

He looked straight through me. 'Yes, I am from Santa Marta', and returned to his book. Conversation over. He was here with a relative, or friend, obviously, worried sick, same as me, an identical jumble of thoughts going through his mind, fearing the worst, not knowing. We could have bonded over that, couldn't we, exchanged stories, talked it through, a problem shared?

I had to get out. I had to speak to someone. But who, my Mum, or brother? My best friend in Spain, Marie from the library group? I could picture them all, their Sunday mornings, their usual routines, doing what they had to do. And what could I say? 'John has been rushed to hospital? Dad has been rushed to hospital? But I have no other details, no information, no idea how he is?' Impossible. Until I have some more details, I have to bear this alone. I reached beside me, instinctively, for my bag, and found it gone. Stifling rising panic, I gripped my palms. Stupid, stupid, how could I have been so utterly stupid? I left it at home of course. We left in a mad hurry. John said…. no I cannot blame him. My bag, my decision, my fault. We thought we were going for a packet of antibiotics of course, not getting rushed to hospital. And now I truly am alone, no phone, no money, stuck here. I couldn't ring someone even if I had some news. Totally alone, in this foreign country. Which made it worse, of course. In Britain I could have found a payphone, reversed the charges, spoke to someone. Got a taxi, paid at the destination. Something, anything. Yet there I was, a thousand miles from our family, completely isolated.

I staggered to my feet and half-ran from the room. If I lose my seat, I lose it. To my left, there was the coffee machine, completely useless to me now of course. Had the bloke opposite been more forthcoming I could have borrowed a euro from him, paid Amador back. Hopeless. To the right was a ward, *the* ward possibly, at the end of the corridor, and my first thought was surprise at how many people were in there, nursing staff, masked and gowned, all frantically busy. I had expected a skeleton staff, on a Sunday, but this looked like a full complement to me. So was John in there? What was he going through, what was he thinking? Could I pop my head around the door? See him, at least? Catch someone's eye? Enquire? The sign over the door read no admission, but was there a reception desk, or a nursing station, where I could at least have asked? Quickly grabbed someone's attention? Hopeless. Fifty yards were all that separated us, which might as well have been fifty miles.

Dejectedly, I turned away, wandering aimlessly, until I found an outside entrance, where I slumped onto a low wall, and completely broke down, let it all out. No arm to comfort me, no tissue to dry my eyes. I have no idea how long I was out there, but eventually pulled myself together, headed back inside, found the ladies toilet, splashed away my tears, took a gulp of the stale, tepid water, then headed back to the waiting room and my uncomfortable chair to wait. Two hours, three, four, and an endless sequence of repeats on the telly, plus interminable adverts for cold and flu remedies, *read the instructions and consult your pharmacist.* Spanish Flockodene no doubt. That evil, cursed Flockodene. If John hadn't wasted a week on that useless rubbish we might have been spared all this. Five hours, six. The relatives ebbed and flowed, sometimes the room was insufferably crowded, other times, as now, almost empty. Seven hours. I plumped up my coat into a pillow, between me and the wall, and closed my eyes.

Suddenly I was aware of footsteps in the corridor, the squeak of rubber-soled shoes on the tiles, louder, and louder, coming my way, and into the room stepped a senior nurse, pale blue bandanna, white surgical mask, only her eyes showing, dark eyes, expressionless, forbidding. *I knew, then.* 'Cristina Reechards?' she whispered, beckoning me to follow, and in total silence she led me along the corridor, and into a little room. John had died, that afternoon. His heart gave way. They had been trying to reach me ever since. The home phone, the mobile. They even sent the local police to the house, to no avail. None of the neighbours knew where we were of course. She kept talking, explaining, and I recall not a single word. I didn't cry. I couldn't cry. Instead I drifted back to nineteen-seventy-five. The second of February. A Sunday. In the local pub where we all used to gather. John was starting a new assignment with the Inland Revenue in west London the following day, and this was his leaving party. A series of leaving parties in fact, stretching across the past week. Cockney Rebel were playing on the jukebox, as John stumbled over to the table where I was sitting, with my best friend Lynn, plonked himself down on a stool, and started to sing. *Come up and see me, make me smi-i-i-le.* And promptly fell to the floor with a sickening thud, like a sack of cement hitting the carpet. Luckily his old partner in crime 'Killer' King was on hand to administer first-aid, in the form of a pickled egg, in a packet of salt and vinegar crisps. Cue instant revival. Then, a year or so later, in my parents' sitting room, kneeling before me, pledging his undying love, thankfully without the pungent aroma of vinegar, asking me to become his wife. And the following evening, same location, as my Mum and I had to magically 'disappear' as he asked my Dad for my hand in marriage. A year later, on our wedding day, as Dad and I approached down the aisle, he uttered those immortal words. *I shot a pig this morning.* A private joke. A few years later, at my bedside in the maternity ward, tears streaming down his face as he cradled our first-born, in that ungainly way all men hold babies, high on his chest. Our Louise. And two years on, an exact repeat, with our second, the quiet one. Our Charlotte.

I slumped sideways in my chair and banged my head painfully on the wall. Instinctively reaching up to rub the affected area, I suddenly realised I had woken from a dream. A nightmare. None of that had happened. Thank you, oh thank you God. With a feeling of overwhelming relief, I glanced around the room, to find I was completely alone. What on earth was going on? Why had nobody come for me? I glanced at the clock. Coming up to seven. Nine hours, almost. Nine hours, with no news. Surely they knew I was here? I leaped to my feet, determined to barge into the ward and demand to know what was happening to John. Didn't they think to check in the room of relations, for any relations?

Suddenly I was aware of footsteps in the corridor, the squeak of rubber-soled shoes on the tiles, louder, and louder, coming my way, and into the room stepped a senior nurse, pale blue bandanna, white surgical mask, only her eyes showing, dark eyes, expressionless, forbidding. The same nurse, identical in every way to the one in my nightmare, even though I'd never previously set eyes on the woman. Those eyes. My stomach lurched. 'Cristina Reechards?' she whispered, beckoning me to follow....

Printed in Great Britain
by Amazon

21774928R00225